MW00343400

THEORY AND
UNDERSTANDING

THEORY AND UNDERSTANDING

A Critique of Interpretive
Social Science

FINN COLLIN

Basil Blackwell

First published in 1985 by Basil Blackwell Ltd.,
108 Cowley Road, Oxford OX4 1JF, UK

Basil Blackwell Inc.
432 Park Avenue South, Suite 1505,
New York, NY 10016, USA

British Library Cataloguing in Publication Data

Collin, Finn
Theory and understanding : a critique of interpretive social
science.
1. Social sciences—Methodology
2. Social sciences—Philosophy
I. Title
300'.1'8   H61

ISBN 0-631-14256-8

Library of Congress Cataloging in Publication Data

Collin, Finn
Theory and understanding

Bibliography: p.
Includes index.
1. Methodology 2. Social sciences—Philosophy.
3. Social sciences—Methodology. I. Title.
BD241.C596 1985   300'.1   85–6143
ISBN 0-631-14256-8

Typeset by Qualitext Abingdon Oxon
Printed in Great Britain by
Billing & Sons Ltd, Worcester

To Catherine and Jonas

Contents

Preface and acknowledgements

The bulk of this book was written while I was the recipient of a research grant from the University of Copenhagen. It contains the fruits of studies undertaken at this institution as well as at the University of California, Berkeley, where I was a graduate student from 1975 to 1978, and Harvard University, which was my host during a stay as a visiting scholar in 1979.

I am indebted to numerous colleagues and friends for commenting upon portions of the manuscript, and for helping me in other ways to find my way through the problems; I especially want to mention Henning Boje Andersen, Jan Faye, Sven Erik Nordenbo, Jens Ravnkilde, Birger Wernerfelt. The present work was submitted to the University of Copenhagen as my doctoral dissertation, and was examined by Professors Mogens Blegvad, Uffe Juul Jensen and Göran Hermerén, from whose suggestions for changes it has benefited. Special thanks are extended to Mogens Blegvad for his long-standing interest in and support for my work.

The publication of this book was sponsored by a grant from the Danish Research Council for the Humanities. It is a pleasure for me to express my gratitude to that institution.

Parts of chapter 3 have previously appeared in *Danish Yearbook of Philosophy*, vol. 19 (Copenhagen 1982) and in Otto Neumaier (ed.), *Mind, Language and Society (Conceptus-Studien*, vol. 2, Vienna 1984). I am grateful to the editors of these publications for permission to reuse this material. Finally, I wish to thank Carol Henriksen and Olivia Cole Collin for their efforts to improve my English prose.

Finn Collin
Copenhagen

Introduction

The statement that social science is currently immersed in methodological crisis has been repeated to the point of boredom, and beyond. Still its truth, if not its news value, seems indisputable: a survey of recent trends will confirm that social science remains the field of many approaches but too few arrivals, as Robert Merton once put it. As a matter of fact, the only ground for opposing the proclamation of a crisis would be the observation that the word 'crisis' implies a discontinuity, a sudden change for the worse. But there is no such change, it might be claimed: the history of social theorizing, at least since Comte, is a monotonous tale of each new generation triumphantly overthrowing the work of its predecessors, declaring that the ground must be cleared so that social theorizing may at last be put on the path of scientific progress; only to find its efforts dismissed by the following generation in the name of the very same slogan.

Still I would agree that the feeling of crisis is more warranted today than at any earlier point in time. In part, this assessment reflects the recognition that the generation against which the current revolt is directed had better grounds than any earlier one for the complacency that it had, finally, brought social science out of its dark prehistory. For the first time in the history of this branch of human enquiry, it had acquired at least the institutional trappings of a mature scientific discipline: generously staffed university departments bearing the name of the discipline or its subdivisions had been created and were producing candidates with accredited degrees on the basis of standardized curricula. And the rapidly growing volume of books, periodicals and research projects generated by workers in the discipline seemed to indicate that these were not just adornments but the true signs of a scientific specialty finally coming of age.

Moreover, this institutionally entrenched discipline, representing a mode of theorizing which has been dubbed the 'orthodox consensus' of the 1950s and 1960s, was strengthened by its alliance with a roughly contemporaneous philosophical movement of great vigour and prestige, namely logical positivism. This school was predominantly occupied with analysing the structure of scientific theorizing, and with promulgating the methodological canons which could be elicited from such studies. This programme was pursued with no regard for the distinction between natural science and the sciences of human action; indeed, positivism explicitly embraced the view that one and the same set of scientific methods must be used in the two fields. The secrets of human action should be unveiled with the same intellectual tools that had proved so powerful in natural science.

Just as the 'orthodox consensus' was a fusion of methodologico-philosophical ideas and substantive sociological efforts, so the reaction against it has been motivated by general philosophical misgivings as well as by dissatisfaction with the actual sociological work produced under its auspices. The philosophical reaction against the orthodox position has assumed different forms in different traditions. In the Anglo-American world, it arose chiefly as an offshoot from the so-called Ordinary Language movement, especially from the branch inspired by Wittgenstein. The main object of this attack was the tenet that explanation of human action involves its subsumption under general causal laws. It was argued that such laws cannot be found; moreover the relationship between action and the psychological states which are its sources—wants, intentions, desires—was claimed to be of a non-causal nature, thus excluding causal explanation of action in such terms. Finally, the positivist conception of the relationship between reality and theory was challenged: social reality was said to be pre-structured by the concepts in which social agents describe it in their everyday dealings. Hence social science must abandon the 'nominalist' stance advocated by positivist epistemology and strive to capture the concepts which are somehow already embedded in the object examined.

This point was anticipated by a methodological school on the Continent, with roots in the phenomenology of Edmund Husserl.

The phenomenological tenet that reality is somehow constituted by the cognitive processes through which it is grasped was applied to social experience to generate the doctrine of the 'social construction of social reality', the thesis that social fact is the product of the 'meanings' which human beings bestow upon their interactions. This conception entailed a methodological corollary to the effect that social science must penetrate the social agents' subjective interpretation of their actions and incorporate it into the scientific picture of the social world. Given its constitutive role, failure to appreciate this interpretation would be a failure to come to grips with social reality altogether.

On the German scene, criticism was primarily directed against the positivists' strict demarcation between descriptive and normative issues and their suggestion that the latter are not amenable to rational discussion and are hence inadmissible in science. Against this, it was maintained that our intellectual attitude to social reality is not that of a detached spectator but of a committed participant; the mode in which we think about the social is critical and evaluative, and the very notions used to grasp it inescapably normative. Hence, instead of trying in vain to purge scientific discourse about society of normative taint, philosophy and social science should endeavour to put normative reasoning on a rational footing and to develop an overall normative interpretation of social reality in terms of which particular social formations could be assessed and criticized.

At a more abstract level, the anti-positivist schools were united in their aversion to the positivist ideal of 'Einheitswissenschaft', the conception that a single set of methodological precepts is valid in all areas of enquiry. The anti-positivists called for a sharp differentiation of methods between natural science and social science and for approaches that respect the *sui generis* character of human action. In this spirit, the anti-positivists urged social science to adopt the patterns of description, reasoning and explanation which are used by social agents in their everyday dealings with one another.

To the working social scientist, at least in the English-speaking world, the main reason for dissatisfaction with the orthodox consensus was the manifest triviality of most of the work undertaken in adherence to its precepts. Such work tended to gravitate towards two equally unpalatable extremes, brilliantly castigated by C. Wright Mills, under the names of 'Grand Theorizing' and 'Abstracted Empiricism'. The former, of which Parsons' *The Social System* is the classical specimen, is theorizing at such lofty heights of abstraction that concrete empirical fact is lost sight of entirely. At its worst, it reduces to an empty algebra of poorly defined neologistic terms, with no implications to be captured in observation. 'Abstracted Empiricism' is the opposite of this, although as often, the extremes are subtly similar. It is the mere hoarding of data, sampled with painstaking attention to the canons of data collection and recorded in a very low-level, 'observational' vocabulary. Unfortunately, the entire effort fails to be informed by any theoretical assumptions and is inspired by no precisely defined problem; hence the only further processing of the data is through statistical manipulation, dooming the outcome to triviality.

Now the representatives of the orthodox consensus and their philosophical backers, of course, have not ceded their positions without firing a shot. A battle has been going on during the last couple of decades, with varying intensity. In this battle, the critics of the orthodox position have profited from an advantageous strategic position. Since little actual work has so far been produced on the basis of the new 'paradigms', they present a smaller target than their adversary: they are as yet vulnerable only to *a priori* arguments, not to charges based upon the way they fare in the actual scientific process. On the other hand, this advantageous position is weakened if it is occupied for too long. As time goes on, the suspicion that the absence of scientific output is not due to the youth of the new paradigms but to inherent defects, begins to grow stronger; a misgiving that the new paradigms offer no guidance once the scientist wants to go beyond attacks upon the positivist position and the issuing of programmatic statements. This suspicion is nourished by the reading of books expounding the new paradigms, which are too often prepared in accordance with the same recipe which leaves the reader quite unsated: we are given introductory chapters in which the weaknesses of positivism are exposed in an entirely convincing manner. Next, the fathers of the various anti-positivist views are introduced and their insights lauded. But after this promising start, we are too often fobbed off with vague suggestions for 'new rules of sociological method', or with minimal guidelines for a 'restructuring of social theory'. Little is done to convince us that these approaches will fare any better than the orthodox one in the crucial test: their ability to generate genuine, substantive theorizing when used in the actual scientific process.

It will surely be objected that there is no way to demonstrate this capacity ahead of time: only the performance of the new paradigms in future scientific work can decide that issue. But while this rejoinder is sound in general, it overlooks the point that the lacklustre career of the orthodox paradigm has taught us quite a bit about the environment in which social theories must deliver their struggle for survival. We know, in a rough way, on which rocks that approach foundered and have a right to learn how the anti-positivist can hope to avoid them. The anti-positivist's obligation to face this challenge is made even more pressing by the observation that the inchoate research efforts within the new paradigms show disturbing symptoms of the very weaknesses that brought down the orthodox approach. Thus, 'critical sociology' embraces a view of human society as a moment in the historical procession of Reason towards the liberation of mankind, a vision every bit as sweeping and as remote from humble empirical fact as Parsons' speculations about the Social System. At the opposite end of the spectrum, the work of symbolic interactionists and ethnomethodologists is no less parochial and restricted than most research guided by the positivist paradigm.

The present book has grown out of reflections upon these events in the recent history of social science. It is inspired by the conviction that it is about time we shifted the lines of battle to escape from the well-trodden ground where the skirmishing has taken place thus far. In the first place, we must get beyond the purely philosophical arguments, the trite impossibility-proofs and their rebuttals, and try instead to assess the fruitfulness of the rival paradigms as instruments of actual research. Secondly, we should grant the anti-positivist the point, if only for the sake of the argument, that the orthodox approach has proved a failure in this respect, but go on to enquire what reason we have to believe that the new paradigms will do any better: for too long, the critics have been allowed to pretend that any point scored against orthodox research in this area is a point in their favour. It is the aim of the present book to undertake an assessment of this kind, adjudicating the outlook for anti-positivist theorizing in a manner which avoids getting bogged down in the familiar philosophical arguments by operating at a more empirical level. Still, our enterprise remains a philosophical one; it will involve arguments that have no place in the simple process of testing a theory against the data. Moreover, the empirical facts that I shall appeal to are, by and large, such as are available to informed common sense. Only rarely shall I invoke the findings of specialized research. This middle ground, I believe, provides a fruitful and as yet largely unexplored field for methodological enquiry. However, I have not been able to resist commenting upon certain standard philosophical issues of human action, the solution to which has never been put quite right, despite the amount of ink expended. In this vein, I shall have something to say about the problem of reason explanation versus causal explanation, the Logical Connection Argument, and the relationship between neurophysiological accounts and intentionalistic accounts.

We have seen that anti-positivist views are legion and highly diverse, as is to be expected with a group of positions that is only negatively defined. Hence, to get a manageable topic at all, we must focus on a narrower and more precisely defined issue. We need to identify a topic which gears into all of the anti-positivist positions without sharing their diversity.

As we noted above, a central common theme of anti-positivist methodologies is the recommendation that social science reflect the *sui generis* properties of human action as embodied in everyday ways of accounting for action. This suggests the following question as a suitable touchstone for the virtues of anti-positivist views: is it possible to devise theories of social action which will support theoretical accounts of action of the kinds used in everyday affairs, and which apply uniquely to action? Is it, in fact, possible to develop theories of social action from which we may derive explanations of action of the very same sorts as used in everyday affairs, but in which concepts from those theories replace their everyday counterparts?

This formulation is acceptable as a provisional statement of the problem which will occupy us in this essay. Only provisional: for that formulation needs substantial tightening and refinement before it identifies a sufficiently precise and manageable topic. But in order to allow the reader to see the relationship between the, unavoidably, rather narrowly circumscribed problem that will concern us here, and the grand themes suggested in my introductory overview, I have found it advisable to start with a more clearcut but not fully adequate formulation, and then gradually take the reader through the steps that will turn it into something precise enough to be answered in a definite way. The reader should be allowed to behold the simple basic issue behind our investigation before I disfigure it with qualifications and provisos. Most of this work of disfiguration will be the task of later chapters; but some of it belongs here and will form the remaining part of this Introduction.

First a terminological point. From now on, our topic is no longer the clash between two opposed approaches to human social action, but rather the merits of one of these approaches. Hence I shall cease to refer to this approach as 'anti-positivism', a tag that was appropriate only as long as we focused upon the critical aspect of this position. Instead, I shall talk about *interpretive* methodologies, and shall mean by this methodologies recommending that social science adopt ways of accounting for action that (1) are used in everyday affairs, and (2) apply to action only. These ways themselves I refer to as *interpretive patterns* of action account, or simply *interpretive accounts*. I have selected the term 'interpretation' because it has a history of use as a tag for various anti-positivist attitudes and positions, while still not being so closely tied to any particular approach as to prevent me from appropriating it here for my own specific purposes.

Now for some elucidation of and some comment upon our rough initial question. In the first place, there are evidently many different grounds on which the prospects of interpretive theorizing might be disputed. One charge might be that the concepts used in everyday action accounts are inescapably normative, or that the accounts themselves have evaluative import; either might be taken as a ground for rejecting theorizing along these lines. Another objection would be that the intentionalistic concepts featured in interpretive accounts resist objective testing and are hence not to be allowed in scientific discourse. A third might be to the effect that social reality is generated by human interaction and exists only in and through such interaction: it cannot be held out at arm's length, as it were, and made the object of disinterested scrutiny. Some of these points, and additional ones, are most likely to be raised by defenders of the orthodox paradigm; others–although there will be considerable overlap–will come from a radical wing of the interpretivist side which espouses the view that no conception of 'theorizing', however liberally construed, will be consonant with the attitude we adopt to human action within the interpretive paradigm; this is considered a strength in that position, a sign of its superior humanity. I shall bypass all these worries here, although issues discussed later in this volume will have repercussions upon some of them. This policy reflects, of course, the conviction that these charges can be met; if not, our entire enterprise would be rather pointless. But an adequate treatment of these problems cannot be given within the compass of the present book, which tries to assess the outlook for interpretive social science in a novel dimension. We must also forego any general discussion of which of the multifarious connotations of the term 'scientific theorizing' are germane to interpretive understanding and may hence form the basis of such assessment. However, in chapter 2, I shall have something to say in defence of the one I select.

This feature is the very notion of *theoreticity,* which I take to be the principal logico-epistemological trait distinguishing scientific knowledge, construed as product rather than process, from common-sense knowledge. It has to do with the power of knowledge systems to organize and integrate our understanding of a given realm. So the question we will pose here is whether we can attain to truly systematic, integrative knowledge of human action of a kind from which we may derive more powerful interpretive accounts of action.

Now our preliminary formulation and the explication just provided, might seem to operate with a notion of 'theory' involving an absolute distinction between theoretical and common-sense knowledge. But while it may be possible to circumscribe the notion of theoretical knowledge, and of theoretical concepts, in a way which makes common-sense knowledge and concepts come out non-theoretical, any such line would be quite arbitrary in terms of the conception proposed here: there is a perfectly gradual transition between typical everyday concepts and those figuring in the most advanced sciences. As we shall see in chapter 2, the characteristic features of theoretical concepts as we understand them here are the properties of all concepts, writ large.

How can we modify the provisional formulation of our query so that it will not commit us to an untenable dichotomy between theoretical and common-sense knowledge? The observation that theoreticity is a graded property might suggest that we construe it as a question whether we can attain a knowledge of social action that is *more theoretical* than common-sense lore, while still using interpretive categories. But this will not do. If we take the question at face value, the answer must be, trivially, *yes*. Any other answer would be equivalent to the assertion that our current ways of describing and explaining action are already pushing against the ultimate limits to their development. But this is hardly credible, on purely *a priori* grounds: there must surely be room for marginal improvements of our everyday action vocabulary, and for infinitesimal increases in the scope of the rough-and-ready action principles which they allow us to express. We cannot circumvent this difficulty by simply demanding that the increase in theoreticity be substantial. This is not primarily because of the vagueness of the word 'substantial' which we might overcome if we could agree, however arbitrarily, upon some particular increment in theoreticity as defining the line between substantial and non-substantial. The real problem is that there are no metrics available to express the exact, absolute discriminations of theoreticity which this proposal involves. Conceptions akin to our present notion of theoreticity, or at least to a dimension thereof, have indeed been worked out by mathematically minded philosophers (normally under the name of 'content measures') ; but the trouble is that these measures are only defined for formalized languages, and nobody has any idea how to apply them to actual languages, be it in science or common sense.

Measurement of relative theoreticity must remain a matter of rough intuitive assessment, which renders formulations like the one just proposed quite meaningless.

A related weakness affects another formulation that would otherwise recommend itself: is it possible to devise theories of social action which are as highly theoretical as the most advanced natural sciences and which support interpretive accounts of human action? Apart from the fact that this formulation makes excessive demands on interpretive theorizing, it suffers from the flaw that we have no way of comparing the theoreticity of such diverse disciplines. Comparison, even in rough intuitive terms, is only possible when one and the same field is dealt with, so that relative ranking on the theoreticity scale can be assessed against one and the same body of data. Only under such conditions–which are satisfied when we compare our everyday knowledge of action with some proposed scientific counterpart–may we produce a meaningful comparison of theoreticity.

Thus, we must refrain from formulations of our query which presuppose the illusory possibility of comparisons of theoreticity in precise quantitative terms. We should settle for something along the following lines as a working formulation: are there considerations of principle militating against the creation of systematizations of our knowledge of social action which are superior in theoreticity to current common-sense understanding of action and which will support theoretically enriched interpretive accounts? This is a very austere and very modest formulation, uncommitted to any presumption that a precise numerical measure of theoreticity can be devised, and innocent of implications that social science must rival the most advanced disciplines of natural science to count as theoretical at all. I propose that we rest content with this formulation for the time being. It will be subject to further comment and refinement in chapters 2 and 5, but will be adequate to guide our steps until then.

Let me briefly indicate two important limitations upon our project. First, the scope of our investigation is restricted to social science; a discipline, however, which I conceive in a liberal fashion to include sociology, social psychology, and social anthropology. The reason for this limitation is not a very profound one; indeed it could hardly be more profound than the very reasons for demarcating social science from such neighbouring disciplines as, for example, psychology: the line separating the two is notoriously drawn in part on the basis of various historical and departmental considerations and does not reflect any deep differences in methodology. However, according to one reasonably systematic way of characterizing the two (to the extent that both deal with individual human action), social science could be described as being concerned with action as socially determined, whereas psychology mainly treats action as determined by factors presumed to be largely independent of cultural moulding; besides it deals with developmental processes shaping action and with pathological as well as normal behaviour. This rough distribution of research interests makes it natural to limit our field of investigation to social science. For some of the modes of account which we shall examine–notably, account by reference to rule, and by specification of linguistic meaning–necessarily apply only to action as socially conditioned.

Secondly, we shall examine only theories supporting explanation of individual human action, paying no attention to social macro-phenomena. This restriction does not indicate any commitment to methodological individualism, but only the conviction that we may elucidate the basic problems concerning the explanation of human action without having to delve into the notorious puzzles relating to the analysis and explanation of social macro-phenomena: we may leave the latter problems alone without suffering distortion or incompleteness in our treatment of the former. This fact gives us sufficient grounds for a restriction: the present study already touches in a tangential manner upon a large number of issues that cannot be given full treatment within the existing limits. Hence any opportunity to circumscribe our topic more narrowly should be resolutely seized.

This book falls into two main parts. The first part, comprising chapters 1–4, deals with philosophical preliminaries to our principal methodological enquiry. However, due to the prominence of these issues in the philosophical debate during the last decades, they receive rather more attention than would be justified by a purely auxiliary role. In chapter 1, I describe certain distinctive features of action and the modes of explanation which they sustain. I go on to investigate, in chapters 2 and 3, a number of traditional problems concerning the relationship between interpretive accounts and causal accounts, in order to gain a better understanding of their differentiating features. In chapter 4, I examine a more radical version of the interpretivist position, to the effect that social science must not only adopt the general explanatory patterns used in common-sense understanding of action, but must incorporate the particular interpretations endorsed by the agents themselves. The second part comprises chapters 5–7. In each of these chapters, I assess the theory-generating potential of one of the three species of interpretive account introduced in chapter 1. Readers with a social science background may want to read the book in the reverse order, studying the methodological results I try to establish in the second part before taking on the philosophical argument in the first part. I do believe, however, that the present book is so tightly knit that the argument of chapters 5–7 will not be fully understandable if divorced from the philosophical background supplied by the earlier chapters. At least, the rationale of the way in which I delimit and structure my topic will be lost.

1

Varieties of interpretive accounts

1

The aim of this investigation is to test the theory-sustaining power of interpretive accounts. The first step will be to single out and examine the basic members of this category. The list which I intend to propose can be subdivided under three headings: (1) accounts indicating the purpose of action; (2) accounts indicating a rule conformed to in action; (3) accounts specifying the semantic meaning of action.

By referring to these as the basic varieties of interpretive accounts, I wish to imply two things. First, these acounts are fundamental in the sense that most other, and ostensibly different patterns, will reduce to one of them when stripped down to essentials. Secondly, they are the significant and interesting types in that they pertain to those features of action which most clearly distinguish it from inanimate processes. The existence of any additional genuinely distinct patterns can safely be presumed to be of little interest judged by this standard. For instance, it might be argued that accounting for action by showing it to be habitual constitutes an autonomous pattern. But whether this claim can be substantiated or not, the fact remains that this is a mode of account attracting minimal interest from the point of view of a social science concerned with human action *qua* action. This attitude is clearly reflected in the writings of interpretation theorists, none of whom devote any attention to habitual action, but focus instead upon ways of accounting for action relating to man's 'higher powers'.

My taxonomy thus represents a compromise between two criteria of admission: on the one hand, a criterion which is simply the application of the definition of interpretive accounts given in the Introduction, requiring that any account is to be included if it is

(1) based upon a feature which distinguishes action from inanimate processes and (2) used in everyday affairs; and on the other hand, a criterion which modifies the first to the effect that only significant and interesting patterns deserve a heading in the present taxonomy; this means, as a practical guideline, that only accounts which have actually been discussed by writers in the field deserve our attention. In brief, my taxonomy represents a compromise between systematic and more historic–pragmatic considerations.

So much for those considerations which determine the outward boundary of the class of accounts that concerns us here; now for those which establish its internal subdivision. The tripartite taxonomy employed in the present study forms the basis of one particular philosophical investigation and must therefore be justified primarily in terms of considerations intrinsic to that investigation. In the present case, justification emerges from the fact that quite divergent lines of reasoning are called for to adjudicate the theory-generating potential of the listed accounts. However, the subdivision is further supported by the manner in which I shall later distinguish between causal accounts and interpretive accounts, namely in terms of the differential force of the two. For when this principle of demarcation is applied within the class of interpretive accounts to generate a subdivision of that class, this is the taxonomy that emerges, at least as long as we are aiming at a rough classification. Finally, the present taxonomy has the advantage of approximately corresponding with the distinctions underlying traditional debate concerning interpretive accounts; although I hope it presents these distinctions in a much clearer fashion than is often the case. Such a correspondence makes the implications of our investigation for that debate more obvious.

Space does not allow me to make good the quasi-exhaustiveness claim made on behalf of my taxonomy, in any case a somewhat unrewarding undertaking. But in the process of characterizing the accounts which fall under these headings I shall attempt to indicate how accounts that might seem *prima facie* to constitute autonomous patterns can really be viewed as variants of the listed types.

In the Introduction, we defined interpretive accounts as accounts based upon the features of human action which distinguish it from inanimate processes. Taking a point of departure in this observation, we will start our enquiry into interpretive accounts by examing these distinctive features of action. Using a traditional terminology, we will look at the *meaningful* aspects of human action. This term is one I have shunned thus far, and I shall make very little use of it in the following. The adoption of this single term to refer in an omnibus fashion to all features of human action by which it sets itself apart from purely physical processes, has done much to prevent adequate analysis and differentiation of these features. This I shall attempt to rectify in the following investigation.

The following list of action characteristics will come as no surprise, having been anticipated in the taxonomy of interpretive accounts. It is not an exhaustive list but merely comprises the characteristics needed to elucidate the types of account that will concern us in this study. As that class of accounts has already been demarcated at another level, the underlying features are not introduced here to achieve such demarcation but rather to provide a deeper understanding of the accounts, something which can only be attained by including a broader background. To put it a little solemnly, the ontological basis of interpretive accounts must be explored. This investigation also serves to stress the obligation of anyone venturing into this area to make clear, at least to some minimal degree, his commitments regarding certain basic metaphysical–logical issues concerning the mentalistic (intentionalistic) vocabulary used in interpretive accounts. In particular, the thorny problem concerning the relationship between a causal and an interpretive account of the same action token cannot be addressed unless one takes sides on these fundamental issues. And this problem cannot be circumvented, since the question of whether interpretive accounts have any actual application to reality rides upon it.

Action is distinctive in that it possesses *inter alia* one or more of the following features: (1) it may be undertaken to accomplish a *purpose*; (2) it may be performed in conformity to *rule*; (3) it may possess *semantic meaning*. Note that this is not a list of different kinds of action but of features characterizing action: one and the same action may exhibit more than one of these features. From a logical point of view, the list is somewhat heterogeneous. Whereas purposiveness and rule-following may be described as types of motivation, semantic meaning, as we shall later characterize it, is primarily a function of the manner in which a certain motive is translated into action. However, this heterogeneity should not concern us: in reflecting our taxonomy of interpretive accounts, the list also reflects the considerations which motivated that taxonomy, as specified on pp. 1–2. There is no reason why these considerations should issue in a logically neat classification.

2

Let us now proceed to a detailed examination of these features of action. To characterize them in a systematic fashion, it is advantageous first to sketch the overall framework of concepts in which they are embedded. And one way to go about this is to look at that feature of action which first comes to mind when one ponders in the abstract the difference between action and inanimate processes. This is the 'goal-directedness' of action, the feature that is captured in the metaphorical idea that action is not pushed into existence from behind, as it were, but is pulled from the front by some future upshot, an end or goal. In contradistinction to inanimate physical processes (with the exception of those of such man-made systems as thermostats and self-guiding missiles), but like animal behaviour in general, human action has a *teleological* character. Animal behaviour, including human behaviour, differs from the teleological manifestations of such artifacts by virtue of its far superior teleological repertoire. And human action sets itself apart from other animal behaviour by the reflexive consciousness of the goal which human agents typically possess, as manifested in their ability to express the goal verbally. Indeed, the paradigm case of human action is one in which we can discern a certain drift or trend in its course, pointing towards a certain upshot, and in which the agent will admit upon request to having that upshot as his goal.

The fact that man has a special non-observational access to his operative desires has done much to lead speculation on the nature of goal-directedness astray, I believe, and thus we must dwell a moment upon this topic here. It has often been suggested that this verbalized consciousness is precisely that which goal-directedness consists in. This is a very unfortunate view. As a matter of fact, if we take this doctrine to call for the agent to have actually at some stage put his goal into words, if only 'in his head', then we are certainly dealing with a rarity, from a purely statistical point of view. Such explicit, albeit private, formulation is reserved for momentous acts and grave decisions ('I'll join the Army tomorrow!'), and is rarely found in everyday action. Instead, everyday action typically features consciousness of the goal in the slightly diluted sense of an ability to express one's goal verbally without the benefit of reflection and without the need for a shift of attention to 'call it to mind'. In typical everyday action, the agent is capable of stating what he is up to immediately and directly, should he be asked, without this statement being the echo of an earlier pronouncement made to himself *in foro interno*. In other cases, the shift of attention needed for the production of such a statement is more substantial. Completely absorbed in thought, I drift into my study to get a particular book. When I suddenly 'come to', it will often require some effort to raise the nature of my objective to the level of explicit verbalized consciousness.

To get the facts right in this area, we must take care not to confuse the agent's verbalized knowledge of his goal with the monitoring attention to the acts by which he implements it. The latter may be present to a high degree without the former; indeed, the latter may crowd out the former: some tricky manual task may so absorb my attention as to blot out all verbalized thought of what I am doing, along the lines of 'Here I go, trying to sew a button onto my old shirt again.' That thought will only occur to me when I look up from my work.

Less trivial types of non-verbalized goal-directed action are those which Freud brought to our attention. Freud demonstrated how certain phenomena which had always been right there under our noses but which had either appeared so insignificant as to call for no special explanation (such as slips, lapses of memory, etc.) or so bizarre as to allow of explanation only in terms of malfunctioning at the somatic level (such as severe neurotic disturbances), could be described and accounted for as goal-directed. Freud forced us to admit that in some cases of behaviour which at first blush seem quite odd and pointless, and which do not seem to tally with any objective avowed by the agent, it will still be possible to discern a hidden goal-directedness. The imputation of that goal will normally not be accepted by the agent when it is suggested to him: in typical cases, he will resist such attribution vehemently. Often, the goal imputed and the manner in which it is pursued will clash with the subject's avowed objectives and with his sense of propriety and rationality. Now if we accept such imputations as sometimes valid, as I think we must, we thereby accept the possibility of goal-directedness divorced from verbalized goal-awareness in a quite radical manner. We admit the possibility of cases in which the agent is not only incapable of volunteering a statement of what he is up to but is even unable to recognize a valid interpretation when it is offered to him.

It is true that practitioners of psychoanalysis generally adhere to the maxim of not resting content with an imputation of a goal (an *interpretation*, in the jargon) until it has received the agent's endorsement; and this principle has actually been declared as a general condition of adequacy for ascriptions of unconscious motives by certain writers on the epistemology and methodology of psychoanalysis.[1] However, this reflection on the practice of psychotherapy does not argue a necessary connection between goal-directedness and reflexive verbalized consciousness of the goal. In the first place, such a clinical maxim hardly reflects any privileged insight into the nature of human action on the part of analysts, but rather an appreciation of the role which the subject's acceptance of an interpretation plays in the dynamics of analytical treatment. Without the subject's endorsement, the diagnosis, even if valid, remains inefficacious. Therapeutic effect is contingent on the patient's acceptance, on his facing the fact that he harbours such motivations; hence insisting on such acceptance is an entirely reasonable maxim where the clinical aspect of psychotherapy is concerned. Secondly, even if we were to accept this principle, not as a practical maxim, but as revealing the nature of human action, it would still not imply any particularly close connection between goal-directed action and reflexive consciousness. The fact that an agent can always be brought to awareness of the objective of his action through a lengthy and obscure process of analytical work hardly proves that goal-directed action is essentially conscious; no more so than the fact that we can always become apprised of our blood pressure through a fairly simple procedure shows that this is something of which we are necessarily conscious.[2]

The point of stressing the existence of various more or less radical kinds of non-conscious action is to clarify the fact that although we tend to consider consciously goal-directed action as the paradigm type, this does not mean that verbalized consciousness of the goal is a necessary condition for the valid imputation of goal-directedness, nor that non-conscious goal-directed action in human beings is so termed only in a defective and secondary sense. Goal-directedness in human action is one and the same thing, whether it is the object of reflexive verbalized consciousness or not. Man's power to put his objectives into words no more adds to the nature of goal-directedness than the physician's knowledge of his gastric processes changes the nature of the latter.

This comparison points to the proper way of viewing the relationship between conscious and non-conscious goal-directedness. We must take pains to conceive of this relationship as one holding between a thing known and the same thing not known. Our common-sense ways of thinking and talking about these matters suggest that the difference between the two consists rather in the existence, in verbalized goal-directed action, of some specific mental *object* of awareness, some picture in the mind's eye of the goal state as already attained. There is no reason here to repeat the arguments, familiar since Wittgenstein's *Philosophical Investigations*, which prove that the existence of such pictures, even if we should grant it, could in no way be that which a person's having a certain purpose consists in. Nor is there any reason to go into the intractable problems, all too familiar, which crop up unless the above construal is adopted. Chief among them is the puzzling relationship between an account of a (bodily) action in terms of its bodily antecedents and in terms of its goal. Since, presumably, the motions which make up a bodily action are explicable in purely physiological terms, possession of a certain goal, construed as an introspectible phenomenal state, is superfluous: the action would have occurred anyway; or at least its bodily component would have occurred, lacking only the concomitance of a conscious goal-in-mind to bestow upon it the epithet of an action. In any case, human intentionality seems to be irrelevant for the occurrence of action.[3] The interpretation proposed above allows us to maintain that what is known in consciously goal-directed action is the very goal-directedness of action, not some introspectible we-know-not-what in competition with the purely bodily processes for the privilege of bringing about action. (The implication that this construal solves the problem is somewhat optimistic. A sophisticated version of the same concern arises even for it. In chapter 3, I will attempt to show how this difficulty can be allayed.)

It may be wondered how an agent can become apprised of the goal-directed tendency of his own behaviour if it is not intimated to him by some introspectible datum. The only alternative would seem to be that he knows about it from observing his own behaviour; but surely this is absurd. We may agree that it is; although hardly more absurd than the suggestion that he derives his information from the inspection of inner pictures, which in turn raises such well-known Wittgensteinian concerns as, 'Is he sure that he has interpreted the picture correctly?', 'Is he sure that the picture shows what he intends to do, rather than what he intends to avoid at all cost?', etc. To dispose of this objection in a more positive manner, we may invoke a causal theory of cognition: in this instance as well as in other cases involving things known without observation, we may explain these specific cognitive abilities by telling a story about the neural hook-up between certain brain states associated with the state known and other brain states associated with the state by which the former state is known. Thus, the capacity for knowing things without observation does not call for any specifically philosophical theory of cognition, but for a straightforwardly scientific explanation.[4]

So much for the relationship between goal-directedness and verbalized consciousness. Now to the notion of goal-directedness itself. In the brief initial characterization of that notion, play was made with the rather fuzzy notion of a 'trend' or 'drift' in behaviour. We must now try to give a more precise content to these conceptions. In the end we will see that goal-directedness is a highly derived, theoretical trait of action opening out into that entire network of intentionalistic concepts in which action is grasped in interpretive accounts.

Intuitively and crudely, goal-directedness consists in the tendency of behaviour to create conditions likely to bring about a certain upshot and to suppress conditions unfavourable to its realization. Perhaps we can capture the import of this thought in a formula of the following kind. An action is directed towards some state G as its goal if it is a member of a class of possible actions which the agent would have performed in counterfactual situations diverging in specified ways from the actual setting of the action; said actions all agreeing in being likely to bring about G, if the agent's beliefs about the setting and his general background assumptions were correct, and in the fact that the agent would not have performed them if they were not likely to bring about G, given the correctness of his beliefs about the setting and of his background assumptions.

This characterization applies immediately only to action issuing in an upshot distinct from the action itself. This is as it should be, since only such upshots are naturally called goals in everyday parlance. Still, there is considerable affinity between these cases, and actions, dubbed *endotychistic* actions by D. S. Shwayder,[5] such as playing music, going for a walk, etc. which involve no detachable upshot but where an action is performed for its own sake. It would be desirable for a characterization of goal-directedness to capture the kinship between these cases. The above account satisfies this requirement if we stretch it slightly. The secret lies in treating such action as a whole as a goal, whereafter the above analysis becomes applicable. A person who wants to play music will antecedently take such steps as he deems necessary for indulging that desire: he will make sure that there is an instrument available and a suitable place to perform, that he has the necessary sheet music, that he will not be interrupted by other people or bothered by street noise, etc. In securing these conditions, before and during his playing, he will perform action displaying goal-directedness in the sense characterized above. But what about cases of endotychistic action for which this notion of bringing about the conditions for successful performance does not apply, such as, for instance, basic acts of wiggling a finger for no ulterior purpose? In this case, stating that the very performance of this action was the agent's goal, amounts to the following two things: first, that the action was really an intentional action and not, say, a reflex, a spasm, or suchlike. There are recognized, if not infallible, ways of checking this. Secondly, that the action had no ulterior goal, a condition to be spelled out by means of the above account of goal-directedness as applied negatively.

These characterizations of goal-directedness are still quite abstract and vague, and I will now point to one reason why this is the case. Let us take a brief look at various attempts to provide a more concrete and precise *analysans* for this notion. For there has been no dearth of suggestions of this kind. We have been offered the analysis of Rosenblueth, Wiener and Bigelow in terms of negative feed-back from the goal object, Braithwaite's analysis in terms of causal plasticity, and many more.[6] In my opinion, these attempts must all be considered unsuccessful. In the first place, each suffers from well-known specific shortcomings.[7] However, these could perhaps be shored up. Far worse is the fact that they all suffer from an overspecificity and over-concreteness springing from the desire for precision motivating them. They fail to do justice to the complexity and the subtle contextuality of our everyday criteria of goal ascription.

The main contributor to this complexity is the familiar logical interdependence of cognitive and conative factors in motivational analysis. If we ascribe a certain goal to an agent, we impute to him a tendency to initiate action of certain sorts, action likely to issue in the production of the goal-state. However, the having of a goal only results in action when conjoined with suitable cognitive states. Even the most nagging bodily desire will lead to nothing but inactivity unless the agent has some idea as to how to satisfy it; and this in turn depends upon his knowledge of the particular situation at hand as well as upon a general familiarity with the ways of the world. Conative states only flow into action through channels shaped by the agent's beliefs. It follows that we can only get at an agent's conative states if we make certain assumptions concerning his beliefs. However, such belief ascriptions must ultimately be anchored in the agent's conduct; unfortunately, the inference of beliefs from action is premised upon certain conjectures concerning the agent's conative make-up. In other words, if we want to identify the goal of an action, we must establish two interdependent parameters at the same time: we have to solve for the agent's conative and cognitive states simultaneously. What rescues this process from circularity is, *inter alia*, the fact that an interpretation can be checked against the agent's further conduct, prior as well as subsequent. The interpretation of any particular action must be consistent with the conative and cognitive states we have imputed to the agent on other occasions. Interpreting action is a holistic matter, involving a large body of data extending far beyond the particular action under scrutiny. Similarly, that which we impute to an agent in ascribing an aim to him is not a simple, concrete property but a highly abstract, theoretical one. No simple formula of the kind offered by the authors listed above can be expected to capture it adequately.

The underestimation of the conceptual complexity of goal ascription is most obvious in the Rosenblueth, Wiener and Bigelow analysis. Their proposal construes goal-directed action as action determined by the 'goal object' via the mechanism of negative feed-back. But this analysis overlooks the fact that human action is not under the direct control of a goal object (which may as we know be non-existent) but is rather governed by the agent's beliefs about that object. The actions which people perform in looking for the Abominable Snowman are not determined by negative feed-back from the Abominable Snowman: for such a creature does not exist. Instead, such actions are determined by beliefs concerning this creature and how to entrap it. The Rosenblueth, Wiener and Bigelow analysis fails by completely shortcircuiting the cognitive aspect of goal ascription.

Braithwaite's theory is similarly flawed, if less blatantly. It should be pointed out at the outset that Braithwaite does not intend his analysis to apply to consciously goal-directed action of the kind found in human beings, but solely to the behaviour of animals. However, I have argued that the goal-directedness of human action is not essentially a conscious, verbalized phenomenon; such verbalized consciousness should rather be construed as the awareness of a condition which is fully capable of existing unaccompanied by verbalization, and which may well be formally identical to the state of goal-directedness found in animals. At any rate, the proposed analysis is inadequate even for animal goal-directedness, as will emerge from the example below.

Braithwaite's proposal is roughly to the effect that an action A is directed towards the goal G iff that action traces a causal path between some intrinsic state e of the agent and G under the borderline conditions f, such that there is a large class of alternative borderline conditions under which e would similarly have caused G. Put more loosely, an action A is directed towards some goal G if there is at that moment a wide range of non-actual, alternative circumstances under which the behaving organism would have attained G. Braithwaite refers to this property as the plasticity of goal-directed action *vis-à-vis* the goal. But this analysis cannot do justice to the fact that agents may have goals which no physically possible chain of events could cause to exist. The dog may station himself behind the door, ready to welcome his master who, alas, has been killed in an accident on his way home. In this case, there is no causal chain between the dog's activity and the situation in which he greets his master, and *a fortiori* no causally productive relationship between these two events (event types) such that the relationship remains stable under varying conditions. It is only when we introduce a cognitive component into the situation, in the form of the dog's belief that his master will soon come to the door, that we get hold of a (counterfactual) situation–that of the master coming to the door–in which the dog's behaviour would be plastic *vis-à-vis* some stable end state, namely that of greeting his master. Only by tapping the animal's beliefs is it possible to see its behaviour as directed towards some such upshot. This point is, of course, much more striking for human action in pursuit of goals springing from some complicated background of mistaken belief, such as, for instance, the alchemist's endeavour to turn lead into gold. It is only possible to see the alchemist's fiddling with retorts and vials as aimed towards producing gold if we read into the situation the whole network of his false theoretical assumptions. There is no physically possible variation of the borderline conditions of his activities under which they could ever result in the production of gold. But the alchemist *believes* that this is so.

The interdependence of conative and cognitive states–of wants and beliefs–precludes a simple dispositional analysis of goal-directedness. Furthermore, a closer look will reveal that this interdependence is only a small corner of the complete picture.

Wanting and believing are just two–admittedly most central–notions in a family of concepts used to describe and account for action in everyday affairs. Together, they make up an intentionalistic proto-theory of action, embedded in and largely constitutive of our everyday ways of thinking about human conduct. The key concepts of this theory are logically interrelated; they cannot be defined in isolation but derive part of their meaning from these mutual logical ties. This entire structure of concepts is grounded extrinsically in non-intentionalistic data, largely of a behavioural nature. However, it is not analytically tied to behaviour, but is supervenient upon it, in the sense that given two identical, non-intentionalistic descriptions of behaviour (of an inclusive sort), and given identical manuals of interpretation, identical intentionalistic descriptions must be assigned to the two stretches of behaviour.[8] By calling the theory intentionalistic I mean to indicate that its core concepts are directed at objects or states or affairs that may suffer 'intentionalistic inexistence': the situation one believes to obtain may not do so; the event that one hopes for may never come to pass; the upshot one desires to bring about may never materialize, etc. By calling it a proto-theory I indicate that it is largely tacit, an implicit structure embedded in our way of thinking about action, and also that its component concepts are rather fuzzy around the edges, making for much looseness and slack in the overall framework.[9]

If we agree to refer to this conceptual system as a (proto-) theory, we may view the logical interrelations between its components as reflecting the axioms of that theory. The central axiom would be the one which ties together the core notions of belief, want, and action, mediated by a handful of additional notions. ('Belief' and 'want' must here be construed as dummies, standing in for the names of the entire range of cognitive and conative factors, respectively.) This central axiom might be expressed (with unavoidable crudity) in this way:

A person who wants U to be the case and who believes that performing the action A will bring about U, will perform A provided the following conditions are jointly satisfied:

(1) He believes that U will not come about unless he takes action.
(2) He is capable of doing A, and knows this.
(3) The external conditions for doing A are satisfied, and he knows this.
(4) He knows of no better way to bring about U than by doing A.
(5) He knows of no reason why he dhould not do A (i.e., he has no fear that the cost of bringing about U will exceed the benefits, or will block the realization of other outcomes higher on his preference list; he does not believe that it infringes some norm to which he subscribes, etc.).

This formulation would need strengthening by numerous additional clauses to express a conceptually tight connection; as it stands, it is open to counter-instances. Moreover, the factors mentioned could be spelled out indefinitely, should we want a finer-grained analysis. But even in its rough version, it serves to illustrate the kind of logical interrelationships existing between the key intentionalistic terms of our proto-theory of action, centrally those of action, want, and belief (the last mentioned to be understood *sensu largissimo*), but also such more abstract background notions as capacity, etc. I shall refer to this conceptual framework as the 'motivational matrix'; the same term will be used to refer to its concrete realizations on particular occasions of action. (The shape of such concrete realizations need not be identical to the above axiom, of course: this axiom reflects only one particular and very simple kind of action, one that is central from the point of view of defining the component terms.)

A better understanding of this proto-theory can perhaps be gained by noting that it corresponds quite accurately to the standard logical positivist conception of theory-building and of theoretical terms. According to this conception, particularly as it is expounded by Carnap, theoretical concepts are implicitly defined by the theoretical postulates or axioms which spell out the connections between them. This entire interrelated conceptual grid is then 'interpreted', at least partially, by means of 'correspondence rules' which tie it to observational data.[10] The neat fit of this analysis with our proto-theory deserves to be pointed out, since it illustrates a crucial difference between the present theory and theories of natural science. It is by now generally agreed that the positivist model is inadequate in the latter domain. By making the meaning of theoretical terms depend on the content of the axioms they serve to express, the positivist analysis implies that the meaning of theoretical concepts must change with every change of theory, and that the terms of competing theories never possess identical meanings. This is an implication which is explicitly drawn and endorsed by some empiristically inclined philosophers (notably Feyerabend). But this doctrine loses ground in the face of the strong intuition that different and competing scientific theories may actually refer to the very same set of phenomena. It goes counter to the deep-rooted idea that science may be seen as a cumulative enterprise in which generation after generation of researchers grapple with the same problems, and to the notion that the scientific advances made today offer solutions to the very same puzzles that occupied earlier generations of researchers.

The above points are familiar from the writings of Putnam and others. And to do justice to this progressive aspect of science, we must resort to a semantics for theoretical terms of the kind developed by Putnam[11] and Kripke.[12] According to that semantics, what are construed as observational *criteria* (if only partial) on the Carnapian model, are really non-definitional ways of *picking out* a certain something-or-other which is causally responsible for the observational phenomena. The identity criteria of this something-or-other are a function of its fine-structural, intrinsic properties, not of its gross macroscopic manifestations. For instance, the identity criteria of chemical substances are a function of their atomic composition, not of their immediately observable properties. This severs the semantical ties between the expressions we use to refer to such things and states and the manifestations by which we single them out, or at least makes them highly flexible. If we discover additional things or properties devoid of these manifestations but of the same intrinsic nature (e.g. with the same atomic fine-structure), the former theoretical terms will refer to these things as well. As a matter of fact, we may subsequently discover that the original sample only displayed certain manifestations because of unrecognized extrinsic circumstances or interfering factors, and still take the term introduced on the basis of these manifestations to apply to the members of that sample. Conversely, if we found things or properties which shared the observable characteristics of the things in our sample, but which differed in their submicroscopic structure, we would refuse to apply the previously established term to them. We refuse, for instance, to call saccarine sugar, although the two are identical to the eye and the palate. On a larger scale, this semantics severs the logical ties between a term and the theory in which it occurs. We may switch our allegiances from one theory to another and still be talking about the very same phenomena. For the terms in which we talk about them are not defined by the theoretical interrelations in which they occur.

If the core theoretical concepts of natural science and the chief notions of our intentionalistic proto-theory diverge as just suggested, we should expect that the identity criteria of intentionalistically described mental states are not a function of the identity criteria of the underlying neurophysiological processes and conditions. This is indeed the way in which we adjudicate these matters on intuitive grounds. We would not begin to doubt the propriety of applying identical intentionalistic descriptions to two human subjects just because we had learned that the neurophysiological goings-on within the two were rather different, not as long as all the manifestations in action showed perfect correspondence. Take an example with some basis in actual clinical fact: we would not hesitate to ascribe the standard meanings to the linguistic output of a person who had suffered a stroke destroying his speech centre, and whose painfully reconstructed speech ability was subserved by areas in the cortex not normally involved with this function.

Another corollary is to the effect that we could not suffer a major shift in the axioms of the intentionalistic theory–such as, centrally, the one listed on pp. 13–14–and still assume ourselves to be talking about the same things. If some psychologist sprang the surprising news upon us that wants have been found to have no tendency to issue in action, we would have to construe him either as saying that it has been established that there are no such things as wants, or as changing the subject. The psychologist could not support his claim to be using the word 'want' in the standard sense by pointing out that the tests employed by him to determine the presence of a want were partly overlapping with those traditionally used by clinical psychologists, such as measurement of pulse rate, blood pressure, psycho-galvanic reflex, etc. of persons exposed to pictures of or conversation about the desired object or state. Once the logical interrelations between the intentional notions are disrupted, the meanings of these notions have been changed, even though large parts of the 'empirical interpretations' are retained. This position is supported by a strong intuition to the effect that the sophisticated tests of the above kinds remain peripheral from the point of view of revealing the nature of wanting. The clinical methods for measuring motivational states could never be allowed to co-determine the meaning of the terms with which we refer to such states on an equal footing with the logical interdependencies between these notions and with the traditional behavioural evidence by which they are interpreted.

I have adumbrated an analysis of goal-directedness which stresses the behavioural implications of goal ascription. But it should be emphasized that this analysis is by no means a behaviourist one (even apart from the endorsement of phenomenal items in note 9). It does not attempt to reduce the notion of goal-directedness, or the remaining components of the motivational matrix, to talk about 'matter-in-motion' in keeping with logical behaviourism. The analysis remains squarely within the ambit of intentionalistic notions, refusing to admit any non-trivial analytic connections between such notions and descriptions of behaviour. As noted above, it explicates the idea of the directedness of a certain action A towards a goal G in terms of reference to a counterfactual class of actions which the agent would have performed in alternative situations. That characterization relies (*inter alia*) on the intentionalistic notion of an action which effectively blocks behaviourist reduction.

But this observation might give rise to the opposite concern, to the effect that the analysis is circular. For presumably the notion of an action cannot be defined without reference to goal-directedness; after all, we introduced the notion of goal-directedness as something characteristic of, and coterminous with, intentional action in the full sense of the word.

This objection must be allowed to stand, in one sense. We have just dwelt at length on the fact that the intentionalistic notions by means of which we describe human action are logically interrelated. Any definition of one of them in terms of the others will eventually lead us back to that very notion if we trace all logical implications. It is a familiar point that there is no way to break out of, or into, this circle. But this does not mean that such definitions are unilluminating, or more specifically, that our explication of goal-directedness is void of interest. This would be the case only if that explication merely featured the two notions of action and goal-directedness, to be characterized symmetrically in terms of each other. But as we have seen, that characterization is merely a part of a larger intentionalistic theory involving many other notions: belief, awareness, ability, etc. A full unpacking of the component terms of that characterization would involve all these notions and would provide illumination of goal-directedness by placing it within this network of intentionalistic concepts.

Moreover, the definition is analytical, and hence informative, also in another sense. It explicates the notion of an action directed towards some goal G (for non-basic acts) by way of reference to a class of actions of a simpler sort, liable to bring about G. This reduction is not rendered uninformative by the fact that the reducing elements are themselves described as actions, i.e. as behaviour-directed-towards-some-goal, and are hence potentially subject to the same analysis. The means-end structures found at the heart of goal-directed action provide genuine insight into this phenomenon.

3

Progressing from an analysis of the notion of goal-directedness, I have offered a sketch of the motivational matrix in which all interpretive accounts are anchored and of the logical nature of the intentionalistic concepts that make up this matrix. This sketch exhibits the general philosophical assumptions underlying the methodological investigation to follow. It will aid us in seeing the nature of interpretive accounts in the proper light and will enable us to cope with certain doubts concerning the very applicability of such accounts in chapter 3. However, our task at present is to use the motivational matrix to characterize the three distinctive properties of human action singled out for special attention. Let us begin with the notion of purposiveness. I employ this term in a narrow technical sense. In everyday parlance, every full-blown human action may be called 'purposive': that is to say it is 'done on purpose', 'with something in mind', and not accidentally, absentmindedly, in a state of somnambulation, etc. For the purposes of this investigation, we are interested in isolating a more narrowly circumscribed property of action. The notion of purposiveness we adopt is a technical one which may, provisionally and crudely, be characterized as the pursuit of an end for its own sake, based on a genuine inclination towards that end. But to arrive at a more precise specification, we must contrast this 'inclination' with various additional modes of conation; that is, we must introduce a number of finer discriminations on the 'want' axis of the motivational matrix.

In the most general sense, a 'want' (a conative attitude) is simply a preference, of whatever kind, for a certain upshot. But additional distinctions can be drawn. In the first place, we may distinguish between 'wanting' a certain upshot for its own sake, versus 'wanting' it as a means towards a further end. Notice that an action can be a means towards some goal in senses other than bringing that goal about causally. It counts as a means towards the goal if it generates it in any of the ways listed and discussed by Goldman in *A Theory of Human Action*.[13] Thus the act of lifting my hat is a 'means' towards greeting you because hat-lifting conventionally counts as a greeting (this is what Goldman calls 'conventional generation'); my jumping eight feet is a 'means' towards breaking the world high-jumping record, since jumping eight feet is equivalent to breaking that record, given the further historical and actual context of my leap (this is 'simple generation' in Goldman's terminology). (In distinguising between actions issuing in an upshot wanted in itself, versus in one wanted only mediately, I make use of a fine-grained criterion of individuation for actions, a criterion that makes all non-equivalent intentionalistic descriptions of action stand for different actions. This choice is motivated by purely pragmatic considerations, since it allows the intended distinction to be expressed in a simpler and more perspicuous manner. No issues are being begged by this policy: the very same distinction may be drawn in terms of a coarse-grained criterion of the type advocated by Davidson.[14] According to Davidson-style individuation, the action whereby I bring about some end state and the actions whereby I take steps on the road towards this state are identical, the former merely being described in a more inclusive manner. To draw the intended distinction on this basis, we must speak, somewhat cumbrously, of actions-under-descriptions: hence the fine-grained criterion is preferable.)

We can also draw an intuitively clear, but otherwise elusive, distinction between 'wants' which embody some genuine preference for a specific outcome and 'wants' which reflect the agent's subscription to a certain norm which obliges him to bring it about. This is a distinction we shall explore in depth in the following section: here an intuitive grasp of the contrast will suffice. It is the contrast between, for example, going to the opera because you like opera or because that is the mandatory thing to do in your social circle, or between helping people in distress because that is your damned duty or because·you have a spontaneous inclination to do so. Notice that in talking about an 'inclination' towards some upshot I mean only a relative one, a preference for one particular outcome with possible alternatives. That outcome may merely be the lesser of two evils; hence, in using the expressions 'liking' or 'preference' I do not imply that the agent is necessarily highly enthusiastic about his choice.

The notion of 'purposiveness' and 'purposive action' I wish to propose can be characterized by means of these contrasts. Purposive action is action aimed at a goal (which may be the action itself, endotychistically) valued in itself and not as a means towards a further end, a goal towards which the agent has a spontaneous inclination (albeit perhaps only a relative one) and not one reflecting his compliance with a norm which bids him pursue it.

The rather complicated reflections involved in the definition of 'purposive action' might suggest that this notion will collect a highly unusual extension. But this is not the case. Let us step back from the detail of the above characterization for a moment and look at the region staked out anew. What we then see is something quite familiar. Purposive action is simply action aimed at an upshot for which the agent has some spontaneous and positive liking, or which he at least prefers to some unpleasant alternative. Paradigm cases of purposive action are acts performed to satisfy bodily needs or to avoid bodily discomfort. But also action performed in the pursuit of more esoteric pleasures, such as those stemming from the contemplation of great works of art, belong in this category, as does action satisfying a liking for solitude, for philosophical discussion, for getting up early in the morning, for going to rugby matches on Saturdays, or the like. Purposive action is not necessarily 'self-regarding': my donating money to the poor counts as a purposive act if I do this out of genuine beneficence rather than out of a sense of duty. Anything which a person wants in itself, not as a means towards some further goal, or which he dislikes in itself, not because of the evils following in its wake, can motivate purposive action when its realization or avoidance is the intended goal of action.

I shall appropriate the term 'desire' to represent the kind of 'want' which motivates a person to undertake purposive action. This term may not be entirely happy, since its everyday connotations suggest a rather violent urge, typically of a bodily nature. On the other hand, it is often used in philosophical discussions in a slightly more general and attenuated sense, devoid of this special implication. The way in which I use the term here is in rough agreement with this semi-technical sense.

Let me emphasize again that the distinctions introduced in this study are drawn solely with the present investigation in mind, and therefore disregard all discriminations not relevant to this context. A motivational psychologist will no doubt find my so-called fine-grained analysis utterly coarse, and perhaps also based on somewhat unusual criteria. What he must appreciate, however, is that the present analysis is meant to serve goals quite different from his.

4

We can now move on to the second distinctive feature of action. To describe action as meaningful may be to indicate that it is performed in compliance with *rule*.

In referring to the feature of action which I have in mind here as compliance with rule, I agree with standard terminology in philosophy. For although the species of action with which we shall deal now is not coincident with what is normally called rule-following conduct in philosophy, it is at least a proper subclass thereof, and indeed a central one. But perhaps a more felicitous designation would have been that of 'norm-governed action'. For that which most clearly sets this particular class of action apart from neighbouring types is its norm-bound nature; and not all rules are normative. However, since the terminology of rules and rule-following is so firmly established, I think it advisable to stick to it. Moreover, by so doing we are able to clear up important distinctions normally passed over lightly in discussion of rule-governed conduct.

Let us begin by listing various salient characteristics of the notion of a rule, in the sense I propose to use it here. As has already been anticipated, the concept of a norm will play a pivotal part. In a way it is misleading to say that the notion I want to adumbrate is that of a rule, *tout court*. For if we ask what a rule is, in the abstract, we should probably have to describe it as a proposition in the prescriptive mood. This answer is hardly informative, not even for those of us who are generally willing to countenance propositions.

Instead, the notion that interests us in the present context is the somewhat less ethereal concept of a rule-conformed-to-in-action. Our primary concern is to gain insight into one particular kind of human motivation and into accounts of action in terms thereof. Thus, we are interested in rules only in as much as they are action-guiding, not in rules in the abstract, considered independently of human cognition and action. Some might object that this is a distinction without a difference: rules are only abstractions from human rule-governed action; they have no existence apart from the concrete phenomenon of which they are an aspect. This objection need not be the trivial point that a rule can only be said to 'exist', in the sense of being in force in some population, if it is generally adhered to by a large segment of that population, but the more subtle claim that the very notion of a rule as something which is normative or prescriptive can only be defined by reference to human practices of sanction, criticism and argument. Normativity, it would be said, is not a part of the furniture of the world but is rather the projection upon the world of certain human practices. But although I have considerable sympathy for this view, which represents a generalized non-cognitivist position, there is no reason for us to accept that position as axiomatic for the present deliberations. There is no reason to commit ourselves to the existence or non-existence of genuine and irreducible normative facts, considered as existentially and definitionally independent of human cognition and human social practices. Our interest here is limited to the notion of a rule-as-conformed-to-in-action. This notion is securely grounded in empirical fact, and may be examined in isolation from the debate concerning a realist interpretation of normative facts. In the light of this, it might have been wise to avoid speaking of rules at all, even rules-as-conformed-to-in-conduct, and preferable simply to deal with the concrete phenomenon of rule-conforming conduct. However, its characterization would call for tortuous circumlocution if we were not allowed to refer to rules in the abstract; and I shall have cause to make liberal use of such reference in the following. Moreover, instead of the cumbrous expression 'rule-as-adhered-to-in-action', I shall simply use the term 'rule', referring throughout to the hyphenated notion.

In order to characterize the concept of a rule, we can proceed in a negative fashion, providing an outline of what it is not. A first, and crucially important, contrast is that between a rule and a mere regularity in conduct. When a rule is adhered to in a certain population, a regularity in action will ensue. To state, for instance, that a particular traffic code is obeyed in a specific community is to imply, minimally, that the conduct of traffic in that community will display a certain pattern, that it will follow a certain repetitive and predictable course. But obviously still more is implied here. A rule is a norm of action. It does not describe action, but prescribes its proper course. To say that a rule is being conformed to in a population is to say that a certain segment of conduct is subject to a standard of right and wrong and that recognition of this fact is a determinant of that conduct.

We may illustrate the point by elaborating upon an example from H. L. A. Hart's *The Concept of Law*.[15] If one watches an intersection controlled by traffic light, one will easily discern a pattern in the flow of traffic. As long as the light is red in a certain direction, motorists coming from that direction will not continue through the intersection but will stop. As soon as the light changes to green they will start up again, and traffic will continue to move through the intersection until the light switches back to red again. This is a fairly valid generalization about the conduct of motorists. But as a sociological description, it fails to capture the essence of the phenomenon, namely, that the observed conduct is based upon a norm. Motorists are aware that a certain standard of correctness applies to their driving and adjust their conduct accordingly.

The traffic code is upheld by an institution of enforcement and sanction. A person who runs a red light, or who parks illegally, is subject to punishment. Less formalized modes of sanction exist to support the rules of etiquette and good manners. Persons who infringe these in a systematic and unrepentant manner risk ostracism; for less serious infractions, there are proportionately milder types of censure, such as verbal rebuke. In many cases, the sanction will just be a certain reserve on the part of the offender's peers.

As we shall see, there is a conceptual connection between the notion of a rule and that of a sanction, at least in the form of reproach or criticism. However, this must not lead us to the view that rules are essentially obeyed out of fear of repercussions. Actions thus motivated will not count as rule-conforming according to the conception adopted here. Action counts as rule-conforming only if carried out with reference to the rule, out of a genuine feeling of obligation. Action motivated by fear of punishment is purposive action in the sense sketched in the previous section; it is motivationally akin to the action of staying away from trees in a thunderstorm to avoid being struck by lightning. Nor should the above observations lead us to the related misconception that rule-following is inherently a social enterprise. It is fully consistent with the notion of a rule proposed here, for example, to speak of a single individual living by his own private moral code, in express and conscious opposition to the sinful ways of the rest of society. True, as we shall see, there is a potential generality at the heart of the notion of a rule; but this generality does not require a plurality of actual rule followers.

An additional negative point. We must distinguish between rules and their explicit formulations. Rules may be followed *tacitly*: their existence is not contingent upon the availability of an explicit canonical formulation against which agents measure their conduct. For instance, the rules of etiquette did not wait for the publication of manuals of the Emily Post variety. Quite the opposite, such tracts depend upon the prior existence of tacit rule-following practices: they are codifications of such practices, purporting to systematize them in an authoritative fashion.

It is true, of course, that in the case of etiquette, most normal subjects will be able to produce a rough statement of a rule which they judge to have been violated on a certain occasion, if they are required to do so; but such explications are likely to suffer from a lack of generality. Nor is this capacity for explicitation upon reflection a condition for action to count as rule-conforming. We may refer to a certain syntactic rule in accounting for a person's use of this or that grammatical construction without implying that he is capable of stating the rule, even upon reflection. As a matter of fact, only a limited number of competent speakers of any natural language are in a position to do this for even a small segment of permitted grammatical constructions. Children are perfectly capable of speaking correctly, and of detecting mistakes in the linguistic performance of others, long before learning in school the explicit formulation of basic rules underlying this competence.

The claim that there is such a thing as tacit rule-following is a contentious one, and we must make a few remarks in its defence. The ground on which the battle over tacit rule-following has primarily been fought is that of transformational grammar. The debate revolves around the propriety of talking about the speaker as *knowing*, albeit implicitly, the deep structure rules which he is said to adhere to. Critics of the notion have maintained that we have no more reason to ascribe to speakers a knowledge of this sort than to ascribe to the digestive system a knowledge of which substances are nutritious and which are harmful, on the basis of its ability to digest the former and eject the latter.[16] But in so arguing, these critics seem to overlook the fact that the discriminatory power of the stomach is keyed to simple chemical properties of the substances that are fed to it, whereas the grammatical faculty handles material, the acceptability of which is often contingent upon semantical properties, at least lexical categorization. These properties are not simple physical parameters, and their recognition involves the processing of highly abstract data. This would seem to warrant our calling the process of grammatical parsing and evaluation a cognitive one, one involving knowledge, since the distinction between cognitive and non-cognitive performance is in part a function of that between abstractness and concreteness.

Gareth Evans has argued against the idea of implicit knowledge (and implicit rule-following) on the grounds that genuine knowledge and belief states have multiple manifestations.[17] Our reluctance to ascribe to a rat the belief that its food pellet is poisonous has to do with the fact that this alleged cognitive state is manifested only in a single type of response, namely, the rat's refusal to eat the pellet. It is not shown, for example, in an endeavour by the rat to keep its next of kin from eating it. According to Evans, the knowledge embodied in tacit rules of language is similarly manifested in one way only: in the production of a corpus of well-formed sentences. It lacks the richness of manifestation which we need to classify it as knowledge proper.

However, the distinction between multi-manifestation and single-manifestation capacities is hardly a clear-cut one. And if it is drawn in a way so as to exclude mastery of language from the domain of knowledge, many additional things that commonly go by that name will be barred too. After all, my knowledge of the rules of language is not merely displayed in my tendency to produce a correct linguistic output but also in my ability to criticize the output of others and to judge whether a sentence is well-formed or not if asked to do so by a linguist. It is difficult to see how this is inferior in variety of manifestation to my knowledge that 'polymers that have several head groups with an affinity for magnetic particles are the most tenacious stabilizers', a piece of information I just picked up from a science journal. For me, the only way to manifest this knowledge is by uttering this sentence or by doing things immediately derived from this linguistic ability. My knowledge equips me with no practical, behavioural competence. If tacit knowledge of the rules of language goes by the board, then so does this piece of explicit knowledge.

We have drawn a handful of distinctions to indicate what rules are not. It is now time to attempt a more positive characterization. Let us begin with a rather superficial observation. An action is motivated by deference to a norm when the agent's answer to the question, 'Why did you do it?' is simply, 'Because this is what you are supposed to do', or 'Because that is the thing to do', or more solemnly, 'Because that is my duty.' This, of course, is not very illuminating; even apart from the fact that the agent could be mistaken about his own motivation, these answers involve notions–those of 'being supposed to do something', 'the thing to do', and 'duty'–which are as much in need of analysis as the notion of a rule; and precisely because they are so closely akin to that notion. Reflection on these answers can, however, bring us a short step forward, if still only in a negative fashion. The answers derive part of their force from what they exclude, especially those answers such as 'Because I want to', 'Because I feel like it', etc. That is, action performed out of deference to a norm is not performed out of a liking for the outcome, nor, as observed above, is it motivated by fear of the evil effects of doing otherwise. Still, this only shows that rule-conforming conduct is not purposive action, in the technical sense introduced in the previous section. And this notion was in part defined in contrast with rule-conforming action. We still do not have a positive, substantive characterization of rule-conforming conduct.

To be able to describe somebody as acting in conformity to rules, certain general conditions must be satisfied which go beyond the concrete instance of rule-conforming action. The agent must exhibit a general mastery of normative considerations in conduct and argument. He must have it in his repertoire to reproach others for failure to abide by rules. Now 'reproach' is itself a normatively tainted expression: reproach is the negative reaction reserved for rule-offenders. It must be distinguished from the simple brutish anger you feel with someone who thwarts your purposes. For a negative reaction to count as a reproach, it must be appropriately sensitive to exonerating arguments on behalf of the offender. It

must be sensitive to arguments claiming such exculpating circumstances as ignorance, inability, etc.; arguments that are not
likely to deflect the assaults of someone who is simply airing the
rage of a frustrated desire. It must also acknowledge the relevance–
which is different from the overriding power, of course–of reference
to generally accepted maxims which endorse the action in question.
The critic must also see the point of reference to precedent, both
general precedent and precedent established by the critic himself
(in other words, the critic must appreciate the weight of *tu quoque*-
arguments). On the other hand, he must remain unmoved by a flat
'I just felt like doing it' from the offender. Similarly, he must reject
as irrelevant any defence to the effect that although the offender did
really fail to take action of the required kind, the upshot to which
that action would have led was attained anyway, through the
activity of other agencies; a rejoinder that would be highly relevant
in attempting to avert a person's anger and frustration at seeing a
desired upshot come to nothing. A person blamed for failing to take
action to save a child caught in a dangerous undertow could not
escape censure by pointing out that the child was later washed
ashore alive by a freak wave. Normative reproach is reproach for
failure to take action, not an expression of anger at an upshot not
attained. (This echoes the Kantian view that the will is the proper
object of moral censure. Notice that the point holds, even if the
norm requires us to bring about some upshot, such as saving other
people's lives.)

The agent must, of course, also adopt an appropriate attitude to
charges directed against himself. He must show awareness that
answers like, 'I just did not feel in the mood for it' are not to the
point, but that ignorance, inability, etc. may be pleaded; equally
effective is reference to generally accepted principles and to
precedent.

In this involvement with critical argument lies the potential
generality and communality of rule-governed action. Although a
person may be the only one to abide by some exacting moral
standard, his way of thinking about his conduct must reserve a
place, so to speak, for the possible existence of others similarly
committed and for the mutual criticism to which they will expose
each other.

So much for the general background needed for rule-conforming action to be attributable to an agent. But, of course, this background does not settle the issue of the motivation of any particular action. For some action token *A* to be motivated by deference to rule, more concrete conditions must be satisfied. In the first place, there are conditions of the general kind sketched above, but bearing directly on *A*: *A* must be an action of a kind which the agent would reproach others for failure to perform, and for which he would accept blame from others if he himself omitted it. Focusing even more narrowly on the concrete instance of action, there exists a counterfactual implication to the effect that if the agent had failed to perform in this situation, he would have accepted the censure of others for this failure. And he would do so even if the upshot which the rule bade him secure was brought about in another way.

I have illustrated my analysis of rule-conforming conduct with examples drawn from the realm of morals, and it might be objected that the points made do not easily transfer to less urgent cases, such as to rules of etiquette. I believe, however, that counterparts to all of these features may be found in conduct determined by etiquette and in all other rule-conforming action, only somewhat weakened in proportion to the importance of the kinds of action regulated. Even in etiquette, there is an institution of reprobation for offenders, and standard ways in which such reprobation may be rebutted. Moreover, although there may not be strong feelings of remorse associated with the infraction of rules of etiquette, there will be acute pangs of embarrassment, as anybody will know who has unwittingly broken such a code.

The point that rule-conforming conduct is conduct motivated by the recognition of obligation is fully compatible, of course, with the fact that rules may be *hypothetical*. The rule specifying the proper attire for court balls is a hypothetical one which restricts you only if you attend such royal festivities. And whether or not you do so is left entirely to your own inclinations.

5

Let me now indicate certain points on which my conception of rule-following conduct deviates from standard philosophical under-standing. As noted already, it does so by being somewhat more restrictive. This deviation saves the notion of rule-conforming action from vacuity: for in the standard version, this notion threatens to become so all-embracing as to allow for no possible contrast.

Suppose you want advice on how to cook your *filet mignon*, which you prefer rare. You check your cookery book and read something along these lines: for *filet mignon* rare, grill for two minutes; for medium rare, grill for three minutes; for well-done, grill for four minutes. You follow the advice and grill the steak for two minutes. Now this conduct would presumably count as rule-conforming, according to the standard conception. But it does not do so, according to the view presented here. The advice in the book is not normatively binding, not even hypothetically; it does not tell you that if you want your meat rare, you are under an obligation to grill it for two minutes. It just informs you that if you want your steak rare, the way to achieve this is to grill it for two minutes. Or even more neutrally: it informs you that if you grill your steak for two minutes, it will come out rare. The 'rule' in the cookery book does not serve as a norm prescribing your kitchen activities: it is a low-level empirical generalization about the changes induced in meat as a result of heating, serving as a perfectly factual premise in that little piece of practical reasoning in which you engage before going about your cooking. If we treat generalizations like this as rules when occurring as premises of action, then all empirical principles and laws will function as rules when so occurring, thus turning almost all action into rule-conforming action. Even the principles of mechanics will count as rules when serving as premises in the computations of a space engineer calculating when to fire the retrorockets to return the wayward spacecraft to its orbit.

The only point of similarity between such principles and rules proper is their generality. Notice, however, that if descriptive generalizations and laws are construed as action-guiding rules, there is no good reason why the same treatment should not be given to singular factual premises of practical reasoning, to the particular facts known by the agent and serving as part of the information basis upon which he acts. As we know from Hare, the descriptive sentence, 'Grimbly Hughes is the largest grocer in Oxford' could be recast as the pseudo-rule (prescription) 'If you want to go to the largest grocer in Oxford, go to Grimbly Hughes.'[18] In this way, all the premises of practical reasoning turn out to be rules, making all action multiply rule-conforming.

On the other hand, these reflections must not lead us to embrace the opposite, equally mistaken position that no premise of action can function as a rule if it has an identical twin of purely descriptive import. For although the statement of some rule may be, so to speak, a mere prescriptive transformation of a descriptive sentence (a 'hypothetical imperative', in Hare's sense), an agent may still treat that principle as a rule or norm: he may still comply with it in the spirit of 'that is what you are supposed to do', with no further reflection. A carpenter's apprentice may fail to recognize the factual underpinning of the rules for handling the tools that are taught him, and abide by them simply because 'that is the thing to do.' In traditional crafts, it is often quite difficult to distinguish between 'hypothetical imperatives' (technical rules) and the non-technical rituals of the trade. Practical routines originating in the first group may gradually move to the second, being fondly adhered to long after their technical *raison d'être* has vanished or been forgotten. One might even treat the sentence, 'If you want to go to the largest grocer in Oxford, go to Grimbly Hughes' as a rule in the strict sense: I, a newcomer to Oxford, and eager to adapt to the local ways, might receive this piece of advice from friendly neighbours and misconstrue it as a page out of the Oxford book of proper conduct. My interpretation of it would be parallel to the principle, 'If you want to go to the largest grocer in Oxford, be sure to wear your Sunday best.' I might so construe it, even though I knew that Grimbly Hughes was the largest grocer in Oxford.

Here is a further difference between the standard conception of rule-following conduct and the one I have proposed. We often call 'rules' those conventions which define, for example, the act of touching one's hat as an act of greeting. The rule states that touching one's hat counts as a greeting, given appropriate circumstances. Yet touching one's hat is not a rule-conforming action in my sense: this is the case only if there is no alternative convention of greeting and if greeting is itself prescribed by rule.

The principle that touching one's hat counts as a greeting does not place us under any obligation or constrain us in any way (with one qualification, see below); rather, it provides us with a tool for carrying out a certain action. It is what is traditionally called a *constitutive* rule, in contradistinction to the regulative rules we have examined thus far. Such 'rules' function in an agent's deliberations, not as maxims which put him under an obligation, but as purely factual–technical premises. The convention, 'Hat-touching counts as a greeting in this community' has much the same role in an agent's practical reasoning as a principle like, 'Waving your hat in the air is an efficient way to attract somebody's attention.'

But, as noted, with one qualification. To say that some action, gesture, sign, or the like, conventionally counts as a greeting is to indicate a state of affairs which involves normative rules. For some action or aspect of action A to 'mean' 'I greet you', A must be reserved for occasions where greeting is in order, that is, for occasions where social encounters are initiated. In general, for some action A to have a conventional meaning M there must exist rules specifying when the performance of A is allowed and when forbidden. The members of a community in which some conventional code of communication is in use are under an obligation to use the symbols of that code only when they believe that the relevant 'conditions of utterance' are satisfied.[19]

This does not imply, however, that all constitutive rules have an underpinning of regulative rules. Constitutive rules that would seem to lack such support are the legal principles specifying the conditions under which individuals may create legally binding instruments such as wills, contracts, etc. The rule which states that a document produced under specific conditions counts as a legally valid will does not imply that persons may only create such legal instruments if they intend the ordinances made in them to become effective. There is nothing unlawful about making a will and at the same time undertaking acts (such as burning all one's belongings) to ensure that one's heirs will never receive a penny of what was bequeathed.

6

Finally, action may be meaningful by possessing *semantic meaning*.

For want of a better term, I shall refer to such action as semantic action. Semantic action is communicative action employing a conventional means of communication. The paradigm type is the speech act, in which a meaningful sentence is put forth orally, addressed at some audience present in the speaker's vicinity. Semantic action involving writing or other media may deviate from this core case by not involving a designated audience: one puts up a poster to be read by anyone who happens to pass by. But as long as the 'speaker' has some potential audience in mind (which may in the limiting case be himself), the appellation 'semantic action' is appropriate.

Action involving such more specialized means of communication as the signalman's pennants, the policeman's gesticulations and whistle blows, and the football umpire's flags and arm gestures, also count as semantic action as this term has been construed thus far. We may feel reluctant to lump such acts together with semantic action of the first type; due, perhaps, to the specialized use and restricted vocabulary of the 'languages' employed in these cases as compared with natural languages. As a matter of fact, I shall soon impose certain further constraints upon the notion of 'semantic action' and 'language' which will exclude such systems from our area of interest. However, my chief concern at present is to establish that languages are conventional vehicles of communication: the words and sentences of language have no 'natural' (e.g. causal) connection with their significata and meanings. The systems mentioned above undoubtedly satisfy this condition.

While the above cases are reasonably clear-cut and uncontroversial examples of semantic action, interpretation theorists often maintain that the class of action embodying semantic meaning is more extensive than this; indeed, some would claim that all social action is really language-like. Human action in general is said to express the agent's intentions and attitudes in much the same way as speech acts express what is on the speaker's mind. Correspondingly, certain aspects of human action and certain human artifacts are described as languages by means of which people communicate various facts about themselves: the clothes they wear, the furniture in their homes, the cars they drive, the food they eat, etc. In brief, the meaningfulness of social action in general, or very broad aspects of it, is equated with the meaningfulness of speech acts in the verbal sense. Of course, such theorists do not always claim that full identity holds between the species of meaning ascribed to speech acts and that ascribed to actions not normally considered to have a linguistic content. More often, they insist that there are significant parallels and overlaps between the two, enough to warrant the extension of semantic methods and concepts to social action in general. (Far too often, the conception of semantic meaningfulness employed by such authors is too loose to give any precise idea as to the exact import of the claim advanced.)

In this book, semantic action will concern us only to the extent that it falls within the wider class just outlined. That is, in assessing the prospects for a social science approach based upon semantic meaningfulness, we shall only examine theories dealing with action that is not normally considered language-like. We shall bypass questions concerning theorizing about the semantic aspect of language as well as the minor semiotic systems mentioned above. This restriction is dictated by the overall objective of the present investigation, as specified in the Introduction. We want to assess the prospects for a theoretical strengthening of *social science* on the basis of interpretive accounts; social science to be distinguished from its more specialized neighbouring disciplines. An examination of the prospects for theoretical advance in such autonomous sister disciplines as linguistics and semiology is outside our scope.

This does not mean, however, that we can leave speech acts and languages completely out of sight, since these constitute the paradigm cases of semantic phenomena. A satisfactory understanding of the phenomenon of semantic meaning and of communication could not be reached without these as a point of departure. For this reason, I shall use them in the following exposition of semantic meaningfulness. But we must continually bear in mind that the concept analysed is one with a presumably much wider application, and that our aim is to assess its power to sustain genuine theorizing within this alleged wider field of application.

Semantic action comprises the production of a sentence or expression in a certain language. By 'language' I mean at this stage any conventional means of communication, regardless of the nature of the vehicle used. The thought that language is conventional is hardly controversial, and the adoption of a terminology that makes this feature a defining property of language would not seem in need of extensive comment. However, this point deserves attention in view of the fact that semantic action falls within a broader class of communicative action not necessarily involving a conventional vehicle of communication. Consider the following situation. Mrs Jones wants to communicate to Mr Jones that rain is to be expected. For some reason or other she cannot convey this information verbally and must resort to other means. She therefore dresses up in an elaborate rain outfit, complete with umbrella, rain coat, and rubber boots, ready to leave home. She does this demonstratively right in front of the chair in which Mr Jones is sitting. In doing so, Mrs Jones not only intends Mr Jones to acquire the belief that rain is to be expected, but also to realize that it is her intention that he acquire this belief. Furthermore, she intends him to reach the former belief on the basis of the latter one; that is, she intends him to believe that rain is expected because he realizes that this is what she intends him to believe. Now if Mrs Jones's intentions are fulfilled and Mr Jones catches on, she may justly be said to have communicated to him the fact that it will soon rain, and she may indeed be said to have *meant* by her rain gear demonstration that it is going to rain. This example illustrates the fact that communication and meaning can exist without convention; since, of course, the donning of a raincoat does not conventionally *mean* rain. The connection between the two is purely causal. Mrs Jones manages to communicate her point without the benefit of a conventional vehicle of meaning. (As we shall see in a moment, this description of Mrs Jones's action does not provide the complete and precise conditions allowing it to count as communicative; but on the most natural way of filling out the gaps in this domestic story, that action will actually satisfy those conditions.)

In the course of the deliberations to follow, we shall deal exclusively with accounts of action employing language, that is, a conventional vehicle of communication. A mode of account will only warrant a separate examination here if the assessment of its theory-generating powers raises unique problems and thus calls for a distinctive argument. Accounts of communicative action do not qualify for independent discussion according to this criterion.

Assessing the theory-sustaining potential of communicative action *qua* communicative would involve the very same considerations needed to answer the identical question for purposive action and rule-governed action in general, of which communicative action is a proper sub-class. Typically, communicative action is a species of purposive action: a man will break silence because he has the desire to achieve a certain effect in an audience. The nature of these effects–we are merely interested in illocutionary effects, since these are the ones determining the meaning of a speech act–is likely to reflect the speaker's concerns in general: what people talk about is likely to represent a cross section of what is on their minds in general. True, such a cross section will hardly constitute a fair sample of a person's concerns, since there are things you may be allowed to do but not to talk about. But on the whole communicative goals are not likely to be so distinct from goals in general that they can be said to create distinctive obstacles or avenues for theorizing. The objection could be raised that in one respect communicative goals represent a very narrow selection of man's desires: by communicating, one can only hope to achieve goals involving the thoughts and action of human beings: only God can create light by uttering the appropriate command. (One can, of course, indirectly bring about changes in the physical world by issuing orders. But these are perlocutionary effects, not illocutionary effects which are the type we are concerned with here.) This point is well taken. However, once we leave this abstract level of specification, diversity returns: the *specific* kinds of belief people want to induce in their audience by uttering constative sentences, or the *specific* kinds of action they order them to carry out by uttering commands, will reflect their overall interests and projects: theorizing in this area holds the same opportunities and faces the same obstacles as theorizing about purposive action in general. Semantic action, on the other hand, offers a distinctive avenue of theorizing: it invites us to investigate the semantic *system* employed in speech acts.

Let me now proceed to outline an account of semantic meaningfulness; certain additional details will be offered in chapter 7. The reader should be aware that the present analysis is not necessarily one that would be accepted by writers who contend that the meaningfulness of action is of a semantic nature. But the only way to assess the prospects for theorizing about social action in terms of its semantic properties, and indeed to test the very appropriateness of semantic description in this field, is to examine these questions in the light of the best theory of semantic meaning available. We hardly have any other option, especially since the advocates of the semantic approach have been remarkably reluctant to reveal how they construe this notion. At times one gets the impression that they take it to be self-explanatory, at other times that they regard it as being so basal that it resists philosophical analysis. The first attitude is woefully wrong; the latter, hopefully, is a bit premature.

I believe that any adequate theory of semantic meaningfulness must contain two elements: (1) it must incorporate sizeable portions of the speech act analysis, originating with H. P. Grice's 'non-natural meaning' and perpetuated by such authors as John Searle and Stephen Schiffer; (2) this element should be combined with relevant insights stemming from current speculation about the abstract form of semantic theories. These two elements are complementary: the speech act theory is essentially an analysis of communicative action, spelling out what we do when we engage in communication. The semantic theory deals with the basic structural features of language as the conventional vehicle of such communicative acts. At the present introductory stage, I shall devote primary attention to the act aspect of semantic meaningfulness, limiting myself to only a few brief remarks on the nature of the semantic system. A more thorough discussion of this aspect will be undertaken in chapter 7.

Let us begin by looking at the Gricean analysis of 'non-natural meaning'. This term is meant to draw a contrast with such 'natural' senses of 'meaning' as in, for example, 'heavy clouds mean rain' and in 'the footprints mean that a burglar has been here'. It also excludes such occurrences of 'mean' as in 'freedom means a lot to me' and 'I meant to return the book to you.'[20] Grice's approach centres around the notion that non-natural meaning as applied to meaning-bearers (i.e. signs) is derived from the idea of a person meaning something in, or by, doing something. This notion, in turn, is dependent upon the phenomenon of communicative intention, that is, the intention of achieving some cognitive or practical effect with reference to one's interlocutors via their recognition of this intention.

We must offer a somewhat more thorough presentation of the development of this proposal, since it underlies the discussion of semantic meaning in this study. I shall provide an account which is specified rather more fully than is required for our purposes. This I do primarily for reasons of exposition: it is impossible to sketch that particular aspect of meaning of interest here without embedding it in a somewhat broader context. However, the account remains a skeleton, which would have to be fleshed out much more fully if we were to use it to attack the problems indigenous to meaning theory. However, this is not our task here.

The account which follows will eclectically combine ideas from the two main Gricean heirs, John Searle and Stephen Schiffer.[21] I will adopt much of Schiffer's technical apparatus but introduce a substantial Searlian modification therein. However, no great store should be set by my deviation from Grice's original proposal or from the later more refined renditions of Schiffer and Searle, this deviation being motivated by considerations irrelevant to our present concerns. The critical–analytical tools I hope to extract from this definition of meaning stem from features which are shared by the original Grice proposal and its successors. In other words, the present analysis is not tailor-made to suit my own critical ends.

First, here is a suggestion for a definition of the notion of speaker's meaning (meaning$_s$), expressed in the locution 'S (= speaker) means that p by doing h'. This definition is subsequently used to characterize the concept of sentence meaning (meaning$_x$), as expressed in the locution 'x (a sentence) means that p'. Finally, I combine the two definitions to provide an explication of the locution 'S says that p by doing h', where 'saying that p' is the act of communicating that p by the use of language, that is, by producing something which means that p in some conventional system of communication. The notion of saying is in a sense the central one in a theory of semantic action, since it is the one that combines the two elements of communicative action and conventional meaning.

The definition of speaker's meaning goes as follows:

S means (means$_s$) that p in doing h iff

(1) S performs h, and
(2) intends (intention$_1$) that S's performance of h produce in A (the audience) the belief that S is committed to it being the case that p, and
(3) intends (intention$_2$) that intention$_1$ be recognized by A and serve at least as part of A's reason for taking S to be committed to it being the case that p, and
(4) intention$_2$ is an iteratively public intention.

(This definition and the two that follow apply directly only to constantive acts of meaning, but will extend to other illocutionary modes when slightly transformed. I shall bypass this complication here.)

For the more general considerations underlying this type of definition, I refer the reader to Schiffer's study, *Meaning*. However, my account differs from Schiffer's on one important point, a point involving that neologistic term, 'iteratively public intention'. This term is introduced to manage a familiar difficulty in framing meaning definitions along Gricean lines. To render my definition intelligible on this point, we must have a brief look at this problem and at the way my proposal comes to grips with it.

A natural first suggestion for the analysis of the locution 'S means that p' (where p is replaceable only by assertoric sentences) might be the following: S means that p by doing h iff in doing h S intends to induce in some audience A the belief that p. We may use Grice's own example to demonstrate that this will not do. [22] S may place B's handkerchief near the site of the murder to induce in the detective ($= A$) the belief that B is the murderer. But clearly we could not say that in performing this act, S *meant that B is the* murderer.

The reason why this example fails to embody meaning is that although S did h intending A to form a belief that p, A was not intended to be aware of this intention in S (indeed, he was not intended to recognize that h was produced by S at all). To resolve this, we must emend the definition to allow S to intend that A recognize S's intention to produce in A the belief that p, and to intend that (at least part of) A's reason for forming this belief be his recognition of that intention.

However, this analysis is open to the following counter-example, originally due to Strawson.[23] S wants to prevent A from buying a house which he, S, knows to be rat-infested. He plans to accomplish this by getting A also to believe that the house is rat-infested. So he turns a rat loose in the house, knowing that A is watching him as he does so, and knowing that A is unaware that S knows that A is watching him. S intends that A should (wrongly) assume that S intends A to take the rat to be natural, genuine evidence that the house is rat-infested. S also knows that A will think that S would not try to produce in A the belief that the house is rat-infested unless S himself was convinced that this is indeed the case.

In this complicated set-up, S satisfies the proposed condition for *meaning* that the house is rat-infested in, or by, turning the rat loose. He performs this act intending to produce in A the belief that the house is rat-infested (p); intending furthermore that A recognize this intention and that this recognition serve as (part of) A's reason for forming the belief that p. Still, it is counter-intuitive to say that by turning the rat loose, S meant that the house is rat-infested.

The way to deal with this counter-example is clear. We must add to the above analysis the condition that S intends that A be aware of S's intention that A recognize S's intention of generating in A the belief that p and that S intends A's recognition of this intention to be A's reason for believing that p.

But, indeed, this emendation is perfectly parallel to the one introduced initially, merely on a higher level. In both cases we reinforce the intentional state specified in the earlier, inadequate definition with a meta-intention to the effect that A recognize the lower-level intentions already cited. And we can now rightfully fear that an additional counter-example could be devised of a kind similar to Strawson's, but at a higher level, and so on *ad infinitum*. Schiffer has, in fact, produced a–highly contrived–counter-example of this kind, thus substantiating such fears.[24]

In *Meaning*, Schiffer tries to overcome this difficulty, partly by introducing the notion of mutual knowledge, involving a recursion upon the speaker's and audience's knowledge of the situation, and partly by adding a clause amounting in effect to a self-reflexive component in the speaker's communicative intention.[25] I doubt the legitimacy of the latter move: such self-reflexiveness appears to block finite specification of the intention. Hence, I propose to handle this difficulty by means of the notion of an *iteratively public intention*. Intuitively, an iteratively public intention that p is an intention with the following content: that p be the case; that it be known to the audience that p is intended to be the case; that it be known to the audience that it is intended to be known to the audience that p is intended to be the case; and so on. The point is that we can dispense with this open-ended characterization in favour of a finite, recursive one: to say that my intention that p is iteratively public is to say that I intend that p and intend this intention to be a member of a class of intentions such that any member of that class is an intention of mine, and such that if any intention i is a member of that class, then so is the intention that i be known to my present audience.[26]

There is a second respect in which we must improve upon the suggested provisional formula, to arrive at our definition on p. 39. The provisional formula calls for a speaker who means that p by some utterance to intend to produce in his audience the belief that p. However, as several critics have pointed out, I may utter something, meaning thereby that p, without the faintest hope of persuading A that p is indeed the case. Or I may alternatively mean that p while fully knowing that A believes that p already, thus pre-empting my generating that belief in him. An example of the latter would be the following exchange. Husband: 'I was working in the office all evening.' Wife: 'You're lying.' This example is Schiffer's.[27] Schiffer is confident that he is able to defend the original Grice analysis against counter-examples of this kind, but I fail to find his ngenious counter-argument fully convincing. However, this is not the place to argue that point. I simply adopt, without further comment, the condition introduced by Searle in *Speech Acts*, according to which a person who means that p by producing some utterance intends that his interlocutor will believe, not that p, but rather that the speaker is committed that p is the case. It should be pointed out that our final analysis as thus emended is closer to Grice's original account, and to the much sharper versions developed by Schiffer, than is immediately apparent. For it may be argued that he who successfully realizes a reflexively public intention of the kind specified in the definition has thereby committed himself to the occurrence of a certain state of affairs p. A speaker who not only intends some audience to form the belief that p, but who also stands by this intention by intending it to be publicly recognized, and who wants *this* intention too to be public, etc., must be taken to have issued a guarantee that p. By making his ground-level intentions public, as well as the total recursive set of meta-intentions, he assumes responsibility for the fact that his audience forms the belief that p. He can no longer excuse himself by claiming that he did not intend his audience to form that belief and that one cannot be held responsible for the beliefs which one's behaviour accidentally leads other people to adopt. Of course, the speaker might be held (morally) responsible even in the absence of such declaration of intention. The point is that by making his intentions public, he has *formally* cut himself off from pleading innocence on the above grounds. His commitment flows from this fact. Still it cannot be said that the Searlian analysis follows logically from the Grice–Schiffer version. For although a commitment to the truth of some proposition p can be said to follow, it does not follow from the analysis that the speaker intends or even recognizes this commitment, nor that he wants this commitment to be known to his audience. However, given the affinities between the two analyses, there is much reason to assume that they are co-extensive: every actual example of a communicative act satisfying the Grice–Schiffer conditions will also satisfy the Searlian analysis. There are, I think, no actual examples of communicators who satisfy the Grice–Schiffer conditions while still not accepting the commitments specified in Searle's analysis.

It follows from our definition of speaker's meaning that such meaning is not dependent upon a conventional vehicle of communication. Indeed, as indicated above, the point of Grice's approach is precisely to show how the notion of linguistic meaning, which *does* imply conventionality, is derived from a more basic, non-conventional notion. However, we now turn to the definition of the locution, 'x means that p', where sentences can be substituted for x. This is the point at which conventions enter the picture. The definition can be formulated as follows.

Sentence meaning (meaning$_x$): *x* means that *p* in a group of people *G* iff it is a convention in *G* that members of *G* produce *x* only if they intend thereby to generate, in the manner specified in the definition of speaker's meaning, a belief in an audience that the speaker is committed to it being the case that *p*.

Finally, the definition of 'saying', the act of communicating something by means of a vehicle that is conventionally reserved for that very communicative act:

Saying: *S* says that *p* in uttering the sentence *x* iff
(1) *S* utters *x*
(2) *x* is a sentence in *S*'s language such that *x* means, that *p* in that language
(3) *S* mean$_s$ that *p*
(4) *S* intends that the intentions involved in (3) be grasped by the audience at least in part by virtue of their knowledge of the conventions of *S*'s language.

So much for the speech act component of semantic meaning. We will now turn to the formal features of the semantic system used in communication as they emerge from current speculation on the form of semantic theories for natural languages. These features are those of *unboundedness*, of *compositeness*, and of *scrutability*. Unboundedness is the property of language permitting the construction of an infinite number of syntactically well-formed and semantically interpretable sentences. For natural languages, this feature is a consequence of their compositeness: simple meaning-bearers may be joined together according to syntactic rules to form new, composite meaning-bearers. (Notice that unboundedness and compositeness are not identical. Unboundedness of a non-composite kind could exist: we could devise a language in which an object held in the hand in a particular fashion would count as a sentence saying that that object, singled out in terms of some standard set of features, exists. Nor does compositeness imply unboundedness, since the rules of composition need only allow a finite number of combinations.) Finally, natural language is scrutable in that a person mastering a finite number of interpretive principles will be capable of interpreting any well-formed sentence of his language (barring lexical and structural ambiguity).

The decision to include this second, formal element in the characterization of linguistic meaning and language involves considerable legislation on these terms, as we shall use them in the following enquiry. The effect of that legislation is one of contraction, excluding from the extension of the terms such sign systems as the policeman's wavings when directing traffic and the football umpire's gesticulations on the field. The purpose here is to exclude sign systems for which a trivial semantics can be given, one that simply lists expressions alongside a specification of their meanings. Such a semantics would not go beyond the language user's explicit grasp of his language, but would simply spell out that grasp, and hence would not represent any advance upon it. By making unboundedness a condition of languagehood and semantic meaning, we exclude such trivial semantics: a simple enumerative semantics for an unbounded language would have to be unbounded itself. But a person, being finite, cannot operate a semantics of this type; he needs a semantics that produces infiniteness through finite devices. The specification of these devices renders the semantics non-trivial. (This specification would admittedly contain nothing beyond what is present in a person's *implicit* grasp of his language. But even making this tacit knowledge explicit is a theoretical achievement.)

7

We have examined certain central ways in which human action may be described as 'meaningful'. The next step is to consider the ways of accounting for action which have been erected upon the former. First, a brief remark is in order concerning the notion of an *account*. That term is employed in an all-embracing manner in everyday parlance, which is precisely why I adopt it here. It seems to embody no slant towards or against any particular approach to action, and should hence offend no one. In general, any description of an action may be said to provide an account of that action. In the present context, however, we will use this notion in a more austere sense. Only answers to questions of the type, 'What did he do?' and 'Why did he do it?' qualify as accounts of action according to the usage I shall adopt. This excludes answers to questions such as, 'When did he do it?', 'Where did he do it?', 'For whom did he do it?', etc.

As we shall see later in this chapter, the different types of interpretive accounts are not equally suited to answering questions of both the 'why' and the 'what'-variety. Purposive accounts and rule accounts are germane to either, whereas accounts in terms of semantic meaning seem appropriate in response to what-questions only. I shall demonstrate in a later chapter that this difference does not argue any deep-seated divergence betweeen the two kinds of accounts, and that the use of a single term for all types of interpretive accounts does not slur distinctions which we would be well advised to heed. This discussion will also show as misguided the radical position, sometimes proposed by interpretation theorists, that no interpretive account really serves to answer why-questions, only what-questions, leaving the former the domain of other types of accounts, primarily causal ones.

The following discussion of purposive accouts and rule accounts will be illustrated mainly by examples of why-accounts (i.e. answers to why-questions). As will be demonstrated in the next chapter, the notion of a why-account is the more demanding one and hence exhibits the distinctive features of interpretive accounts better than what-accounts do. Inevitably, the discussion of semantic accounts must be conducted primarily in terms of answers to what-questions (what-accounts).

8

In what ways has the purposiveness of human action been utilized in accounts of action at the everyday level? Before answering that question, we would do well to broaden briefly the scope of our discussion in a manner echoing our original treatment of purposiveness. We characterized this notion by contrasting it with other modes of motivation, all of which represented ways of filling out the general want–belief matrix of motivation. One contrast was that between action issuing in upshots wanted in themselves versus action issuing in states wanted only mediately, *qua* steps on the way to ultimate goals. We placed purposive action on the side of action issuing in a state wanted in itself. Secondly, within the class of action so motivated, we contrasted purposive action with action performed in deference to rule. Joining the two, we can say that purposive action is characterized as action issuing in an upshot wanted in itself and for which that agent has a genuine liking, if perhaps only a relative one.

Putting on one side action motivated by deference to rule, which will occupy us in the next section, these contrasts within the overall class of goal-directed action suggest the following two modes of interpretive account.

First, a mode which might be dubbed the 'means–end' pattern. It illuminates action by exhibiting it as a means for the realization of some upshot wanted by the agent in an inclusive sense; that is, by showing it is (believed by the agent to be) likely to generate (causally, or otherwise) some state of affairs to which the agent has some favourable attitude. It does not give any indication as to whether that state is wanted in itself or merely mediately, as a means towards achieving still further goals, nor does it indicate whether the ultimate goal is pursued out of genuine inclination or in deference to rule.

The second mode is that of purposive accounts. It generates understanding of action by identifying the 'intrinsic' upshot of an action–that is, the upshot cited in the intentionalistic specification of that action–as desired *per se* by the agent: desire to be understood in the exacting sense of p. 21 as signifying a genuine, if perhaps only relative, liking for some upshot, as contrasted with one derived from rule. (This way of defining purposive accounts presupposes the fine-grained manner of individuating action which we adopted on p. 19. With a coarse-grained criterion, we would have to relativize purposive accounts to descriptions of action: we would have to define such accounts as statements which account for an action under some description D by identifying the intentional object specified in D as an object of the agent's desire. This is somewhat cumbersome, but otherwise equivalent to the fine-grained formulation in all respects relevant to our investigation.)

Succinctly put, means–end accounts thus possess the following form (in response to the question, 'Why did X bring about the upshot U_1?'):

X brough about U_1 because he wanted (*sensu largissimo*) that the upshot U_2 come to be, and because he believed that U_1 would be likely to generate U_2.

Whereas purposive accounts may be spelled out like this (in response to the same question):

X brought about U_2 because he desired (in the stringent sense) that U_2 come to be.

Still, as foreshadowed by the number of headings in our taxonomy, we shall not give separate treatment to means–end accounts as a possible basis for interpretive theorizing. This is so because means–end accounts are of necessity *intermediate* accounts. The proffering of an account of this type necessarily leaves room for an additional question as to the agent's motivation: why did he want to bring about the second upshot (U_2 above)? This question, of course, may elicit still another means–end account; but eventually some other kind of interpretive account must terminate the regress. (Naturally, there will always be the possibility of raising further questions, answerable only in non-interpretive, causal terms. That regress is open-ended.) But this means that the theoretico-systematizing power of means–end accounts is a function of that of the terminating accounts: an examination of the former will inevitably issue in an examination of the latter. Means–end accounts borrow their theoretical power from the principles and concepts employed in the terminating accounts. Thus, a separate discussion of the theory-generating power of means–end accounts becomes impossible: there is no such thing as an assessment of their theory-generating power distinct from an examination of the theoretical power of the terminating accounts to which they point. We may therefore forgo further concern with this type of account and instead focus on purposive accounts.

This is the policy I shall adopt in this book. With one significant

qualification, however: the type of interpretive account whose
theory-generating power we shall examine in chapter 5 will not be
the pure purposive pattern, but rather a hybrid between this
pattern and the means–end pattern. Like the former pattern, it
makes action intelligible by relating it to some end state desired in
itself; but unlike that pattern, it does not necessarily relate action to
that state as its intrinsic upshot, but allows that relation to be
mediate, the upshot being just a means towards achieving the
ultimate goal. In this it agrees with means–end accounts. In other
words, hybrid purposive accounts make action intelligible by
relating it to some desired upshot which it either realizes
immediately or as a station on the way.

Why trouble ourselves with this hybrid, when its theory-
generating potential is of necessity identical with that of its pure-
bred cousin, the pure purposive account? The answer lies in the
fact that the hybrid displays much more clearly than the pure type
a number of logical–structural features common to both. These
features are relevant to an appreciation of the distinctive power of
such accounts and raise crucial problems that will occupy us at
various points in the following investigation. One of these problems
regards the strength of the notion of practical rationality involved
in such accounts (to be discussed in chapter 5). Another regards
the very logical status of this rationality principle (to be touched
upon in chapter 2). A further, more general problem best discussed
in terms of the hybrid is that of the logical entanglement of
cognitive and conative elements in the interpretation of action. We
have already dealt with this topic earlier in the present chapter and
shall do so again in chapter 7.

The reason pure purposive accounts are so poorly suited when it
comes to illustrating these problems is that they may be viewed as a
limiting case of the hybrid notion, a case in which the means–end
nexus between the immediate upshot of action and the ultimate
goal approaches zero. My bringing about U_2 because I desire that
U_2 come about is the zero case of my bringing about U_1 because I
desire that U_2 come about, and believe that U_1 is likely to generate
(causally, or otherwise) the coming about of U_2. As the gap
between U_1 and U_2 approaches zero, so does the number of possible
interpretations of the practical rationality relation which links them

together. The same is true regarding the number of alternative beliefs that may be attributed to the agent to account for his bringing about U_1 in order to achieve U_2.

When I speak of purposive accounts in the following, I shall be referring to the hybrid, not to the pure type. I hope that the above remarks have served to assure the reader that although this notion is indeed a bastard, from the point of view of an ultimate taxonomy, it is not a monstrosity. Nor does it collect a highly peculiar class of accounts, judged by intuitive standards. As a matter of fact, the extension of this concept will be found to coincide quite well with standard examples of what is traditionally, but loosely, called 'purposive acconts' elsewhere in philosophical literature. However, the reader must also bear in mind that the term is used here in a technical sense which excludes many cases belonging to its everyday extension.

If we outline the structure of a purposive account of an action consisting in the bringing about of an upshot U_1 in the format used earlier, we find the following elements: a desire in the agent for some upshot U_2 *per se*, plus a set of beliefs about the world, centrally a belief to the effect that if U_1 is brought about, U_2 will thereby be generated. In the limiting case, $U_1 = U_2$ (the case of a pure purposive account).

There is no doubt that this general pattern forms the backbone of a large number of everyday accounts of action. However, it is not always easy to catch sight of this anatomical structure beneath the surface form of such accounts. In some clear cases, the elements of the motivational matrix, or some of them, are mentioned directly. When we explain that Peter bought a new motorbike because he wanted to impress his fiancée, Peter's conative state is mentioned explicitly. But not all purposive accounts are equally obliging in revealing their underlying structure. Some indicate it only indirectly, by specifying the intentional object of the conative state, but without explicitly referring to or indicating the specific nature of that state. They still qualify as purposive accounts if the context makes it clear that that state is of the required kind. Such accounts may speak of the agent's 'goals', 'aims', or 'objectives'. Another construction which explicitly cites only the intentional object of action involves the 'in order to'-locution and its cognates, such as 'for the sake of', 'in the interest of', etc.

Notice that I do not claim that these locutions are reserved for purposive accounts and hence signal that some such is being offered. The grammatical constructions mentioned may all be used to express what we called (pure) means–end accounts and do not in themselves reveal whether or not anything stronger is intended. Whether this is indeed the case must be gleaned from the context.

In other kinds of purposive accounts, the motivational matrix is even more effectively veiled. This is true for what is commonly termed *motive*-accounts. These point to a character trait of the agent such as ambition, vanity, or greed; or to a more transient state of emotion such as jealousy or envy. As pointed out by Ryle in the *Concept of Mind*, such terms denote dispositional properties, certain standing or short-term tendencies to engage in action of specified sorts. However, Ryle overlooks the fact that these states are conative states, involving a preference for certain more or less precisely circumscribed upshots (typically rather loosely circums-cribed: part of the rationale of the motive-idiom is to allow us to refer to loose clusters of related preferences in an economical manner). The actions which manifest, say, a man's *ambition* are actions directed at the attainment of power, wealth, prestige, etc. Hence, explaining his actions by citing ambition as his motive is to proffer a purposive account, if only a very imprecise one.

All the above variations on the theme of purposive accounts are normally stated in an elliptic manner in everyday discourse. They will merely indicate the conative vector of motivation, leaving the cognitive factors unspecified. But some accounts may show ellipsis of a converse kind. They attribute a certain belief, or appreciation of a certain fact, to the agent, but say nothing of the conative states which combine with that belief to generate action. Still, they can only manage to make action intelligible if this other element is tacitly supplied. Its nature will typically be obvious from the specification of the cognitive factor; hence the permissibility of leaving it implicit. If we are told that Guiseppe left town because he had received news that the mob had put a contract on his head, we need not be told in addition that Guiseppe cherishes being alive and that these two factors jointly motivated his disappearance.

The final version of purposive accounts that I shall touch upon is that of reason-accounts. Reason-accounts are an extremely unspecialized mode; they may refer to any of the elements of the motivational matrix, with no special affinities. The formula, 'The reason Mr N. N. did *A* was . . .' may be completed just as naturally by a sentence indicating a belief as by one indicating a desire. Someone asks: why did Norbert sell his shop and leave town? The answer, beginning pedantically with the phrase 'The reason Norbert sold his shop and left town was . . .' may be finished in either of the following ways: 'because he wanted to move to a climate more agreeable to his tuberculosis'; 'because he needed to put as many miles as possible between himself and his mother-in-law'; 'because he believes that the West Coast climate is better for his tuberculosis.' The first two answers indicate a conative attitude, the latter a cognitive state. (Again I do not suggest that the 'reason'-terminology is used only to express purposive accounts, merely that it is one of the grammatical forms which such accounts may assume.)

I have dealt with only a few of the guises in which purposive accounts appear. Many more could be added, and a much fuller story could be told about the distinctive features of such accounts extending beyond their shared underlying structure, as well as about the considerations which make one type more appropriate in a given context than another. However, such an examination would be of primary interest to the lexicographer and would not further our present aims. Besides, careful studies of the fine nuances of meaning and subtle differences in use between these notions abound in the literature following in the wake of Ryle's *Concept of Mind*. The objectives here have been reached if we have succeeded in showing that the notion of a purposive account captures a way of elucidating action that is ubiquitous in everyday discourse.

9

The way in which *rules* figure in everyday action accounts are many and varied. Yet only one particular mode of occurrence qualifies an account as a rule account, in the sense I propose to use this word.

That mode, of course, will reflect our characterization of rule-conforming conduct in section 4, where we attempted to adumbrate a way in which the consideration of rules might motivate action, a way which we described as manifesting 'deference to the rule'. I need only repeat a few salient negative points in that characterization.

A person who acts out of deference to the rule does not act to achieve something for which he has a liking, nor in order to avoid hardship. In particular, he does not act in order to avoid the sanctions attending infraction, nor to gain the esteem reserved for the scrupulously rule-abiding. Thus, the conduct of a motorist who sticks to the rules of the road because he fears getting caught and prosecuted should he do otherwise, or because he is aware of the higher accident rate associated with unlawful driving, does not invite account in terms of rule-conformity, based upon the present conception. His action will call for purposive account in the sense previously defined.

Another negative point: a person who adapts his conduct to a rule need not be able to state that rule. Hence this ability is not required for the propriety of accounting for his action in terms of rules. We may account for certain features of people's speaking habits by pointing out that they adapt their verbal behaviour to the rules of the language spoken in their community without implying that they are capable of stating these rules, much less that they rehearse them in their heads prior to speaking. All that is required, generally, is that they be capable of spotting deviations from the rules as a practical accomplishment.

We need a terminological device to mark the distinction between action performed in deference to rule, and action which accords with rule but is not necessarily motivated by deference but by other concerns, and which, in fact, may even be performed in perfect ignorance of the existence of the rule. I have used the term 'rule-conforming conduct' to refer to the former and shall continue to do so. For the latter, I shall coin the term 'rule-consonant conduct'. Notice that rule-conforming conduct is a proper subclass of rule-consonant conduct.

Let me emphasize that in presenting my conception of rule-conforming conduct, and of rule-accounts, I make no empirical claims concerning the distribution of such conduct. I do not imply, for instance, that most rule-consonant conduct is actually rule-conforming, nor that conduct normally taken to be rule-conforming actually is so. On the other hand, this conception would clearly suffer from loss of interest if it were never instantiated in human conduct. Hence, by introducing it, I imply–if only pragmatically–that it is actually sometimes instantiated. Such a commitment is hardly hazardous. True, there is a tendency in social theorizing to account for all action by citing the hope of gratification or the fear of distress. This stance, I believe, springs in part from a resolve to display scientific sophistication by not taking the official interpretation of social conduct at face value. Social science, it is felt, must look behind the facade, unflinchingly reporting what it sees no matter how embarrassing these findings may be to our most fondly held beliefs about the origins of our actions. However, in this case I am convinced that genuine sophistication will bear out the naive view as often as not. There is actually a phenomenon called following a rule out of deference, with no eye to rewards or punishments. And this kind of motivation is at least a powerful co-determinant of much rule-consonant conduct. Indeed, if rule-consonant conduct were merely undertaken out of fear of repercussions, it is doubtful whether such conduct could ever be sufficiently common to keep society from disintegrating.

10

Finally, we come to accounts in terms of semantic meaning. The idea that we understand speech acts in the sense of grasping the meaning of what is said is hardly in need of support; nor is the suggestion that there is such a thing as accounting for speech acts by stating their semantic content. It is merely the suggestion that this kind of meaning and the use of this kind of account extend much wider than is normally recognized that is contentious. However, the validity of this proposal is not to be discussed here: that topic will be reserved for chapter 7.

To understand a semantic account is to identify the speaker's (as I shall call him for convenience) communicative intentions, and to appreciate that he intended those intentions to be known to his interlocutors as result of that act. The interlocutor grasps the speaker's intentions by virtue of his command of the conventions which tie the uttered expression to this particular communicative intention. Correspondingly, accounting for a semantic act in terms of its meaning is to indicate the speaker's communicative intentions and to spell out the semantically relevant conventions which govern the sentence uttered and which make it a vehicle for precisely this intention.

This notion of an account of semantic meaning is quite a stringent one. It is not satisfied by an *oratio obliqua* account, indicating merely what somebody said or meant without identifying and analysing the expressions by means of which he said it. Perhaps we would do well to loosen this notion somewhat, to comprise pure *oratio obliqua* accounts as well: that is, we may allow an utterance like 'Mark Antony said that Brutus is an honourable man' to count as a semantic account. Still, we must maintain that the kind of account which exhibits and analyses the speaker's actual statement is primary to *oratio obliqua* accounts. The latter could not be given unless the former could. Knowledge about what somebody said or meant by some utterance without knowledge of the actual expression used must, in the end, be anchored in information about what words were actually spoken and about what those words mean. (I shall henceforth refer to those statements which supply the latter kind of information as *mixed (semantic) accounts*, since they combine elements from (pure) *oratio recta* and *oratio obliqua* accounts: they indicate what the speaker actually said (i.e. what words were actually mouthed) as well as what he *meant*, deriving the latter from a semantic analysis of the former).

There is a further reason for taking mixed accounts to be primary to pure *oratio obliqua* accounts: the latter merely indicate the speaker's communicative intentions without troubling themselves with the vehicle of communication used. Hence they deal with semantic action only *qua* communicative. We have already argued (pp. 35–36) that communicative action is not suficiently distinctive to form the basis of an autonomous pattern of interpretive account. The messages which people convey to each other in linguistic interaction may be presumed to reflect their sundry projects and overall concerns in life: they must be presumed to be a function of those further goals for which communication serves as one means. This suggests that communicative action *qua* communicative is best treated as a species of purposive action or rule-conforming action when it comes to assessing the theory-generating powers of the first.

The above reflections may become clearer when considered in terms of a distinction familiar from linguistics, namely that between *langue* and *parole*. *Langue* is the abstract semantic system, a system of timeless meanings. *Parole* is the sum total of messages actually expressed by means of that system as actual historical occurrences. Recast in this terminology, we can rephrase the point made above as follows: when construed as dealing with semantic acts only as elements of *parole*, semantic accounts are not distinctive enough to generate special avenues for theorizing. They do so, however, when they are taken to deal with semantic acts *qua* describable in the terminology developed to analyse *langue*.

I must add a few remarks in order to avert a misunderstanding to which these observations might easily lead. When we provide a semantic account of a speech act, the object we are concerned with is that concrete act, that instance of *parole*. It is not the abstract sentence, a constitutent of the *langue* which it embodies. This is apparent from the fact that should we for some reason suspect that the sentence spoken was somehow a slip and hence did not express the speaker's real meaning, we would not rest content with simply indicating the standard meaning of that sentence; we would try to get at what the speaker really meant by it, and would thus produce a double account, one part specifying what he actually said and one specifying what he meant to say. The point of the preceding deliberations was merely that semantic accounts are only distinctive–and this means essentially: only pose distinctive problems for theorizing–because they utilize purely semantic categories, categories developed to analyse the *langue*.

It has been implicit in what I have said thus far that semantic accounts are typically answers to what-questions. They are accounts given in response to queries of the kind 'What did he say', 'What did he mean', etc. Moreover, it might appear as if such accounts were altogether inapposite as answers to why-questions. What way of filling in the blank could turn the following exchange into an intelligible dialogue: 'Why did Jones . . . ?' 'He said that it was three o'clock.' If this impression is right, it might be taken to indicate a heterogeneity in the class of statements I have termed 'interpretive accounts', and hence might suggest that the project of assessing the theoretical powers of such accounts is an ill-conceived one.

In chapter 3, I shall attempt to justify the view that the differences between why- and what-accounts are quite insignificant, largely reflecting differences in the background information of the addressees. Hence, even if it were true that semantic accounts are never appropriate in response to questions initiated with a 'why', this would not indicate that the category of interpretive accounts is infirm. Still, it is reassuring to observe that the asymmetry intuition is not entirely warranted. Consider the following case. *A* walks up to *B* and goes through a rapid series of odd finger movements before the eyes of *B*. *B* makes a remark to *A* who walks away, apparently satisfied. Rather puzzled, you ask *B* why *A* twisted his hands in this peculiar manner. *B* answers that *A* asked what time it was in sign language and goes on to specify the meanings of the individual gestures used. This would be a semantic account, yet it would clearly provide an adequate answer to your why-question.

2

A critique of the covering law model of explanation

1

In the preceding chapter, we outlined a number of everyday ways of accounting for action, all reflecting the 'meaningful' features of human action. No attempt was made to provide an analysis of the notion of an account. Indeed our use of that term was meant to reflect faithfully its everyday use, which is so liberal that little of interest could be expected from such an analysis. This term's all-embracing nature was precisely that which recommended it to us. It allowed us to introduce our present topic in a manner which would not be biased against any approach to human action.

However, given the role played by the concept of an account in the formulation of our project, it is inevitable that at some point we will be forced to provide a substantive characterization of those intellectual tools vaguely referred to as 'accounts'. The present chapter, and the next, are primarily dedicated to that task. The crucial step towards this more precise characterization lies in the division of the class of accounts into two sub-classes, as already suggested in the previous chapter, namely, into why-accounts and what-accounts. As we shall see, the former permit analysis in fairly precise and substantive terms, whereas the latter retain all the vagueness of the parent class. Hence we will concentrate our efforts on the characterization of why-accounts. One major aim of the analysis will be to show that the traditional positivist theory of why-accounts (under the name of *explanations*) is misguided and that interpretive why-accounts are genuinely distinct from causal why-accounts. Thus, the following deliberations are not primarily intended as a contribution to the theory of explanation in the abstract, but rather as an attempt to highlight those features of causal and interpretive accounts which warrant a differential classification of the two.

A couple of further notions figuring in the formulation of our project call for particular clarification, namely those of *common-sense knowledge* and of *theoreticity*. I shall deal with these first, as this can be done fairly briefly, turning subsequently to the more involved and controversial issue of why-accounts.

2

For the purposes of the present enquiry, I will define 'common-sense knowledge' (or 'everyday knowledge') as knowledge which the average person could establish or test for himself, given time and patience, without relying on any specialized education or sophisticated techniques, let alone on exotic measuring devices and other laboratory equipment. A definition in terms of the establishment of knowledge is forced upon us by the fact that with today's rapid dissemination of the latest scientific break-throughs via semi-popular books and magazines, no distinction can be drawn between scientific and everyday knowledge as merely passive possessions. The average citizen may have conversational knowledge about quasars, white dwarfs, unconscious wishes, cognitive dissonance, or whatever; still the establishment and testing of such knowledge transcend his powers, thus providing a foothold for a more precise means of drawing this intuitively plausible distinction. (Needless to say, the mere drawing of this distinction in the abstract does not guarantee that there is scientific knowledge to be had in any particular field, and hence does not presage a negative answer to our question.)

Notice that in the specification of the project of this study, we ask whether there are considerations militating against progress beyond *current* common-sense knowledge of social action in interpretive terms, that is, beyond *currently* available lore about action which could be established by the average person. We are not asking the broader question whether interpretive social science may progress beyond what in principle can be attained by everyday methods; although that broader question will of course be answered should we come up with a positive answer to the narrower one. The reason for raising the narrower issue is that it might be possible to achieve a more integrated, more systematic grasp of the facts of human motivation by a sustained and disciplined use of the methods available to common sense. This would count as an advance in theoreticity, as we shall define that notion in a moment, and we should therefore construe our investigation in such a way as to acknowledge this possibility alongside advances that go beyond anything achievable by common sense. This liberal policy is especially to be recommended in an investigation of the interpretive approach to action, an approach which might seem somewhat at odds with the idea of sophisticated research techniques and laboratory testing and other such marks of science.

Let me emphasize that I do not take the contrast drawn between common-sense knowledge and scientific knowledge to reflect some deep epistemological difference, as should be evident from the very difficulty of effecting that demarcation. We only managed to characterize common-sense knowledge—a category that no doubt remains very fuzzy—by reference to circumstances that are quite accidental by the standards of general epistemology, namely, facts having to do with the educational level of the average citizen and the data-gathering equipment available to him. Such things are quite open to historical change: there was a time when only a smallish number of the most highly educated people could handle the mathematics needed to balance a ledger. Thus my distinction here does not signal a commitment to a Metaphysics of Common Sense, the idea that common-sense knowledge is *sui generis* and essentially divergent from the knowledge found in the specialized sciences. Here in the initial stages of our investigation, current common-sense knowledge merely serves as a benchmark for measuring possible scope of theoretical progress in interpretive social science. On the other hand, the possibility remains that our investigation will show that mark to be more than accidental after all in this particular field.

With the notion of common-sense knowledge suitably fixed, and with it the contrasting notion of scientific knowledge, we may now use the two to introduce the concept of *theoreticity*. In the present study, this term is not used in the familiar epistemological sense, marking an opposition to the notion of observationality.[1] Indeed, as used here, the term does not mark any contrast at all within the category of knowledge systems, but rather points to a dimension along which all such systems may be ordered. Theoreticity is the major dimension in which scientific knowledge differs from, and surpasses, everyday knowledge as defined above. It is the dimension measuring the integrative, organizing power of knowledge systems, their power to compress information into an easily surveyable form. Any knowledge system that goes beyond a mere list of names possesses that property to some extent. Still, there is considerable difference in the degree to which that property is manifested by common sense and scientific knowledge. Let us use physics as an example of scientific knowledge in order to illustrate this point. The distinguishing mark of the physicist's knowledge does not reside in his command of a larger store of facts of the kind to which the layman is also privy. Rather, it lies in the greater generality and abstractness of that knowledge. The layman may know about the tides, about the way that heavy things fall to the ground, and he may know the positions of the moon on the firmament throughout the seasons. But this falls far short, both in scope and abstractness, of the physicist's grasp of the very same phenomena. The physicist knows that these superficially very diverse phenomena are describable in a single narrow set of concepts and are explicable in terms of a handful of theoretical principles, centrally the principles describing the motion of a body in a gravitational field. The physicist's knowledge integrates facts which to common sense are perfectly unrelated. In general, the physicist is in a position to describe and explain events of the physical world through the use of a much more economical vocabulary and with a much narrower array of principles than are available to common sense.

To illustrate the same point with an example from the sciences of man, we might take the psychoanalyst's theory of suppressed wishes. This theory unites a large and heterogeneous class of phenomena that to common sense are utterly disparate: occasional actions suitable for implementing the wish, without the agent having any conscious intention to this effect; the recurrent appearance of the wish object, often suitably veiled, in the subject's dreams; lapses of speech and memory in matters pertaining to that object; the aggressive denial of the existence of the wish when it is pointed out to the subject; and finally his conscious recognition and admission of the wish after he has been subjected to psychoanalytic treatment. In this latter feature in particular, the notion of a suppressed wish goes beyond that which can be established through everyday procedures.[2]

Before I go on to provide a more careful account of the notion of theoreticity illustrated by these examples, I must briefly point to another notion with which it is tied up, namely that of explanation. Explanation enters the picture by virtue of the fact that knowledge which ranks high on the theoreticity scale is typically explanatory and provides deeper insight than everyday lore. By subsuming a broad range of diverse phenomena under a narrow set of abstract principles and concepts, a knowledge system high in theoreticity offers a more powerful explanation of such phenomena. The introduction of Newtonian mechanics and of the concept of universal gravitational attraction made possible a deeper explanation of the free fall of bodies near the surface of the earth than was hitherto available; Freud's discovery of unconscious mental processes paved the way for a much more revealing account of certain kinds of puzzling action.

We can distinguish two aspects of theoretical integration, each of them to be assessed along two dimensions. I shall refer to the two aspects as the *integration of principles* and the *integration of ontology*, respectively. The two dimensions I dub the *dimension of generality* and the *dimension of parsimony*. By the integration of principles, I mean the power of knowledge systems high in theoreticity to reduce the number of laws and principles needed to account for the data, replacing a large class of narrow-scope principles with a smaller class of more general ones. This explication captures both dimensions of generality and parsimony of the notion under examination, and points to the connection between them: it is by virtue of introducing principles of superior generality that highly theoretical knowledge effects the systematization which allows us to get by on a smaller number of principles. Still, the two dimensions do not necessarily interact like this: we may at times achieve a gain in the generality dimension by adding principles of high generality to our knowledge structure, without this resulting in the dispensability of the old, narrow-scope principles. In such a case, the gain in the generality dimension results in a loss of parsimony.

The notion of theoretical integration of principles which I am trying to work out here is clearly related to Hempel's notion of theoretical systematization as presented in the article 'The Theoretician's Dilemma'.[3] Both have to do with the power of theories to organize our knowledge. One minor difference would seem to be that Hempel's notion is related to mine as a process is related to the tool employed to carry it out: Hempel's notion refers to the process of establishing links between different parts of a body of knowledge by means of inferences in accordance with general empirical principles (laws of nature). The notion I have introduced rather describes features of the tools used in this activity, namely the very principles which sustain the systematizing inferences. Of course Hempel's notion and mine deal with the same activity, but we view it from slightly different angles.

Another difference between the two concepts is more significant. Hempel recognizes two varieties of theoretical systematization, which he terms *deductive* and *inductive* systematization, respectively. In deductive systematization, certain data are inferred from other data through the mediation of general laws which specify an exceptionless connection between data of the two kinds. In inductive systematization, laws of statistical form replace the strictly general laws of deductive systematizations. Such laws do not permit the deduction of particular fact from particular fact, but only manage to make the inferred fact more or less likely. Now I believe we should weaken still further the inferential nexus between a theory and the facts it systematizes. Talk of 'systematization' or 'integration' is still in order in cases where a theory suggests a possible explanation of a certain phenomenon, but does not permit us to infer the occurrence of that phenomenon, whether deductively or inductively. An example is Darwin's theory of natural selection. That theory does not enable us to infer, for any species and for some feature which would be adaptive for that species in its current environment, that the species will develop that feature: it might develop some functionally equivalent trait instead, or might just fail to adapt and be penalized with extinction. Still it can hardly be disputed that Darwin's theory has the power to explain countless biological phenomena, integrating them in terms of one over-arching conception. So, but for its lack of truth, would Freud's hypothesis that all human endeavours can be traced back to the twin forces of Eros and Thanatos. Still that theory does not allow us to infer the occurrence of any particular action. (Later in this chapter, we shall treat at length the possibility of explanation without inferential ties between the explanans and the explanan-dum. And we return to the topic of systematization without inferential power in chapter 5.)

There are two basic ways in which gains in the integration of principles can be achieved. The first is through the subsumption of previously known, less general principles under higher-order principles from which they may be deduced, given suitable additional premises. Notice that what we deal with here is the deduction of principles (laws) from other principles, not the inference of particular fact from particular fact through the mediation of universal or statistical laws which we have just discussed. (Talk of deduction here is somewhat misleading. It is commonly recognized that the relation between everyday gener-alizations and the theories to which they are 'reduced' is not one of strict deduction, even in cases where the two employ the same vocabulary. (I here bypass everyday generalizations based upon 'facts' that are simply false.) The theoretically inferred description of a certain phenomenon will often be slightly divergent from that embodied in the low-level generalization. Reduction should not be taken to require the strict deduction of the generalization but only the demonstration that the latter can be seen as an approximation to the theory, as applied to the same limited field of data.) The second way concerns other cases, where less inclusive principles may be replaced by more general ones from which they cannot be inferred, being incompatible with those principles. Here, replace-ment is still legitimate when the original narrow-scope laws are seen to be false in the light of their theoretical rivals. The replace-ment corrects the mistaken conception embodied in the narrower principles.

We now turn to the second aspect of theoretical integration, namely ontological integration, or the power of a knowledge system to order the facts of a specified domain in terms of principles involving ontological commitments which are more sparse than those of the previously prevailing understanding. More precisely, this explication captures the *parsimony* dimension of ontological integration. In a more careful formulation, ontological integration in the parsimony dimension is a theory's effect of systematizing the facts in a manner which commits us to the existence of fewer kinds of basic entities than the alternative conception. Putting the point in the 'formal mode', this is to say that the theory allows us to make do with a more limited vocabulary of undefined terms. It typically accomplishes this by introducing concepts broader in scope than their low-theoretical counterparts, thus replacing a multitude of terms with a single or a few notions of at least equal overall explanatory power. This introduction of terms with wider extension is what is meant by gains in the *generality* dimension of ontological integration. Note that a point previously made concerning the integration of principles holds here, too: the two dimensions of ontological integration, although interrelated, do not necessarily support each other. The introduction of broad-scope concepts does not necessarily bring a gain in parsimony in its train, since such concepts may still need a rich vocabulary of auxiliary notions to handle the given body of data. Observe also that ontological integration need not (and indeed rarely will) take the form of definitional elimination of the concepts of the 'reduced' conception. Only an extensional equivalence may be involved, and a rough one at that. A theory of a given domain may even show that some of the terms previously used to describe it have no genuine application at all.

The concept of theoreticity is *comparative* and *local*. It is comparative in that it does not involve an opposition between knowledge which is, and knowledge which is not, theoretical, but only a difference between grades of theoreticity. For all knowledge possesses this feature to some extent. The concept is local in the sense that it does not permit us to rank every body of knowledge on a single, all-encompassing scale, but only knowledge systems with strong affinities. For a global ranking to be possible, there would have to exist a common measure of extension for the concepts used in different areas of knowledge; this again would presuppose that every bit of knowledge could be expressed in a common language with a fixed stock of referring expressions. But the dream of a universal experiential language in which all of science can be expressed, a true *characteristica universalis*, has long been abandoned in philosophy. Thus all we can hope for is a measure of theoreticity applicable to bodies of knowledge described in the same language, or at least closely related ones.

Theoreticity as I have sketched it here is primarily a predicate of knowledge systems: it is knowledge systems as overall structures that achieve integration of the two sorts outlined. But we may extend that predicate in an obvious fashion to concepts if those concepts are part of a knowledge system high in theoreticity. Such extension is natural by virtue of the fact that the integrative power of the system is directly reflected in the generality of its concepts. But we should be aware that even a highly general concept may count as low in theoreticity in the sense adopted here if it cannot be incorporated into an overall knowledge system which ranks high on the theoreticity scale. Conversely, a narrow-scope concept may earn the distinction of high theoreticity by being an essential part of a knowledge system which possesses it.

Having managed, I hope, to bestow reasonably clear meaning upon the notion of 'theoreticity', I will now grant myself a relaxation of terminology in order to make this essay easier reading. The concept of theoreticity I have introduced is a comparative one which locates every body of knowledge on a scale, although not on a single, all-encompassing one: every body of knowledge that goes beyond a mere tagging of objects has a place on some such scale and thus counts as a 'theory' in the strict sense. However, the present study centres around a difference in theoreticity between the everyday conception of action and one which we might hope would result from systematic scientific study, and we are hence in need of a simple way to refer to this contrast. So, in keeping with a familiar means of expression—one that has already crept in surreptitiously at various points above—I shall refer to the products of such systematic study as 'theories' *simpliciter*, thus deriving a classificatory concept of theoreticity from the comparative one. In other words, I propose to call 'theories' those knowledge systems that are superior in theoreticity to the common-sense conception and to use grammatical derivatives of this term with the same absolute meaning, where this can be done without risk of confusion with the comparative notion. (Why not mark the contrast with the pair, 'common-sense knowledge'/'scientific knowledge' which we used above for a roughly coincident distinction? But our aim here is to test the potential of interpretive methods only in the dimension of theoreticity. We take no interest in the question whether such methods could be made more 'scientific' in various other senses of this broad notion; whether, say, the concepts on which such methods rely may be purged of normative taint; whether their findings could be put into more precise, mathematical form; or whether they could be strengthened with rigorous laboratory procedures. And besides, the very word 'scientific' is wedded to a naturalistic approach to human action quite alien to the one we wish to examine here.)

3

At this stage, one might suspect that by adopting integrative power, as characterized above, as our yardstick, we have loaded the dice heavily against interpretive methodologies. A few comments to dispel such suspicions are in order.

One source of concern can be dismissed easily as it embodies an excessively narrow reading of the above remarks on theoretical integration: when speaking of the explanatory power of theories, we used 'explanation' in a liberal sense to cover all kinds of why-accounts, not restricting this term to causal accounts. Hence there is no basis for the accusation that we have already committed ourselves to a non-interpretive methodology by stressing the ties between integration and explanation.

Another misgiving might spring from the link forged between theorizing and ontological integration. Is not the latter conception at home only in natural science, where micro-reduction is possible and desirable? Thus, does it not favour a reductive, causal approach to action? But 'ontological reduction' need not be micro-reduction. For instance, the classical attempt to derive the multitude of human motivating factors from a limited number of basic 'instincts' or 'drives' does not reduce that multitude in the manner of a micro-reduction. Still, an obvious integration of ontology (or of principles: it matters little which expression we choose here) would be accomplished if this effort were to succeed. And this achievement would respect our preference for interpretive ways of accounting for action.

A more powerful objection can be raised on the basis of the distinction between *nomothetic* and *idiographic* disciplines. Social science, it might be ventured, belongs to the latter group, endeavouring to grasp the individual social phenomenon in a manner which gives maximum attention to its unique features and puts a premium on fullness of detail. Social science is concerned with whatever distinguishes one social phenomenon from another, its individual physiognomy, so to speak, rather than with the features which it shares with the rest of its kin. Social science tries to capture the distinctive traits of *this* revolution, *this* governmental system, *this* kinship structure; as well as the unique features which these social entities bestow upon the individual human actions performed within their respective frameworks. Hence 'theoretical integration', being the metamorphosis of concrete, rich data into rarefied general formulae, is quite inapposite as a standard of excellence in social science, and can thus only be imposed as a desideratum at the cost of total distortion of work traditionally undertaken under such a label. Relevant desiderata in this field would rather have to do with the *comprehensiveness*, *clarity* and *depth* of the picture which social science paints of the individual social phenomenon.

This allegation might be supported by the invocation of a currently popular doctrine concerning the interdependence of human cognition and certain abstract human interests, as championed by such authors as Jürgen Habermas and Karl-Otto Apel.[4] As this doctrine has it, cognition is the tool of certain *a priori* interests of man as a species which define what counts as knowledge in the various departments of human experience. The chief line of division runs between knowledge concerning physical reality and knowledge concerning the world of man. Knowledge of the former kind is shaped and conditioned by man's need to be able to manipulate and control physical nature so as to maintain his existence *qua* physical existent among other physical existents. At the everyday level, this need is satisfied by 'recipe knowledge', rules-of-thumb which tell us that if we do so-and-so, such-and-such will ensue. And physical science, according to this view, is simply recipe knowledge writ large. The understanding of the world of man, on the other hand, is governed by an entirely different cognitive interest. The ultimate goal of such understanding is the establishment of a consensus on norms and values among men so as to facilitate unencumbered social commerce. Now this doctrine could be appealed to to support the claim that generality is a virtue in natural science but undesirable in social science. Principles of superior generality are *eo ipso* more powerful and more versatile tools for the technical subjugation of nature, permitting us to control physical nature with a more economical use of cognitive resources. Theoretical integration, the systematization of knowledge into a compact set of interrelated laws, is an obvious virtue in a mode of cognition aimed at the mastery of reality, and may even be said to define what 'theory' *means* for cognition with this aim. The concern underlying the understanding of human action, on the other hand, does not call for general recipes for the handling of recurrent situations, but rather for the cultivation of an ability to appreciate the other person's unique objectives, values, and overall vision of the world; it calls for subtlety of judgement and a feel for significant difference. In brief, it calls for an idiographic approach to social reality.

Now this argument, and the metaphysico-epistemological doctrine on which it is based, may not be regarded very highly; and at any rate its conclusion could hardly fail to be an overstatement. For clearly, generalizing disciplines concerned with human action do exist—take, for example, economics. And to suggest that their existence is somehow illegitimate would be a futile claim. However, the above objection gains in force when read as making a more moderate claim, to the effect that although there are indeed branches of social science which adopt the nomothetic approach, there are others which do not; hence we cannot apply the integration yardstick of theoreticity across the board. In particular, we cannot apply it to interpretive theories, which typically embody the idiographic attitude.

The distinction between nomothetic and idiographic disciplines invoked here is indeed a genuine one. That is, there are in fact scientific disciplines which are concerned with individual objects of study *qua* individual. *History* is an idiographic discipline; and certain historians would indeed appear to be aiming at an understanding of their subject matter that transcends and improves upon the everyday conception. An example from outside the realm of human action might be the branch of astronomy occupied with our own solar system. The trouble here, however, is that the features by which these disciplines surpass everyday understanding are all borrowed from some corresponding generalizing discipline. Idiographic disciplines do not boast their own distinct brand of theoreticity, but use whatever tools they can find in the storehouse of nomothetic science; indeed the very difference between nomothetic and idiographic approaches has been quite fittingly expressed in the statement that the former produce general principles, whereas the latter use them. Hence we do no injustice by applying the above conception of theoreticity to social science, even if it should most properly be classified as an idiographic discipline (a conception I would resist): for although, according to this view, social science does not aim at producing general verities, it makes use of them and of the concepts in which they are couched. Hence, the prospects of a theoretical social science, even as an idiographic discipline, stand or fall together with the prospects of generalizing theorizing in this field, by whatever name.

This view is born out by the above example of a genuinely idiographic discipline: the principles and concepts employed by the astronomer studying our solar system are borrowed from a generalizing discipline, namely, theoretical physics. Let me sketch an argument showing that this is no accidental feature of the concrete example. A would-be idiographic science is obliged to indicate how it is different from, and superior to, common-sense lore about the same matters. Wherein does its superiority consist, if not in the use of concepts and principles of greater systematizing power? We have already suggested a possible answer: the picture offered by the idiographic theorist is more *comprehensive, clearer,* and *deeper* than the common-sense one. Comprehensiveness, however, counts for very little by itself, as we realize when we remind ourselves that this quality would often be present in the work of 'abstracted empiricists' scorned by interpretivists. The social scientists who thought that the method of true science is meticulous data collection would often satisfy the requirement of comprehensiveness. Indeed, what could be more 'comprehensive' than the picture of society contained in statistical yearbooks? Yet statistical almanacs hardly count as theoretical treatises, by the interpretivist's or anybody else's standards. How about *clarity?* It might seem as if we can simply repeat the above argument: the data gathered by 'barefoot empiricists' were nothing if not clear, if by clarity we mean the absence of that vagueness which typically clings to everyday lore about society and social action. But perhaps the interpretivist has something else in mind: there is another way, he might insist, to attain clarity than through operationalist regimentation. This is the method of ideal types proposed by Max Weber. The method of ideal types is highly germane to concept formation in an idiographic science. The social scientist starts out with a body of data. Out of this, he endeavours to extract a conception of what is typical of that phenomenon and to integrate the typical features into a purified concept, an ideal type purged of the accidental properties and imperfections inevitably clinging to the actual empirical object. In the generation and deployment of such idealized individual concepts lies the theoreticity of idiographic disciplines; or so the interpretivist would conclude.

The response to this proposal might be to refer the critic to Hempel's careful study of ideal types in 'Typological Methods in the Natural and the Social Sciences'[5], which argues that such constructs must be derived from nomothetic theories and hence do not represent an autonomous mode of theorizing. However, Hempel's reasoning, which proceeds by way of an analysis of ideal types in natural science, is vulnerable to the observation that economics has enjoyed considerable success in operating with the ideal type of *homo economicus.* For although certain economists declare that this creature has by now outlived its usefulness, it can hardly be denied that the theory which has grown up around it possesses a strength and rigour that other branches of social science can only dream about. And the point is that *homo economicus* is not derived from some comprehensive theory of economic conduct, there being no such theory. It is the other way around: microeconomical theory is largely generated by means of reflection upon *homo economicus*.[6]

Unfortunately, the procedure of theoretical economics cannot be generalized into a methodology available to all of social science. Quite specific circumstances pertain to the use of *homo economicus*, who is better called by his English alias, Rational Man. To see why this is so, we must examine a feature of the intentionalistic framework of description as outlined in chapter 1. We made the point that the core concepts of this framework, those of want and belief, unfold into talk about action: wants and beliefs are theoretical states which manifest themselves in action. We might now ask how an observer gets from a certain body of action data to the ascription of a suitable want/belief pair to the agent. A clue to a crude first answer is provided by the fact that a valid attribution will serve to *rationalize* the observed conduct. This suggests the answer that we generate intentionalistic descriptions by imputing to the agent such wants and beliefs as will make his recorded conduct appear rational. That is, we ascribe to him such wants and beliefs that, if he were to act rationally on this basis, the upshot would be conduct of the kind which we have observed in him. But this means that in Rational Man theory, we explore and articulate the conceptual matrix in which we grasp human action as action. The rationality principles which sustain this matrix are *a priori* valid as long as we move within its bounds. (This is not to say, of course, that agents will always come out fully rational when we apply the action framework to them, but only that we must construe recalcitrant cases as deviations from full rationality, to be blamed on shortage of information, intelligence, willpower, etc. in the agent.) To abandon the way of vectoring out the determinants of action which is dictated by the rationality principles would be to cease to speak of it as *action*. Due to their special status, the rationality principles and the ideal model which embodies them need not be anchored in a global empirical theory of human conduct, the way that the laws for ideal gases are anchored in the kinetic theory of gases. (We shall return to the relationship between rationality and intentionalistic description in chapters 5 and 7.) The embarrassment for ideal type methodology is that the concept of rationality is unique in this respect. Or we had better say, rationality-*cum*-logical-consistency is unique: for the notion of consistency plays a similar constitutive role in the framework of intentionalistic description. In any case the number of constitutive notions is strictly limited and cannot serve as the basis for a universal methodology of social science. The attempt to construct ideal types for other, non-constitutive notions will result in nothing but tautologous explications of meaning with no guaranteed application to social reality. (It is a significant fact that Max Weber, the father of ideal type theory, constantly had recourse to rational models to explicate and defend his view, and never presented any other ideal model of comparable power.)[7]

How about *depth?* This notion is an obscure one; but we could perhaps agree to understand a 'deep' treatment of some phenomenon as one which deals with its 'deep' features; these we could then construe as those features in terms of which the surface traits as grasped in common-sense understanding may be explained. This proposal would stress the point that explanation need not be theoretical in the generality-sense adopted here in order to improve upon the common-sense view. To support this contention, such a proposal might appeal to the case of historiography. The scientific historian's account of the outbreak of the First World War, to use this as an example, will be deeper than the layman's, by focusing less upon the dramatic incident in Sarajevo than upon such underlying factors as the jockeying of the Hapsburg empire and Russia for control of the Balkans, and the overall political situation in Europe with the Triple Alliance pitted against the *Entente Cordiale*. The historian's account goes deeper by tracing the chain of events issuing in war further back than does the layman's story, thereby anchoring that account in a more fundamental stratum of events than the layman's. Still, the critic would go on, the historian's account is no more general than the everyday one: the scheming of the Hapsburg empire to subjugate the Balkans is as individual a phenomenon as the confused stirrings in the minds of those Bosnian students who planned the assassination of the Archduke.

However, I believe that this way of putting it is not quite fair to the facts. The superior power of the historian's account does not lie merely in its adding further chapters to the explanatory narrative by describing earlier links in the chain of events leading to war. Beyond this augmentation, the historian also adds generality to the account: he relates the Sarajevo incident and Austria's reaction to it to the more general pattern of a power seeking to extend its influence and looking for a way to put a thin veneer of legitimacy upon its brutal exercise in *Realpolitik*. This is a sadly familiar theme in the history of mankind and provides that unifying power which raises the historian's account above the layman's story. Thus even the historian must deal in general verities if he wants to improve upon common sense. Without that aspect, history reduces to mere chronicle.

The upshot of this discussion is that there is no alternative brand of theorizing specific to the idiographic approach, or more generally, to the study of man. Theoreticity as characterized above remains the most significant dimension in which scientific knowledge, considered as a product rather than as a procedure, sets itself apart from everyday lore.

4

Let us now turn to the second topic of the present chapter, one that will spill over into the next one, namely, the analysis of accounts. In order to get a handle upon this topic, we must first bring into play the distinction, already introduced in chapter 1, between why-accounts and what-accounts. The distinction is a general one, and we shall draw it in a manner which applies across the board. In the present context, however, we are primarily interested in this distinction as it applies to the understanding of human action.

Some accounts are proffered in response to why-questions. Why did Jones quit his job? The answer may be, in order to devote his time to his all-consuming interest in stamp collecting (or: because he wanted to devote his time to stamp collecting; or again: for the purpose of devoting his time to stamp collecting). The reply, whatever its grammatical form, offers a purposive account in response. Other why-questions may be answered by the citing of rules. Why do motorists stop when a light suspended above certain intersections changes from green to red? Because some paragraph in the traffic laws requires them to do so.

Other accounts are elicited by what-questions. The report, 'He said it is going to rain' will typically be the response to some such question as, 'What did he say?', rather than to some why-question. Indeed we would have to strain the imagination to come up with a why-question, enquiring about the speaker's conduct, to which this would be a suitable reply. This partiality to what-accounts holds for meaning-accounts in general. But purposes and rules may figure in what-accounts as well. We ask, 'What is Freddy doing underneath the car?', and get the answer, 'He wants to check the brake cylinders.' Or we ask, 'What are the natives doing, rubbing their noses against each other?', and receive an answer like, 'You are supposed to rub noses with your next of kin when you welcome them in the house' (or: 'rubbing noses is the required greeting ceremony between next-of-kin').

We have drawn a distinction between two types of account on the basis of grammatical-cum-pragmatic considerations. Now clearly this criterion provides no insight into the essential features of these two kinds of account. It merely secures a preliminary structuring of our subject matter, preparing for the work of explication from which a more satisfactory characterization will eventually emerge. But already at this stage it should be pointed out that the explication will do nothing to dispose of the large overlap between the two classes of accounts which, as a moment's reflection will show, follows from the grammatical means of demarcating them. This is a welcome upshot, since it helps discredit the position, sometimes championed, that why-accounts (explanations) and what-accounts of human action are so utterly disparate as to defy analysis within the same framework.

As mentioned above, we shall focus on why-accounts, since these allow of rather more substantive explication. An attack upon the positivist doctrine of explanation will be central, more precisely, an attack upon the positivist construal of explanation of singular events; the explanation of general laws and theoretical principles will not concern us here. This critical effort takes up the major portion of the present chapter, the next will attempt to outline alternative modes of explaining.

According to the positivist conception, explanation is causal explanation or a generalization thereof, called covering law explanation, to the effect that we explain a phenomenon by showing that, as conjoined with certain further phenomena in its surroundings, it instantiates a general law. The relevance of this doctrine to our present concerns lies in the consideration that positivist writers single out explanations by the very same test which we used to pick out why-accounts above: in most standard expositions, explanations are charaterized as answers to why-questions (this criterion of course has the same provisional status in the positivist approach as in ours).[8] In other words, according to the positivist view, why-questions concerning human action must be answered by specifying a general law of human conduct of which the action to be explained is an instance.

This doctrine, if true, confronts the interpretive theorist with a dilemma. One option is to accept the obligation to reconstruct interpretive accounts as causal accounts, or covering law accounts, with a resulting deflation of the interpretivist programme. The interpretivist position would forfeit much of its status as a genuinely distinct approach to human action if interpretive accounts did not represent autonomous patterns. True, there would still be a more than merely grammatical difference between causal accounts and interpretive accounts. Interpretive patterns impose a tight restriction upon the terms permitted in accounts of action: only intentionalistic terms may be used to designate the central action-generating states. The positivist position, on the other hand, admits all kinds of terms (such as those of neuro-physiology) as long as the states referred to are nomologically relevant, and as long as they satisfy the general metaphysical strictures of positivism. But this difference would hardly bear out the interpretivist's pretension that his favoured mode of explana-tion is non-trivially different from that appropriate to natural science. The occurrence of a special class of terms in interpretive accounts–intentionalistic terms such as 'belief', 'desire', 'want', 'norm', 'rule', etc.–no more renders interpretive social science a *sui generis* discipline than meteorology is made a *sui generis* discipline by its unique use of such terms as 'conversion layer', 'cold front', and so forth.

The other option available to the interpretivist is to stick with his claim that interpretive accounts ae not covering law accounts, or causal accounts, at the cost of conceding that such accounts do not answer why-questions about action at all; that is, they do not explain why some action would occur. This is a price that few interpretivists have been willing to pay; and quite understandably so.

The only way for the interpretivist to salvage his programme is by jumping between the horns of dilemma. To do this, he must challenge the positivist analysis of explanation. I believe that such a challenge may succeed and shall now provide an argument to support it. In what follows, I shall talk about 'explanations' and 'why-accounts' indiscriminately (and I shall often simply use the word 'account' when there is no danger of confusion with what-accounts). This usage is warranted by our observation that the term, 'why-accounts', has the same extension as that traditional philosophical notion, 'explanation'. Thus, 'explanation' in the following does not refer to the narrower class of causal accounts or covering law accounts, as is often the case when these conceptions are pitted against interpretive accounts.

There are a handful of well-worn arguments designed to show that interpretive accounts are not identical to causal accounts, or to their generalized kin, covering law accounts. I shall make no use of these arguments: I believe that they overshoot their mark entirely in trying to show that interpretive accounts are *incompatible* with the existence of causal ties between actions and agents' motivational states. This is not a tenable position, as our investigation will reveal that causal ties are essentially involved in all explanation. However, this result does not force us to conclude that interpretive accounts are causal accounts after all. The mere fact that a certain sentential structure implies the existence of a causal tie between specified events is not enough to make that sentential structure a causal explanation, or indeed an explanation at all. What our findings suggest is rather what we might call a *causal theory of explanation* to indicate its kinship with recent causal theories of perception, knowledge, and reference. Such a theory captures those sound points in both positivist and anti-positivist views which have made neither side willing to cede its position, and the reasons versus causes debate so distressingly interminable. It allows us to maintain, with the positivist, that causal ties are a *sine qua non* of explanation, while still agreeing with the interpretivist that telling a causal story is not the heart of (all kinds of) explanation.

These remarks anticipate a crucial point in the case which I am about to present, and we must dwell upon them a little longer. Adherents of the covering law analysis have traditionally argued as if the demonstration that causal ties (or general laws) are involved in interpretive accounts were enough to render them causal accounts (or covering law accounts); this assumption was shared by their opponents, who thus found themselves forced to argue that interpretive accounts do not involve causality (or covering laws) at all. The mistake inherent in this reasoning is basically that of assuming that an adequate analysis of explanation can be given in terms of the purely syntactic or semantic properties of explanatory sentence schemata. But to get a proper characterization of this notion, we need to look at the use to which (the things we call) explanations are put. Explanations, after all, are intellectual tools; and it is normally the case that the use to which a given tool is put forms part of the concept of that tool. A can opener cannot simply be characterized as an object of this or that geometrical form or material composition: reference must be made to the fact that it is an implement designed and used for the opening of cans.

The point is actually often admitted by covering law theorists, who, however, fail to draw the full implications of such a concession. Hempel, for instance, makes the remark that the chief difference between explanations and predictions is one of use. Both are deductive (or inductive-statistical) arguments. However, when the conclusion of the argument refers to an event in the future, and when our only grounds for believing that such an event will occur is the information contained in the argument, we call the overall reasoning a *prediction*, whereas, if the conclusion describes a present or past phenomenon, one of which we have independent knowledge, we call it an *explanation*.[9]

But this concession does not go far enough. We cannot get the use aspect of explanations under control in this semi-formal way.

For it is simply not true that every argument which has the proper deductive or inductive-statistical form and which satisfies the further conditions for being an explanation serves as an explanation. Suppose a physicist puts forth a daring new hypothesis. His colleagues point out to him that a certain well-entrenched experimental fact contradicts his proposal. The physicist refuses to admit defeat and sets out to prove that his theory is not merely consistent with that fact but actually implies it, given some additional assumptions. Now could we say that the physicist sets out to *explain* that fact? Hardly: we have already stated what he is trying to do, namely, to show that his theory actually implies, and is thus corroborated by, the fact that was supposed to falsify it. Nor if he actually succeeds will it be proper to say that he has succeeded in explaining that fact; not even if his theory is true. What he has achieved is what he set out to do, which has nothing to do with explanation. (It is useless to maintain that what the physicist sets out to do is to show that his theory is *capable of* explaining the recalcitrant fact. Why say this rather than maintaining, conversely, that a physicist working to explain some fact is really trying to show that that fact is capable of corroborating his theory?)

In writings expounding the covering law model, we often find that concessions are made on one page to the use aspect of explanation, only to be rescinded on the next. The need to purge the concept of explanation of 'pragmatic' impurities is solemnly impressed upon us. Thus Hempel, having previously ceded the crucial points to the use aspect of explanation, cited in note 9, later goes on to say the following:

> [S]cientific research seeks to account for empirical phenomena by means of laws and theories which are objective in the sense that their empirical implications and their evidential support are independent of what particular individuals happen to test or to apply them; and the explanations, as well as predictions, based upon such laws and theories are meant to be objective in an analogous sense. This ideal intent suggests the problem of construing a nonpragmatic concept of scientific explanation–a concept which is abstracted, as it were, from the pragmatic one, and

which does not require relativization to questioning individuals any more than does the concept of mathematical proof. It is this nonpragmatic conception of explanation which the covering-law model is meant to explicate.[10]

This argument looks quite imposing at first sight. It loses its bite, however, the minute we discover that it intermingles two different claims: the claim that we need to introduce considerations of use as *part* of the characterization of explanation; and the claim that 'pragmatic' considerations *exhaust* the notion of an explanation, such that no 'objective' constraints need be imposed at all. Hempel's comparison of explanation with the notion of mathematical proof weighs heavily against the latter proposal; it fails entirely to address the former, which is the one I intend to advocate here. I fully agree with Hempel that it will not do to propose a purely pragmatic concept of explanation. By this I mean a conception which starts out from some prior, independently defined notion of 'understanding' or 'insight' and then proceeds to define explanations as whatever brings about this cognitive state. The sterility of this approach is evidenced by the rather poor record of those who have attemped to make use of it.[11] The difficulty lies in the fact that the required notion of understanding is far too intertwined with that which provides such understanding to allow of independent explication. Such understanding must inevitably be defined as something which results from the pondering of explanatory structures. The point remains that reference to the use of explanatory structures has some independent import and is indeed indispensable for the proper characterization of the latter notion. For we can still distinguish different ways of using the information comprised in an explanatory sentential structure.

We may prove the clarifying powers of the distinction between a purely pragmatic notion of explanation and a partially pragmatic one, by looking at the simple example of a clock. I assume that no one would want to oppose the view that explication of the concept of a clock need involve reference to pragmatic considerations. A clock is something used for telling the time. The attempt to 'construe a nonpragmatic concept of a clock—a concept which is abstracted, as it were, from the pragmatic one, and which does not require relativization to time-keeping individuals' (to offer a travesty of Hempel's above argument) would clearly be a most unfortunate project. It remains true, however, that to fulfill its, humanly imposed, role as a gauge of time, any physical system must satisfy certain 'objective' requirements. First of all, its workings must exhibit a dependable regularity and continuity. You cannot make something a clock just by treating it as one: you cannot turn a compass into a clock by writing the numerals from 1 to 12 on its face, and conducting your daily business according to its readings. In a similar fashion, you cannot turn any old bit of information into an explanation by treating it as one, or by insisting that it gives you some feeling of 'insight'. To serve as an explanation, any sentential structure must satisfy certain objective conditions. It does not follow, however, that any structure satisfying these requirements counts as an explanation, nor indeed that this notion can be defined simply by amassing a sufficient number of such formal constraints. You can no more define explanation in this way than you can define the notion of a clock by listing at length the objective physical conditions that a physical system has to satisfy to serve as a dependable time-piece.

This point is rather obvious, I think, once it is properly stated; and I would not belabour it were it not for the fact that Hempel's (and other covering law theorists') failure to appreciate it results in a truncated analysis of explanation. This is not simply a charge that the covering law model is incomplete by leaving out the pragmatic dimension, a charge which its advocates could, perhaps, take fairly lightly: it is rather a complaint that this oversight results in an incomplete analysis even of the formal aspect of explanatory structures. By dismissing all the features of acccounts that go beyond their deductive-nomological skeleton as merely 'pragmatic', the positivist view overlooks the fact that the 'pragmatic' aspect consists *inter alia* in the selection among a number of additional properties of explanations which allow of formal analysis just as much as does the deductive-nomological framework.

In the preceding sections I have occasionally placed scare-quotes around the word 'pragmatic'. This is to warn the reader that care must be taken with this word which, in my opinion, has been used with certain false connotations which in turn have lent specious support to the positivist theory of explanation. We must distinguish carefully between the pragmatics of explanation and the pragmatics of 'explanation'. In the philosophical explication of a concept, we want to capture its semantic import, dismissing its merely pragmatic features. However, the pragmatics of explanation, that is, the way in which explanatory information is used, may well be a part of the *semantics* of 'explanation' rather than of its pragmatics. This is parallel to the way in which the pragmatics (use) of can openers is a part of the semantics of 'can opener'. If the two uses of 'pragmatics' are merged, the legitimate concern for avoiding pragmatic elements in the explication of 'explanation' is turned into an unwarranted injunction against proper recognition of the use aspect of explanations.

5

Roughly outlined, the plan of my campaign against the positivist conception of explanation is as follows: first, I attack the covering law analysis which, as indicated earlier, I consider a refined version of causal explanation. This version deserves special scrutiny, as it imposes much more stringent conditions upon explanations than does the parent conception of causal explanation; conditions which are particularly inimical to interpretive explanation and the kind of theorizing it sustains. Now the covering law model has been under fire ever since Carl Hempel and Paul Oppenheim first gave it a definite form, with the most important criticism revolving around the doctrine that explanations are evidential arguments which bestow a certain rational credibility upon the explanandum.[12] Step by step, the advocates of covering law explanation have yielded to this criticism, and in retreating have produced a sequence of modified versions in which the evidential aspect of explanation is progressively played down. In part, the critique I will present simply perpetuates and consummates this trend, securing a definitive break with the idea that an explanation is an argument which provides grounds for the explanandum. This will return us to the position that explanations in the realm with which the positivists primarily concerned themselves–that is, natural science–are essentially causal explanations, providing understanding by identifying the factors causally responsible for the event to be explained. However, the distinction between the covering law model and the causal model will remain precarious as long as we hold on to the Humean regularity theory of causation which, I believe, is one of the main supports of the covering law model. For reflection upon the regularity interpretation leads straight to that model. Therefore, I point to an alternative conception of causality with which to bolster our rival analysis of (causal) explanation. Beyond the critical aim, I also use the discussion of the covering law model to introduce the notion of *explanatory tightness* which will prove useful to characterize the difference between causal accounts and the various types of interpretive accounts in chapter 3.

As the second stage of my anti-positivist campaign, I argue that interpretive explanation is not identical with causal explanation even on the more liberal analysis which emerges from the ashes of the covering law model. This undertaking, which is deferred until chapter 3, I approach by providing a sketch of purposive explanation, as a paradigm of interpretive accounts, and then taking issue with the classical argument which has been thought to show that such accounts cannot possibly possess explanatory import unless reconstrued as causal accounts.

For the purposes of the following investigation, I shall presume the reader to be familiar with the covering law account; no presentation of that model will be supplied here. Let me repeat, however, that we shall be dealing with the explanation of particular fact only: explanation of general regularities and theoretical principles remains outside out present scope.

Our point of departure will be the emphasis placed upon *deduction* in early statements of the model, the idea that giving an explanation is essentially producing a deductive argument with a description of the fact to be explained as its conclusion. (In the following, I shall use the term 'explanandum' to refer ambiguously to the event explained and its description; in most contexts, there is little need to distinguish between the two since the same points and arguments can be put in either the 'material' or the 'formal' mode.) The concern with deduction is bound to the idea that an explanation must give us good or indeed conclusive grounds for accepting the explanandum. The connection is readily apparent from the following quotation from Hempel's classical article, 'Studies in the Logic of Explanation' (co-authored by Paul Oppenheim), in which it expresses a 'logical condition of adequacy' upon explanations: 'The explanandum must be a logical consequence of the explanans; in other words, the explanandum must be logically deducible from the information contained in the explanans; for otherwise, the explanans would not constitute adequate grounds for the explanandum'.[13] Yet, later in the essay we find scattered remarks which open the door for the recognition of accounts in which statistical, inductive ties replace deductive entailments.[14] But no analysis of such accounts is provided; and Hempel only came to grips with non-deductive explanation in his 1962 article, 'Deductive-Nomological vs Statistical Explanation'.[15] Much of the material from this article was integrated into the more general examination of explanation undertaken in the 1965 essay, 'Aspects of Scientific Explanation', which remains Hempel's most complete statement on the topic.[16]

Hempel construes explanations which fall short of deductiveness as statistical accounts. Like their deductive counterparts, they indicate how a description of the event to be explained may be inferred from some general law (or laws) plus additional singular premises. But in statistical accounts, the inference is not deductive but inductive; hence Hempel refers to such accounts as inductive-statistical accounts. In inductive-statistical accounts (hereafter referred to as i-s accounts) the deterministic laws featured in deductive accounts are replaced by statistical, probabilistic ones.

Statistical laws may be of different shapes and varying complexity; but essentially they state that the probability that an event of a given kind E will also be of kind F is of magnitude r. We may express it thus in a traditional formalism:

$$p(F,E) = r$$

Now if r is very close to 1—in everyday parlance, if the occurrence of an event of type F is highly likely, given the occurrence of an event of type E—we may construct an explanatory argument of the following form for a concrete event, m:

$p(F,E)$ is close to 1
Em

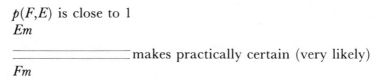

makes practically certain (very likely)

Fm

(I follow Hempel's convention of using a double line between premises and conclusion to signal that the inference is not deductively valid.)

This analysis assimilates inductive-statistical accounts and deductive accounts. For deductive accounts (which Hempel calls deductive-nomological accounts, d-n accounts hereafter) could be exhibited in the following schema:

All E are F
Em

———————————————makes absolutely certain

Fm

The difference between the two accounts lies simply in the fact that d-n accounts make their conclusion necessary, given the premises, whereas i-s accounts only render the conclusion highly probable, given the premises.[17] This suggests a general notion of explanation of which d-n explanation and i-s explanation may be seen as two closely related species: very roughly, an explanation is an argument with at least one of its premises being a universally quantified sentence, from which the occurrence of the event to be explained may be inferred with at least reasonable probability. Even more colloquially put, we might say that we explain a phenomenon by supplying information showing that its occurrence was to be expected.

And as a matter of fact, Hempel uses a formulation very close to this last one to express a 'general condition of adequacy for any rationally acceptable explanation of a particular event'. It goes as follows:

Any rationally acceptable answer to the question 'Why did event X occur?' must offer information which shows that X

was to be expected–if not definitely, as in the case of *D–N* explanation, then at least with reasonable probability. Thus, the explanatory information must provide good grounds for believing that *X* did indeed occur; otherwise, that information would give us no adequate reason for saying: 'That explains it–that does show why *X* occurred.' And an explanatory account that satisfies this condition constitutes, of course, a potential prediction in the sense that it could have served to predict the occurrence of *X* (deductively or with more or less high probability) if the information contained in the explanans had been available at a suitable earlier time.[18]

This adequacy condition is a counterpart of, and a replacement for, the deductiveness requirement of the original Hempel–Oppenheim analysis, involving a relaxation of the inferential connection between the explanans and the explanandum. It brings out even more clearly than that requirement the postulated kinship between explanation and evidential reasoning: the power of a covering law account is represented as a function of the 'rational credibility' it bestows upon the explanandum, its evidential impact upon the latter. Explanatory why-accounts are depicted as a species of what Hempel calls 'epistemic why-accounts', i.e. accounts giving reasons in support of assertions. And he indeed declares that 'any adequate answer to an explanation-seeking question "Why is it the case that *p*?" must also provide a potential answer to the corresponding epistemic question "What are the grounds for believing that *p*?" '[19]

However, even in the eyes of those who favour the general conception, Hempel's explication is flawed by its reliance upon the vague notion of a 'reasonable probability', and is seen to be threatened with the charge of arbitrariness if the vagueness is removed by the stipulation of a particular probability value as the cut-off point for explanatory power. The task of remedying these defects has been taken up by other explanation theorists, a particularly careful analysis being provided by Nicholas Rescher in *Scientific Explanation*. Rescher makes a point of not admitting any threshold for the probability values that count as explanatory. Instead, he arranges statistical accounts into three levels according to their explanatory power. At the first level, the explanatory information bestows the probability 1 on the explanandum, and thus satisfies even Hempel's original requirement of deductive linkage. Explanations at the second level assign a probability value to the explanandum which exceeds the summed probability values of all its alternatives. This means that the probability value of the event to be explained is >0.50, and thus that this event is more likely to happen than not. The third level is the one which most strongly marks Rescher's departure from Hempel. Here, the probability of the explanandum drops below 0.50, and may indeed approximate 0 as closely as you like; still Rescher insists that such low-probability accounts must be granted explanatory import. He proposes two relative measures of the power of explanations in this bracket.[20] One represents explanatory power as proportional to the degree in which the account shows the probability of the explanandum to exceed the probabilities of alternative individual outcomes (although not the probability of their disjunction). The other measures the power of an explanation by the difference between the probability value it assigns to the explanandum and the probability values conferred upon that event by rival explanations.[21] An especially pertinent comparison here–but one which Rescher does not specifically explore–would contrast the probability which the explanandum receives from the explanans with its prior probability, that is, its probability on the information available before the explanation was offered. As measured by this comparison, the power of an explanation is proportional to the degree in which it raises the probability of the explanandum above its prior probability; intuitively speaking, explanation is represented as a matter of showing that the event to be explained was more likely to happen than we thought antecedently, although it need not have been likely to occur in an absolute sense.[22]

However, all such attempts to identify explanatory power with (relative) positive evidential relevance have been effectively discredited by Wesley Salmon. In his 1970 article, 'Statistical Explanation', and elsewhere, Salmon argues on the basis of convincing counter-examples that explanation is the product of information singling out the factors which are statistically *relevant* to the occurrence of the explanandum in the given setting, the factors which 'make a difference' to the probability value assigned to it. The identification of those factors need not confer a high probability upon the explanandum; it need not even raise the prior probability of that event, or indeed satisfy any other of Rescher's conditions for explanatory import.

Here is an example which supports Salmon's case against analyses such as Rescher's (and *a fortiori* against the original Hempel model); it freely combines and elaborates upon elements from Salmon's own examples in the article cited: the Geiger counter in the laboratory emits a solitary click. We ask, Why? Suppose the setting in which this query is raised bestows a certain non-negligible prior probability upon this happening: there has been some recurrent malfunction in the apparatus, resulting in a probability of 0.005 that the detector will pick up a spurious 'emission' during the course of, say, one second. Still, it turns out that the instrument was not to blame this time: subsequent check of the record of a monitoring device shows no evidence of any malfunction. Instead, it is discovered that the Geiger counter picked up a radioactive emission from the phosphorescent dots on the face of a laboratory technician's watch as he moved his hand close to the apparatus. I think we are perfectly willing to accept this as an explanation, and that we do so in the absence of any indication, from the way the situation is described, that the prior probability of a recording (a click) was *raised* by the information comprised in the explanans. We may set the probability that the instrument would pick up an emission from the watch during the one-second period of proximity well below the prior probability of a recording–say, at 0.001–and still have no scruples about citing the laboratory technician's introduction of his wrist watch on the scene as an explanation of this event. (To have the explanation lower the probability, we must take the explanans to include the information that no malfunction occurred.) Explanation is provided by the very link-up of the recording with a particular feature of the setting, not by any increase in the likelihood of such an occurrence implied by the explanatory information.

Now it is unavoidable that we should think of this link-up as a causal one; and Salmon himself supports this interpretation through his recognition that a statistical correlation must have nomological status to be explanatory, and through his efforts to handle the problem posed by statistically relevant but non-explanatory information of the kind which connects a barometer drop with a subsequent storm.[23] It is natural to describe this problem as that of separating causally productive ties from causally non-productive but statistically significant correlations. Still, at the time of writing 'Statistical Explanation', Salmon was not yet prepared to concede that only causal relationships are explana-torily relevant.[24] He has since taken this step and has tried to work out a statistical theory of causality to go with his statistical theory of explanation.[25] This is a wise move, since a commitment to the standard Humean position on causation would soon force us back to the covering law model once again. However, I do not think we need to trouble ourselves with the difficulties inherent in a statistical concept of causality, not the least of which concerns the very interpretation of statistical concepts. A much simpler theory will do the trick, and I shall point to such a theory in the next section.

But first I want to argue that even Salmon's contribution to debunking the covering law model fails to take this process to its natural conclusion. The dissociation of the notions of explanation and of evidential reasoning has not been effected with sufficient resoluteness. For although Salmon rejects the idea that explanation is an argument which provides good grounds for accepting the explanandum as true, or at least better grounds than we had before, he still asserts that the cognitive function of explanation is to provide evidential information about that event.[26] In this vein, he even endorses Hempel's view that explanation and prediction are logically symmetrical:

> The problem of symmetry of explanation and prediction, which is one of the most hotly debated issues in discussions of explanation, is easily answered in the present theory. To explain an event is to provide the best possible grounds we could have had for making predictions concerning it. An explanation does not show that the event was to be expected; it shows what sorts of expectations would have been reasonable and under what circumstances it was to be

expected. To explain an event is to show to what degree it
was to be expected, and this degree may be translated into
practical predictive behaviour such as wagering on it. In
some cases the explanation will show that the explanandum
event was not to be expected, but that does not destroy the
symmetry of explanation and prediction. The symmetry
consists in the fact that the explanatory facts constitute the
fullest possible basis for making a prediction of whether or
not the event would occur.[27]

In his later writings, Salmon still stands by the position expressed
here. Thus, despite the break with the Hempelian model, explanation continues to be construed as a mode of evidential reasoning;
only explanatory power is no longer taken to be proportional to the
degree of rational expectability bestowed upon the explanandum,
but–to put it rather crudely–to the precision with which the
explanation captures the 'true' probability value of the explanandum in the given setting.[28] But once it is granted, as Salmon has
lately been willing to do, that explanation is a matter of linking the
explanandum to a causally relevant factor, the evidential power of
the explanans is seen to be a by-product of explanation, not its very
essence. This is apparent from the fact that the explanation of the
Geiger counter incident above would not be detrimentally affected
if we happened to be ignorant of the exact probabilities of an
emission from the watch and of a malfunction in the measuring
apparatus. As long as we learn which of the two kinds of events
caused the recording, our explanatory needs are satisfied. Information specifying the degree to which it would have been rational to
expect that event in advance, on either mode of generation, adds
nothing to the account. It is true that any non-quantitative
statistical–causal explanation can in principle be turned into a full
inductive-statistical argument, assigning a determinate probability
to the explanandum. But this fact plays no role in our appreciation
of the power of the non-quantitative account. Besides, if the
symmetry thesis were sound, the mere *possibility* of assigning a
determinate probability would not satisfy us. For certainly more is
required for rational prediction than the naked assurance that
information could *in principle* be obtained which would reveal the

likelihood of the future event. For intelligent prediction, we need real live information, not the mere conviction that such information exists.

To bring out the irrelevance of statistical information to explanation in a radical manner, we may ask whether our Geiger counter explanation would be undercut by the discovery that no determinate statistical probability could be assigned to the event of an emission from the watch. The answer would appear to be no: the solution to the laboratory crew's puzzle, 'Why did the Geiger counter click?', would still be, 'Because the junior assistant put his wrist watch with its radioactive trimmings next to it.' Nor is there any worry abut the testability of that claim after the assumption of a definite probability value is dropped. The crew could still have compelling evidence, observational and theoretical, for the assumption that the recording would not have occurred save for the introduction of the watch and its phosphorescent dots. This information links the recording to the introduction of the watch in a manner which justifies the crew in citing the latter as an explanation of the former. (A theory of causality to support this intuition will be sketched in the next section.)

If the question is raised how an event (type) could fail to possess a determinate statistical probability, the answer is that for the probability calculus to apply to some empirical event (type), whether according to the standard frequency interpretation or the propensity interpretation, the ratio of that event in long sequences of cases must approach some limiting value. But there is no *a priori* reason, mathematical or otherwise, why this must always be the case; although it does seem to hold as a matter of brute fact for all known processes in the universe. The feeling that some such limiting frequency must inevitably exist may betray the lingering hold of the dogma of determinism which, having been forced to give up its claim upon singular events, still retains a grip upon generic events: although the state of some lump of radioactive matter does not determinately fix the next alpha-decay, still it is thought to fix some dispositional property, a tendency of that matter to undergo alpha-decay at a particular specifiable rate, varying from one substance to the other, and capturable in terms of a specific limiting frequency value. But the assumption that such determinate frequencies must necessarily exist would seem as ill-founded as its ancestor to the effect that determinism holds for singular events with *a priori* necessity. At any rate, it is not obvious how the assumption that some such frequency exists is supposed to gear into the machinery of explanation in cases like the one examined above: how that assumption makes any difference to the truth of the claim that the laboratory assistant's wearing of a watch explains the activation of the Geiger counter.

6

We stated above that any alternative to the covering law model, considered now as an explication of *causal* explanation, must be accompanied by a non-Humean theory of causation. Failing such a theory, we must eventually relapse into the Hempelian position, the plausibility of the amassed counterexamples notwithstanding. According to the Humean regularity interpretation, when we say that A caused B (A and B being particulars), we imply the existence of a law linking events similar to A to events similar to B (in some relevant respect). That is, we imply, minimally, the existence of some predicate F of A, and of some predicate G of B, such that the following sentence is true: $\forall x(Fx \supset Gx)$. Given this analysis of causality, the covering law model follows as a matter of course, as long as we are explicitly or implicitly concerned with causal explanation. To explain B by citing A as its cause is to say that the sequence AB is an instance of some regularity; and to say this is to imply that given the verbal expression of this regularity in the form of a universally quantified conditional, we may infer a description of B if we plug in a description of A in the antecedent of that conditional. But this is the essence of the covering law model, in its strong deductive version.

The affinity of the regularity theory for the covering law model is no incidental matter, as far as the acceptance of the latter is concerned: this theory of causality has frequently been used as a premise in arguments supporting that model. However, such use has mainly been implicit. A good example is Hempel's rebuttal of a certain standard type of counterexample, the thrust of which is to show that we may often be absolutely certain of the truth of an explanation without being aware of any general law subsuming it. Michael Scriven's version of this example is as follows: reaching for the dictionary, you accidentally knock over the table, thus turning over the ink bottle standing on top of it and spilling its contents all over the carpet. If you are later asked to explain the presence of the ink stains, you may relate this sad story, *without* being able to cite any general laws linking the pushing of tables with tables turning over; or the turning over of tables with bottles toppling; or the toppling of bottles with liquids spilling over.[29] To this, Hempel makes the following comment:

> Presumably the explanation [Scriven] has in mind would be expressed by a statement roughly to the effect that the carpet was stained with ink because the table was knocked. But, surely, this statement claims by implication that the antecedent circumstances invoked were of a kind which generally yields effects of the sort to be explained. *Indeed, it is just this implicit claim of covering uniform connections which distinguishes the causal attribution here made from a mere sequential narrative* to the effect that first the table was knocked, then the bottle tipped over, and finally the ink dripped on the rug.[30]

This passage clearly, albeit implicitly, appeals to the regularity theory of causation to support the claim that explanation must involve the existence of general laws stating 'uniform connections' which subsume the explanans and the explanandum. It indicates why we shall never lay the ghost of the covering law doctrine until we introduce a theory of causality to replace the Humean analysis.

A theory to fill this bill is in fact available, proposed by J. L. Mackie in *The Cement of the Universe*. I accept the central idea in Mackie's position, namely, that the minimal notion of a cause is that of a *necessary condition* for an event, in a strong, counterfactual sense. Mackie thus directly opposes the conception of causes as a species of sufficient conditions which follows from the regularity theory.

Let me hasten to emphasize, however, that my endorsement of Mackie's position extends only to the conditional analysis of causality which, I think, he succeeds in rendering highly attractive. It ·does not apply to the other controversial elements in that position such as the analysis of the direction of causation, of 'fixity', of causal necessity, and of counterfactual conditionals. This does not necessarily mean that I would reject Mackie's contributions here, only that they are independent of the conditional analysis which remains our central interest; hence we will simply adopt a non-committal stance on them, justified by the fact that the problems which these conceptions are meant to deal with must be faced by the regularity interpretation as well. Thus, if we should find Mackie's answer unsatisfactory on the mentioned points, this would not jeopardize his position *vis-à-vis* the latter interpretation. These remarks are especially pertinent with regard to Mackie's reliance upon the notion of counterfactual conditionals, which some critics might view as the weakest spot in his analysis. This problem has a perfect counterpart in the regularity view, namely that of demarcating truly *nomic* principles from accidental regularities. For it is generally recognized that this problem could be solved easily if the regularity theorist allowed himself free use of counterfactual conditionals. He could then simply characterize nomic regularities as regularities expressed in sentences which sustain counterfactual conditionals. However, most regularity theorists, consistent with their empiricist leanings, eschew the deployment of such intensional notions and try instead to construct some extensional substitute. If this effort were to succeed, the resulting analysis could be implemented in Mackie's theory as well: it could be used to draw that line between merely accidental and nomically necessary conditions which is an indispensible part of his theory.

Thus, what I shall provide in the following is not a fully-fledged presentation of Mackie's theory of causality, but merely a partial picture, serving as a corrective to the orthodox regularity view on a single point. It circumvents most of the really deep and troublesome questions of causality which, however, also infest the orthodox view (and indeed every analysis of causality with which I am familiar). I shall refer to Mackie's position as the '*sine qua non*' theory; this seems preferable to the designation which Mackie applies to it, namely, the 'conditional analysis', an appellation that is somewhat infelicitous in view of the fact that the regularity theory, too, may be expressed in terms of conditionals: as causes being *sufficient* conditions for their effects.

Let me first sketch the argument with which Mackie supports his main thesis: that the standard philosophical idea of a cause as a sufficient condition for its effect should be rejected. Mackie invites us to consider three different slot machines for which the insertion of a coin is, respectively, a *necessary and sufficient* condition, a *necessary* condition, and a *sufficient* condition for the emergence of a chocolate bar. We shall look only at Mackie's discussion of the first two cases, by means of which he establishes his main point. He shows that event *A*'s being a necessary condition for event *B* is sufficient for *A* being the cause of *B* (given certain provisos, it goes without saying). Mackie's discussion of the third machine, with which he tries to demonstrate that an event's being a necessary condition is not only sufficient for causality but is also necessary, features complications that are not relevant in the present context. I shall replace it by a related example, one that is traditionally used as an argument against the necessary condition analysis. The upshot of the discussion will support Mackie's contention that causes must at least be necessary conditions, but will point to the need for an additional clause in his definition to the effect that we must sometimes construe causes as *both* necessary and sufficient conditions. (Mackie himself admits what he considers a broader concept of causality, according to which causes are necessary *and* sufficient conditions. But he does not associate this notion with the special case of causality which we shall point out below.)

Let me now present Mackie's argument. We have two slot machines, K and L, both offering chocolate bars in return for 25p. K is a deterministic machine, and dutifully ejects a chocolate bar when fed 25p unless prevented by some malfunction. It never ejects a chocolate bar unless fed 25p. For K, the insertion of 25p is a necessary and sufficient condition for the appearance of a chocolate bar, *ceteris paribus* (that is, provided everything works properly).

L is a genuinely indeterministic machine (we may, if we like, imagine that its internal mechanism is somehow linked up with a device recording the emission of particles from a radioactive source). It will normally produce a chocolate bar when coins are inserted, but will sometimes fail to do so. Thus for *L*, the insertion of 25p is a *necessary* condition for the appearance of chocolate. But it is not a *sufficient* condition: *L* might have been in exactly the same condition, the coins might have been inserted, and yet nothing might have happened.

Now, imagine that on some occasion 25p is put into *K*. A bar of chocolate appears. Given the description of *K*, we know that the insertion was necessary for that happening, in the counterfactual sense that the chocolate would not have been ejected if the coins had not been inserted. The insertion of the coins is also a sufficient condition for that event, not only in the trivial sense of, insertion of coins $\supset$ appearance of chocolate (which is trivially true since the two events are actual ones) but also in a stronger, counterfactual sense, to the effect that the insertion would not have occurred if the chocolate had not been going to appear (or, as we might prefer to put it, the insertion could not have occurred if the chocolate had not been going to appear). These two counterfactuals give us ample grounds for asserting that the insertion *caused* the appearance of the chocolate.

Next coins are inserted into *L*, and again a bar of chocolate appears. *Ex hypothesi*, the insertion is necessary for that event, in the counterfactual sense that the chocolate would not have appeared if the coins had not been inserted. The insertion is also sufficient in the weak sense of material implication; however, it is not sufficient in a counterfactual sense. It is not true that if the chocolate bar had not been going to appear, the coins would not (or: could not) have been inserted. For, *ex hypothesi*, the machine might have been in exactly the same state, including the insertion of the coins, and yet no chocolate would have appeared, due to the action of the non-deterministic component.

Now Mackie's point is that although the insertion of the coins is not a sufficient condition for the emergence of chocolate, we would still not hesitate to say that the insertion *caused* the appearance of the chocolate. We are justified in ascribing causal power to the insertion of the coins by the fact that if the coins had not been inserted, the bar would not have appeared: the two events are related in a more than just contingent manner. We conclude that being a necessary condition (of a certain specifiable sort) is sufficient for causality. Mackie's argument disposes of the idea that causes necessitate their effects. There may be a non-deterministic connection between the two.

As mentioned, Mackie continues to examine a third machine to demonstrate that being a necessary condition is necessary for causehood and not merely sufficient as just shown. I think that Mackie is correct regarding this claim, although it needs some modification. However, I disagree with the way in which he supports this position; moreover, to handle the counter-examples that have been adduced against views of this kind, a minor addition to the Mackian characterization of causality is required. I will not attack Mackie's own slot-machine example, which features an unnecessary complication in the assumption of an indeterministic component, but will instead make my point in terms of a type of example which is often adduced to refute the *sine qua non* analysis. The example is orginally due to Marc-Wogau.[31]

A tramp is hiding from the thunderstorm in a barn stacked with straw. Having finished his cigarette, he throws the butt into the straw which ignites. In the same instant, lightning strikes the straw in the very same spot.

If we say now that the throwing of the cigarette butt was a cause of the fire, we undercut Mackie's analysis, to the extent that it pretends to offer a necessary condition for causehood (its claim to provide a sufficient condition is unaffected). For in the situation as described, the throwing of the butt was not necessary for the fire: it would have come about anyway, due to the lightning. And this and further such cases of *causal overdetermination* have indeed been taken to refute the *sine qua non* analysis by several authors.

Now the counter-instance has force only if we should actually say, intuitively, that the butt caused the fire. Mackie suggests that we should not naturally do this. Is he right? There may be some ambiguity in the question here. Of course, we could not say that the but was *the* cause of the fire, but this is simply because the definite article implies uniqueness. Would we hesitate to say that the butt caused the fire? And if so, is this simply because this locution hides a proposition which calls for uniqueness? It seems as if our intuitions are not quite confident here, with an inclination, I think, towards counting both events as causes, severally. If we yield to this inclination, we are compelled to accept Marc-Wogau's example as a genuine counter-instance to Mackie's theory of causality. However, a modest revision of the theory will allow it to accommodate this example. Cases of joint overdetermination have the following structure, when set out in counterfactual conditional analysis. *C* is jointly determined by *A* and *B* iff *C* would not have occurred if neither *A* nor *B* had occurred, but would still have occurred if *A* but not *B* had occurred, or if *B* but not *A* had occurred (this needs strengthening with additional provisos to exclude alternative overdetermination, so-called 'fail-safe' causes. But we cannot go into this here). Now could we not simply agree that this kind of conditional relationship between *A*, *B*, and *C* warrants our calling *A* and *B* causes of *C*, severally? To do so would not mark a very large departure from Mackie's analysis. The central idea of causes as necessary conditions is retained, although in a less simple form, in the stipulation that *C* would not have occurred if *neither A nor B* had occurred. The chief difference between the two is that the new one reinstates the sufficiency-aspect of causality. The analysis amounts to saying that in joint overdetermination of *C* by *A* and *B*, *A* and *B* may still be termed causes of *C* if either would have been a sufficient condition of *C* in the absence of the other. (Notice that the above conditional is not intended as a rival to Mackie's analysis as a general theory of causality. It is only meant to supplement the latter for a particular kind of case which Mackie, somewhat counter-intuitively in . my opinion, refuses to term 'causal'. Mackie's analysis still stands as applied to simple causation.)

The above definition does not allow us to speak of causal determination in situations of joint overdetermination by merely necessary conditions. But does it not make sense to say that, for instance, the introduction of a lump *X* of radioactive matter (call this event *A*) and the introduction of another lump *Y* of radioactive matter (event *B*) severally caused one and the same event, namely a recording in a Geiger counter (event *C*)? Maybe so. In that case, we need a conception of causality that goes beyond conditional analysis altogether. All that can be said about such a situation, in purely conditional terms, would be captured in the following cumbrous statement: C would not have occurred in setting S if neither A nor B had occurred. Moreover, situations obtain in which A and C occur in setting S while B fails to do so; on such occasions, C would not have occurred if not for the occurrence of A. Conversely, situations exist in which B and C occur in setting S while A fails to do so; and in such situations C would not have occurred save for the occurrence of B (in this analysis, the letters stand for event types, not tokens, in the last two clauses). The trouble with this conditional, as a suggested explicans of causal overdetermination by purely necessary conditions, is that, intuitively speaking, it is consistent with either A or B having 'failed to exercise' its causal power on the actual occasion, the production of C being due solely to the activity of the other. That is, it fails to explain what it means, in an instance of this type, that A and B severally cause C. And no further emendation of the conditionals will suffice to capture this intuitive idea.

Given the dubious character of the situation suggested, we may perhaps be justified in returning the ball to the opponent's court, challenging him to produce an alternative theory of causation to prove that causal overdetermination by purely necessary conditions is indeed a conceptual possibility. In the meantime, we may rest content with the observation that such an analysis, if forthcoming, could not fail to be as divergent from the regularity interpretation as the *sine qua non* analysis, and would thus do nothing to reinstate that interpretation.

So we have reached the following partial characterization of causality: to say that event A caused event B is to say, minimally, that A is a necessary condition for B, or (in cases of overdetermination), a necessary and sufficient condition for B, all in a strong, counterfactual sense. Let me stress once more that this is not a definition, but a partial specification. What is most urgently needed to turn it into a full definition is additional information about the conditional relationships involved. There are many kinds of counterfactual relationships between events which we should not count as causal. We need a demarcation between the two kinds.

Jaegwon Kim has presented the following list of examples which are clear counter-instances to the counterfactual theory unless strengthened with such provisos.[32]

If yesterday had not been Monday, today would not be Tuesday.

If George had not been born in 1950, he would not have reached the age of twenty-one in 1971.

If I had not written 'r' twice in succession, I would not have written 'Larry'.

(As it stands, the first example is not about events, and hence not a counter-example in the strict sense. But it is easy to produce a similar example in terms of events. For instance: if yesterday's sunrise had not been a Monday's sunrise, today's sunrise would not have been a Tuesday's sunrise.)

The task of formulating constraints that will absorb such counter-instances is not all that difficult. Kim himself suggests how it can be done by pointing out that the first two examples are based upon a 'logical' or 'analytical' connection. Hence they may be handled by a proviso excluding such relations. The third case would be taken care of by an injunction against part-whole relationships. But the main reason why these counter-examples need not cause us much concern is one that we have emphasized earlier: they all affect the regularity interpretation as much as the counterfactual theory. All these examples may be reformulated such that they refer to regular connections. Thus, all Monday mornings are followed by Tuesday mornings. All persons born in 1950 turn twenty-one in 1971. All writings of 'Larry' are writings containing two consecutive 'r's. Given our limited, critical objectives in introducing the counterfactual theory, we need not worry about problems that are common to both interpretations.

I have sketched a slightly emended version of Mackie's analysis of causality to serve as an alternative to the governing view of that notion. This analysis, I hope, will serve to undercut the basic prop of the covering law model of explanation. It will check the familiar argument that if we delete reference to general covering laws stating suficient conditions, we shall have no way to distinguish between mere narrative and explanation, no way to tell mere coincidences from non-contingent, explanatory relationships. It will equally dispose of the semantic version of the same objection to the effect that if explanatory (causal) claims are not taken to have a 'general implicate' along these lines, it is unclear precisely what is being implied with the statement that one event causally explains another one. The counterfactual analysis provides us with the answer that what is implied is, minimally, the existence of a counterfactual dependence of one event upon the other. (Notice that the conception I advocate need not adopt a realist position on counterfactuals, nor need it dispute Hume's insight that causality cannot be detected by a mere examination of a single case. The counterfactual theorist may–and, I believe, must–accept the point that a causal claim has a general implicate of sorts; but this implicate need not deal in *sufficient* conditions. Rather, what is implied is a law stating necessary conditions for the effect to occur, that is, a law of the form: when *C* is absent, *E* never occurs.)

7

We must return to reflect for a moment upon the vicissitudes of the covering law model. Was this magnificent edifice erected upon nothing more solid than an erroneous analysis of causality? Certainly not: behind it was also a very powerful intuition which any theory of explanation must accommodate. Unfortunately, this intuition reflects not the essence of explanation but rather a condition we impose in certain employments of explanations; and at any rate the covering law theorists only recognized this condition as it applies to causal accounts. The intuition has to do with a feature we might dub *explanatory tightness*.

On many occasions, we put a premium on explanations which do not permit the explanandum to 'rattle around' within the framework supplied by the explanans (to borrow a metaphor from Harold Greenstein).[33] The restriction of this freedom (continuing the metaphor) I refer to as 'explanatory tightness'. The intuitive idea is that the explanans may fit more or less tightly around the explanandum; at the limit, it will fit so accurately that no other outcome could fit the explanandum equally well. Cashing the metaphor of 'fitting', explanatory tightness is properly described as a matter of the extension of the set of different events that are consonant with the information contained in the explanans. A maximally tight account is one in which only one specific event is so consonant. (The precise import of the notion of 'consonance' must remain unexplained until the next chapter.)

The trouble wih explanations which suffer from explanatory slack is that a plurality of different possible explananda will fit them equally well. This means that the explanation cannot discriminate between these explananda and tell us why any particular one of them would actually happen. In situations where explanatory tightness is cherished, the ideal explanation is a maximally tight explanation: an explanation which permits us to identify the actual event to be explained as solely consonant with the explanans. Indeed, in this type of situation, it may even be felt that information that does not single out a unique potential explanandum fails to explain altogether: if our explanation of A is also consonant with the occurrence of its complement $\bar{A}$, it thus must fail to explain why A occurs, by not showing why A rather than $\bar{A}$ would come about. For to explain why A happened, it would be said, is to explain why $\bar{A}$ did not. Hence the explanation of A must be inconsonant with $\bar{A}$, and thus must point determinately to A; or, failing that, must at least favour it strongly over $\bar{A}$. We might call the principle thus expressed the Exclusion Condition.

It is easy to see how a one-sided appreciation of explanatory tightness and the Exclusion Condition would serve to entrench the covering law theory with its conception of explanation as a species of evidential reasoning, whether deductive or inductive. In causal accounts–which, as I have suggested, were the real explicata of the covering law model–explanatory tightness means causal tightness: the strength of the generative relation between cause and effect. This strength is naturally measured by the probability of the occurrence of the effect, given the occurrence of the cause. The ideal is a fully deterministic correlation in which one specific (type of) event must occur, given the events cited in the explanans. For this is tantamount to a unique specification of the explanandum and thus renders the account maximally tight. In the absence of a deterministic tie, we prefer that the probability bestowed by the explanans upon the explanandum be as high as possible. (The lack of a deterministic tie will normally be due to the fact that only a partial specification of the cause is provided. It may, however, be due to the presence of a genuine non-deterministic relation between the events themselves, as in radioactive decay.) Now when the premises of an optimally tight, that is, deterministic, causal account are fully stated, they permit the deduction of the explanandum. From this flows additional encouragement to insist on deductiveness in causal accounts, or at least on strong inductive support. Such insistence tallies perfectly with the covering law model and with the regularity theory of causation, which supply the logical framework within which the idea of explanatory tightness can be given a precise formal expression. But despite the harmony between these ideas, and the support they lend each other, the doctrine remains a mistake. Deductiveness is the mark of the optimal (causal) explanation in so far as we value tightness in the concrete use to which the account is put. But it is not the essence of explanation, not even of causal explanation. And despite the intuitive power of the Exclusion Condition, it remains the articulation of a particular practical interest in explanation in certain uses. An example of such a use might be this: you want someone to explain to you why your neighbour's apple trees bear a bountiful harvest while yours stand naked. Here, you will insist on a maximally tight account, since you want to know the full set of causally relevant factors which will bring forth a rich harvest for you, too, when you manipulate them according to your neighbour's recipe. You want an explanation of your neighbour's success which excludes the possibility of failure. However, seeing how the requirement of tightness was dictated by the specific concerns behind your query, we should not be surprised to find that in other situations, that requirement is absent. The Geiger counter incident is a case in point: here, there is no demand for an explanation which will allow the reproduction of the explanandum, and accordingly no feeling that the occurrence has not been explained until sufficient conditions have been found. Similarly, there is no tendency to deny the explanatory import of the account on the grounds that it is compatible with the non-occurrence of the explanandum. The powerful intuition articulated in the Exclusion Condition evaporates in the face of such examples, and is revealed as the mere reflection of a particular explanatory interest.

I have tried to show that the covering law model represents the intersection of two convergent and mutually supporting ideas: the regularity (sufficient condition) analysis of causation and the notion of explanatory tightness. The first leads directly to the covering law model when conjoined with the premise, often more or less explicitly endorsed by covering law theorists, that all explanation is causal explanation, or a generalization thereof. The second notion involves the idea that an explanation should point uniquely to a single possible explanandum; this is formally expressed (for causal accounts) in the requirement that an explanation be an argument in which the premises imply the conclusion deductively or at least with high inductive probability. I have tried to show that the regularity theory fails, and that the notion of explanatory tightness is an occasional desideratum of explanations, not their essence. We shall return to the concept of explanatory tightness in the next chapter, where it will be employed to draw the distinction between causal accounts and the different varieties of interpretive accounts. As part of this undertaking, I shall provide a sketch of the analysis of causal explanation implicit in the preceding deliberations.

3

An analysis of
interpretive accounts

1

In the preceding chapter we criticized the positivist construal of explanation. If that criticism is sound, its immediate yield is a better understanding of causal accounts. But its primary value in the present connection lies elsewhere, namely in the freedom to recognize other modes of explanation obtained by eliminating the covering law model. This freedom is produced when we abandon the deductiveness requirement and its weaker epistemic relative to the effect that an explanation must offer us good grounds for expecting the occurrence of the explanandum, or at least better grounds than we had before. The insistence that explanations are arguments which imply the explanandum deductively or with high inductive probability has often been used as a weapon against alternative models, or as a tool for transforming them into something that fits the covering law schema. It is not evident on the face of it that an account like 'I went to the garage to have my spark plugs checked' hides an argument with the description of that action as its conclusion. Strict adherence to the deductiveness or high probability criterion thus forces us either to withhold the title of 'explanation' from such statements or to justify the use of it through a demonstration that such accounts are deductive after all, at the cost of utter distortion (as I will show later).

However, the realization that the covering law model does not even provide a faithful explication of causal accounts means that in disposing of that model, we have not demonstrated that interpretive accounts are not a species of causal accounts, construed according to some more liberal analysis. That is, the interpretive theorist must be prepared to face the claim that interpretive accounts are indeed causal accounts, while not conforming to the covering law model. The present chapter deals with this challenge. It does so *pari passu* with an attempt to explicate the nature of interpretive accounts, using purposive accounts as an exemplar.

In arguing that purposive accounts are not causal accounts, I shall not try to show that the idea of causal connection is somehow at odds with purposive explanation. On the contrary, I shall adopt the position that causal ties are indispensable for purposive explanation. But the point is that this does not make them causal accounts; no more so than a perceptual statement is made a causal account of the perceiver's current sensory state by the fact that a perceptual statement implies the existence of a causal connection between this state and the object of perception. Thus, what I shall propose is a causal theory of purposive, and more generally interpretive, explanation, analogous to certain current theories of perception, knowledge, and reference in which causal ties play a crucial role.

2

Let us begin with purposive accounts. My explication of the relationship from which purposive accounts derive their explanatory power will be quite traditional; and I would be imposing upon the patience of the reader in presenting it were it not for the fact that most recent writers in the field agree that this view, despite its air of commonplace, is open to a fatal objection. I shall first provide a superficial statement of the commonplace view, then I shall carefully examine the celebrated objection to it; and finally I shall offer an improved statement of the commonplace view modified so as to accommodate the objection.

Succinctly put, purposive accounts illuminate an action by citing the agent's goal in action, and by showing how, given his beliefs, the action performed would appear to him to bring him closer to its realization. In a more careful formulation, we might say that purposive accounts explain by placing the action in a means–end framework, constituted by the agent's operative desire (or desires), and by his relevant beliefs about the situation he is in and about the world in general. The account specifies the motivational matrix out of which the action arose, in a way permitting us to see that based on this matrix, the action performed was practically rational.

Some may have difficulty accepting the claim that purposive accounts contain information concerning the agent's action-relevant beliefs. Most purposive accounts offered in an everyday context cite only the agent's goal (his relevant desire), not the beliefs which determine how it is to be pursued successfully. What is the justification for saying that the cognitive component is a part of purposive accounts? The answer is that most everyday purposive accounts are simply elliptic versions of the full story (cf. p. 50). In most day-to-day situations, there will be little doubt as to the general nature of the beliefs in the light of which the action was undertaken, and hence no point in spelling them out. The need for such additional information arises, however, in situations in which the efficacy of an action *vis-à-vis* the stated goal is not apparent. The point is brought out nicely in an example provided by Charles Taylor.[1] Someone who answered the question, 'Why are you mowing the lawn?' by revealing a desire to see Naples and die would not be thought to have given us much by way of explanation. We spot no means–end connection between the action and the professed goal. But now suppose this person adds that he has taken up lawn-mowing as a way to raise money for the airfare to Naples. Now we see the connection: we see how lawn-mowing constitutes a step towards that person's goal, given his beliefs about the world.

Now let us turn to the reasoning which has been accepted as proof that the above picture is entirely misguided, despite its platitudinous appearance. The *locus classicus* of this objection is Davidson's article, 'Actions, Reasons, and Causes'. A succinct statement of that criticism is contained in the following passage:

> If rationalization is, as I want to argue, a species of causal explanation, then justification . . . is at least one differentiating property. How about the other claim: that justifying is a kind of explaining, so that the ordinary notion of cause need not be brought in? Here it is necessary to decide what is being included under justification. Perhaps

it means only . . . that the agent has certain beliefs and attitudes in the light of which the action is reasonable. But then something essential has certainly been left out, for a person can have a reason for an action, and perform the action, and yet the reason not be the reason why he did it. Central to the relation between a reason and an action it explains is the idea that the agent performed the action *because* he had the reason. Of course, we can include this idea too in justification; but then the notion of justification becomes as dark as the notion of reason until we can account for the force of that 'because'.[2]

First an important remark on terminology to avert misunderstanding of the position that I am about to argue here. Quite misleadingly, Davidson speaks about the explanatory power of *justifying* action. However, from the quotation itself, and from what precedes it, it is clear that Davidson uses this word synonymously with the term 'rationalizing', which he has just introduced in an earlier paragraph. So what is being discussed is the explanatory power of showing that an action is reasonable and worthwhile, given the agent's concerns, not the explanatory power of the spectator's deeming the action justified according to his own standards. I am in agreement with Davidson that the latter could not possibly constitute an explanation of action, if only because the spectator's grounds for endorsing the action might be totally different from the considerations which motivated the agent. Unfortunately, Davidson vacillates somewhat on this crucially important distinction. In an earlier passage, he makes the point that rationalization may be called 'justification', albeit in an 'anaemic' sense. This is a highly misleading statement. Rationalization is not a weak relative of justification. To 'rationalize' an action is to realize that, and how, that action would seem reasonable and rational according to the agent's interests and beliefs; we might also say, *realize* how it would be justified relative to those interests and beliefs. The same relationship exists between the two as exists between your realization that somebody else has a headache, and your having a headache yourself. The former realization does not amount to an ache in your head, no matter how anaemic the sense of the word. Similarly, your realization that some action is justified in terms of the agent's concerns (not excluding his moral and other standards) does not amount to an endorsement of that action on your part, not even in a weak sense.

Now back to Davidson's argument. The passage cited may be reconstructed as follows. It has been suggested that rationalization explains action. But this cannot be so: for the presence of a rational connection between the agent's motivational state and his action only explains the latter if the agent acted *because of* his realization of this connection. Rationalization without this tie is non-explanatory. Now, what could be the nature of the tie indicated by the word, 'because', if not a causal one? No satisfactory alternative analysis is available. We conclude that the nexus is indeed causal and that purposive explanations are therefore causal explanations.

I agree with everything in Davidson's argument, as thus parsed, with the exception of the final step. He is right that rationalization alone does not explain, but that the explanatory power of purposive accounts is contingent upon some 'because' relation between the motivational states and the action. I agree with him, moreover, that this 'because' indicates a causal tie. I disagree, however, with the inference drawn from this realization that purposive accounts are causal accounts. That conclusion is a *non sequitur*. It commits the fallacy of assuming that a purely semantic analysis of a body of explanatory information suffices to establish the nature of the explanation. But we must also consider the force with which the explanation is proffered. We recall that the general notion of an explanation itself required reference to the force of the statement in which it was proffered. A body of information which satisfies the semantic conditions for being an explanation may nevertheless be adduced with the force of prediction or corroboration (cf. p. 78). Thus we should be wary of accepting the observation that a body of information involves causal ties as proof that that information counts as a causal explanation: for perhaps the distinction between causal explanation and non-causal explanation should also be drawn in terms of the force of statements. To my mind, this is clearly the case. When we refer to something as a causal explanation, we are not merely saying that it is an explanation and that it involves causation: we are saying that it is *explanation by causation*, that it is precisely the demonstration of a causal tie that delivers the explanatory power, and further, that this is the sole source of such power. If this is the case, then to demonstrate that some mode of explanation is causal explanation, we must show that it has the force of causal explanation: that, in its typical use, its explanatory power derives from the causal ties indicated, and from these alone.

I shall now adduce a pair of contrasting cases to illustrate that purposive accounts, as measured by this test, are not a species of causal accounts. Their explanatory power does not emerge solely from the causal information provided. I shall go about this by contrasting two accounts which are identical on the causal side, but which are clearly different in force. The example to be used as well as the contrast it illustrates will be familiar from a related discussion, namely, that of a causal theory of action.[3]

Bill calls on his uncle, whose estate he is to inherit, with the purpose of doing the old man in. At the appropriate moment, he produces a gun and points it at his uncle. A shot is fired and his uncle falls dead to the floor. However, the firing came about in the following way: Bill's desire to get at the old man's money, combined with his knowledge that he could achieve this by firing the gun, put him in a state of nervous tension. This state resulted in the jerking of his finger which triggered the gun.

The explanatory point of this account is quite different from that of another one from which it ought to be indistinguishable, given the causalist's position. This is the account we should have used to explain the outcome which Bill had planned: his pulling out the gun at some appropriate moment and coolly and deliberately dispatching his uncle. Here again we explain by pointing to Bill's desire for the money and to his belief that killing his uncle is a step towards the satisfaction of this desire.

In both accounts, a causal tie is pointed out between Bill's conative and cognitive condition and his action, and in the causal sense the accounts may be assumed to be equally tight. Hence, if they both were to be construed as causal accounts, they should provide the very same illumination. But obviously they do not: the force of the two accounts is entirely different. In the first case, Bill's action is presented as a mere causal offshoot of his wants and beliefs. In the second case, a goal is indicated via the specification of Bill's operative desire, and a belief is indicated on the basis of which his action can be seen as a means towards this goal. The account provides understanding by demonstrating this relationship to us.

The fact that both accounts involve the same intentionalistic states averts an objection to which the example would have been vulnerable if we had compared a neurophysiological account and a purposive account, namely, the objection that the difference in the two accounts reflects a difference in the terms figured in them, and that this has nothing to do with explanatory power. Unlike a neurophysiological account, so it might be argued, an account employing intentionalistic terms invites some kind of 'empathy' which gives it its special flavour but which is entirely without explanatory import. But in the example given here, both accounts are equally open to such empathy. The difference between them cannot be put down to such irrelevant features.

Nor will it help the causalist to blame the difference between the two accounts on the fact that the two explananda are slightly different: in the first example, he might point out that Bill only 'shoots the uncle' in a tenuous and secondary sense, one that does not presuppose that he fired the shot *in order to* dispatch his uncle, whereas in the second case his action is a fully-fledged intentional one. (The way the incident is described, the causalist might even be tempted to argue that the happening was not an action at all, but a mere nervous spasm. We may stipulate that Bill's finger-jerking was of the same kind as someone's nervous drumming on the table with his fingers. We would not hesitate to call this an action, although a very low-grade one.) But this difference is one that the causalist can hardly use in his defence. If the causalist is correct in maintaining that purposive explanations are causal explanations; that is, that the explanatory power of such explanations derives from the causal links indicated, it cannot be allowed to make any difference with respect to their powers that their explananda diverge in this manner. To propose this diagnosis would really be playing into the interpretivist's hands. It invites the rejoinder that the difference in explanatory power is indeed due to the difference in explananda, a difference, however, which removes one of these accounts from the class of causal accounts altogether: since one of the explananda is a purposive action, we are in a position to account for it, and do indeed account for it, by pointing to this teleological aspect.

But could Davidson not handle the situation with a rejoinder related to the hypothetical objection of two paragraphs back to a different pair of contrasting cases? That is, could he not concede that there is a difference in force between the two accounts, that this difference springs from the rationalizing effect of the second one, and still deny that this effect has anything to do with explanation? The first account, he might maintain, is an unadorned causal explanation, whereas the second combines the force of a causal explanation with that of a rationalizing argument. But here we may turn the tables on Davidson by confronting him with an argument quite similar to his case against the provisional analysis of purposive explanation. Rationalization cannot mean the mere observation that an action is rational in the light of the agent's concerns: for in that case, the two accounts above would be identical once more. In both, Bill's act receives identical marks for suitability with reference to his ends. Rationalization must thus involve such appreciation of rational suitability, *plus* recognition of the fact that the action was caused in the appropriate manner by the cognitive and conative states of the agent.[4] But given this interpretation, it is no longer obvious that rationalization has nothing to do with explanation. It no longer means the mere appreciation of certain abstract rational connections, but in addition the recognition of certain mental states as causally operative in the situation.

Moreover, a certain troublesome reduplication would be generated in Davidson's analysis by this rejoinder. Proffering a purposive account would seem to involve the following two elements, according to that analysis: (1) giving an unadorned causal account of the action; (2) demonstrating how the action was worthwhile to the agent, adding that his appreciation of this fact caused the action in a standard, non-deviant manner: the manner which licenses our saying that the agent acted in order to bring about the upshot. The second item in this analysis amounts to an improved statement of our original analysis of purposive accounts, a statement which concedes the necessity that action and motivating states be causally connected. What justifies Davidson in saying that in addition to this element, purposive accounts involve another, distinct one, a full-blown causal account? Is it not as if Davidson were saying that in proffering a purposive account of action, we do the following two things: (1) we proffer a causal explanation; (2) we proffer a purposive explanation?

The causalist's response to this might be to question the confident manner in which cognitive activities are being singled out and listed. We have no firm criteria for counting such different parts of what goes on when we adduce an explanation, he might object. He might go on to suggest that the proper way to express the difference between standard causal accounts and purposive accounts (as he would put it) is in terms of differences in the criteria of adequacy to which they are subject. All explanations are subject to the condition that they establish causal ties between the explanans and the explanandum; and this is what renders them all causal accounts. Upon accounts of human action we impose the additional requirement that they show action to be rational, given the agent's beliefs and desires. This is the *differentia* which sets them apart from other kinds of causal accounts. But claims concerning which specific functions are performed by explanatory information and the charge that the causalist position gets the number wrong can only generate confusion.

But this rejoinder does not harmonize very well with our previous conclusion that the overall notion of an explanation cannot be captured in such formal terms. It resists explication using the method of adding up the conditions upon those sentential structures we call explanations. Instead, it calls for reference to the force with which explanatory statements are put forth. But the causalist's suggestion is equivalent to the proposal that we do without the notion of force. In other words, were the causalist to defend his construal of purposive accounts in the manner indicated, he would thereby be retreating to an overly austere framework of description in terms of which we could not even distinguish between explanation and, say, corroboration, in the first place. He would have salvaged the claim that there is no essential difference between causal accounts and purposive accounts, but at the cost of implying that there is no essential difference between explanation and corroboration, either. The causalist's victory would be won at the price of abolishing the very topic he set out to investigate.

Why speak about the force of an explanation instead of simply referring to the speaker's intentions as to how the information he submits is to be taken? For clearly the force of an explanation, as of any other type of statement, must be a function of such intentions. But the notion of force is adopted here to indicate that we are dealing with a highly idealized and restricted segment of the speaker's intentions: most of what passes through his mind at the moment of producing the explanation is irrelevant to its force. Moreover, the term is also meant to suggest that a direct report of the speaker's intentions, formulated in his own terms, is likely to be unilluminating. For that report may well contain the very notions that we want to explicate. The speaker may simply report that he intended his account as a purposive account. We need to transcend such answers, producing instead a rational reconstruction of the intentions which they reflect. The situation is familiar from the analysis of meaning in the Gricean tradition: when we want to capture the illocutionary force of, say, assertions, it will do us little good to record what people say they are up to when using assertoric language. For they are likely to say that they mean what they say as an assertion. The notion of force reminds us that we are dealing with a highly idealized and reconstructed model of a speaker's intentions.

For the benefit of those who become somewhat impatient with talk about the force of statements,and who believe that any point worth making in philosophical analysis can be made in terms of semantic properties alone, I would like to adduce a consideration in further support of the claim that we cannot dispense with the notion of the force of an explanation in its concrete use. I shall go about this by comparing the role of causality in purposive explanation with its role in another notion for which a causal analysis has recently been offered.

According to a very plausible theory of perception advocated by H. P. Grice and P. F. Strawson, among others, the notion of perception involves a causal link-up between the object perceived and the sensory state in or through which it is perceived. If I am to say truly, 'I see a deer in the thicket', it must be the case that

(1) I have certain visual experiences as of a deer in the thicket (whatever this means exactly).

(2) There is actually a deer in the thicket.
(3) The presence of the deer causes the mental state indicated in (1).

If the mental state had been caused by some neural malfunctioning in my brain, causally unconnected with the object in front of me, we could hardly say that my experiential state was a perception of that object.

Now notice first that although the truth of a perceptual claim implies the existence of causal ties, there would be no plausibility in saying that making such a claim is tantamount to proffering a causal account of the current phenomenal state of the perceiver. If I catch a glimpse of what looks like a deer hiding in the thicket, but, not being quite certain, I sneak up closer to make sure, my eventual report, 'So I did really see a deer in the thicket' does not offer an explanation, not even a highly elliptical explanation, of my phenomenal state when it first looked to me as if there were a deer in the thicket. This is the case despite the fact that the temporal relationship between the 'explanans' and the 'explanandum' is, or at least may be, as required by the Hempelian analysis of explanation: the phenomenal description of my perceptual state will be known prior to, and certainly independently of, knowledge of the nature of the events which caused it. But the force of the claim is still not that of a causal explanation.

What, then, is the force of a perceptual claim? The answer is that it is an epistemic claim. Perception is basically a physical process in which external objects or events effect systematically correlated neurophysiological changes in the perceiver (I disregard here the phenomenal (but non-epistemic) component of perception which I believe to be irreducible to physiological terms.) But by calling this a perceptual process, we apply to it what I shall dub a *privileged description* in part supervenient upon the physiological description. We indicate that that process is also describable within a higher-level conceptual framework comprising epistemic notions such as truth, falsify, corroboration, evidence, etc. We grant it the status of a source of information about reality, a revealer of truth about the world. Correspondingly, individual perceptual claims do not have the force of declarations that one's experiential state at some particular time was causally explicable through reference to some specified event or state. They are moves within the privileged conceptual system, claims to the effect that one has a certain kind of evidence for what one asserts. When someone asks me, 'How do you know that Sinatra is in town?', my reply, 'I saw him this afternoon', is not meant to indicate that some phenomenal event occurring in me this afternoon can be traced back causally to Sinatra and thereby be explained. It indicates my grounds for believing that Sinatra is in town.

Of course, not all perceptual statements carry a heavy epistemic load: I may simply report what I saw in town today, with no intention of supporting further claims. Such a report is still a move within the privileged descriptive framework: it is a record of the world as experienced by me today, not a record of psychological changes in me throughout the day, with an appended explanation. Whether intended as evidential support or as mere narrative, perceptual claims do not amount to causal explanations.

There is a feature of perception which serves further to highlight the special role of causality in perceptual claims. Perception is susceptible to deviant causal chains. In perception, a deviant causal chain is one which, despite connecting some object in the external world and some suitably corresponding experiential state, still will not permit that state to count as a perception of the object.

An example of this might be the following. Lying on the operation table in local anaesthesia, I have vivid impressions as of an operation room teeming with activity. These impressions match precisely what is actually going on in the room around me. However, they are not generated in the standard way: by the physical impact of the events around me upon my visual receptors. Instead, the causal chain runs via the person of the head neurosurgeon, who stimulates the visual cortex of my exposed brain with delicate electrodes in such a manner that perfect correspondence is maintained between my visual impressions and what goes on in the room. (The neurosurgeon's knowledge of what happens derives from vision, i.e. from the goings-on in the room impinging upon his visual receptors. In this way, the causal chains responsible for my visual impressions are secured to the right objects at the other end; but deviantly.) Our intuitive reaction to this set-up is to deny that what goes on counts as seeing.

These observations concerning perception carry over to purposive explanation. Purposive accounts imply the existence of a causal link between the action to be explained and the motivational states listed in the explanans. The agent acts *because* he is in such-and-such a state; and this 'because' is a causal one. If no causal tie obtains, the account will be false. However, the force of the account is not a causal one. Instead, it is that of a move within the privileged descriptive framework of purposive action. The conceptual system of action is another higher-level framework supervenient upon a segment of reality which is, from another point of view, a mere physical one. Within the higher framework, we apply such notions as goal, purpose, reason, rationality, as well as those of decision, freedom, and responsibility. The point of purposive accounts is to make a move within this framework, not to provide causal explanation.

The affinity between the role of causality in perception and in purposive explanation is strengthened by the observation that causal deviancy may afflict the latter as well. We have actually met this phenomenon already: the first version of the shooting story on p. 109 was obviously a case of deviantly caused action. Since the causal chain which linked Bill's motivational state to his action was of a non-standard kind, the privileged conceptual framework of purposive explanation became inapplicable. For contrast, we may observe that causal explanation is immune to causal deviancy. The route traced by the causal chain between some causative state and its effect may be as complicated and bizarre as you like without affecting the truth or propriety of the causal account in which it is cited.

Thus Davidson's argument does not demonstrate that purposive accounts are causal accounts, but rather supports a *causal theory of purposive explanation*. The role of causality in purposive explanation which we have uncovered is analogous to that assigned to it in recent causal theories of perception, knowledge, and reference, a kinship revealed by the susceptibility to causal deviancy which these concepts have in common. The analysis of all these notions will bring to light specific 'intrinsic' connections between certain events or states: my perceptual state tallies with the event perceived by a relation of isomorphism; my cognitive state is 'true of' a given state of the world. But we also need a brute extrinsic connection between these items as well. For my experience to count as a perception of *this* very state, that state must be tied to my subjective condition by some purely factual nexus: and causality provides that nexus. Similarly, for my action to be explicable through reference to *this* current desire of mine, the action must be linked to it by some factual connection. Again, causality establishes the connection. I believe that what holds for purposive explanation is only a special case of a more general causal theory of explanation which allows us to reconcile the traditional pluralist and monist (=causalist) positions in the theory of explanation. The former theory has it that explanation is a matter of fitting the explanandum into some pattern with which it is seen to mesh, and claims that there are numerous such patterns: the purposive pattern, the functionalist pattern in sociology, the pattern of rule and rule following, the pattern of evolution and selection, etc. The rival view insists that only the demonstration of causal ties is explanatory and uses arguments analogous to Davidson's above to bring this out. A causal theory of explanation allows us to harmonize the two traditions by granting the causalists that causal ties are indeed involved in all explanation, while still insisting, with the pluralists, that this tie does not exhaust the explanatory power of all types of accounts. This is not the place to work out the details of such a mediatory theory. I do believe, however, that any adequate theory of explanation must incorporate the idea of an explanatory pattern, and shall go on to use this terminology in characterizing purposive accounts and rule accounts below.

3

With all these points properly digested, we may now offer a characterization of purposive explanation which will incorporate the insights won in the struggle with Davidson's objection. For contrast, we shall also provide an account of causal explanation in the same format.

First an explication of purposive accounts. A purposive account is an account in which the explanatory point resides in the specification of a certain conative state in the agent, of the kind we termed a *desire* in chapter 1, in a slightly technical sense, and in the specification of certain beliefs about the world entertained by him; the two elements together allowing us to see a means–end connection between these states and his action. To be added is the condition between these states and his action. To be added is the condition that these motivational states cause the action in a non-deviant manner. In somewhat more detail, we may specify the motivational states as follows:

(1) A desire that some upshot U come to be.
(2) A belief to the effect that the action A has at least some likelihood of bringing about U.
(3) A belief that there is no better way to achieve U in the setting, given the cost constraints and the limitations set by the agent's further interests; or at least the absence of any contrary belief.
(4) A belief that there is no overriding reason why A should not be performed; or at least the absence of any contrary belief.

It is apparent that the information comprised in a purposive account gives only a very abstract and very selective picture of the agent's motivational matrix, especially on the cognitive side. The account cites the agent's second-order belief that there is no better way to achieve U, but is silent about the first-order beliefs from which that belief is an inference. Nor does it cite the first-order beliefs which support the agent's conclusion that there is no reason why he should not perform A: a belief to the effect, say, that there are no rules bearing upon the situation which forbid A; that he has not promised to refrain from A; that A will have no overriding negative side-effects, etc. In this feature, purposive accounts differ from what might be called rationality accounts, which represent a scientific expansion and idealization of the everyday pattern of purposive explanation, and which we shall meet in chapter 5. There, we shall also comment briefly upon the psychological realism of the above explication of purposive explanation.

The schema offered above explicates the minimal core common to all purposive accounts. But at times we want to go beyond this minimum in the interest of *explanatory tightness*. In purposive accounts this means the tightness of the means–end relationship, as measured by the extension of the class of alternative actions that embody equally good solutions to the agent's decision problem. When explanatory tightness is aimed at, the ideal is a unique solution, that is, a solution that is not equalled or surpassed by any other one. Failing uniqueness, we want the class of equivalent alternatives to be as narrow as possible. Given the concern for tightness, non-uniqueness represents a lacuna in the account since it implies the existence of a class of possible actions $A_1 A_2 A_3 A_4 \ldots A_n$ for which the question, 'Why did the agent perform A_i instead of A_j' has no answer in purposive terms. (Note that uniqueness is not guaranteed by the fact that purposive accounts deal in optimization (by the third clause in the schema). An optimal solution–a solution that cannot be improved upon–need not be unique.) Now when we aim for explanatory tightness in a purposive account–henceforth to be referred to as *rational tightness*–we need additional information making the alternatives which the agent considered and his assessment of their relative merits explicit. This is the information which is merely summarized in the third clause of the schema. The situation is parallel to that which we found in causal accounts: when we want a tight causal account, we must have more than the minimal information that some specified event is a cause of the explanandum (i.e. is a nomically necessary condition for its existence): we must fill in additional information that allows us to infer the explanandum deductively or with high inductive probability.

There is also another case in which we will want to go beyond the basic schema. Often, the addressee of an account will have background beliefs, true or false, about the agent or the setting which render a purposive account by the minimal scheme unilluminating to him. To answer his query, information will often have to be supplied about the first-order beliefs summed up in the third clause. This phenomenon may be illustrated by means of Charles Taylor's example above: the explanation why a certain person–let us call him Norbert–is mowing a lawn, citing his desire to see Naples and die and his belief that he can earn the money for the airfare by mowing lawns, will be unsatisfactory if you happen to know that Norbert is a millionaire who could pay several hundred times that sum out of his bank account. To restore explanatory power to the story, you require supplementary information to the effect, for instance, that (Norbert knows that) a charge of fraudulent financial transactions has been raised against him and that his liquid assets have been frozen by court order. Now you become illuminated, because you no longer see any obstacle to the telling of a story which would show Norbert's action to be an optimal way to realize his goal. This does not mean that in order to appreciate a purposive account, you have to be able to sketch, if only in rough outline, the agent's first-order beliefs showing his action to be optimal: I may derive insight from being told that the activities I observe in the laboratory are aimed at producing deuterium, although I have not the faintest idea how deuterium is produced. But I cannot have positive grounds for wondering how the participants could ever expect their activities to have such an outcome.

The observation that the addressee's background beliefs determine the propriety of an explanation further supports the view that explanation is a pragmatic notion.[5] The addressee's needs determine not only which kind of explanation is required–say, a purposive rather than a causal explanation–but matter even after the proper kind has been selected. Reference to user's needs has a place even in the fine detail of the explication of explanation. Note that the formalist's favourite move to block the intrusion of pragmatics is a non-starter here: he will introduce the notion of a *complete* explanation, comprising a specification of every dynamic factor co-determining the explanandum, and will then go on to dismiss the pragmatic considerations as pertaining merely to the *selection* of specific bits of information especially salient to the user. But the notion of a complete account has no clear sense in interpretive explanation, since we cannot produce a complete, finite list of operative motivational factors. This is due to the liberal nature of the criteria for ascription of implicit beliefs, which permits us to assign such cognitive states if their propositional content follows logically from the content of other beliefs entertained by the agent. Thus, to cite Hempel, if we know that a person believes that seven and five make twelve, we will feel justified to attribute to him the (implicit) belief that seven speckled hens and five speckled hens make twelve speckled hens, although he may never have pondered this piece of applied mathematics. (Of course this criterion is subject to overruling by the agent's explicit repudiation of that proposition.)[6] In this way, a person is the subject of an indefinite number of implicit beliefs. The point is that any one of these beliefs may become relevant in an explanation of action, given sufficiently bizarre background beliefs in the addressee. Suppose the question about Norbert were raised by a child who believes that the good fairy will put money under your pillow if you wish for it badly enough. To make sense of Norbert's toiling, this child would have to be told that Norbert does not believe in fairies. In the light of such background beliefs, and the accounts which they call forth, the idea of a complete explanation is seen to be an illusion.

Now for causal accounts. An account is a causal account if it derives its explanatory power from identification of a causal tie between an event cited in the explanans and the explanandum event. In the miminal case, this tie consists in the former being a nomically necessary condition for the latter; a more complicated relationship obtains in cases of overdetermination (cf. chapter 2, section 6). Explanatory tightness in causal accounts means the strength of the causal connection: the likelihood that the effect will happen, given the occurrence of the cause. If we desire a causally tight account, we must add further information to the basic schema of the explanation, rendering it a sufficient or near-sufficient condition for the explanandum, thus bestowing at least a high probability upon the latter. When tightness is minimal, as in pure necessary condition accounts, the causal link-up is only explanatory if it is viewed against some contrast case, normally left unspecified, which is roughly similar to the actual course of events but diverges from it by *not* issuing in (an event of the same type as) the explanandum event, and by *not* featuring the necessary condition singled out in the explanans. For instance, explaining why Smith won the auto race by pointing out that he had petrol in his tank will work if, but only if, all the other drivers had for some absurd reason failed to fill up theirs. The condition cited in the explanans must not only be necessary for the explanandum to occur, but must be one which *makes the difference* between the actual course of events and some, normally implicit, contrast case.

Frequently, the contrast case is simply the standard or normal state of affairs. Finally, it is a feature of causal accounts that the intrinsic nature of the causative states is immaterial to explanatory power, as is the nature of the causal chain joining cause and effect: in other words, the notion of causal deviancy has no foothold in causal accounts.

To appreciate the unity of causal accounts, underneath their variation in tightness, we must remember that the necessary condition aspect is present even in tight accounts; thus a high degree of tightness is something additional to, and not something which replaces, the necessary condition aspect. The explanation of the breaking of a car radiator during a frosty night, citing the relevant initial conditions and physical laws which entail that such a thing would happen, would not be satisfactory if we knew that the radiator would have ruptured even in the absence of freezing temperatures, due to the agency of other causal factors. Even a maximally tight account involves the assumption that in the absence of the explanatory facts cited, the explanandum would not have occurred.

Given a complete statement of the explanans of a maximally tight causal explanation, we may deduce the explanandum. Rational tightness, on the other hand, does not permit such deduction, even when maximal. For even when a unique solution to the agent's decision problem exists, and he appreciates this fact, there may still be extrinsic, non-rational factors which prevent action from ensuing. Countless things may happen to prevent the execution of the act. This is why I spoke rather vaguely about the 'consonance' of the explanans and the explanandum on p. 100. In general, this relationship is not one of logical implication or inductive support, but of 'agreement' according to the specific nature of the principles involved in the explanation: principles of means–end rationality in purposive accounts, and the notion of conformity to rule in the case of rule accounts. But note that we can establish a purely deductive connection in such accounts (when maximally tight) if we take as their conclusion not a sentence stating the occurrence of the explanandum-event, but instead one expressing the verdict that the action is the rational or obligatory thing to do in the given situation. This brings out the basic unity of the notion of explanatory tightness in all types of account: its central meaning is that of a unique way of completing the explanatory pattern. Such uniqueness must always allow for formal expression in a deductive argument when that pattern is put into propositional form, if perhaps only after a transformation of the logical mode of the component statements.

Let me stress emphatically that these last remarks do not imply that purposive accounts explain only why some action was 'the thing to do' by the agent's own standards rather than why that action occurred: purposive accounts explain the occurrence of action-events. This is why such accounts are only explanatory if the agent's desires and deliberations, as recorded in the explanation, actually brought about the action in a causal sense. The point of the above remarks was simply that we can recognize the basic kinship between explanatory tightness in all types of account by observing that this phenomenon may be expressed in terms of deductiveness (in the optimal case); however, this expository device may call for a shift in the mode of the explanandum sentence from descriptive to normative.

To highlight the difference between rational and causal tightness, and to show that only the former is relevant in purposive accounts, let us take a look at an example. Suppose someone asks why Caesar invaded Britain. In answering that question, we would list the strategic considerations that may be assumed to have been at the forefront of the Consul's mind: the need to curb hostile interventions from the British tribes in newly conquered Gaul, and the need to put an end to any safe breeding-ground for rebelliousness against the Romans that might spread from the Celtic tribes on the islands to their kin on the Continent. We would also look for evidence that the prospect of booty and conquest played a role, as well as the glory of victory. In view of the dramatic nature of Caersar's undertaking, we would probably seek a maximally tight account, in the rational sense: we would attempt to explain why Caesar chose to achieve his primary military objectives by a punitive invasion rather than, say, by the building of a navy to control the channel, or by fortifying the friendly coastline. Ideally, we should like to present an account that would point to the invasion as a uniquely good solution to Caesar's strategic problem.

On the other hand, we should be uninterested in the information needed to make our account *causally* tight. We would derive no further understanding from additional data permitting us to deduce that there was such an event as Caesar's invasion of Britain. Minute specification of that lucky combination of geographic, meteorological, sociological, organizational, psychological, technological, etc. circumstances which enabled Caesar to succeed in his enterprise would create nothing but boredom, if our question were still the one with which we set out; nor would we be interested in learning about the general laws (if any) which would have to be applied to these data to infer the existence of that historical event. To put the point in a slightly misleading fashion, we are interested in Caesar's deliberations (his motivational matrix) and in the fact that *these* desires and assumptions prompted (caused) his undertaking, but not in the myriad further circumstances which caused that undertaking to succeed. Still, if purposive explanation is construed as a species of causal explanation, and if, with the covering law theorists, we maintain that the secret of causal explanation lies in causal tightness, then specification of all these factors is required in an adequate explanation.

To counter suspicions that this is a misrepresentation of anything ever claimed by covering law theorists, we may cite statements, such as the following, by A. J. Ayer:

> The ground for arguing [that motive explanation (=purposive explanation) requires deterministic laws, permitting deduction of the explanandum] is that otherwise the ascription of the motive would not properly account for the action: we should have to allow that even granting the agent's motive and the rest of the attendant circumstances, including all the other aspects of the agent's mental and physical condition at that time, we could not entirely rely on the action's taking place; and to this extent its occurrence will still be unexplained and indeed inexplicable. There may, however, be those who are prepared to accept this consequence, so long as they can hold that there is a high probability in this situation of the action's taking place: that is, they may be satisfied with the hypothesis that

if the situation were repeated a great number of times the action would take place very much more often than not. But since this leaves an element of arbitrariness, in that we have no answer to the question why it should ever not take place, it seems preferable to make the stronger claim, unless it can be shown to be untenable. The suggestion would then be that whenever an agent can properly be said to have acted exclusively from a given motive, the circumstances must be such that in any situation of this kind, indispensably including the presence of such a motive, an action of this kind invariably follows.[7]

To be truly explanatory, by Ayer's standards, a purposive account must provide such details of the situation and offer such a list of general explanatory principles that it can be established that the action could not but occur, given the situation as it was. Included in this information must be all sorts of data concerning the mode of operation of the means–physical, institutional, or whatever–which the agent used to implement his intentions. The historical example above takes this position at face value, exhibiting its weaknesess to optimal effect by picking an example in which the path leading from the intention formed to the act accomplished is especially long and perilous, and in which the irrelevance of the additional information needed to secure causal tightness is therefore especially obvious.

Of course, Ayer did not have this kind of action in mind when he wrote the passage quoted above. He was clearly thinking of actions like popping out to buy a newspaper. Still, invading Britain is as good an action as any, if not exactly an everyday occurrence, and on top of that eminently deserving of explanation. To disregard it and its kin in an examination of action explanation can only lead to a skewed analysis. (It will not do to dismiss invading Britain as an action on the grounds that it is not really one action but a collective effort involving the activities of countless Roman legionaries: for even the act of buying a newspaper requires the kind collaboration of other people, minimally the newsagent.)

Ayer may have been persuaded to accept his position by the observation that in certain cases, it would indeed point to a lacuna in a purposive account if, on some further, roughly similar occasion, a similar action did not occur, despite the agent's motivational state being exactly as specified in the explanans. The troublesome cases are ones in which the failure cannot be blamed on problems of execution; that is, cases in which nothing prevents the agent from implementing his plans. This kind of failure would indicate that the agent's motivational state was not fully specified in the original account. Some additional, unrecognized motivational state was present on that occasion but absent on the second one. The failure to record this state would represent a gap in a purposive account *qua* purposive.

However, for those who want to retain deductive tightness in purposive accounts, the above deliberations suggest an obvious way to achieve this. Instead of adding to the explanans, we may salvage deductiveness by paring down the explanandum: what we have to explain is not really how action was successfully completed, but why it was embarked upon. In other words, all we need to explain is the *initiation* of action, not its *consummation*.

This way out of the dilemma is taken by von Wright, among others. According to von Wright, a purposive account of an action A implies deductively, not that the agent performed A, but that he performed the action of setting himself to do A (cf. *Explanation and Understanding*, chapter 3). With this approach we may skip all those tiresome references to the specific features of the situation which assist the agent in carrying out his plans. These features are not prerequisite to his setting himself to do the action.

Now 'setting oneself to do something' must be understood in a truly minimal sense to save deductiveness. Since it is not obvious what is involved in setting oneself to invade Britain, let us leave our historical example and instead look at a case closer to home to illustrate the point. Jack drives Mary to the hospital in the middle of the night, with great haste. We ask, Why? and receive the answer that Mary had gone into labour and that Jack thought it was high time to get her to the maternity ward. Now Jack's setting himself to drive Mary to the hospital cannot mean, say, his getting dressed for the drive; for the sight of Mary's agony might trigger an attack of total motor paralysis, putting even this action beyond him. Thus his 'setting himself to drive Mary to the hospital' can mean no more than his attempt to move his body in a way conducive, as a first step, to getting Mary to the hospital.

But now the relationship between this account and the event to be explained—Jack's driving his wife to the hospital with no difficulty or mishap—would seem to be getting rather tenuous. It seems as if we have substituted another explanandum for the original one, one which is not even a part of it. Jack's frantic struggle to get his paralysed legs to push him out of bed has no counterpart in what actually takes place: Jack's slipping out of bed without more ado, getting into his clothes, and rushing out the door to start the car. This is simply Wittgenstein's point that *trying* is not a minimal action involved in all full-blown actions, their common core, so to speak, but is rather a distinct kind of action on a par with these. We set out to explain one action and wound up explaining a perfectly different one; and an action of a rather shadowy nature at that. The situation is hardly improved if, instead of tryings, we speak about 'volitions' or any other of the dubious goings-on conjured up by philosophers to bridge the gap between motivational states and action.

Thus, we recognize the necessity of carefully distinguishing between rational tightness and causal tightness. Conflating them leads to either of two related distortions of purposive accounts: either the explanans is inflated way beyond what our explanatory concerns require, or the explanandum is shrunk so as to bear no obvious similarity or relationship to the action we actually want to explain.

4

I have argued that purposive accounts are genuinely distinct from causal accounts. Clearly a parallel line of reasoning could be presented to show that rule accounts and semantic accounts (when serving as why-accounts) are also non-causal modes. Indeed, within traditional discussion, these accounts have all been heaped together under some such label as 'reason accounts' or 'purposive accounts' (in a sense more inclusive than mine). Hence, the entire prior exchange between the causalist and his opponent could be rerun here, with an example of a rule account or a semantic account replacing the purposive account. I shall spare the reader, and simply indicate the crucial turns in the argument.

First, rule accounts. In his opening formulation the interpretivist asserts that rule accounts explain by stating a certain rule or normative principle subscribed to by the agent and by indicating that the action to be explained is taken by him to conform to this rule. The causalist retorts that this does not suffice as an explanation: somebody might perform an action which was prescribed by his norms and known by him to be so prescribed, but still not perform that action *because* of this insight: he might do it for an entirely different reason, or just by accident. To preclude this possibility, we need to assume that the agent's performance was caused by his insight into the dictates of the norm and by his resolve to abide by it.

The interpretivist will agree that some such causal connection is involved in rule accounts. But he will deny that this makes them causal accounts. The force of rule accounts does not reside in the specification of that tie, but rather in the specification of the rule and the observation that the action conforms to it. He might go on to tell a story involving a deviantly caused rule-consonant action to prove his point.

Summing up the upshot of the argument, we might characterize rule accounts as accounts which explain action by placing it in a motivational framework which comprises the following components:

(1) an attitude of obedience to some rule R;
(2) a belief that, in the situation at hand, the rule dictates the agent to perform an action of type T;
(3) a belief that the action A is of type T;
(4) a belief that there is no overriding reason why A should not be performed; or at least the absence of any contrary belief.

To this we must add the condition that these motivational states cause the action in a non-deviant manner.

Explanatory tightness in rule accounts is measured by the extension of the class T: the class of alternative actions which all count as obeying R. In the optimal case, there is a unique solution to the agent's normative decision problem: the rule dictates one single line of conduct. Church liturgy and similar ceremonial rules approximate to this ideal. Still, even these do not ordain everything: not the way the pastor places his feet when blessing the congregation or similar petty details. Failing uniqueness, we want the class of alternatives to be as narrow as possible. When we aim at explanatory tightness, such alternatives represent gaps in the account which can only be closed by reference to other models of explanation. (I have treated 'explanatory tightness' as a one-place predicate of accounts here. Clearly, in a formally adequate characterization of that notion, it must be construed as at least a three-place predicate. First, it has to be relativized to a certain level of detail of action descriptions: we need a stipulation of how much it takes for one action to be qualitatively different from another. Secondly, it must be relativized to a particular aspect of action. Here, I am merely concerned with getting across an intuitive grasp of the notion and have to bypass all such technical details.)

The above characterization of rule accounts establishes a distinction between rule accounts and causal accounts. It also marks a distinction between rule accounts and purposive accounts: the explanatory pattern in which action is placed diverges between the two models, being the pattern of rule and rule-conforming action in the one, and the pattern of means–end rationality in the other. But clearly the difference between rule accounts and purposive accounts is much less significant than that between rule accounts and causal accounts. The latter difference coincides with the general distinction between causal accounts and interpretive accounts, whereas the former merely effects a division within interpretive accounts. Still this is a distinction that should be drawn, being justified by the way that accounts conforming to each pattern will often command differential interest in concrete situations of use. This is especially striking in the case of mixed action, that is, action determined by rules as well as by purposive concerns (as is indeed most action). When, for instance, an anthropologist examines a native sacrificial custom, he will often merely be concerned with the rule-governed aspect of that phenomenon: he will for instance explain the composition of the sacrificial meal only to the extent that it is dictated by norms, and will care little about those features that are determined by purposive considerations, such as which foodstuffs are available at reasonable cost.

Let me emphasize once again at this stage, however, that the tripartition of interpretive accounts with which I operate in this book is not primarily based upon such intrinsic differences. Rather, it reflects the fact that different modes of account offer varying options for theorizing and hence call for different considerations to assess their theory-sustaining potential. This point is especially important to bear in mind when we turn to the final mode of account, which is semantic account. This could hardly be said to constitute a distinct mode if we looked solely at the pattern which it embodies. For that pattern will be found to be either that of a purposive account or a rule account, typically the former. A semantic why-account will typically indicate some goal which the agent wants to achieve, notably some cognitive change in the listener or some action to be performed by the latter, plus the belief that he can achieve this by uttering certain sentences which are tied to those upshots by the conventions of his language. Hence, the form of a semantic why-account will most often be that of a purposive account as spelled out on p. 118. Its only distinctiveness will lie in the way in which the second clause of the schema would be filled out, in the present case by information concerning the agent's knowledge of his language and his expectation that by uttering a particular sentence in the language, he will achieve his goal. I shall have nothing more to say about this mode of account, since we have already examined the purposive pattern. But the thing to appreciate here is the fact that although semantic why-accounts do not embody a unique explanatory pattern, and hence cannot boast a distinctive explanatory force, they qualify as a special mode of explanation by the criterion adopted in chapter 1, which concerns itself with the opportunities for theorizing offered by different types of explanation.

5

Let us look at a consideration that might appear to imperil the proposed analysis of purposive accounts and rule accounts. For that analysis to work, motivational states must be causative *qua* intentionalistic states. Citing my desire for a swim as a purposive explanation of my going to the beach will only work if that desire causes my going to the beach *qua* a desire for a swim. The desire must be causally relevant under its intentionalistic description. If not, the statement that I went to the beach because I wanted a swim will be as useless for explanation as the statement, 'The disaster happened because of the events mentioned in today's headlines.'[8] The intentionalistic description must satisfy what we might call the Causal Relevance Condition. As a first suggestion, we might take this condition to call for the description under which a causative event is introduced to be such that had it not satisfied that description, the effect would not have occurred. This will take care of the 'headlines' case. However, an examination of a more sophisticated example shows that we need something still stronger. Suppose we introduce a cause-event C_1, which has the effect E_1, under the description 'is similar to C_2', where C_2 is an event causally productive of the event E_2. We may now infer that if C_1 had not been similar to C_2, it would not have brought about E_1. Still this does not intuitively make 'is similar to C_2' a causally relevant description. This is apparently due to the fact that we can explain why an event similar to C_2 would issue in an event similar to E_2 in terms of general laws that mention neither C_2 nor similarity: being similar to C_2, C_1 will share with it some property P for which general laws exist, tying possession of P with the generation of effects of type E. We cannot conversely explain why an event with the property P will generate an effect of type E by pointing out that in possessing P, this event agrees with C_2, and will therefore, by some law of nature, produce the same kind of effects as C_2. There are no laws of nature to the effect that events emulate certain other, similar, events in the effects they produce (which is not to say that this is a conceptual impossiblity). In brief, 'being similar to C_2' is causally irrelevant and explanatorily impotent because there are general principles, not themselves referring to C_2 or to similarity, that will allow us to explain why an event describable in that manner will be tied by a counterfactual conditional to the occurrence of an event of type E. Broadening our scope somewhat, and adding a little extra detail, we might define a causally relevant description of a cause–effect sequence as one for which it is true that, had the cause-part of that description not applied to the sequence, the effect-part would not have applied either; and of such a kind that there is no alternative description under which that sequence can be subsumed which would permit us to explain why that counterfactual conditional holds.

We must add a further clause to the Causal Relevance Condition. A causally relevant description must establish a *contingent* connection between the cause and effect. This clause is needed to block such non-causal relationships as were cited on p. 99: the sentence 'If yesterday had not been Monday, today would not be Tuesday', does not count as a causally relevant description of a sequence of states, nor does 'If I had not written "r" twice in succession, I would not have written "Larry".'

So much by way of setting the stage for the argument. The first scruple concerning the causal relevance of intentionalistic descriptions stems from the fact that they fail to satisfy the contingency-clause. This worry arises from a reflection on the nature of the intentionalistic framework as outlined in chapter 1. We found that framework to constitute a proto-theory, its central notions implicitly defined through the 'axioms' which they serve to express. Ultimately, the meaning of these notions is provided by the actions which they explain, since there are implications from the ascription of intentionalistic states to the occurrence of action. But perhaps the claim that such inferential ties exist needs to be defended. For it has often been pointed out that attempts to capture these alleged implications in rigorous formulae have always failed: given sufficient time and ingenuity, it always seems possible to think up counter-examples to any proposed formula licensing inference from a desire–belief pair to action. (In my statement of the core axiom of the intentionalistic theory in chapter 1 (pp. 13–14) I expressly indicated that it is not complete as it stands, and thus does not amount to a watertight rule of inference.) But the discussion of such concrete examples is rather futile: the present issues cannot be decided at this level. The core notions of the intentionalistic proto-theory are, after all, everyday concepts, with all the vagueness and open-endedness which accompanies that status. Add to this the holistic nature of the theory which implicitly defines these notions, and the fruitlessness of the attempt to crystallize the logical interrelations between them into hard and fast rules of inference becomes obvious. Exceptionless rules can only be hoped for if we allow ourselves liberal use of such highly elastic linguistic devices as, 'under normal circumstances', '*ceteris paribus*, 'unless extrinsic factors interfere', etc., in the formulation of the principles. These devices do not rob the principles in which they occur of all rigidity, and hence of all informativeness: there will often be considerable consensus among language users as to what constitutes a 'normal' situation. However, there is about as much hope of spelling out this intuitive grasp in more precise and unqualified terms as there is of spelling out the implications of other everyday terms in this manner.

Instead, this issue should be settled in the light of the general reflection upon the semantic structure of the intentionalistic theory as sketched in chapter 1. We argued that there is no other source of meaning for the core motivational notions than their mutual logical interrelations and their collective impingement upon observational fact in terms of the actions which they explain. Their ultimate source of empirical import is the actions which they serve to rationalize. In the light of this observation, and of the fact that exceptionless rules of implication can actually be formulated if we avail ourselves of the formulational safeguards mentioned above, we seem to be justified in saying that the attribution of motivational states implies the occurrence of action. (Given the way that the conceptual ties between motivational states and action will be exploited in the argument below, it would not really matter if we were to concede that there are other ways of (conclusively) verifying the presence of such states, for example, in terms of the agent's sincere avowals. See below p. 135.)

We might also make this point by saying that when we attribute a desire–belief pair to an agent, we ascribe to him a *disposition* to engage in action of a certain sort, a sort rationalizable in the light of that pair. (By 'disposition', I mean no more at this stage than a state or property which can be expressed by a universally quantified hypothetical sentence with counterfactual force; this is what I shall later call a *bare* disposition.)

To see how this analysis spells trouble for the ascription of causal relevance to intentionalistic states, *qua* intentionalistic, *vis-à-vis* action, we may ponder the fact that a desire–belief pair can be used not only to explain actual conduct, but hypothetical conduct as well. We might tell a hypothetical story about some person, based upon our knowledge of his actual motivational make-up, and within the scope of that story explain the hypothetical actions attributed to him by referring to those same motivational states. Now if we put together all the actions, actual and hypothetical, explicable in terms of reference to a particular belief–desire pair, plus indications of the conditions under which they occurred or would occur, their aggregated specification would be equivalent to the specification of a disposition in the agent to engage in action which could be rationalized in a certain manner, in the minimal sense of 'disposition' introduced above. But this disposition is precisely what that belief–desire pair consists in, according to the above analysis. The upshot seems to be that the complete class of actions which can be rationalized in a specified manner is represented as self-causative when explained interpretively. This consequence seems to make nonsense of the idea of explaining action by means of reference to intentionalistic states.

This objection shows the rationale of the much-debated Logical Connection Argument (LCA) against the causal status of intentionalistic states. There are several versions of this argument, most of them quite without merit. But one is generally recognized to possess a certain power, namely, the variant from verification. According to this variant an event E_1 cannot be allowed to be the cause of E_2 if, in order to verify the presence of E_1, we have to verify the presence of E_2. Infraction of this principle may come about in other ways than by ascribing causal power to a bare disposition (a disposition which can only be characterized in conditional terms) *vis-à-vis* its manifestations; and I shall not try to assess the general validity of the principle here. However, when used as a weapon against such ascription, and more specifically as an argument against the ascription of causal power to intentionalistic states, its cutting edge lies in the above consideration. Infraction of the LCA is in this case the symptom of a causal ascription by which a phenomenon is stated to cause itself.

Locating the force of the LCA in the necessity of avoiding self-causation is especially advisable, given that we accept the *sine qua non* analysis of causation. Applied to this analysis, the LCA must be understood to bar counterfactually necessary conditions that are non-contingently necessary. However, it is questionable whether intentionalistic states actually infringe this principle. If a person has a strong desire for some state of affairs *S*, and believes that the action *A* will lead to it, it follows that he will perform *A*, *ceteris paribus*. But it does not follow as a matter of logic that if he had not had that desire, he would not have performed *A*: the desire is not guaranteed to be a *necessary* condition for that action. Hence the relevance of the LCA for this case becomes questionable on its traditional reading. But it retains its bite when construed as an injunction against self-causation, since this charge, if valid against intentionalistic states at all, is also valid according to the *sine qua non* analysis. Moreover, if we construe the force of the LCA in this manner, we see that it does not really matter if we sometimes allow a person's sincere say-so to count as sufficient evidence that he harbours a certain desire, even though appropriate action may not be forthcoming. For unless that avowal is construed as a report of some categorical internal state, whether physiological or phenomenal, the ability of agents to produce such avowals merely shows the need for a further axiom in the intentionalistic proto-theory, an axiom specifying one more manifestation of that dispositional property which we attribute to people when we ascribe a desire–belief pair to them. The use of intentionalistic terms in explanation will still be open to the objection, now in a generalized version, that when we refer to such states to account for people's actions *and for their avowals of desire*, we involve ourselves in the incoherent notion of self-causation.[9]

To salvage intentionalistic causation, and hence interpretive explanation, we may start by making a few general observations on dispostions. We operated above with the notion of a bare disposi-tion, a disposition which could be expressed exhaustively in terms of conditional sentences. It is now time to introduce the notion of a grounded disposition, as I shall call it, a disposition which cannot be defined exhaustively by such means but which also requires reference to a 'categorical basis' for its characterization. I shall argue that the problems faced by the explanatory use of intentionalistic notions dissolve when we appreciate the fact that motivational states are grounded dispositions. *That* motivational states are grounded (in neurophysiological states, as it happens) I simply accept here as an utterly well-attested empirical fact. There is a dispute of long standing as to whether the notion of a bare disposition is an intelligible one, or whether dispositions must ultimately rest upon a categorical basis. Fortunately, we may bypass this thorny issue here: we need not demonstrate that all dispositions must be grounded in order to maintain that motivational states are. There is plenty of independent empirical evidence in support of this view. Indeed, another traditional challenge to the use of intentionalistic notions in action explanations is the accusation that their explanatory role is pre-empted by accounts referring to the categorical basis, that is, to neurophysiological states. We shall return to that challenge presently.

The disposition $D_{n,m}$ of O (i.e. the disposition of O to display reactions of type n in situations of type m) is grounded iff there is some mechanism in O, describable in categorical terms, which causes O to mainfest n in situations m. The thing to appreciate here is the fact that in many, or perhaps all, grounded dispositions, the existence of the categorical basis (mechanism) is strongly integrated logically with the meaning of the statements we make about these dispositions. Many of the things we want to say about them will only make sense in terms of reference to the underlying mechanism.

A simple example from outside the realm of human action may illustrate this point. If we are to say that Socrates' death is a manifestation of the toxicity of hemlock, it is not enough for Socrates to die after having imbibed hemlock, nor even for it to hold counterfactually that he would not have died if he had not taken hemlock: his death must be caused in the manner, whatever it is, in which hemlock typically kills people. If Socrates were actually immune to the poisonous effect of hemlock, and his death the effect of hemlock mixing with some food ingredient in his stomach to form a new deadly compound, we should not say that it was the toxicity of hemlock that caused his death. The notion of toxicity imposes a restriction on the causal paths which are allowed to connect the ingestion of the toxic substance and the consequent death. That notion, in other words, invites application of the notion of 'deviant causal chains'. And the precise import of deviancy for toxicity can hardly be made explicit without reference to the fine detail of the causal processes involved.

Notoriously, deviant causal chains may infest action, too. On p. 109 we sketched a case where Bill kills his uncle as a causal consequence of a desire for his uncle's money and a belief that he can get hold of it by killing him; a causal consequence mediated, however, by deviant causal chains. In the case of action, too, full sense can only be given to the notion of a non-deviant causal chain by attending to details of the mechanism through which action is generated. If this is not obvious from the example involving Bill, it will be clear from the case where we discount as deviantly caused, a piece of behaviour prompted by an electrode operated into the agent's brain, hooked up with a radio receiver on his skull through which his conduct is controlled by some other person who monitors the flow of the subject's motivational states and makes his bodily motions mimic the 'natural' manifestations of those states.

These observations reveal that, when a disposition is grounded, the statements we make about that disposition will be enriched by reference to features of its categorical basis, an enrichment permitting us to describe the disposition (or its subject) in ways that cannot be rendered meaningful in purely conditional terms. When we say of some object O that it has the disposition $D_{n,m}$, where $D_{n,m}$ is grounded, what we imply, then, is that O has some property X which causes it to manifest n in situations of type m, the causal chain being of a standard kind, more or less narrowly specifiable, characteristic of $D_{n,m}$. (What is said here can be somewhat misleading: it is not to be understood as if we await the demonstration that a certain disposition is grounded before talking about it in such enriched terms. Our naive assumptions about dispositions are staunchly realist: we will talk about dispositions using the rich terminology until it can be demonstrated that they are not grounded, whereupon we will fall back upon a weaker descriptive framework.)

If the import of the attribution of a grounded dispositional property is as indicated, this suggests a very natural interpretation of the statement that a grounded disposition causes a certain phenomenon, where that phenomenon is of the sort which manifests the disposition: to say that the grounded disposition $D_{n,m}$ of O causes the event E, where E is itself of type $T_{n,m}$, is to say that the state or property X of O, which normally causes O to display n in situations m, causes E in the standard manner in which O causes n. This is really no more than saying that E is a manifestation of $D_{n,m}$ in a manner stressing the causal import of that predication.

The point is that this construal saves us from running afoul of the LCA: because a grounded disposition involves a categorical basis, it is not identical to the sum of its manifestations, actual and hypothetical. A grounded disposition cannot be exhaustively analysed into a cluster of conditional sentences of counterfactual force specifying its manifestations: the categorical basis prevents such dissolution. Looking more specifically at the intentionalistic states by means of which we explain action, we see that talk about these is more than just oblique talk about action. It refers to something that functions as a genuine cause of action. (Note that the proposed analysis of grounded dispositions does not involve the identification of such dispositions (dispositional properties) with that in which they are grounded. It does not imply, that is, that the identity conditions for dispositional properties are a function of those of the underlying categorical basis. More specifically, the analysis does not imply that intentionalistic states are identical to their neurophysiological basis. The argument to show that such an implication does not hold is familiar from writings espousing 'functionalism'.)[10]

Someone might suspect that this way of salvaging interpretive explanation secretly sacrifices the intentionalistic vocabulary it set out to defend. For does not the above analysis trace the causal power of intentionalistic states to their categorical basis, that is, presumably to certain neurophysiological states? Does it not actually show the intentionalistic description to be causally irrelevant? This suspicion is unfounded. To impugn the causal relevance of intentionalistic descriptions, it would have to be shown that causative states are really introduced under a neurophysiological or some other non-intentionalistic description in interpretive accounts. But this is patently not the case according to the analysis just provided. For although that for which X stands in the formula of two paragraphs back, is presumably a neurophysiological state or process when that formula is applied to intentionalistic causation, that state is not being introduced under a neurophysiological decription. 'X' is not a dummy neurophysiological description, but a variable; the force of the entire phrase in everyday terms would be something like 'that state or process, whatever it may be, which normally causes the agent to perform actions of such-and-such a kind'. This string of words contains no neurophysiological vocabulary, merely intentionalistic terms, plus what used to be called 'topic-neutral' expressions.

It might still seem puzzling that there is room for a causally relevant intentionalistic description of the action-producing state, given, as we assume, that this state has a causally relevant neurophysiological description. How could there be two non-equivalent, causally relevant descriptions of a causative state? The solution to this puzzle is that the intentionalistic description, *qua* dispositional, really provides information not primarily about the cause, but about the effect. It refers to the cause, but characterizes it in a manner which provides insight into the effect. A complete, causally relevant description of a cause–effect sequence must provide a characterization of the effect as well as of the cause. Hence, even if we already possess a causally relevant description of the cause, there is still room for causally relevant information about that sequence, namely about the effect. An intentionalistic description of the agent's motivational state supplies that kind of information: by telling us that Moe's manoeuvres on the Stock Exchange are motivated by a desire to corner the copper market, it tells us that his action of buying stock was caused *qua* being likely to bring it about that Moe will get the copper market cornered. This is causally relevant information about the effect, but logically transformed so as to serve as a predicate of the cause. Intentionalistic descriptions of motivational states supply a different part of the causal story than the one they are ostensibly concerned with; hence they may exist alongside an intrinsic, causally relevant description of the cause.

But now another worry concerning the causal relevance of intentionalistic terms arises. The description of a cause, via oblique description of the effect, will only count as causally relevant if the latter description is causally relevant as pertaining to the effect. But there is a familiar line of reasoning that seems to show that this condition is not satisfied in the action case. Human action, at least of the bodily sort, consists of selected parts of bodily motion described within the framework of intentionalistic notions. And it is a plausible assumption that bodily motion is fully causally determined by prior physiological events in the agent's body. But this means that the connection between the agent's motivational state, intentionalistically described, and the ensuing action, similarly described, can be explained by reference to the agent's bodily condition and the effects of that condition, conceived as mere bodily motion (more precisely, what is explained is the (contingent, non-conceptual) relationship between the action and the further manifestations of the agent's motivational state). The intentionalistic description of action is thus shown to be causally irrelevant in the same way as is identical to C_2' above (cf. p. 131). And, as a consequence, so is the intentionalistic description of motivational states. For these must be construed as dispositions to perform actions, not dispositions to carry out movements.

Before we respond to this argument, let me make a few comments in defence of the assumption that bodily motion terms are causally relevant in the case of action. Charles Taylor has argued that this is no *a priori* truth, not even if we grant that every intentionalistically described phenomenon also has a physiological description.[11] (As it happens, Taylor focuses on the causal relevance of intentionalistic descriptions of motivational states, rather than of action. The issues involved remain the same, however.) Now Taylor is correct in his assumption that there is no *a priori* principle to the effect that, to put it in the terms adopted here, supervenient descriptions must be causally inert. Such descriptions may well be causally prior to the descriptions upon which they supervene. Still, this assumption presents difficulties in the present case due to the dispositional nature of intentionalistic predicates. What makes a particular bodily motion an action is the fact that it is a member of a class of alternative, hypothetical sequences of bodily motion which, taken together, display a certain directedness (to speak very crudely) inviting us to describe the phenomenon within the teleological framework of action. What makes the movement an action is thus something which, from the point of view of logic, is a dispositional property of the agent. Now if we want to avoid the unattractive position that dispositions may be barely true (to use Dummett's term)[12]–that is, may be true without there being some categorical fact which makes them true–we must accept the fact that this dispositional property belongs to the agent by virtue of certain non-dispositional facts that are true of him. These are, no doubt, facts about the physiological condition of his body, in combination with laws which permit us to predict the agent's future bodily movements on the basis of his present state. But now we come to the problem: these laws cannot be the familiar laws for processes in living animal tissue: for according to the hypothesis proposed by Taylor, physiological processes are governed by laws that make them out to be the function of *intentionalistic* states of agents. That is, these processes are hypothesized to be explicable in terms of laws the antecedents of which refer to intentionalistic states. This means that these laws cannot get a grip upon the physiological processes until a suitable intentionalistic interpretation has been adopted. But at this point we are clearly moving around in a circle: we invoked the laws to fix the truth value of (counterfactual) sentences about bodily motion; such truth values were needed in order to fix the truth value of intentionalistic descriptions of the agent. And now we have been forced back to fixing intentionalistic truth values again. The problem is, of course, that we have a paradox of mutual determination in Taylor's proposal: the intentionalistic description is said to fix the truth value of the physiological description by causal determination; on the other hand, the neurophysiological description fixes the truth value of the intentionalistic description through the supervenience relation. The intentionalistic and the physiological description are doomed to chase each other in vain, with no hope of a determination ever emerging.

If we cannot take Taylor's route out of this quandary, I believe that the above argumentation against the intentionalistic framework must be allowed to stand, as long as we stick to our original definition of the Causal Relevance Condition. But perhaps this condition is too strict. We introduced it to bar the citing of causes under such descriptions as 'the events mentioned in today's headlines' and 'similar to C_2'; cases for which we have strong intuitions of inadmissibility. However, this condition has no justification so far when applied outside this range of cases; hence if we should resolve, for some novel range of descriptions barred by the condition, that they are intuitively admissible, then we should modify our formula. I believe that supervenient descriptions count intuitively as causally relevant, if the descriptions on which they supervene are also causally relevant. Consider an example: P is a pattern of black dots on a piece of paper, and D an exhaustive geometrical description of that pattern. But P also forms the likeness of a horse's head. The description H which attributes this property to P is supervenient upon D: it introduces an immediately observable property of P which is determined by, but cannot be analysed into, the geometrical facts comprised in D. Now suppose a photograph is taken of P. This involves *inter alia* the fact that P causes a pattern of dots to form on a negative. This pattern will also correspond to the description H. It would surely be overly stringent to insist that H is causally irrelevant to the generation of a horse-head shaped pattern of dots on the negative, and that only description D is causally relevant, on the grounds that the application of the former description can be explained in terms of general principles that do not refer to the property of being horse-head shaped at all. It seems that the supervenience relation is intimate enough to allow causal relevance to be transmitted from one description to the other. In a similar vein, we should grant causal relevance to intentionalistic action descriptions *qua* supervenient upon descriptions of movement.

6

Considerable space has been devoted to the task of providing analyses of interpretive why-accounts (interpretive explanations). Much less can be said on the topic to which we now turn, the nature of interpretive what-accounts. The aim of such an analysis is to obtain a non-grammatical characterization of what-accounts, and as part of this a non-grammatical way to distinguish what-accounts from why-accounts.

An obvious starting point lies in the exploitation of the insight gained into why-accounts to effect a demarcation between these two types. We have found that interpretive why-accounts work by placing the explanandum in either of two kinds of patterns, the means–end pattern or the pattern of rule and rule conformity. Returning to a point made in chapter 2, we may add that in an explanation the explanandum must be known in advance of, or at least independently of, knowledge of the information comprised in the explanans. Thus, interpretive why-accounts place an action, under a description independently known to apply to it, in a context of states or events which embody either the means–end or the rule pattern. Using this clue, we might simply distinguish the two kinds of account by stipulating that all accounts which divide up into two sets of components (i.e. an explanandum and an explanans) answering this description count as why-accounts, whereas the rest count as what-accounts.

This criterion works well for many examples; that is, it places the distinction where we intuitively want it to be. You ask, 'What is Sally doing tonight?' This cannot be intuitively construed as a request for an explanation for anything: the answer ('She is studying for her finals') will most naturally be construed as a what-account. The proposed criterion delivers the same verdict, thanks to the clause specifying that explanation (the providing of why-accounts) requires the explanandum-event to be known to the asker (i.e. some description thereof to be known to him) independently of the account: in the natural way of construing the above episode, you, the asker, have no prior information about Sally's doings which you can insert into a wider pattern.

However, trouble lies ahead. You ask, 'What is Sally doing with that newspaper?' This question suggests that you are in possession of some vague prior description of Sally's behaviour ('Sally is sneaking around with a folded newspaper in her hand'). Hence, an answer to your question like 'She is trying to swat a fly', will qualify as a why-account. It places the action, under this implicit description, in a wider means–end framework. However, this characterization is somewhat counter-intuitive. The answer reveals the nature of the action, we would like to say, rather than the reason why it was performed.

Should we defer to our criterion, or should we let our intuition prevail? We might prefer the latter, if we could give some explanation of this intuitive verdict in more general terms. Here is a suggestion: an account may satisfy the above conditions for qualifying as an explanation and still serve as a what-account if the (implicit or explicit) explanandum is expressed in very low-level or vague terms, or is otherwise trivial. In the above case, the description under which you know Sally's action ('Sally is sneaking around with a newspaper in her hand') is a very low-level, 'behavioral' one. You do not yet know *what* Sally is up to, the nature of her action, but only purely trivial manifestations thereof. Hence the answer to your question is meant to provide you with this information: it is meant to inform you of the *what*, the *nature* of the action.

It follows from this observation that, for a wide range of cases, there is no sharp distinction between what-accounts and why-accounts. Sharp demarcation is only possible for accounts that fail to satisfy the prior knowledge condition, or that cannot be divided into sub-elements related as explanans and explanandum. But for the large class of cases that do satisfy these conditions, the decision whether to label them why-accounts or what-accounts hangs on quite flimsy intuitions as to the substantiveness of the description under which the action accounted for is known. It would be futile to press the distinction for such cases.

However, this upshot is not something to be lamented. To the contrary, it is highly welcome. It serves to undermine the attitude, sometimes evidenced by interpretive theorists, that an investigation aimed at answering why-questions is *toto coelo* different from one answering what-questions, and that the former is rather inappropriate in an interpretive approach to action: the task of an interpretive science is to understand the nature (the 'what') of the individual action, not to explain the fact that it was performed. The demonstration that these two kinds of account shade off into each other and that they can be distinguished, for a large range of cases, only by fine discriminations of the substantiveness of action descriptions, serves to undermine this misconception. No crucial methodological distinctions could be presumed to hinge upon differences of this kind.

The distinction between these two kinds of accounts has been advocated most insistently for accounts in terms of linguistic meaning. We recall from chapter 1 that it was indeed the existence of this kind of account that forced us to operate with a separate category of what-accounts. For accounts in terms of linguistic meaning cannot very naturally be construed as answers to why-questions. It is gratifying to see, however, how this intuition is captured and explained by the above demarcation of why-accounts and what-accounts, its significance thus being diminished. Any query of the form, 'Why is he doing so-and-so', asked about a speech act and with the same force as the question, 'What is he saying?', would presuppose a very low-level, 'behaviouristic' action-description to replace the 'so-and-so' (such as, 'Why is he producing those oral noises?'). When our anterior knowledge of an action is this minimal, we cannot be allowed to know yet *what* action is being performed. Hence the answer to our question will be construed as supplying us with that information: it will be construed as a what-account. This analysis shows that the partiality of meaning-accounts for what-questions does not, by itself, argue any profound methodological difference between that kind of account and the others which we have examined.

Nor, as we pointed out in chapter 1, is the intuition that meaning-accounts are somehow incongruous with why-questions fully born out by the facts. Pointing to the man yelling and gesticulating at you from the bank of the river, you ask, 'Why is that man yelling at us?' The answer might be, 'He is shouting that the ice is unsafe.' This answer indicates the linguistic meaning of the man's utterances; it would have been equally apposite as an answer to the question, '*What* is that man yelling to us?' Still it counts as a perfectly adequate answer to the why-question as well. The notion that accounts in terms of linguistic meaning are germane only to what-accounts cannot be upheld.

We have presented the outlines of a non-grammatical criterion for the distinction between why-accounts and what-accounts. Obviously, this effort still leaves the latter quite undefined in other respects. Thus, what-accounts, like why-accounts, need to be distinguished from predictions, retrodictions, and other more specialized uses of information (although there is presumably an even looser sense of 'account' in which anything at all may count as a what-account, even predictions, etc.). I shall not attempt to provide the distinguishing features which would secure such demarcation. It is obvious that such an effort could produce very little by way of positive, substantive characterization of what-accounts. The required demarcations, as the one we have just worked out, provide only negative characterization of what-accounts. They draw the dividing line from without, so to speak, from the position of a more specific, bordering notion, leaving the tag, 'what-account', to apply to the residual class. No matter how many such demarcations we introduce, they will not add up to an intrinsic, substantive characterization of what-accounts of the kind we managed to produce for why-accounts. The notion of a what-account, in general, is purely pragmatically defined, that is, in terms of the use to which a certain piece of information is put. And even at the pragmatic level, only a negative characterization can be provided.

The above merely amounts to a somewhat more technical statement of the commonplace that any old description of a phenomenon may be called an account of that phenomenon, given appropriate circumstances. More specifically, a what-question about some action could be a request for any old bit of information concerning that action; no formal restrictions can be placed upon the answers that can be classified correctly as what-accounts. When the counsel for the defence asks the witness to give an account of the defendant's conduct on the night of the murder, only the concrete interests of the court determine what counts as an admissible and proper answer. Any piece of information filling a gap in the judge's and the jurors' picture of what happened on that fateful night deserves to be called an account of those events.

Does this upshot threaten our project with vacuity, to the extent that it deals with meaning-accounts which, as we have seen, are largely to be construed as what-accounts? Does it imply that when we ask whether theoretical meaning-accounts are possible, we are asking a perfectly indefinite question? Fortunately, the answer is emphatically no. That question receives all the definiteness we could ask for from the word 'theoretical' (and a lot from 'meaning' as well). The query concerning theoreticity imposes very strict conditions upon what could pass as an acceptable meaning-account, even though such accounts are (most naturally) to be construed as what-accounts. Chapter 7 will be dedicated to the task of examining what a theory of meaning might look like and what implications this may have for the proper form of meaning-accounts.

4

The authority of agents' self-interpretations

1

In the Introduction, we mentioned that a crucial motive behind interpretive social science is the concern that social enquiry should present a picture of social reality in which the agents can recognize themselves and their actions. This concern is taken to commit social science to using the same type of concepts and explanatory patterns as are employed in common-sense understanding of society. However, numerous philosophers of social science have taken the additional step of insisting, in the name of the same concern, that social enquiry adopt the same *particular* interpretations and explanations that the agents themselves embrace. Social science, so it is asserted, must defer to and somehow incorporate the social agents' own interpretations of their actions. This precept is intimately tied to the doctrine of the 'social construction of social reality', the idea that social fact is a product of the agents' conceptions and 'meanings'. This is a central theme in the writings of symbolic interactionists, ethnomethodologists and other phenomenologically-orientated sociologists, as well as in much Anglo-American anthropology.

The present chapter is dedicated to determining the precise import of this doctrine, and to evaluating its merits. Such an investigation has obvious relevance for our project, since an obligation to accommodate the agents' everyday interpretations could hardly fail to influence detrimentally the prospects of a genuinely theoretical understanding of action. And although in the main we shall reject the proposed methodological precept, certain results will be established which will prove important later.

2

I shall introduce our present topic by quoting a passage by the sociologist–philosopher Alfred Schütz, in which the requirement of faithfulness to the agents' own interpretations is enunciated with particular force. I choose Schütz as a foil for our investigation, not only because he put so much store by that principle, but also because he recognized that it constitutes a threat to social science which he tried to find a way to counter. In this, he differs favourably from other philosophers who endorse principles similar to his own, but who regard them as the solution to the social scientist's methodological worries, rather than as part of the problem.[1]

In the article 'Common-Sense and Scientific Interpretation of Human Action', Schütz formulates the following 'Postulate of Adequacy' for theory and concept formation in social science:[2]

> Each term in a scientific model of human action must be constructed in such a way that a human act performed within the life-world by an individual actor in the way indicated by the typical construct would be understandable for the actor himself as well as for his fellow-men in terms of common-sense interpretation of everyday life. Compliance with this postulate warrants the consistency of the constructs of the social scientist with the constructs of common-sense experience of the social reality.

Thus, the fate of a scientific interpretation of action hinges on its conformity with the everyday interpretation as provided by the agents involved. The reason Schütz offers for his adequacy requirement is the idealist conception hinted at above: social reality does not have the independent mode of existence enjoyed by sticks and stones, but is constituted by the interpretations which social agents put upon their own and their fellows' conduct. Hence, a failure to incorporate the interpretation adopted by the agents would be tantamount to a failure to deal with the social reality constituted by that interpretation. Since social reality is socially constituted, to explore social reality means to explore the constitutive interpretations.[3]

Our task in this chapter is to evaluate Schütz's Postulate of Adequacy (hereafter the Postulate). But before we can take aim at that principle, we must impose a precise interpretation upon it: in the above wording, it is ambiguous on crucial points. The purpose of the disambiguation is not to contribute to Schützian scholarship, but rather to reach a precise and *prima facie* plausible position to serve as a point of departure for the subsequent discussion. First, Schütz's talk of 'constructs', scientific or common-sense, must be taken to refer to items of propositional form and not merely to concepts. Schütz urges that social theory be compatible with the agents' interpretations, not merely that the concepts in which the two are couched be somehow compatible. Secondly, when it is demanded that an action performed in accordance with the scientist's model be 'understandable for the actor himself as well as for his fellow-men in terms of common-sense interpretation of everyday life', we should take this to call for action to be thus understandable under the description which the theory assigns to it, not under some other, weaker description true of it. Unless this interpretation be adopted, the Postulate will be incapable of doing the job it was designed to do. For instance, it will not be able to block typical Freudian interpretations of action, although these certainly sin against the spirit of that principle.[4] Psychoanalysis may explain a housewife's excessive care in checking that the stove has been turned off as a reaction formation against a repressed wish to dispose of her husband by means of gas 'accidentally' leaked from the stove. However, the same action under some weaker description–detailing, for instance, how the woman returns to the kitchen every ten minutes to inspect the stove–would clearly be amenable to common-sense interpretation and explanation, according to which she is just a person who is overly worried about gas leaks.

But what precisely does it mean to say that an action as described by social theory is understandable in terms of the common-sense interpretation? Certainly more than mere logical compatibility is involved here; for a (true) behaviourist description will be logically compatible with a (true) everyday interpretation of the same action. But Schütz repeatedly denounces behaviourism as directly antithetical to his approach.[5] On the other hand, the relationship must be less than logical equivalence or the deducibility of the theoretical account from the everyday one, since the concepts involved in the two interpretations are allowed to differ, thus precluding the mentioned relationships. I believe that what Schütz has in mind is captured in the relationship between an everyday concept and the 'rational reconstruction' thereof, as we know it from philosophical analysis of vague everyday concepts, and in the relationship between an everyday sentence and a counterpart in which such concepts have been replaced by their reconstructed explicata. This interpretation jibes with Schütz's remark that '. . . their strictly logical character is one of the most important features by which scientific thought objects are distinguished from the thought objects constructed by common-sense thinking in daily life which they have to supersede'[6] ('Logical' here must mean something like 'reconstructed in some logically regimented language'.) More importantly, this interpretation secures a perfect correspondence between the Postulate and the master argument with which Schütz supports it. If the appeal to the 'social construction of social reality' is sound, and if the investigation of social reality is thus the investigation of the social agents' own action interpretations, social enquiry must operate within a constraint of precisely this import. To capture the social reality constituted by the agents' interpretations, social science must adopt the very same concepts that are used in those interpretations, apart from some logical streamlining, and must even incorporate everyday lore about social reality, similarly transformed.

There is a further point on which we might wish to tighten, or at least make unambiguous, Schütz's position. Precisely with whose interpretation must a theory of social action be consonant? With that of the individual agent, or the group, or perhaps of society at large? In the statement of the Postulate, Schütz includes the first two. But it would seem to be a fact with which all social theorizing must come to terms that there is sometimes systematic divergency between the individual agent's 'definition of the situation', as it is traditionally called, and that of his interactants. Social science must not cut itself off, methodologically, from recognizing the existence of such discrepancies. In Schütz's methodological writings, a somewhat naive conception of social reality often appears to be communicated: everything is what it claims to be, everything is to be taken at face value. There is no systematic and pervasive deception, no largescale attempt to hide the true nature of some aspect of social interaction. (It is tempting to point out that ethnomethodology, one of the heirs to Schützian sociology, has redressed this flaw, with a vengeance: in ethnomethodological writings, one gets the impression that social action is never what it pretends to be, but always an illusion staged to take in the next man.) I am not suggesting, or course, that Schütz was unaware of this kind of social phenomenon, nor that he would want to back up a methodological principle that would bar its theoretical recognition. Still, as it stands, the Postulate does not allow for it, and we are left without guidance as to how to cope with such cases. The first way which comes to mind if we wish to amend this principle would be to let it call solely for the individual actor's endorsement of the theoretical interpretation of his conduct. Yet this construal will be somewhat at odds with the argument which Schütz suggests in support of his Postulate, since it makes play with the idea of a *social* constitution of reality. I shall evade this difficulty by taking the principle to commit us to the common-sense interpretation only when that interpretation is agreed upon by the agent and society at large. This proviso also guarantees that those common-sense interpretations to which social science is committed will not be rash, spontaneous opinions but considered, reflective views.

It transpires from his general discussion of the Postulate that Schütz wants us to respect agents' everyday interpretations only to the extent that these deal with actions and motivations.[7] But, of course, any everyday proto-theory of social reality will embody elements which are not of this kind. It will, *inter alia*, contain sentences detailing 'what there is' in social reality. A native theory of the social world might, for instance, involve a claim to the effect that certain people are witches: beings with supernatural powers. This is a contention which social theory will want to dispute: clearly the Postulate would be absurd if it did not allow for discrepancies of this kind. Hence we must put a restriction on the scope of the Postulate to the effect that it applies only in as much as the sociological theory and its everyday counterpart are concerned with action and motivation. Yet even this formulation must be tightened, for actions and motives may be referred to by all kinds of locutions, some of them with undesirable implications. Thus, for instance, the everyday interpretation of some action might refer to it as the 'performance of a ritual which is efficient in warding off evil spells'. Again it would not do to insist upon consonance between this proposition and social theory. To avoid this implication, we need to insist that consonance may only be required with propositions in the everyday 'theory' which characterize action in purely intentionalistic terms. This will be a characterization in which all truth claims and all existential commitments of referring expressions in sentences following the intentionalistic operators, 'intends that . . . ', 'believes that . . . ', 'brings it about that . . . ' are suppressed. The statement that an individual is engaged in a ritual antidotal against evil spells, construed according to this recipe, comes out as a claim that the agent believes that there are such things as evil spells; desires to defend himself against them; believes that he can achieve this by performing the ritual; and acts accordingly. In the following I shall refer to such inferentially bowdlerized descriptions as *neutralized descriptions*.

Some of the writers advocating positions akin to Schütz's view assign a wider scope to the Postulate. They insist that social theorizing abide by it even when dealing with the causes of motivation and belief (although they may not realize that this is what their ruling amounts to). There is very little to be said in favour of such a principle, and Schütz had the better sense in granting it only a limited scope. However, we should not bypass the stronger position entirely, and I shall have a few words to say about it after having investigated Schütz's version of the doctrine.[8]

3

In the present section, I shall try to develop the idealist argument suggested by Schütz in favour of the Postulate, and afterwards evaluate its power. But let me begin by indicating two issues which I shall evade in the following investigation.

First, the commitment to incorporate the common-sense interpretation would be vacuous if that interpretation could not always be recaptured. There is considerable literature espousing the position that full understanding is not possible in cases where the target community belongs to a culture radically foreign to the interpreter.[9] This view builds typically upon an unstated premise to the effect that linguistic meaning is holistic in two different ways. First, words and sentences do not possess meaning in isolation, but only as constituents of the language as a whole. Secondly, language is meaningful only as an abstract aspect of the community's life in general; it can only be decoded when viewed against the background of the native world view, since it embodies and crystallizes that view and serves as a repository for explications of native desires and concerns. When these two points are held together, we get the upshot that only he who shares the native world view, the overall native 'theory' of the world's constitution, understands the native language: indeed, understands even a single sentence of that language. Since native interpretations of action are expressed in their own language, it follows that these too are only accessible to those who share that world view. But since *ex hypothesi* the social scientist from a foreign culture embraces a different world view, he is barred from penetrating native self-interpretations and hence from abiding by the Postulate.

There are difficulties in this view, since the holism which keeps the outsider from penetrating the native language would also keep the budding insider from ever learning it; in other words, it will be impossible for children born into the community to learn the language of their parents and to assimilate their culture.[10] Moreover, the contention that in order to grasp the native language one has to share native beliefs, is too strong: an appreciation of the contents of those beliefs is all that can be asked of the interpreter, not that he actually embrace them. However, these brief remarks will have to suffice as an indication of the direction in which the solution to these puzzles may be sought. For reasons of space, I cannot pursue them any further here but shall simply assume, somewhat dogmatically, that the view of alien cultures as monadically impenetrable to each other may be refuted in the way suggested, or in some other fashion.

The second issue has to do with the extent to which an investigation of social action, expecially of a primitive, tribal society, may be forced to dismiss the everyday self-interpretation of the agents, not as shallow or false, but as meaningless or incoherent. In the following, I shall discuss only common-sense interpretations assumed to have already passed the test of meaningfulness. Now this might be thought to be an ill-conceived policy since our weightiest reason for quarrelling with an everyday interpretation is the suspicion that it is somehow incoherent or unintelligible. This happens most frequently to the social anthropologist: it is the occasional weirdness and senselessness of native interpretations that warrant the adoption of an alternative theoretical interpretation. Once the native interpretations are cleared on this charge, there is little ground left for disputing them.

I think this attitude errs in the extent to which the everyday conception is vulnerable to the charge of meaninglessness. That position springs perhaps from the belief that whenever some sentence P can be seen for *a priori* reasons to be incapable of having a truth value, then P cannot occur in an intentionalistic context $I(\ )$. Hence the expression $I(P)$ will fail to single out any intentionalistic state at all.

However, we grow sceptical of this reasoning when we remind ourselves that $I(P)$ might be, 'N.N. has devised an argument showing that P is incoherent', thus bringing it home to us that in calling sentences such as P incoherent or 'meaningless', we do not imply that we meet them with blank incomprehension. We understand them in some sense, and it is precisely this understanding which allows us to decide that they are somehow not up to standard. But then why should we ask for more intelligibility in P in order to allow that P might be used to express a native belief or desire? The critic of the native ways must concede that 'meaningfulness' is a graded property, and he must supply an argument to explain why the particular degree or kind of meaninglessness sometimes suffered by the sentences ostensibly expressing native beliefs is so severe as to disqualify them from having any reporting function.

Now to Schütz's central argument in favour of respecting the agents' own interpretations of action. This, we recall, is the tenet that social reality is 'pre-interpreted' by common-sense proto-theories and beliefs. These provide the structure and form of social reality. Hence social science must somehow capture, and embody, the native interpretation if it wants to come to grips with social reality as structured in this way. This, however, is hardly an argument, but merely a sketch for one. And we lose faith in it right at the outset when we realize that as it stands, it also applies to physical reality. Physical reality is equally 'structured' by the concepts of human beings, who are inhabitants of physical reality just as much as of the social world. True, as Schütz points out,[11] physical reality is not structured by 'meanings' which atoms and molecules ascribe to their motions. But then treatises of physics are written for human beings, not for atoms and molecules. It is to human beings that science exhibits its picture of the world, and to whom it must take pains not to present a 'fictitious' world instead of the real one in which they live. Physical reality is as much part of the *Lebenswelt* of human beings as is social reality, and it was conceptualized by man long before the advent of natural science and the aspiration to investigate nature in systematic ways. Despite this, physics has succeeded marvellously in grasping reality in its own terms, radically divergent from those of common sense. And, to my knowledge, no philosopher of science of any standing has ever been daring enough to insist that physics reflect and embody the concepts and theories of common sense.

Thus, we need a more powerful argument if we want to retain the common-sense interpretation. Such an argument might lie in a stronger construal of the reasoning just examined. The criticism of this reasoning presupposed a moderately realist conception of truth which allows us to distinguish between reality and our conception thereof, even when the latter cannot be improved upon within its particular mode of discourse: the counter-example of physics only worked because we assumed that we may replace the common-sense view of physical reality with some scientific theory and still be talking about the same reality. However, it might be argued, although this conception may be valid for the physical world, it is not tenable in the realm of human action. It is valid in the physical realm because talk about this realm, in the final analysis, is just highly derived talk about observational data expressed in a neutral observational vocabulary which is common to the everyday picture and to theoretical physics. Observational sentences, not being wed to any particular theory, not even the proto-theory of common sense, provide a neutral body of data which may be taken as the common object of all theorizing about the natural world, whether in science or in common sense. Not so in social science: there is no unvarnished description of human action to serve as the common ground, or object, for rival social theories, including the common-sense interpretation. One might assume that a language of 'basic acts' could serve as an intentionalistic observation language. But there may well be disagreement, of a theoretically inspired kind, as to whether a certain bodily movement should count as an action *at all*. Not even the basic action language qualifies as an observation language.

Thus we arrive at the thought that no class of sentences about human action is truly observational, that is, comprises sentences, the truth value of which may be ascertained by mere sensory inspection. All truth about human action is theoretical in the standard, epistemological sense: it can only be established by aligning it with our global interpretation of social reality. Add to this the idealist (anti-realist) position inherent in Schütz's reasoning, and you get a radical coherency interpretation of truth for the intentionalistic language. According to this interpretation, reality is not something independent of language or theory and something to which language or theory corresponds (or fails to correspond). Rather, 'reality' is an 'intrinsic' object of theorizing, and talk about it is just a picturesque and economical way of referring collectively to those sentences which mesh optimally with our best global theory.

In the following, I shall refer to the proponent of this argument as the *phenomenologist*, to avoid any misrepresentation of the historical Schütz. Is the phenomenologist's reasoning helpful? I do not think so. The suggested coherency interpretation of truth falls foul of the learnability constraint upon semantic theories. Conflict with that principle arises because meaning is plausibly taken to be a function of truth conditions (whether or not these be construed as epistemically accessible). In a radical coherency interpretation of truth, no type of sentences are especially sensitive, with regard to their truth value, to the kinds of occasions on which they are uttered, or assented to. In brief, there are no observation sentences. Hence, there is no class of sentences such that their meaning reflects in a simple manner the nature of the settings in which they are observed to be uttered, or assented to. But this means that there is no basis in observational fact for semantic interpretations: there is no way to break into a language if the radical coherency interpretation is valid. Language would be strictly hermetic, and unlearnable.

Notice that the phenomenologist's relativist objectives bar a possible way out of this predicament. The above reasoning might be resisted on the grounds that language will be learnable despite the holistic nature of meaning if human beings are endowed with strong inductive (or 'abductive') procedures which permit them to extrapolate from records of the use of a certain expression in a limited class of settings and linguistic contexts to its use in other kinds of settings, without at any stage linking that expression up with observational meanings. Such an endowment would consist of two components. First, a theory about the way the linguistic community interprets reality, i.e. about the nature of the beliefs they form about it. Secondly, a theory about the ways in which their linguistic output links up with these beliefs. In the interpretation of intentionalistic vocabulary, the first component amounts to a theory about the way the linguistic community interprets action. This theory must be a very strong one, since it must make up for the lack of observational access to those interpretations. Now the interpretive canons this theory ascribes to the linguistic community must be identical to the ones employed in that theory itself: we can hardly make sense of a theory of interpretation involving the *a priori* assumption that the people examined use a different theory (which is not to deny that this may be the *upshot* of the examination); at least such an assumption would run counter to the celebrated Principle of Charity. This means that we must ascribe to the person trying to learn the intentionalistic language a very strong schematism for action interpretation. But the assumption of some such schematism is incompatible with the idea that different societies endorse radically different interpretations. The very strong *a priori* constraints on interpretation necessitated by the coherency assumption leave very little slack for such divergencies.

In any case, the semantics of the intentionalistic language is not insulated in the way the phenomenologist would have us believe. Purely behavioural data offer an entering wedge into it. It is not a valid objection to this claim to point out that there is no logical connection between behavioural and intentionalistic descriptions of action: because then no theoretical description follows logically from its basis in observational fact. Behavioural data provide a common ground for rival intentionalistic descriptions and thus give the lie to the idea that competing interpretations of action are semantically and epistemically insulated.

But perhaps the idealist argument can be upheld even without the assumption of the full insulation of social realities. The phenomenologist's original thought was that the separation of social worlds springs from the absence of a shared data base for divergent interpretations; this was the feature cited as distinguishing the status of rival interpretations of social reality from that of rival interpretations of physical reality. However, even if we grant the existence of a shared observational base, the fact remains, of course, that there is a gulf between that base and the interpretations erected upon it. The data do not by themselves determine an interpretation, but leave a gap to be bridged by inferential processes of various kinds. To say this is just to repeat the fact that the intentionalistic description is theoretical *vis-à-vis* the behavioural one. This observation might be thought to provide an opening for the relativist argument: different societies use different canons of theoretical inference to get from the behavioural data to action interpretations, canons which respectively generate a separate social reality for which alternative canons are simply irrelevant. The reason why physics can be allowed to deal with the same reality as common sense is that the canons of theoretical inference in physics can be viewed as refinements of those employed in common sense. This is not the case for action interpretations, or at least for those action interpretations which the phenomenologist wants to block. For these are of a kind which impugn the very canons of interpretation involved in the agent's own understanding of his action.

A critic might object that we can still give meaning to the notion of divergent interpretations of one and the same social reality if we construe the real object of such interpretations as that picture which would emerge from the application of the universally and uniquely *true* principles of interpretation. The phenomenologist's rejoinder will be to dispute the idea of a notion of truth for such principles which goes beyond what may be established by the community in which they are used. He would offer some such argument as this: on anti-realist principles, standards of reasoning, too, must be cognitively accessible, that is, it must be possible for users to establish their truth. Now assume that in some social group A there is firm consensus that some principle of inference I is valid; that is, a consensus that cannot be swayed by arguments trying to discredit I. What would justify a member of another community B, in which there is consensus to the effect that I is invalid, in maintaining that I is not valid even in A? What would justify him in giving priority to the consensus in B over that in A, if both of them are indeed firmly established? According to anti-realist principles, this would presuppose an argument to support the privileged position of B. But typically, such an argument will not be available; and if it is, it is *ex hypothesi* one which will fail to impress the community A. So we are back where we started. The only way to render such incurable disagreement consistent with an anti-realist position is to allow that the divergent interpretations are dealing with different realities. The monistic notion of reality must be given up in the social sphere.

Thus, the picture which the phenomenologist invites us to accept is as follows: reality is the sum total of the facts that are cognitively accessible to man. Accessibility is of two kinds, direct observational accessibility, and accessibility via various received principles of 'data processing': of theoretical inference from observational fact. 'Reality' is the correlate of that overall theory which ensues when we apply our canons of inference to the totality of available data. Now add to this standard anti-realist picture the observation that different cultures subscribe to divergent canons of inference in the interpretation of social reality, and the fact that this is a disagreement that cannot be resolved: the modes of thought of one culture are characteristically resistant to argument in favour of those of another. The arguments *pro et con* simply bypass each other. Since, according to anti-realist principles, we cannot ascribe exclusive validity to one of the rival canons of reasoning failing a meta-argument in its favour, we have to grant them equal validity and to allow that they are dealing with different realities. To gain access to each separate social world, the social scientist must therefore grasp and adopt those reality-constituting interpretive canons from which it springs, and he must endorse the native interpretations which issue from those canons.

The above is a reconstruction of an argument in favour of cultural relativism present in nascent form in Schütz, Winch, and many other methodologists. There are numerous dubious moves in this reasoning, and for many it would be disqualified merely by its anti-realist stance. However, this is not the place to join in the battle over realism versus anti-realism, nor do I believe it is fruitful to pick away at the minor soft spots in the argument. Instead, I shall try to present a constructive argument showing that the thesis of a social constitution of reality cannot be upheld.

As a preparatory move, we must separate two versions of the relativist position. In the first version, action interpretations are what Crispin Wright has dubbed *investigation-independent*.[12] To say that an interpretation is investigation-independent is to say that there is a fact of the matter as to whether that interpretation is true or false, prior to, and independently of, the actual undertaking of an interpretive act. Since investigation-independence is a matter of the character of the principles used in interpretation, it must reflect a property of those principles; I name that property the *application-independence* of the principles, and mean thereby the characteristic that the principles are fully determinate prior to their actual application; that is, for any body of behavioural data (as set against a background of further such data), the principles will fix the interpretation to be placed upon such data prior to and independently of their actual application to the data. Application-independent principles and rules determine their own application and do not require any (non-rule-governed) 'discretion' on the part of the user.

The other version denies the application-independence of interpretive principles. That is, it refuses to countenance the idea that there is such a thing as the content of a principle being fixed in advance of its actual employment. Only the actual, communal use of the principle determines what that principle really comes to on that occasion. Only the actual use of the rule bridges the gap between its abstract formulation (or the record of its previous applications) and any new situation of application.

I now want to demonstrate that the anti-realist argument for relativism faces serious difficulties in both interpretations. Let me start with the interpretation which embraces application-dependence. This is the one most germane to the spirit of Schütz's position, since it is the only version that gives full meaning to the idea that reality is *socially* constituted. In the application-independent view, the process of interpretation—which has a fixed outcome independently of its actual execution—might presumably be undertaken by a single individual: reference to communal use or consensus plays no essential part in fixing the contents of the interpretive canon. It merely serves to single out the particular canon which must be adhered to. On the basis of application-dependence, however, communal agreement plays an integral role as the final tribunal to which divergent interpretations may be appealed. Such divergencies cannot be resolved by reference to the canon itself, since the disagreement may be presumed precisely to reflect its application-dependence. Communal discussion and resulting agreement become the final arbiter of truth.

The unfortunate thing about this view is that it will assign an indeterminate truth value to almost all action descriptions; that is, it will make almost all action descriptions come out neither determinately true nor determinately false. Thus, we pay for the pleasing proliferation of social worlds with a shrinking of those worlds: if a social world is defined by the class of sentences which are determinately true or determinately false in it, then the social worlds which emerge in this picture are so impoverished as to almost vanish. To see why this is so, we must first appreciate the fact that most action descriptions, of course, are never put on the ballot of a general referendum: their truth value will never be the object of an actual community-wide consensus. This observation might not concern the adherent of this view in the first instance, since he may have recourse to the notion of a *counterfactual* consensus: such consensus as would have ensued if the matter had been made the topic of a community-wide discussion.[13] Unfortunately, the application-dependence of interpretive principles prohibits this move. According to this conception, there is no fact of the matter as to whether a counterfactual consensus would be forthcoming and what its content would be. It follows from the very definition of the notion of application-dependence that such consensus could not be fixed beforehand by the rule itself, for the rule itself has no determinate implications prior to its application. Nor could the outcome of the hypothetical discussion be fixed purely causally. It seems to me to be true, and would certainly be accepted by the relativist due to his anti-realist leanings, that a counterfactual conditional cannot be barely true, in Dummett's sense. There must be something actually existing in the world which makes it true. And perhaps the relativist would suggest that what makes counterfactual statements about human consensus true is the present state of the world plus our nomological knowledge about it. That knowledge—namely, information about how people generally act and judge—allows us to anticipate what would be the outcome of a hypothetical community-wide discussion in which the nature of this or that action was up for assessment.

But this suggestion cannot be upheld in the face of the assumed investigation-dependence. If information of the kind cited suffices to fix the nature of counterfactually hypothesized human actions such as the 'communal agreement that Mr N. N.'s conduct is to be described as a fit of anger', then there is at least one intentional state, or set of such states, which is fixed independently of any agreement about it, namely that very state of agreement. And then why not others? Why not the very state of Mr N. N.'s anger, since presumably we may have equally good grounds for predicting that state on the basis of our general knowledge of human reactions? The only way in which the consensus-theory which embraces investigation-dependence can allow that a counterfactual consensus is fixed is by another counterfactual consensus that the first one counts as a consensus. But this, of course, is the first step of an infinite regress.

Let us turn to the second version of the argument, the one based upon a more traditional anti-realist position which concedes the application-independence of interpretive canons. It grants that an intentionalistic action description does not await an actual community-wide consensus to become true or false, but already possesses a fixed truth value by agreeing or disagreeing with the available behavioural data, viewed in the light of the interpretive canons subscribed to in the community; these canons are assumed to have a definite content prior to their actual application. In this view, reference to the community plays a more indirect role, serving only to single out the relevant canon of interpretation without being necessary for defining its contents. (Notice that the proposed doctrine is still an anti-realist one: the truth conditions of interpretive sentences are still taken to be necessarily accessible to human cognition. The truth or falsity of interpretive sentences are assumed to be fixed independently of actual interpretive efforts, not of the possibility of such efforts.)

The snag in this suggestion is how there could be a fact of the matter as to which canons of interpretation are being used by some community independently of the availability of a canonical interpretation of conduct in that community, and that means: independently of a ruling upon which principles of interpretation should be employed in making sense of that conduct.

To bring out the difficulty, let me treat it first as an impasse at the level of epistemology and then show how the epistemological problem is a reflection of a deeper logical one. The epistemological problem is this: how do we get at the principles of interpretation used by the natives upon their own conduct? The answer which is provided by the relativist view is, locate native acts of describing native conduct, interpret them, and see what canons of interpretation they embody. But how do we decide on which canons of interpretation to invoke in decoding native acts of action interpretation? The answer will be, again, locate native acts of action interpretation, interpret them to see what principles of interpretation they involve, and apply them to native acts of action interpretation. We have been caught in an infinite regress.

It might occur to us that the task we are facing is really that of solving an equation with two unknown quantities and that we have run aground only because we are going about it in the wrong fashion, tacking back and forth between the two unknowns. The way to do it is to pool the information and to solve for both of them simultaneously. When set out in this format, our assignment goes as follows:

Locate an interpretation manual X for the community C (which is given) which

(1) assigns an interpretation to any item in the class of native actions A (which is also presumed to be given);
and which

(2) singles out a subclass Y of A, the members of which, when interpreted in the light of X, come out as native acts of interpretation using X for their interpretation manual.

Or, put more simply: find an interpretation manual such that it turns out that the people interpreted use that very same manual.

But this solution to the epistemological problem forces the logical problem to the surface. The information about the two unknowns is exceedingly weak and will certainly allow an infinite or indefinite number of solutions; that is, the constraints upon the interpretive canon sought are utterly lax and will conform with an indefinite number of different manuals. Indeed, presumably *any* manual of interpretation can be made consistent with this condition if we expend sufficient ingenuity on cooking up outlandish beliefs and inference patterns to impute to the natives (remember that no further restrictions are being placed on these parameters).[14] According to the anti-realist premises embraced by the relativist, this upshot does not indicate that we can never know which manual is actually used by the natives, and also to be used by the social scientist: it means that there is no fact of the matter as to which one is used and ought to be used. This result leads to a commensurate indeterminacy in the interpretation of other native actions, an indeterminacy of quite a different order of magnitude than that envisaged by Quine. Where Quine warns us that there may be no truth of the matter as to whether the natives talk about rabbits or rabbit time-slices, in the present view there will be no truth of the matter as to whether they talk about rabbits, the weather, about

Avogadro's number, or about the outlook for the world Communist movement. With this much indeterminacy, the intentionalistic framework of description simply collapses. There is really no recognizable aspect of the world to be reported in that language. The relativist view does away with intentionalistic interpretation altogether.

The basic flaw underlying both versions of the relativist argument is that the stratum of facts to which social reality is traced back belongs itself to the social sphere. Compare the case of anti-realism in mathematics (intuitionism). Here the truth value of mathematical statements is grounded in the truth of sentences referring to items of another kind, namely, *proofs*, considered as actually existing mental or physical structures. But in the above view, the truth of sentences about social reality is made to depend on the incidence of human consensus, which is a social phenomenon to boot. Hence the circularity and the threat that social reality will become entirely evanescent.[15]

4

The idealist argument in favour of the Postulate will not do. But this does not mean that this principle cannot be salvaged in the light of other considerations. In the following, an alternative reasoning in support of the Postulate will be essayed. That reasoning takes its inspiration from the observation that the Postulate implies a crucial difference between natural and social science. It is obvious that we are not committed to anything resembling it in natural science. Hence it might be fruitful to examine the ways in which physical accounts replace and supersede everyday accounts of natural phenomena. This investigation might bring to light presuppositions which are not satisfied in social science.

Let us first have a look, in the abstract, at the scope left for the theoretical redescription of a physical phenomenon for which an everyday description is available. Two different cases may be distinguished. First, the everyday description may leave room for a theoretical description by being *false*, thus calling for another description to put things right. This case is uninteresting since it does not throw light upon the specific relationship between theoretical and everyday descriptions: replacement of an invalid description by a true one does not require the latter to be theoretical. The second, more interesting case is that in which a true everyday description leaves room for a theoretical description which provides a deeper insight than the everyday one, without showing the latter to be invalid. Such compatibility is typically the case for theoretical redescriptions in physics. Physics does not teach us that the common-sense conception of natural events is wrong, on the whole. Let us illustrate the point with the example of *heat*. Physical investigation into heat does not impugn the everyday conviction that there is such a thing as heat, nor show the invalidity of everyday accounts of certain natural events as the effects of heat. The physical concept of heat is not different from the everyday one; 'heat' means the same in the physicist's mouth as in the layman's. This is so because the term 'heat' is not defined by the test which we use in an everyday context to single out heat (namely, the power to generate certain sensations). Rather, this test serves to fix the reference of the term, 'heat'. It fixes the reference as being that something-or-other in objects which causes them to generate certain characteristic sensations. What physics does is to tell us what this something-or-other is, namely, molecular motion. This description expresses the essence of heat in the sense that any physically different phenomenon in a possible world different from our actual one will not count as heat, even though it should happen to produce the very same sensation in human beings.[16]

The nature of the relationship between the everyday and the theoretical description is most clearly exhibited when these descriptions figure in explanations of the same phenomenon. For the context of explanation greatly narrows the margin of compatibility. We observe that the everyday account–the account featuring the everyday designation–is not falsified by the theoretical one, because they both single out the same parameters as causally relevant. True, they do so in different ways: by means of non-synonymous linguistic devices; and one might think that the opacity of explanation-contexts would bar substitution of the theoretical expression for its everyday counterpart and thus render the two accounts incompatible. But we are saved by the consideration that the everyday account does not single out the causative state under any description at all, strictly speaking. The everyday designation may be backed up by descriptions, but it is not synonymous with these descriptions, which merely serve to pin down its reference. Hence substitution works because we are not dealing with two non-synonymous expressions which will be incompatible in the opaque context of explanation, but with a description and a non-description. There is no incompatibility between the everyday account which says, for example, that the heat from the sunshine caused the snowman to melt, and the physical one to the effect that the electromagnetic radiation emitted from the sun sped up the motions of the H_2O molecules in the crystalline structures composing the snowman, thus breaking them up and causing them to assume liquid form. The everyday, non-connotative ways of referring to the physical parameters involved ('heat from the sunshine', 'melting (of the snowman)', etc.) are replaced by their theoretical equivalents ('electromagnetic radiation emitted by the sun', 'breaking up of crystalline structures of H_2O molecules', etc.).

The above narrative involves considerable idealization. The possibility of smooth theoretical replacement in the above fashion presupposes that the everyday account is maximally specified: that it selects the very aspect of the cause-phenomenon by virtue of which it possesses causal power. If it fails to do so, the intensionality of causal accounts will block substitution. But in day-to-day affairs, we rarely bother to put accounts in this strict form. We will be happy to say, for instance, that the window broke because it was hit by a cricket ball. Here the cause event is overspecified: it was not *qua* cricket ball that the object caused the window to break, but *qua* a hard and heavy object. However, the resources of everyday knowledge are normally rich enough to effect the required specification. It is part of common-sense knowledge that cricket balls break windows *qua* being hard and heavy. Laziness aside, common sense is capable of providing maximally specified accounts.

Let us look at the prospects for a similar theory-loading of everyday intentionalistic descriptions of action. That is, let us look at the possibility of replacing everyday references to intentions, goals, desires and beliefs with theoretical counterparts. In the first place, we observe that we cannot effect such improvement by replacing intentionalistic descriptions with micro-reductive descriptions of the physiological realizations of motivational states. The point I am making here is not primarily that such substitution is not formally permitted, given the dubious status of the psychophysical identity theory. It is rather that our major concern is with finding redescriptions that will result in enriched *interpretive* explanations. The accounts resulting from substitution of the kind mentioned would no longer be interpretive accounts. They would no longer allow us to see action as a rational move towards a goal, as being required by some rule, or as embodying linguistic meaning. They would have been transformed into purely causal accounts.

This result is quite trivial, and simply reminds us that interpretive accounts are not causal accounts. Substitution of the kind mentioned is licensed, and indeed recommended, in causal accounts, because knowledge of the fine-structure of physical magnitudes provides increased insight into the causal processes involved in physical events. On the other hand, facts about physiological fine-structure are irrelevant to interpretive accounts. The counterpart, for interpretive accounts, to the theory-loading of everyday accounts of natural phenomena would clearly be a substitution of the everyday intentionalistic terms with other intentionalistic terms which better capture the 'real nature' of the motivational states involved.

We might indeed be led to believe that such redescription is actually possible. We engage in this kind of redescription when we declare that the smoker's desire for cigarettes is *really* a desire for the blissful state of security he enjoyed when sucking at mother's breast; that the little boy's phobic fear of horses is *really* the fear of castration which has been transferred from its original object–the revengeful father–to another object which is easier for the child to avoid; or that the girl's desire to please her sister is *really* a strong animosity which has been transformed, through reaction formation, into the opposite attitude. These descriptions reveal the real nature of these motivational states, the one behind their superficial manifestations which alone are accessible to everyday understanding. They are genuinely theoretical descriptions since they allow deeper explanations of the agents' conduct than their everyday counterparts.

However, this construal will not withstand closer scrutiny. The identity of intentionalistic states is a function of the identities of the propositions which are their contents. If p and q are different propositions, then so are the intentionalistic states I_p and I_q which have them as their objects. Hence, since the intentional contents of the theoretical descriptions are not identical with the ones they are meant to replace, they do not offer a deeper characterization, in intentionalistic terms, of the same motivational state. Rather, they introduce a different state. This means that when such descriptions occur in the context of interpretive explanations, the result of plugging in the alleged theoretical description will be incompatible with the everyday account, on two assumptions. First, that the everyday account is intended to be maximally specified, indicating the very aspect of the goal state under which it is desired. Again, we do not normally bother, in everyday contexts, to provide maximally specified accounts. I may inform you that I went to the library to get a book without letting on whether I want it *qua* reading material or *qua* something suitable for stabilizing my wobbly desk. But we believe ourselves capable of producing maximal specifications should we be required to do so. (We must of course take the Postulate to call for adherence only to accounts intended to be maximally specified.) Secondly, the assumption that the everyday account is meant to provide the *full* explanation of the action. If not, compatibility of a trivial sort can be established by taking the theoretical description to refer to a further motivational factor bypassed in the everyday account. If the everyday accounts of the smoker's hankering for cigarettes, the boy's avoidance of horses and the girl's ministrations to her sister satisfy these conditions, they will be inconsistent with the explanations that emerge when we plug the alleged theoretical redescriptions into the places occupied by their everyday counterparts.

But is not the above reasoning a neat specimen of the deplorable philosophical tendency to legislate *a priori* about empirical matters? Certainly the findings of Freud and other great observers of human conduct cannot be spirited away by purely philosophical sleight of hand? To dispel this suspicion of foul play, two remarks should be made. In the first place, what I have argued above is merely that the alleged theoretical redescriptions are incompatible with their everyday counterparts *if* they are taken to characterize the very same mental state or are thought to offer a deeper interpretive explanation of the same facts accounted for by the everyday account. But although this is the way they are often construed by psychologists given to the formula, '*x* (altruism, love, etc.) is really nothing but *y* (disguised self-love, fear of being alone, death wishes, or what not)', this is not the way we have to take them and not the way in which they are understood by more circumspect psychologists. The actual relationships between the facts expressed in the everyday vocabulary and in the theoretical one are multifarious and not to be captured in a single formula; but frequently they make up a causal–genetical sequence. The boy's fear of horses is the causal outcome of his Oedipal jealousy towards his father, an emotion which triggers a complicated mechanism of reaction formation, displacement and other defensive mechanisms on the part of the ego (if Freud is to be trusted), to issue eventually in equinophobia. This emotion is not identical to the one that set off the whole psychological process, nor to any of those that emerged as intermediate products. This is so even if some sense could be given to the (Freudian) idea that it is somehow the same libido-energy which, in turn, animates all these desires or fears, although with changing sign and direction. For the identity of a desire is determined by its direction, that is, its intentional object. But if this is the nature of the theoretically postulated states, they are not to figure in rival interpretive accounts, but rather in causal accounts which explain the emergence of those motivational states that are referred to in everyday accounts. The theoretical account and the everyday one are of different kinds and addressed to different questions. There is no rivalry between them.

The second reason why the above reflections do not fly in the face of established scientific fact is that what is being claimed is merely that if we construe the theoretical descriptions as intended replacements for everyday ones as figuring in interpretive accounts, then those descriptions are *incompatible* with their everyday counterparts, used in the same way. It does not follow that this discrepancy renders the theoretical description false, nor have I pretended that it does: for the rivalry may well be taken as proof that the everyday description should be abandoned. Rejection of the theoretical description follows only if the everyday one is assumed to be true. To what extent this is the case will be discussed in a moment.

The upshot of the above reasoning is as follows: of the two avenues for theoretical strengthening of common-sense knowledge cited in p. 167, one seems to be greatly restricted in social science. This is the one which replaces everyday accounts of action with theoretical conceptions which are still compatible with their everyday counterparts. The margin of compatibility is very narrow in the sciences of human action: only expressions roughly equivalent semantically with the everyday ones may be substituted for the latter in accounts of action, *salva veritate*. This is a step towards vindicating the Postulate, since this principle calls for precisely such an affinity between everyday and theoretical accounts. However, the Postulate needs a second leg to stand on: if the everyday interpretation of action could be shown to be largely wrong, or incomplete, there would still be room for non-equivalent theoretical redescription to improve upon that invalid and partial picture. Thus the injunction against redescription requires the further premise that the everyday story is true, and complete. We shall assess that premise shortly, restricting ourselves, however, to the assumption of truth. For the import of the Postulate is to secure the compatibility of the theoretical and the everyday accounts, as far as the latter go, but not to assert that the latter are necessarily complete. Hence we need not try to support the premise of completeness in order to validate the Postulate.

Before we examine the truth assumption, however, we should have a brief look at a suggestion for a less trivial mode of term substitution in interpretive accounts. We noted earlier that substitution of theoretical terms is a fact of life in the description of natural processes. Perhaps this fact can provide an opening for substitution in intentionalistic descriptions. Can we not replace everyday natural kind terms occurring in propositions governed by intentionalistic notions with theoretical terms expressing their essential natures in micro-reductive terms? Thus, can we not say that a person who desires a swig of water desires a swig of H_2O? To make this suggestion, one need not be oblivious of the fact that on a strongly intensional reading of the desire-operator, this substitution is not valid. One might only dispute that this is the reading we want when we explain human action. The strongly intensional notion of desire (and belief, etc.), it would be said, is a specialized semantic device which allows us to describe human conduct and its sources in a manner accommodating human ignorance and obtuseness. It allows us to state that someone desires a glass of water without implying that he displays any interest in a bottle labelled H_2O, since he may not know that water is H_2O. But if we are looking for a theoretical insight into the sources of human action, we are better served by a language which permits substitution of the kind mentioned, it might be maintained. Suppose we examine the organism of a person who desires water: who declares that he wants some water and manifests appropriate water-seeking behaviour. That examination might well be capable of demonstrating how those behavioural manifestations were set off by a state of dehydration of the subject's organism, and of showing, in precise chemical terms, how consumption of a quantum of H_2O would set the situation right again. Would it not here be utterly pedantic to insist that the subject does not desire H_2O just because, due to his ignorance of chemistry, he does not ask for H_2O and displays no interest in liquids so marked? The opacity that blocks substitution reflects a purely cognitive circumstance, namely that people do not know every description under which a desired object may be subsumed; but this opacity should be overridden when we specify objects of *desire* rather than *belief*.

This argument shows, I would concede, the propriety of disregarding the extreme intensional interpretation of 'desire' in certain contexts of investigation (the resulting notion is still intensional, of course: 'water' could be replaced by 'H_2O' but not, say, by 'the liquid ubiquitous on the earth's surface'). But I doubt whether interpretive social science represents such a context. The little story we had to present in order to make substitution seem permissible does not suggest a social science investigation but rather one germane to the categories of biology or physiologically-orientated psychology. Within these frameworks, we may aspire to explanations of human action using homeostatic models referring to physiological states; and it is legitimate to characterize the objects desired in a vocabulary which ties in with such reference. But this is a different ambition than that which inspires interpretive social science. This is so even for socially conditioned action directed towards objects with essential redescriptions. Suppose that, influenced by social custom, Norma wants her engagement ring to be made of gold. We cannot here replace this term by the physicist's theoretical description of gold as a substance with the specific atomic structure S. This is brought out by contrasting Norma's case with that of a physicist who is also interested in gold; however, his interest is precisely in gold *qua* the element with the atomic composition S which he finds especially fascinating. This case generates a strong reading of the phrase 'being interested in the substance with the atomic structure S' in which it is wrong to say that Norma has this interest and hence wrong to substitute a description of S for the word 'gold' in the specification of her conative condition. Note that the opacity involved here has nothing to do with a cognitive shortcoming in Norma: it would hold even if she knew that gold has the atomic composition in question. The conclusion that physical redescription is typically inimical to the understanding we seek in interpretive social science is strengthened by the observation that many of the most important motivations with which social science deals–moral sentiments, religious zeal, political ideals, etc.–are not directed at objects with an essential physicalist redescription. In brief, the proposed technique for replacing everyday motivational descriptions with theoretical counterparts represents a step away from interpretive explanation and towards homeostatic and other physiological accounts which have no standing in interpretive social science.

Thus we have strengthened our previous conclusion that in the sciences of human action, only trivial replacement of everyday descriptive terms is possible, *salva veritate*, in the context of interpretive accounts. However, as noted above, this observation only imposes restrictions upon our specific practice if we admit that everyday accounts do actually contain truth to be preserved. To vindicate the Postulate, we need an additional premise to the effect that everyday accounts are *true*.

And apparently that premise is indeed available. Remember that by our definition, the everyday interpretation is one which is endorsed, *inter alia*, by the agent himself. Now as a matter of fact, in everyday situations, we do grant special weight to the agent's sincere avowals of motivation. In everyday affairs, the agent's sincere say-so settles the matter as to the nature of the action performed and the motives at play. This authority presumably has something to do with the direct, non-inferential character of first-person knowledge of motives. The agent does not have to observe his own behaviour and to make perilous inferences from his recordings to know what he is up to. Hence that knowledge is not susceptible of the weaknesses which afflict our knowledge of the physical world and of other people's conduct, such as lack of observational data, poor conditions of observation, faulty inferences, etc. True, we have learned from psychoanalysis that there are limits to this authority. It may be overridden by a sufficient amount of other, notably behavioural, evidence. But the existence of such exceptions would seem of little moment to social science. The type of behaviour examined by Freud falls outside the scope of this discipline. Social science, as I understand this term (cf. the discussion in the Introduction), deals with behaviour which is socially conditioned or with behaviour *qua* socially conditioned. The behaviour investigated by psychoanalysis and kindred disciplines spring from innate developmental processes which run their course independently of social conditioning; they are not social phenomena at root. Consequently, there is a quite specific explanation of the agent's misconstrual of his own action in typical Freudian cases: special mechanisms of repression are at work to blind the agent to the truth about his own motivation. There is little likelihood that similar mechanisms could be at work in socially conditioned action; or so it might be argued.

Thus, we now have the premises needed to make what I consider the best case for the Postulate. First, we have the result that social science does not have the option of improving everyday accounts while still respecting their truth by substituting non-synonymous 'essential redescriptions' of the motivational states. No intentionalistic description d_n may express the 'essence' of the intentionalistic state correctly described by the non-synonymous expression d_m

(provided both are fully specified). Secondly, we have the strong presumption in favour of the truth of agents' self-interpretations. Combining these two premises, we conclude that only a very narrow range of redescriptions of action and motivation, all of them roughly equivalent to the one provided by the agents themselves, are permissible in social science. And this is indeed the force of the Postulate.

5

Should we accept Schütz's Postulate, on the strength of the above reasoning? In my opinion, the answer can only be that although this principle involves some sound points, it suffers pervasive exceptions. This is so because the second premise in the above argument on its behalf has only limited validity. There are, as a matter of fact, situations in which the scientific observer will be warranted in overriding the agents' interpretations of their action. I shall adduce a couple of examples to establish the point. But first an observation of a more general kind.

We saw in chapter 1 that agents may often be innocent of explicit knowledge of the rules which govern their conduct. Such knowledge is not introspectively given, the way that knowledge about the goal of purposive action is. Rather, at least for sophisticated rule-guided conduct, such knowledge derives from observation of behaviour and the formulation of a suitable explanatory hypothesis. Now presumably some such hypothesis adopted by the agents themselves might be simply false. Thus, if taken to apply to human action across the board, the Postulate must be deemed untenable. But perhaps a wiser policy would be to restrict it to purposive action.

However, here are a couple of examples to suggest that the Postulate is invalid even if it is thus restricted. In certain parts of the world, the notion of demoniacal possession is still legal tender in the explanation of behaviour. Not only are people accused of being possessed by evil spirits, or of being witches, to account for their actual or imagined wrongdoings; more surprisingly, this charge is sometimes even accepted by the accused. Now whatever our favourite theory of this phenomenon may be, there is no question, of course, of the social scientist endorsing the afflicted person's claim that he or she is acting under the control of some supernatural being. The social theorist's attitude will not just reflect his doubts as to the existence of evil spirits: it is of a different kind than his disagreement with the native who engages, for example, in ritual ceremony to protect his household from black magic. This disagreement will be over the very existence of black magic and will not be relevant to the explanation of the native's conduct, since it does not impugn the native's neutralized description of his own action. The scientist's quarrel with the possessed person, on the other hand, is precisely over the correct neutralized description of the latter's motivation. During the moments that he is in control, the victim will claim that he was forced to act against his own will or to follow some compact with the evil spirit; or he may deny outright that he was really acting at all: something else was acting with his body as its instrument. The social scientist will think differently. He will see the possessed person as enacting a social role, or as fulfilling the desires of a split-off part of his personality.

Research into witchcraft and demoniacal possession in social anthropology and sociology has focused primarily upon the social factors behind the institution of witchcraft accusation, neglecting the perhaps even more fascinating mechanisms which lead to self-confessions of witchhood. Thus we have no canonical theory of witchcraft confession to appeal to in support of the above contention (which is not to imply that there exists a consensus on the explanation of witchcraft accusations, for that matter.)[17] However, we cannot go too far astray if we assume that in many cases, the explanation, at least a partial one, will depict the victim as acting out repressed urges, of a kind subject to strong social disapproval, in a way which, while not endorsed by society, still serves to deflect the reprobation away from the agent himself. This explanation will probably have to deal in pyschological mechanisms of a trans-cultural kind. But it will refer essentially to social determinants as well, and thus be a *bona fide* element of social theorizing. The very notions of demons and witches are characteristic of human thinking at a particular stage of socio-cultural development; they offer a ready-made, socially engendered framework within which a disturbed person may express his neurotic urges. Demoniacal possession and witchcraft are evidently phenomena that call for social categories for their full explanation. They constitute genuine examples of fallacious self-interpretation within the territory of social science, and bring home to us the futility of trying to uphold agents' self-descriptions in social science once they are admitted to be overridable in psychology. For, of course, these two disciplines are no more insulated than the realms of action with which they deal. It could hardly fail to be the case that the materials out of which pathological human conduct is built are gathered from among the conceptions and ideas current in the victim's culture.

There are other and less dramatic, but then more common examples of self-interpretations which the social scientist will want to override. Goffman and his colloborators have taught us that much social interaction possesses an aspect of which the conventional, socially endorsed interpretation is naive.[18] Besides the official aim of such interactions, there is often a subsidiary one, manifested in the specific way in which the interaction is 'managed' (to use the favourite jargon). By and large, this aim is to get across a certain image of the agent: social agents communicate a certain picture–sometimes true, but often false, and usually somewhat inflated–of their social status, abilities, wealth, etc. by the way they comport themselves in social encounters.

It is clear that these aspects of social conduct are denied by the official interpretation. For instance, the goings-on during a surgical operation, under its canonical interpretation, are aimed solely at the care of the patient. The official version does not allow elements of the procedure–such as the way the surgical instruments are handed to the surgeon by the nurse; the way members of the surgical team address each other; the way they are supposed to dress, etc.–to be meant to symbolize and manifest differences in status between doctors and nurses, between different kinds of nurses, between doctors and interns, etc.

One might object that although these aspects are not admitted by the canonical interpretation, they may well be fully recognized in the individual agent's interpretation of his own conduct. Those persons to whom a lowly status is assigned in such social games may be particularly, and painfully, aware of what goes on. Hence the Postulate does not apply to this case, and is thus not wrecked upon it, since we agreed to take this principle to call for loyalty to the socially sanctioned interpretation only when it conforms to the individual agent's self-understanding.

However, while the Goffmanian account may capture the self-conception of a few cynics, it is hardly in accord with the naive interpretation of the majority of social agents. Most social agents will offer, in full sincerity, interpretations of such social encounters, including their own roles therein, which take them entirely at face value, wholly dedicated to their ostensible and official purpose. They thus fall within the scope of the Postulate, adherence to which will hence commit us to a shallow and naive account of what goes on. The conclusion can only be to abandon the principle in the light of such cases. Alternative stories like the ones told by Goffman are sometimes sufficiently persuasive to make us realize that we cannot stick to the naive interpretation.

The reader may wonder why I bother with the rather recondite example of demoniacal possession and the somewhat trivial facts detailed by Goffman and consorts, instead of adducing the Marxist doctrine of *ideology* which is a scientific theory of mistaken self-interpretation of a socially conditioned kind. An ideology is a set of beliefs or values shared by a social group and of a nature suitable for protecting and legitimizing the interests of that group. As this doctrine has it, we will often be in a position to point out, for instance, that a minister preaching quiescence to his parishioners in the face of oppressive conditions, holding out the prospect of an afterlife in which those inequalities will be rectified, is really acting in order to stifle social discontent and thus to protect the interests of the governing social class to which he himself belongs. We may impute this motive to him even against his sincere protests that he has only the spiritual salvation of his flock in mind.

However, I doubt that the doctrine of ideology will bear a reading strong enough to license the general reinterpretation of motivation along these lines. It may well be true that certain social mechanisms tend to generate intellectual doctrines favourable to the social *status quo*, and hence favourable to the interests of the social group in power. It may also be true that individuals are more prone to embracing doctrines which defend their group interests. It cannot be inferred, however, that actions springing from such beliefs are performed with the aim of protecting these underlying interests. For this inference to be valid, we would have to construe the agent's acceptance of the ideological belief either as sham, or as sincere, but still of the nature of an *act* rather than something that happens to him, the way that we normally simply find ourselves subscribing to a certain belief. Moreover, we would have to construe this action as performed in bad faith, against the better judgement of the agent. Now there are cases which will sustain some such interpretation. A person who believes that he is in the best of shape in the face of clear indications that he is mortally ill may well be said to adopt this soothing belief, as an *action* on his part. He deliberately turns a blind eye on the unwelcome evidence, allowing only favourable information to have an impact. But this is not normally the situation where ideological beliefs are concerned, nor was it claimed to be so in Marx's original doctrine. These beliefs are not adopted or defended by an individual in the face of evidence which is overwhelmingly negative, even by his own standards, when properly considered. Rather they are typically instilled in him during the process of socialization, conditioning the way he thinks so thoroughly that conflicting evidence simply cannot be seen for what it is. If this is so, the adoption of an ideological belief cannot be construed as an action at all, aimed at the protection of the class interests which would profit from the general adoption of that belief. Nor may particular actions performed on the basis of such beliefs be construed as aimed at that purpose.

These remarks indicate that the reasoning in favour of the Postulate does not, in general, count against the adoption of functionalist theorizing. Functionalist theories are not to be construed as offering interpretive accounts, and hence are not rivals to everyday interpretive accounts. The Durkheimian doctrine that religious ceremony has the function of affirming and strengthening social bonds does not, properly construed, allow the inference that individual participants in a ritual are inspired by that goal. Rather, it says something about the conditions which generate and sustain religious beliefs and practices.[19] Hence there is no direct clash between functionalist theory and the everyday understanding of religious action. There may still be a tension at a higher level, however, since subjects embracing a given belief system will normally harbour a meta-belief to the effect that that system is somehow rationally grounded. And a functionalist theory tends to show that the adoption of a certain belief is not governed by considerations of evidence but by non-cognitive factors. To the extent that functionalist theorizing conflicts with the everyday interpretation in this manner, the argument we have developed in favour of the Postulate is powerless to defend it, however.

6

We have had to recognize the existence of counter-examples to the Postulate. I shall conclude this chapter by examining various proposals for a weakening of this maxim so as to render it immune to these examples. If the Postulate could be salvaged by non-trivializing modifications, it would still point to a crucial difference between physics and social science and would tell us something about the conditions for social theorizing..

An obvious modification of the Postulate would make it call for the scientific interpretation to be acceptable to the agent himself, but not necessarily as judged by his original, naive self-interpretation: for it might be possible for the social scientist to persuade the agent that the scientific interpretation offers the truer picture. This methodological maxim would be reminiscent of one adhered to in psychoanalysis. The interpretation proposed by the analyst will typically be highly divergent from the patient's conception, in content as well as in form. Still, that interpretation is only allowed if it eventually receives the patient's endorsement.

A methodological principle of this kind would be sound, I believe, and indeed an improvement upon Schütz's Postulate. Still, it should be treated not as an unbending rule, but merely as a useful heuristic maxim. The social scientist may at times be justified in sticking with his own interpretation in the face of the agent's refusal to sanction it. Thus, for instance, there is probably not much chance of getting a 'possessed' person to underwrite the sociological interpretation, at least not through any method short of actually removing him from his native background and entirely acculturing him in our ways of thought.

However, I shall make no attempt to assess the strength of this weakened version of the Postulate. To do so would lead us into methodological issues of rather limited philosophical import. The Postulate in its original form dealt with the relationship between social reality and the theories and concepts in which it is naively grasped by everyday social agents. This is an aspect of the general problem of the relationship between theory and reality which occupies a centre-stage position in philosophy. The issue raised by the weakened version concerns the relative weights to be accorded to the agent's sincere avowals of motivation and conflicting behavioural evidence (in situations, that is, where the behavioural evidence is not complete; as it is unlikely to be in any actual case). After the rather inflated claims made on behalf of the agent's authority in a previous decade have now been abandoned, I think it must be recognized that there is no simple answer that philosophy can give here: this issue is a corner of the huge and rationally rather intractable problem of how to rank hypotheses in the light of empirical evidence. We may be forgiven for not pursuing this widely ramified issue any further here.

Finally, let me make a few remarks concerning an alternative way to weaken the Postulate. Doctrines akin to this maxim have sometimes stated that the social scientist must respect the agents' concepts, rather than their judgements; that to express his theory about their conduct, he must adopt the concepts used by the people studied, or at least concepts understandable to them.[20]

If we take this maxim to call for adherence to the notions actually used by the people studied, it. is undermined by one of the very examples that disposed of the previous, stronger interpretation. The individual—say, an illiterate Catholic woman from a rural region of Sicily—whom we describe as satisfying repressed sexual urges by adopting the symptoms of 'possession', will not only refuse to accept such an interpretation: the very concepts in which it is couched will be foreign to her. The sociologist's explanation embodies a biological, secular conception of sexuality, whereas the subject may conceive of it in ethico-religious terms, as a ruse with which the forces of evil lure man away from the road to salvation. If, on the other hand, the maxim simply requires the scientist to employ only concepts which the people studied can be brought to grasp, after suitable indoctrination, it is unclear whether this will impose any limitations whatsoever upon social scientific practice.

This does not mean that there are no constraints at all upon the interpretations we may adopt when we reject the agents' own understanding, or upon the concepts in which they are couched. But I doubt whether anything resembling a simple rule can be produced here. In discussions of radical interpretation of human action, the point is often made that it counts against an interpretation of language and action if it imputes beliefs and desires which the subjects could not possibly possess, given their channels of information about the world. Thus, we should be highly suspicious of an interpretation which would impute a detailed knowledge about the nuclear composition of matter to illiterate South Sea islanders. The trouble is that this principle must be hedged considerably in order not to block recognition of such magic and religious beliefs for which the natives cannot possess adequate evidence either. Magico-religious conceptions typically contain elements which are explicitly declared to be beyond the cognitive powers of mortal men.

But perhaps some restrictions upon reinterpretation may still be derived from these considerations. We are only allowed, it might be said, to describe beliefs and desires by means of notions that are not cognitively accessible to the agents if the latter entertain higher-level reflections that explain why they are not thus accessible (pronouncements to the effect that spirits are invisible, etc.). When we deal with conduct for which we reject the official interpretation, and when our interpretation is couched in concepts not used by the agents, such meta-commentary will necessarily be lacking. In this case we are obliged to describe motivation only by means of concepts, a (tacit) grasp of which can be manifested in ground-level conduct, unaided by commentary. The reinterpretation in terms of sexual gratification satisfies this restriction, since a person's conduct may supply sufficient evidence that a certain activity is sexually gratifying to him, and is pursued for that reason. But other interpretations might be barred by this principle; such as perhaps an interpretation to the effect that the natives engage in religious ritual in order to strengthen social cohesion.

Thus we can propose that in interpreting action, our theories must be couched in terms either explicitly used by the agents, or in terms, an implicit command of which may be manifested in non-verbal conduct. This suggestion has considerable plausibility. Still I am not certain it can be adopted as it stands. Perhaps in some cases we should be justified in importing elements from the agents' explicit discourse into descriptions of their non-verbal conduct which would not be sustained by that conduct in isolation. This might lead to the use of other concepts which are parts neither of the agents' explicit discourse nor of the conceptual framework applicable on the basis of their non-verbal behaviour alone.

But we must leave these questions, as they lead away from our original topic and into the largely uncharted waters of radical interpretation. The problem we have tried to tackle in this chapter was a different one, concerning the relationship between social scientific theorizing and the interpretation endorsed by the people studied. We have concluded that the Postulate in its original formulation is undermined by the infirmity of its second premise to the effect that everyday interpretations are true. Still, the investigation also showed that there are strict limitations of principle to the improvement of an everyday interpretation if its truth is not questioned. This result will assume a certain importance in the next chapter.

5

Purposive accounts

1

Having dealt with a number of preliminary issues in the preceding chapters, we have at long last reached the point where we can examine the merits, from the point of view of theory construction, of the three varieties of action accounts outlined in chapter 1. We begin with purposive accounts. What is the potential of purposive accounts for serving as the focus of a genuinely theoretical approach to human action? Or, to put it in the slightly more precise manner employed in the Introduction, are there considerations of principle which militate against the generation of theoretical systematizations of our knowledge of human action capable of supporting theoretically enriched purposive accounts? But before we proceed to answering that question, it must be subjected to further comment and refinement.

The above formulation makes calculated use of a vague term when referring to a theory 'supporting' an account. That locution is employed in order to counteract the idea that the relationship between a theory and an account based upon it is necessarily one of deriving the latter through some rigid formal procedure, typically that of logical deduction. But it may not be possible to derive accounts from theories by simply plugging additional information into their blank spaces. Instead, a theory may only be suggestive of a possible explanation, leaving it for a detailed investigation of the concrete case to determine whether that explanation actually applies.

An example of this weak relationship between theory and explanation is provided by Darwin's theory of evolution. This theory does not license the *a priori* verdict, with reference to any given anatomical trait of some currently existing species, that this particular trait emerged through a process of adaptation to the environment governed by the mechanism of 'survival of the fittest'. It fails to do so, even if the trait is clearly adaptive for the species today. For even complicated anatomical structures may develop 'accidentally', that is, unrelated to any adaptive function, as long as they are not positively detrimental to survival; moreover, an anatomical structure developed in this fashion may suddenly acquire survival value after some change in the habitat of the species. Darwin's hypothesis merely serves to bring a possible type of account to our attention, directing us to look for evidence confirming or invalidating it in any concrete case.

The reason for dwelling upon this point is that it helps focus our attention upon that feature of theories which is our sole concern here, namely, their very theoreticity, their degree of integrative power; disregarding the question of their inferential power, their power to serve as tools for prediction or retrodiction. Darwin's theory is high in integrative power, permitting us to see a large class of diverse phenomena as springing from the same generative processes. But it is weak in inferential power: it does not allow us to predict with any precision the future evolution of some current life form, nor to retrodict the contingencies of selectional pressure that led to the emergence of that form as we meet it today. It does not even allow us to state, with reference to any concrete feature of that species, that it emerged through a selectional process. (Notice that the notion of inferential power introduced here is somewhat broader than the one which occupied us chapter 2. There, we dealt with the power of a theory to license inference of the explanandum, given additional premises, whereas we are now concerned with the possibility of deriving an explanation from the theory (plus additional premises). The two conceptions overlap, of course: for where we can infer the explanandum from the theory, we can also, trivially, derive the complete explanation from the same premises. However, there are cases where an explanation may be derived in the absence of derivability of the explanandum. For instance, the mosquito theory of malaria does not allow us to infer that Jones, who has just been bitten by a vector, will develop the disease, since being bitten is only a necessary condition. However, the theory allows us to infer, from an observed case of malaria, that a mosquito attack preceded it and caused its occurrence. In other words, the theory enables us to infer the relevant account, and to do so even in the absence of any further information.)

In the present investigation, we are concerned with the integrative power of theories, not their inferential powers. The traditional debate about the possibility of establishing a science of human action has focused for the most part upon the outlook for theories strong enough to license prediction or retrodiction. This possibility depends largely upon our ability to discriminate and pin down the factors influencing conduct, and to introduce suitable operational tests to measure their strength. It may well be possible to succeed in this endeavour without producing 'theory' proper, that is, without offering a more parsimonious, more systematic picture of human action than the everyday one. Conversely, it is possible to produce theories which effect some integration of their subject matter, but without their being formulated in such a way as to license inferences about concrete events. A prominent example of such theories is what might be termed *taxonomico-reductive* theories. In the field of human purposive action, they might take the form of a list of the dynamic factors behind action, but without specifying these, or the conditions under which they are activated, in such detail that inferential power ensues. The second component in the designation, taxonomico-reductive, is meant to remind us that in order to possess theoretical power, such systems must not be purely classificatory. They must effect some systematization or condensation of their subject matter, as compared to the common-sense conception. (Of course every classification effects some 'reduction' of the data dealt with, minimally a systematization relative to a mere list of the particulars classified in the taxonomy. But here we ask for a reduction beyond that attained in common-sense descriptions and classifications.)

In the following explorations, I shall often speak as if our present concern were whether a taxonomico-reductive theory of purposive action is possible. The reason for focusing on this mode of theorizing is twofold. In the first place, actual historical attempts at interpretive theorizing in this field have mainly been taxonomico-reductive. Thus, when we want to illustrate the abstract argument with some concrete material, this is the kind of doctrine we must turn to. Secondly, it is a convenient expositional device, permitting us to talk about the problems of theoretical integration in a more concrete manner than is possible if we stick to the canonical formulation. It is a legitimate device, given two conditions of which the one reflects the particular structure of the following discussion, whereas the other holds generally. The first condition is that in our investigation, we shall be concerned primarily with ontological integration. This will be the case because, as I shall argue, it is here that interpretive theorizing is up against its chief obstacle, whereas I grant that some headway can be made with the integration of principles. The second condition is that the question of whether a taxonomico-reductive theory is possible in some realm is equivalent to the question of whether ontological integration can be obtained in this same realm. For the question as to whether *this* taxonomico-reductive theory holds in some particular realm is, so to speak, the 'material mode'-version of the question as to whether *this* theoretical vocabulary suffices to explain all data of that realm. We might also say that a taxonomico-reductive theory is the smallest common denominator between theories which employ the same theoretical vocabulary, but diverge in inferential power. Thus, the results arrived at for taxonomico-reductive theories are valid for theories of higher inferential power as well. Focusing on this kind of theory has the additional advantage of helping us stay clear of issues regarding the inferential tightness of action theories.

It must be firmly kept in mind that this approach is an expositional tool only: we are investigating the prospects of theoretical advance for any kind of theory that will support purposive accounts, inferentially strong ones as well as purely taxonomico-reductive ones. This deserves emphasis lest my approach be taken to signal subscription to the view, quite widespread among interpretive theorists, that inferentially strong theories are somehow inappropriate in the realm of human action; that the special cognitive interest that we take in matters humane makes such theorizing out of place.[1] This position seems to me quite unsupported. If inferentially strong theories of human action could be devised, couched in theoretical intentionalistic terms–and whether such theories can be found is not at issue here–they would be highly interesting even from the standpoint of a methodological position which insists that action be grasped in interpretive categories. Certainly we should often be interested, while adopting this attitude, in being able to predict what other people will do, and for what reasons.

There is a further point upon which the formulation of our project calls for comment, and tightening. Imagine that we succeed in producing an ideally refined theory of the working of the human body, including the central nervous system, enabling us to predict, to within any desired degree of precision, the external, behavioural aspect of action as well as its inner concomitants in the central nervous system. Assume, furthermore, that we managed to devise a set of bridge laws, in Nagel's sense, spanning the gap between the neurophysiological descriptions of action and their intentionalistic counterparts. What is suggested is a class of statements which join a description of the agent's bodily movements, plus information about the condition of his central nervous system, with a specification of what the agent is up to, couched in intentionalistic terms (we bypass any scruples about the feasibility of such a project). Combining the physiological theory and the bridge principles, we get a device which enables us, in two steps, to produce interpretive accounts of action. Now these accounts would be theoretically enriched ones: the neurophysiological component of the compound would provide a theoretical description of the neural conditions which subserve various motivational states which could then be imported into interpretive accounts. For instance, the neurophysiological theory might reveal a certain difference between classes of human desires in terms of the brain structures subserving them. One class might primarily be associated with processes in the hypothalamus, say, whereas another would involve cortical processes as well. Designate the two classes as X-desires and Y-desires, respectively. Armed with this distinction, we might now produce purposive accounts of the following kind: Mr N. N. did so-and-so because he had a Y-desire that such-and-such be the case. This is a theoretical redescription of Mr N. N.'s conative state, but clearly not the kind we are looking for here. This is the case even though the redescription is impeccably intentionalistic: when we talk of Mr N. N.'s Y-desire to become a junior member of the firm, that desire is being introduced under an intentionalistic description and fits neatly into an interpretive account. To block this kind of redescription, and to capture more clearly what we have in mind when we speak about the theory-loading of interpretive accounts, we must require that the theoretical substitutions be made within the scope of intentionalistic expressions. In other words, the enriched descriptions must occur in the blanks of such expressions as: 'Mr N. N. desires that. . . ', 'Mr N. N. believes that. . . ', and 'Mr N. N. abides by the rule that. . . '

This brings us to the following final formulation of the question which occupies us in the present study: are there considerations of principle militating against the creation of systematizations of our knowledge of social action which are superior in theoreticity to the current common-sense conception of action, and which will support—in the sense of 'support' outlined above—interpretive accounts which embody theoretically enriched concepts within the scope of intentionalistic expressions?

Is this formulation not somewhat redundant? Could we not simply have asked about the possibility of producing theoretically enriched interpretive accounts, leaving unstated the truism that theoretical notions derive from theories? We could indeed. I have chosen this formulation because it acts as a reminder that in the sense of 'theoretical' used in this study, as opposed to that defined by the traditional theoretical–observational distinction, theoreticity is a property which a concept earns in the full sense only on the basis of a detailed examination of the theory in which it occurs, and of the merits of this theory relative to a previous body of knowledge which it replaces. Theoreticity cannot be established by a simple test performed on an isolated concept. Some scientific notion might have wider scope than its intuitive everyday counterpart and still fail to count as theoretical in the full sense, because the overall explanatory system of which it is a part is not superior to the everyday picture.

Finally, a brief note on the 'everyday' or 'common-sense' understanding of action. I sketched the overall distinction between the common-sense view and the scientific view in chapter 1, and have nothing to add to that account in a general vein. I shall only stress the point that when talking about the 'common-sense view', I do not mean the agent's spontaneous or unreflected description of his own action, but his considered, studied opinion.

2

We have now decided on the canonical formulation of the question which occupies us in the present study. It is time to start answering that question for purposive accounts. Let us jump *in medias res* by looking at a conception which has often been held to be the proper way to introduce theory in social science. This is an approach using the notion of *practical rationality* as its chief conceptual tool.

An exponent of this approach is Karl Popper. In the article, 'Rationalité et le statut de principe de rationalité',[2] Popper compares the role of the rationality principle–that 'people act appropriately to the situation they are in'–to the role of the Newtonian principles in mechanics. Popper invites us to observe how in order to explain particular physical phenomena–for example, solar eclipses–we may construct miniature models of the physical systems involved, *in casu* the solar system. Such a model might consist of an electric lamp, symbolizing the sun, with little wooden balls around it, representing the earth and the moon. In the same manner, according to Popper, we might construe models of social situations (although these would hardly be material models); he dubs them 'situational analyses'. Popper points out that Newtonian mechanics provides the dynamics of the solar model: to set that model in motion, we assume that the elements of the model behave the way that real celestial bodies would behave according to the principles of mechanics. What, then, is the counterpart of Newton's law in the situational analyses? Popper's answer is, the rationality principle. This, as already mentioned, he construes somewhat vaguely, saying that 'people act appropriately to their situation'. The situational model of the agent placed in a particular social situation contains all relevant information about the agent's goals and beliefs. All we need to add to inject dynamics into the model is the axiom that the agent acts rationally. When animated by this principle, the model enables us to account for human action by depicting it as the appropriate response to the situation in which the agent finds himself.

However, the notion of an 'appropriate' action in a given setting is so loose as to rob Popper's suggestion of much of its initial attraction. It is, in general, simply not very clear what counts as the 'appropriate' move for an agent in a given situation; indeed, this notion may be suspected of being ineradicably subjective, thus undermining the objective validity of action accounts. Fortunately, however, for the general idea, the notion of situational logic may be strengthened by importing into it the very precise and exacting notions of practical rationality developed in economics and its more recent sister disciplines, known under such names as decision theory and game theory. One crucial assumption which serves to bestow rigidity on the notion of a rational action, as it is understood in these disciplines, is that a practically rational action is a *maximizing* action–an action that seeks the highest point on some measurable scale. Another advance in the economist's model, as compared to that proposed by Popper, lies in the much greater explicitness and precision of the former as to the motivational factors which the agent himself brings to the situation. Popper states, in the article cited, that the 'situation', as he uses that term, already contains all relevant aims and all the available relevant knowledge on the part of the agent.[3] Still it is not very clear how this information enters the model.[4] The economist's model embodies these facts in a particularly complete and perspicuous form. The agent's *conative* states (his desires) are captured in a preference ordering of the outcomes of the actions open to him (his so-called 'feasible set'). That ordering is normally required to satisfy certain intuitively natural conditions. In the first place, the ordering is required to be *complete*, in the sense that for any pair of outcomes, O_1 and O_2, O_1 is preferred to O_2 or O_2 is preferred to O_1. Secondly, the ordering must be asymmetric, such that for any pair of outcomes, O_1 and O_2, the agent will not both prefer O_1 to O_2 and O_2 to O_1. Thirdly, the ordering should be transitive, which means that for any triad of outcomes, O_1, O_2 and O_3, if O_1 is preferred to O_2 and O_2 is preferred to O_3, then O_1 is preferred to O_3. (These conditions are sometimes relaxed to allow relations of indifference as well, resulting in a so-called weak ordering. We need not go into these issues here.)

As for the *cognitive* factors which the agent contributes to the situation–his beliefs about the situation–it is assumed in the strongest version of the economic decision model that the agent has full and correct information about his feasible set, and about the outcomes of the actions in this set. In a weaker version, the agent lacks definite information as to which actions lead to which outcomes; he is merely taken to assign to these outcomes certain probabilities of occurrence. In an even weaker model, there is not even such statistical information available to the agent; still, it is possible to assign to him so-called 'subjective probabilities', which, intuitively speaking, are numerical assessments of his degree of conviction, for any specified upshot, that that upshot will be forthcoming.

Given this apparatus, it is now possible to provide an extremely precise content for the idea of a practically rational action, considered as a critical–normative ideal. The central idea, as noted before, is that of an action that maximizes some property, on the background of the agent's 'preference function' (his desires) and his 'feasible set' (as reflected in his beliefs). A number of different canons of rationality have been developed, corresponding to different kinds of decision situations. The simplest rationality principle is to be deployed in situations of so-called 'decision under certainty', that is, situations where the information available to the agent singles out the outcomes of his feasible set in definite, non-statistical terms. The principle simply calls for the agent to 'maximize his utility'–to pick the action issuing in the highest ranking outcome on his preference scale. A slightly more complicated situation obtains in cases of 'decision under risk'–cases where the available information does not guarantee an invariable connection between the agent's options and their outcomes, but only provides probability figures. For this kind of case, the rationality principle prescribes selection of the option which 'maximizes expected utility', that is, the option for which the sum of the products of each possible outcome and its associated probability is not exceeded by any other option. The same maxim applies in instances where the agent is not even apprised of objective probabilities, 'subjective probabilities' being substituted instead.

It follows from the above remarks that in order to reach a

rational decision in accordance with the expected utility maxim, the agent must be capable of establishing a cardinal ordering of his preferences, not merely an ordinal one. Such an ordering is not normally introspectively available to agents; and it is one of the major achievements of decision theory to have devised a metric for cardinal utility, in the form of an operational procedure which issues in, and hence gives precise meaning to, numerical estimates of preference.

The previous two maxims of rational choice presuppose that the agent is capable of assigning at least a 'subjective probability' to the happenings which are the outcomes of his feasible actions. However, there are situations of choice in which not even such assignments are available.[5] In such instances, dubbed 'decision under uncertainty', an even weaker notion of rationality must be resorted to. Or rather: one or another of a number of alternative rationality canons must be resorted to. For in the case of decision under uncertainty, there is no single generally agreed-upon canon of rational choice, but rather a number of different and incompatible proposals. Moreover, it may well be that the notion of practical rationality has no unique interpretation for such cases; the different proposals may all have an equally valid claim to the title. A maxim often promulgated is the so-called minimax (or maximin) rule, which urges the agent to maximize his smallest possible gain, that is, to choose the option for which the least fortunate outcome is better, or at least as good, as the least fortunate outcome of the alternative options. Another, more optimistic rule has also been proposed, the so-called maximax rule, which calls upon the agent to choose the option for which the most favourable outcome is not exceeded by the most favourable outcome of other options. Moreover, hybrid versions of these two rules have also been devised. Unless an argument is forthcoming in the future which knocks out all but one of these canons, we have to admit, it would seem, that they are all equally valid strategies in situations of decision under uncertainty.

Thus, in order to develop the potentials of Popper's methodological suggestion, we should strengthen it by replacing the woolly notion of acting 'appropriately to the situation' with the canons of rational choice developed by economics and decision theory. We should use these notions, which were originally developed as axioms of a *normative* theory of decision, as explanatory principles. Or perhaps we should rather view Popper's proposal as a call for broader implementation of these notions for explanatory purposes: for clearly something very close to the method sketched is already being used in one branch of economics, namely microeconomics. Microeconomics predicts and explains the actions of the individual consumer by assigning to him a decision basis of the kind just outlined and by seeing him as striving to maximize his utility, that is, to spend his budget in such a way as to get maximum satisfaction in return for his expenditure. Popper's suggestion might be construed as an incitement to extend the scope to all sectors of human action, even such that do not involve an economic aspect. Man should be conceived as a utility maximizer, equipped with desires and goals organized in a preference ordering, fitted with a store of information geared to the attainment of these goals, and propelled by the principle of utility maximation. The respectable pedigree of this kind of theorizing would seem to license the hope that its general adoption could lead to theoretical advances in social science comparable to those in economics.

3

Before we turn to an evaluation of the merits of rationality theory (as I shall henceforth call the approach sketched above) we must indicate why an examination of this mode of theorizing is relevant to an assessment of the theory-generating potentials of purposive accounts. What is the relationship between the two? This query might be prompted by the observation that the accounts provided by economists are not ostensibly a species of purposive accounts. As we have seen, such accounts–let us call them rationality accounts–will typically depict the agent as being involved in a choice between ends, that is, as engaged in the process of determining which of the options open to him will result in the highest valued outcome. Purposive accounts, on the other hand, merely involve the relationship between one single end and the means to realize it. Or, in cases where rationality accounts merely deal with one end, they at least show the agent as being engaged in a choice between different ways of reaching this end and as making the optimal choice (the canons of practical rationality can easily be transformed to handle means as well as ends). Moreover, rationality accounts show the outcome of action to be maximizing, given the agent's concerns and beliefs, whereas the notion of maximizing seems to play no role in purposive accounts.

These scruples call for two remarks. In the first place, no claim has been made in the preceding discussion that purposive accounts are identical to rationality accounts. Our concern above was with rationality *theory*, not rationality accounts. Rationality theory was introduced because it is capable of supporting purposive accounts; but clearly this move does not presuppose the thought that purposive accounts are a species of rationality accounts. Rationality accounts, as developed by economists, constitute a different, more powerful pattern and utilize more of the information embodied in rationality theory. But our interest in rationality theory is justified if it is indeed true that this kind of theorizing will also support purposive accounts. And this claim is hardly controversial: if we possess a theory which indicates a person's preference structure and his knowledge as to which of the actions open to him lead to which valued upshots, then that theory is certainly capable of generating purposive accounts. A purposive account makes a selection within the information contained in the rationality account of the same action, disregarding information about the non-realized alternatives to the action which was chosen. It represents a restriction in another sense as well. We characterized 'purposive action' somewhat more narrowly than is generally the case, taking the term to stand for action undertaken to achieve some goal which the agent wants *per se*, not as a means towards some more distant goal; and as action motivated by a genuine inclination rather than by a sense of obligation. Both stipulations represent restrictions upon rationality accounts. (It is true that there is a tendency among economists to regard rule-following conduct as being out of reach for the utility-maximation model. But this is not necessarily the case where the purely technical apparatus of such accounts is concerned.)[6]

As my second remark to the query above, I would submit that

purposive accounts and rationality accounts are closer in nature than is allowed by the critic. The opposite position might spring from the notion that purposive accounts deal solely in means–end relationships and that these have nothing specifically to do with rationality. But this position is hardly tenable. If purposive accounts simply cited means–end relationships, it would not detract from their explanatory power if *prima facie* superior, alternative ways of reaching the goal were available to the agent. The existence of such alternatives would not change the fact that the option chosen was *one* way of reaching the goal. Still the little scene with Norbert on pp. 119–20 showed that such alternatives do undermine explanations and require additional information demonstrating why the option chosen was, all things considered, the best one after all. (Clearly, if it is true that maximizing reasoning is built right into the intentionalistic framework, the observer knows *a priori* that the agent must regard the strategy chosen as optimal, or at least cannot harbour the opposite belief. But he does not know the *particular* way in which the motivational matrix is filled out so as to satisfy this *a priori* condition.)

There is an ever-present danger of overstatement here. Many reconstructions of purposive accounts feature a clause attributing to the agent a positive belief to the effect that the action is optimal, all things considered (taking into consideration the 'cost constraints', the side- and after-effects, etc.). This, I fear, gives a much too rationalistic picture of what goes on in much purposive action. Many instances of spontaneous purposive action, especially in infants, cannot plausibly be taken to spring from a piece of practical reasoning involving such a belief, however implicit. This scepticism does not reflect the idea that beliefs, to be relevant to action explanation, must have been explicitly entertained prior to action. On the contrary, I would insist that to make sense of human action, we must ascribe to agents numerous beliefs which they have never and will never formulate explicitly: the confident way I step out my front door manifests *inter alia* the belief that an abyss has not opened up there during the night, although this is a matter to which I have never paid any explicit thought. The sceptical attitude rather reflects a doubt as to whether such an abstract and sophisticated belief can be ascribed to young infants at all. There would certainly seem to be an age at which we would be willing to ascribe purposive action to infants while still hesitating to attribute to them such esoteric beliefs, explicit or implicit. It is to avoid this pitfall that my parsing of purposive accounts on p. 118 offers a dual condition in certain clauses, a stronger condition calling for the presence of some positive belief and a weaker one calling only for the absence of any contrary belief. In other words, I admit the existence of a minimal version of purposive accounts applicable to action in which the agent does not entertain the belief that the course selected is one that cannot be improved upon, but merely fails to believe the contrary. (However, there is still reason in listing the stronger condition as well, since the kind of action for which it is satisfied is justly thought to be more intelligible, and to be more fully action, than the type for which the weaker condition holds.)

On the other hand, the above remarks also signal an opposition to a conception of purposive accounts which allows that they deal in rationality, but still resists the view proposed here. According to that conception, the kind of rationality involved in purposive accounts is not maximizing rationality, but is rather akin to the notion of satisficing developed by Herbert Simon.[7] The notion of a satisficing choice involves the idea of picking an outcome which is *good enough*, but not (necessarily) the optimal one available in the situation. It shows us the agent as deciding upon some minimal level of acceptability which the outcome must satisfy, and then choosing the first best option to come along which is on or above this level. According to Simon, this notion gives a much more faithful picture of the decision-making of actual entrepreneurs in the marketplace (apart from offering less utopian counsel when used as a normative conception); he would no doubt also maintain that it gives a better idea of the decisions behind trivial non-economic everyday actions. And, the critic would go on, it is something like this, rather than maximizing reasoning, which is found in purposive accounts. To be satisfactory, a purposive account must show that the course adopted is 'good enough', given the agent's concerns; that it satisfies some not too precisely defined minimal requirement of adequacy. This jibes with our reaction to the example involving Norbert: the problem with that explanation, the critic would suggest, was precisely that it is not clear, lacking further information, how mowing a lawn could ever be considered a 'good enough' way for a millionaire to raise money for an airline ticket. A full account must include information which shows his action to be good enough after all. But it is not a part of the account to show that the strategy chosen was the optimal one. (This conception need not dispute the view that maximizing rationality is built into the intentionalistic framework. It need only maintain that purposive accounts list only a fragment of the total decision basis, a fragment sufficient to demonstrate that the action chosen is 'good enough' but omitting that additional information which singles it out as optimal.)

However, it is possible to give other examples of purposive explanations being undermined by background information, examples which indicate that the satisficing proposal does not account for this sensitivity in the right manner. In other words, it is possible to embarrass that proposal with examples of the same general kind used to discredit the view that purposive accounts do not involve considerations of rationality at all (cf. p. 197 above). To make this kind of example bear on the satisficing proposal, we must introduce a slight modification rendering the contrast involved one between a satisficing but non-maximizing strategy adopted by the agent and a maximizing alternative of which he must be presumed to be aware. Once again, this will raise the puzzle as to why the agent did not choose the superior solution, with accompanying adverse effects upon the explanatory power of the account; effects that are inexplicable from the standpoint of the satisficing proposal.[8]

Besides, a second look at the satisficing view reveals that the psychological realism which is its *prima facie* advantage over the maximizing position is largely an illusion. I would venture the guess that a person who fully satisfies the conditions of Simon's conception in an everyday situation of action is almost as rare as the person fulfilling the conditions of maximizing reasoning as set out by decision theory. We do not, in preparation for doing our everyday shopping, fix for ourselves some price threshold above which we refuse to buy, nor do we set up corresponding quality standards below which we will not drop.

It remains a fact, of course, that the practical reasoning behind everyday action is different from that which is presented in full-blooded rationality accounts. However, the difference does not lie in the strength of the canons of reasoning employed, but in the richness of the decision basis. Whereas rational choice as set out in rationality accounts involves explicit consideration of all the options open to the agent in the given setting, the decision scheme behind trivial workaday action will be exceedingly simplified. The agent may not explicitly ponder any specific alternative way of reaching the goal; instead, his decision basis features a general implicit premise to the effect that most likely, there is no better way of bringing about the goal than the one at hand (which will presumably be the standard way, the way to which the agent is accustomed, or in some other manner pre-selected by experience or tradition). Thus the rationality principle does not operate directly upon information about specific alternatives, but rather upon abstract generalizations about such alternatives.

This consideration shows that maximizing reasoning plays a different, more modest role in purposive accounts than in rationality accounts. Although optimizing reasoning is involved in purposive accounts, it is not the point of such accounts to demonstrate how the action chosen is maximizing relative to a very comprehensive decision basis available to the agent. The maximization condition of practical reasoning is satisfied in an utterly trivial way: the account specifies the upshot towards which the action is a means and simply *states* that the agent judges it optimal in the situation (or at least does not judge it inferior to any concrete alternative), but without citing the premises of that judgement. Those premises only become relevant if we possess background information making it unclear how sufficient grounds could possibly exist. This case is interesting because it shows that the maximization condition is indeed at play in purposive accounts; making itself felt, however, only when it is hard to see how it could be satisfied.

4

We have sketched a kind of theorizing which has enjoyed considerable success in economics, and on which we might pin our hopes for a theoretical breakthrough in social science. Rationality theory, it might be hoped, could permit a systematization of the facts of human action in terms of a handful of theoretical notions of high integrating power. The technical notions of rationality developed by economics and decision theory and the associated concepts of subjective probability and cardinal utility make possible a much more sophisticated interpretation of action than that available to common-sense thinking. Utilization of these terms opens the door to genuine theorizing in social science, based upon an interpretive mode of account.

It is now time to assess this claim. In the rest of this chapter, I shall argue the position that although rationality theory does represent an obvious advance over everyday understanding of action, this advance is smaller than it may appear at first glance. It is only partial, leaving aside an entire dimension in which rationality theory is in no way superior to its everyday counterpart. Moreover, I shall try to show that there are reasons why this situation cannot be improved upon.

But first we must ask what it is that comprises the advantage of rationality theory over the everyday conception. Indeed, how could rationality theory constitute an advance if we are right in what we have been claiming all along, namely, that rationality is embedded in the very conceptual framework in which we talk about human action? How can rationality theory be more than a mere explication of something which is already implicit in the common-sense picture of action?

This objection has considerable force. And I think it is indeed true that when we deal with the simplest case of action and decision, namely, decision under certainty, rationality theory simply spells out the rationality conception implicit in intentionalistic talk about action. For in this case, rationality theory tells us that human agents will choose the option which maximizes their utility, that is, the option which ranks the highest on their preference scales. This is simply a technical way of stating the axiom governing intentionalistic interpretation of action, to the effect that, in situations where the agent knows for certain the outcomes of his actions, the action he adopts will be the one leading to the upshot he likes the best (all things considered, and perhaps only at the very moment of action). This is the principle which allows us to reason backwards from a man's actions to the desires and beliefs from which they sprang. Moreover, it is no doubt the case that much of our everyday knowledge of action is already organized by means of the rationality principle. The very principle that people act rationally, given their desires and beliefs, and given the absence of corrupting influences, is of course a vacuous one, given the way these terms are defined. However, accumulating experience allows us to replace this quasi-analytical version with more informative ones in which the blanket reference to interfering factors is replaced by substantive specification of the nature of the deviations and of the conditions under which they occur. The rationality principle serves as a skeleton upon which such empirical findings can be hung. (This is the insight behind Max Weber's ideal type methodology, but one that holds only for the rationality principle, as I argued in chapter 2.)

However, the relationship between rationality theory and the everyday conception is somewhat less straightforward when we turn to the other, more complicated situations of choice and action. Here, it will not do to say that rationality theory is simply an explication and clarification of the everyday view. We have seen that the application of rationality theory to cases of decision under risk requires the operational fixation of the notions of cardinal utility and subjective probability. And although these two concepts may well be seen as reconstructions of certain everyday notions—of (degree of) liking and (strength of) belief, respectively—it must still be admitted that rationality theory goes beyond mere explication when combining these notions in the principle of rational choice for decision under risk, that is, the principle that people act so as to maximize expected utility. Because this principle (and its normative counterpart) stands and falls with the numerical expressibility of the two parameters, it makes no sense to talk about the maximization of expected utility as long as only an ordinal ranking of outcomes is available, and no metric at all for the strength of belief. With the quantification of these notions, rationality theory extends to a range of action that was not previously within its scope.

The same point holds even more strongly for decision under

uncertainty; although here we must add the qualification that rationality theory offers us no unique principle by which to describe and explain behaviour, but a choice between several. But perhaps this matters less for the explanatory use of rationality than for the normative use, since we may resort to empirical observation to decide which of the maxims are actually adhered to in human conduct. At any rate, it seems clear that none of the rationality canons developed by decision theory and game theory can be construed as mere explications of something already implicit in the everyday way of talking about action. Neither the minimax principle, the maximax principle, nor the remaining canons proposed for decision under uncertainty can be said to be constitutive of the intentionalistic framework of description. They are not employed as *a priori* principles of the interpretation of action.

We may conclude that the apparent theoretical advance made by rationality theory is not pre-empted by the special status of rationality in intentionalistic description. Nor is it fatally under-mined by the circumstance, which we must hasten to mention, that rationality theory does not enjoy a perfect fit with the facts of human conduct. It has been pointed out already, and hardly needs saying anyway, that most everyday action does not spring from decision bases with anything resembling the comprehensiveness presupposed in rationality theory. Human beings hardly ever possess complete knowledge of their feasible set, the range of options open to them, nor do they have fully reliable information about the outcomes of those actions. They normally decide on the basis of a highly restricted body of information. More seriously, the requirements imposed upon preference orderings are normally not fully satisfied. The condition of completeness will rarely be met fully; worse yet, empirical research has revealed that the condition of transitivity sometimes is not met either.[9] But the point is that these snags do not argue the rejection of rationality theory. Rather, they argue that the concept of fully rational action should be embedded in a more comprehensive theory identifying the factors which make actual conduct diverge from that conception. Given the crucial role which the rationality assumption plays in the intentionalistic framework, at least for the central case of riskless

action, attacks upon the basic presuppositions of rationality theory
are really attacks upon that framework. The problem of non-
transitive preferences, for instance, is not just a problem for one
particular theoretical approach to human action: it strikes at the
very heart of the everyday notion of an agent desiring a particular
upshot. And the various attempts by economists to overcome failure
of transitivity are not attempts at salvaging a theory that has got into
trouble, but at vindicating an entire mode of talking about action.
Through this association, rationality theory acquires a certain
immunity against attack, at least as far as its central components
are concerned. And I believe that once we introduce the technical
notions of cardinal utility and subjective probability in the
description of human action, the notion of rationality which
thereby becomes statable (namely, the principle of expected utility
maximation) will be constitutive of the superior mode of description which is thereby created. These considerations suggest that the
way to handle the shortcomings of rationality theory is the one
recommended by Weber–to use the concept of perfect rationality as
an ideal model and to describe and explain actual conduct as
falling more or less short of that ideal.

However, rationality theory suffers still another kind of shortcoming which is more pertinent to our present point of view. Its
theoretical gains are only partial and limited. I shall now try to
demonstrate the existence and nature of this limitation.

Let us return to our point of departure in Popper's comparison of
the principle of rationality to the Newtonian principles of
dynamics, or to dynamic theorizing in physics in general. This
comparison would seem appropriate, since the theory of motivation
is traditionally conceived as the study of the 'forces' which propel
human action. First, we may draw attention to a crucial similarity
between rationality theory and mechanics in order to highlight the
differences which will appear presently. The principle of
rationality–the principle that people act in a practically rational
manner, given their aims and beliefs–and the axioms of mechanics
possess a similar systematic status. Both may be seen as partly
constitutive of the conceptual system in which these respective
theories are couched. It is a well-known fact that the axioms of
mechanics may be treated as, and are *de facto* often used as, implicit

definitions of the notions used therein. The second axiom especially, to the effect that the acceleration of a body is proportional to
the force exerted upon it and has the same direction as that in
which the force is impressed, is often met in this role. This reflects
the fact that there is no other general criterion for establishing the
presence of a force than the occurrence of acceleration. Hence we
use the second axiom as a general device for detecting and
measuring force, computing the magnitude of a force by the
product of acceleration and mass.[10] This procedure is closely
reminiscent of the way in which we employ the rationality principle
to interpret action, identifying the dynamic factors of belief and
desire involved on the basis of the assumption that an agent seeks
to maximize the satisfaction of desires, given his beliefs. Such
logical interrelatedness and quasi *a priori* status are distinguishing
marks of the notions at the core of theoretical systems and thus
encourage optimism on behalf of rationality theory.

But here we find the crucial difference between rationality theory
and physical dynamics. In physics, the number of different forces,
or 'force functions', which we are led to recognize when we apply
the force criterion, is strictly limited. Recent physical speculation
has it that all physical forces may be reducible to only four, namely
strong and weak interaction, electromagnetism, and gravity; and
the latest word is that electromagnetism and weak interaction can
be collapsed into one. But even if this radical reduction should turn
out to be unattainable, there is little doubt that a relatively small
number of 'force functions' will suffice to integrate all the dynamic
phenomena dealt with in physics.

In physics, we thus have integration not only at the level of the
basic 'framework' concepts—force, mass, acceleration—and of the
principles that describe their interrelations. We also have
integration at the secondary level at which specific forces, and the
principles which describe their working, are introduced. Such
concepts as that of electromagnetism, and of strong interaction,
clearly represent an advance over common sense. They exceed by
far the systematizing powers of the concepts indigenous to common
sense. (Clearly, the former concept is by now firmly established in
common-sense. It remains true that it appears in the common-
sense vocabulary through the courtesy of physics, in the sense that

most of the statements made about electricity, even in an everyday context, can only be established by means of experimental procedures not available to common-sense. See, and compare, the remarks on p. 58.) To a common-sense conception as yet unadulterated by modern physics–in concrete historical terms, that of fourteenth-century man, say–there is nothing in common between the phenomenon of lightning and that of the attraction between a bit of amber and a piece of fur which has been rubbed against it. To this view, the two are due to distinct powers or agencies. Nor, to that same view, is there anything in common between such gravitational phenomena as the tides, a leaf's falling to the ground, and the moon's revolutions around the earth. Widely divergent mechanisms and agencies will be posited to account for them.

It is my contention that rationality theory leaves us at a stage comparable to that of fourteenth-century man *vis-à-vis* physical nature. Application of the technical rationality conceptions in conjunction with the notions of subjective probability and cardinal utility provides a general framework of concepts and principles for the interpretive explanation of human action of a wider scope than that of which common sense avails itself. But rationality theory fails to provide the secondary-level systematization which we get in physics.

It might be contended, perhaps, that the rationality principle which defines the general interrelationship between the core concepts of the action framework also effects some systematization at the secondary level. Any particular desire is governed by the principle, roughly, that when propelled by that desire, the agent will, *ceteris paribus*, do that which is rational, relative to the goal identified by that desire. We might agree to this formulation. The point remains, however, that we are still talking about a highly formal property of desires: we have not yet come to the task of examining the kinds of desires that propel human beings and of presenting them in the form of a taxonomico-reductive theory.

Before we proceed, we must locate the issue more firmly within the framework developed to characterize theoretical integration in chapter 2. The notion of a desire does not fit very neatly into the division between the integration of principles and the integration of ontology. The conception of desires as 'forces' might lead us to place them in the first group, on the grounds that talk of forces is really reifying talk about dynamic principles, *in casu* low-level laws of human action. But desires may also be construed as more or less transient properties of human beings. I do not think it matters which alternative we choose here, as long as we stick to a consistent classification. So here I shall classify desires as states or properties of human beings. The shortcoming of rationality theory then becomes one of ontological integration: we agree that the rationality maxims effect a considerable integration of principles, but complain that they fail to provide a corresponding integration of ontology. Progress along this line would minimally require a taxonomico-reductive theory of the conative states which propel action. But rationality theory traditionally takes no interest in this project. It may even be said that rationality theory embodies a somewhat anti-theoretical, 'atomistic' approach to human desires. Its only aspiration, as far as the conative side of motivation is concerned, is to assign a certain determinate utility to each precisely specified outcome of the actions available to the agent. By so doing, it may be said to postulate a corresponding number of precisely specified desires, each with a particular outcome (type) for its object. Economics has no ambitions as to factoring out these atomistic preferences as functions of deeper, underlying desires. Indeed, neo-classical marginalist theory, which first introduced the technical rationality apparatus into economics, embodied an assumption which militated against any such reduction. Neo-classical theory, represented by such names as Jevons, Menger and Marshall, assumed that the utility of a combination of different goods can be computed by a simple addition of the utilities of the component goods. This is tantamount to the assumption that utilities are independent across commodities: if you assign five utiles to an apple, and four utiles to a pear, the latter assignment is thought to be independent of whether or not you are already in possession of an apple. Having an apple does not diminish the utility that a pear will have to you. The principle of diminishing marginal utility operates only within each narrowly delineated type of goods, not between types. This means that it would be futile to look for classes of goods with interdependent utility values, that is, classes of goods of such a kind that possession of any one of these goods diminishes the utility assigned to all the other goods in that class. Yet the identification of such classes is a crucial first move in the process of identifying the basic desires underlying the boundless variety of human preferences, on the assumption that each class of interdependent goods represents different ways of satisfying one and the same desire. A common, if not invariable, feature of purposive action is the phenomenon of satiation: the fact that obtaining the coveted upshot or object will lower the intensity of the desire; that is to say, diminish the zeal with which further things of that type are sought after. When satiation obtains, a desire may be defined by the class of its actual and potential satisfiers.

The assumption of independence is no longer accepted by modern economic theory. Still this change has not brought with it any endeavour towards producing a theory of the goals of human action; even despite the fact that economists are keenly aware that such a theory would increase immensely the predictive and explanatory power of rationality theory. In the present situation, economists have to take the preference structure of human beings simply as a brute datum that must be supplied from outside the theory. More seriously, economical predictions are typically based upon the assumption that utility functions are stable, an assumption that is known to be generally invalid but which economic theory has to adopt willy-nilly since it has no means at its disposal to predict changes. A theory of human desires would help overcome this obstacle (that theory would obviously have to be an inferentially strong one to permit prediction). Indeed, economists frequently stress the need for co-operation with social science and psychology in the hope of gathering such information.

The trouble is that no other branch of behavioural science has been overly eager to pursue the kind of theorizing needed by economics. Or rather, that kind of theorizing is one that has gone out of fashion. For a brief period around the turn of the century, there was indeed considerable enthusiasm for a kind of theorizing that would at least begin to fill the bill. Speculation about human motivation revolved around the idea of defining the basic sources of human action, commonly referred to as 'instincts'. These were conceived in intentionalistic fashion, being defined in terms of the general kinds of goals towards which they were directed. Thus, what was aimed at was a taxonomico-reductive theory of the dynamic factors behind human action, described in intentionalistic terms. The trend was started by William James's *Psychology* from 1890, in which he offered a list of basic 'instincts' presumed to be innate to man. It gained momentum through the publication of William McDougall's *Social Psychology* in 1908, a work which ushered in a spate of books listing and defining human 'instincts' and trying to utilize them to explain the basic facts of human conduct. Among the more prominent members of the movement were E. L. Thorndike and R. S. Woodworth.

However, this trend turned out to be a very short-lived one. Already in the next generation of psychologists, a change of interest is apparent. This shift was a highly heterogeneous one, as far as positive aims were concerned; but it was invariably a change away from the kind of interpretive theorizing found in James and McDougall. It abandoned the concern with human goals, with the *direction* of human action, in favour of an interest in the *determinants* of action. Special interest was taken, by such figures as Tolman and Hull, in questions of the dependency of behaviour upon simple experimentally manipulable parameters. The connection between the intensity of behaviour (as measured by rate of response) and strength of motivating desires ('drives' or 'needs') as measured by duration of preceding deprivation, was much in focus. So was the connection between volume of action and 'reinforcement', that is, rewards given to spontaneously emitted action leading to an increase in its frequency. The observation that behaviour could be modified by suitable reinforcement led to a general interest in the phenomenon of learning. Associated with this was a concern with the mechanisms, strongly tied up with the phenomenon of reinforcement, through which new motives are acquired. In general, the psychologists of this generation were highly sceptical of the innateness doctrine of the instinct theorists, and tried to show how many of man's more rarefied desires may be construed as secondary, learned ones, resting upon the foundation of a few innate impulses.

The shift initiated by Tolman, Hull, and their followers, did not just reflect changing research interests. It also reflected deliberations on the methodology of the sciences of human action, and the endeavour to render them more 'scientific'. The standards of testing, of the operational definition of terms, and of mathematical expression set by natural science were to be emulated in the other field as well, as was the general causal approach of natural science. We may venture the guess, however, that the apparent sterility of the 'instinct' approach had a lot to do with the shift as well. When L. L. Bernard reviewed the literature in his 1924 monograph, *Instinct,* he could report that no fewer than 849 distinct 'instincts' had been introduced by different authors in the field. Not the mere proliferation of 'instincts', but also the character of the various lists of such motivational factors, led to the eventual demise of the approach. Those lists have an air of arbitrariness to them, a charge born out by the observation that they differ greatly in the number of items listed as well as in the way they are specified (to the extent that the normally somewhat vague vocabulary permits meaningful comparison). So the following generation of behavioural scientists resolved that James's and McDougall's mode of theorizing was a dead end. The approach was silently abandoned and has remained dormant to this day, with a few exceptions.[11] The kind of doctrine with which rationality theory needs to be supplemented to turn it into a complete and fully integrative theory of human action does not exist.

So far, this has merely been a report of historical developments and an observation on the current state of the game. For our present purposes, we need to show that this disappointing upshot was inevitable and did not merely reflect the ineptness of the instinct theorists. For, after all, the apparent open-endedness of the lists of instincts and the abundancy of rival theories might merely have been taken as the growing pains of a discipline still in its infancy; a consequence merely of the enthusiasm with which the new territory was explored. Here one might point to the current situation in elementary particle physics for a comparison: the rapid multiplication of 'elementary particles' is clearly a sign that our present theories are not good enough; that we have still not reached ground level in the process of splitting up matter. But it is not taken as a sign that the whole idea of explaining the behaviour of molar units by viewing them as aggregates of simpler units is mistaken; and for good reasons. So perhaps the ontological extravagance of instinct theorizing was just as temporary a feature as we assume that of current nuclear physics to be.

In the following section, I shall try to show that such optimism is unwarranted and that motivation theory of the 1930s and 1940s did well in abandoning the instinct approach. We shall of course be concerned only with the problems which the instinct theory faces *qua* a taxonomico-reductive theory of human desires, bypassing the criticisms it drew upon itself by virtue of its specific features, in particular the innateness hypothesis. Furthermore, it should be kept in mind that even the wider class of theories merely serves as an exemplar. The argument we shall present bears upon all types of interpretive theories of purposive action, whatever their inferential power.

5

As an opening move, let us look at the conceptual tools employed by physics and see if we can discern the feature or features to which it owes its immense potential for theoretical integration. Afterwards, we may compare this with the situation in the theory of action in order to pin down the points on which the latter falls short.

A feature which immediately leaps to the eye is the highly *decompositional* nature of physical accounts. In the process of explaining a phenomenon, physics typically analyses it into an aggregate of parts, aspects or properties that are not singled out in the everyday conception. These parts or aspects typically display a certain homogeneity which allows them to be explicable in terms of a limited number of principles. By aggregating the explanations of the part-phenomena, the overall phenomenon is finally explained.

Let me illustrate this with an example. Physics cannot engage the phenomenon of *tides* under its everyday description; (roughly) that of periodical changes of the sea level. As a preliminary to explaining the tides, physics must analyse this phenomenon as a bulge on the surface of the sea, located roughly on the line connecting the centres of the earth and the moon. This bulge must be further analysed as the shifting of the water molecules towards the centre of the moon. Given this decomposition, the tides may now be explained as a vertical motion of water molecules, caused by the gravitational pull of the moon as the earth's rotation moves the sea surface through its field of gravitation.

In brief, explanation in physics follows the pattern already recognized by Galileo: analysis of the phenomenon to be explained into simpler elements or aspects ('resolution'), followed by aggregation ('composition') of the explanations of the part-phenomena to reach an explanation of the overall phenomenon.

If we have a closer look at the above sketch, we realize that there are two distinct conditions responsible for the success of theorizing in physics. In the first place, the fact that everyday descriptions of physical phenomena can be replaced by descriptions which reveal the 'real natures' of the items referred to by the former descriptions. (As we saw in chapter 4, replacement is typically of a kind which will respect the truth of the everyday description. However, it does not matter for the point made here whether a complementary or a rival description is involved.) Secondly, the fact that this description is more highly analytical than the everyday one, revealing structure not recognized by the everyday conception. The theoretical integration achieved by physics depends upon the satisfaction of both conditions.

If we now turn to interpretive theorizing concerning purposive action with this lesson in mind, we immediately spot a crucial obstacle to the success of such a programme. This lies in the limited room for improvement upon the agents' descriptions of their own actions. In intentionalistic description of action, we do not have that substitutivity of an everyday term in favour of a non-synonymous but compatible term expressing the 'real essence' of the former, which we have in physics: intentionalistic descriptions do not have such counterparts. Thus, replacement is restricted to the cases where the everyday description is false or incompletely specified. But there is a general presumption that common-sense action descriptions are true and maximally specified, at least if we agree to mean by the 'common sense view' the reflective view, the understanding that a person will only attain after a certain amount of soul-searching, not the first best interpretation that will come to mind. Human agents possess a direct, non-inferential access to their own motivations which is immune to many of the vicissitudes of empirical cognition at large. True, we concluded in the previous chapter that agents' self-interpretations are not inviolable, not even when dressed up in socially generated categories and when socially endorsed. Still, although it is hardly possible to make any *a priori* assessment of the scope of mistaken self-interpretation, it is safe to say that the special nature of self-interpretation places a large segment of everyday action descriptions beyond improvement (but without rendering any type of self-interpretation equally immune). This segment must necessarily exert a considerable inertial influence upon an interpretive theory of purposive action, imposing narrow—although not *a priori* specifiable—limits upon its theoretical gains.

Let us demonstrate in more concrete detail how loyalty to the everyday descriptions of action creates trouble for theorizing. Before we begin, we must briefly recapitulate the characterization we provided of ontological integration in chapter 2. (It is only ontological integration that concerns us here, since we have already granted the possibility of some integration of principles.) Ontological integration has two dimensions, the dimension of parsimony and the dimension of generality. The two dimensions are conveniently measured by the magnitude of the conceptual apparatus needed to deal with the given realm, and by the scope of the concepts which make up that apparatus, respectively. On the one hand, ontological integration means the introduction of concepts of higher generality and greater inclusiveness; on the other hand, it means the reduction of the total number of concepts needed to explain the facts. The two dimensions are, of course, interrelated: it is the introduction of broader-scope concepts which allows us to manage with a smaller conceptual tool-box. However, this connection is not invariable. The introduction of more general concepts need not necessarily permit the elimination of the prior conceptual system and the distinctions embodied in it. To be entirely successful, theoretical integration must make progress in both dimensions. I shall show that loyalty to everyday descriptions of action creates trouble in both dimensions. Let us first look at the obstacles to the use of more inclusive concepts.

Perhaps it is not obvious on the face of it why commitment to the everyday descriptions should preclude theoretical generalization upon these descriptions. Does not the action language allow us to introduce a more general term as long as this term *subsumes* the relevant class of more concrete, everyday action descriptions? Such subsumption would not impugn the validity of these descriptions; on the contrary, it would presuppose it. Unfortunately, the answer is no. The action accounts we want to improve upon are presumed to be maximally specified, that is, they cite the very description under which the goal is desired. If this condition is satisfied, there is no room for a more general characterization, if that characterization is to occur within the scope of intentionalistic expressions. A true, maximally specified everyday action description will not merely indicate the specific desirability properties of the action (or its upshot), but will cite its generic desirability properties as well. And if the specification is indeed maximal, no more universal term may be added to it. The specification will already provide the most inclusive category under which the action or its upshot may be subsumed, for the purposes of interpretive explanation.

It is true, of course, that there may be even more general rubrics into which that action falls, as a matter of brute classification. But they will not refer to a more general desirability characteristic of the action. Suppose I have a desire for a glass of cold milk and a desire for a new automobile. Call a thing which is either a glass of cold milk or a new automobile a mobilk. We cannot now conclude that I have a desire for a mobilk: for we noted previously that when the notion of satiation applies to a desire, specification of that desire as directed towards some type of upshot (or object: it does not matter what we say here) implies that the attainment of some such upshot decreases the vigour with which further upshots of the same kind are pursued. My putative desire for mobilks does not satisfy this condition: having a glass of milk will not still my longing for a car, or vice versa. The composite class, although counterfactually identical with the disjunction of the two classes, both of which I desire, is not itself an object of desire.

A real-life example of the infraction of this semantic principle, and a radical one at that, is found in R. S. Woodworth. (Woodworth speaks about 'drives' rather than desires. The logical point remains the same, however.) According to Woodworth, the tendency to *deal with the environment* is the primary conative factor behind human action; there is a general *behaviour drive* to which the specific drives add up and from which they are somehow derived.[12] Now it is a fact that many desires (or 'drives') have for their object a certain activity, typically involving handling of items in the environment. Such acts as eating (at least some of the time), making love (most of the time), playing chess, gardening, etc. belong to this group. And let us forget about the fact that an equally large or even larger class of desires are aimed at some *upshot* detachable from the action, not at the latter itself. It does not follow that every desire in the former class may be described as a drive to deal with the environment: to think this is to commit the mobilk fallacy. My playing the piano is not motivated by a general desire to interact with the surrounding world; if it were, I would afterwards, having been successful in that endeavour, be less eager to pursue other ways of manipulating reality, such as making love, eating, or what have you. The performance of any (endotychistic) action would sate the craving for any other such action. We know that this is not the case.

However, when these points have been made, we must also note that among the ways in which everyday action descriptions fall short of full specificity, lack of complete generality is probably the most frequent one; hence a door is left ajar for theoretical improvement. It would seem that the concrete *differentiae* of our operative motives are more readily available, introspectively, than the higher-level, abstract characterizations. Hence they may escape detection, even by reflective self-understanding. I may be fully aware that I quit my job because I resented the way that my superiors ordered me around to do menial tasks and still fail to see that I generally try to flee from situations where people exercise authority over me.

It should also be kept in mind that the intentionalistic framework grants us a certain latitude with agents' own descriptions when these are vague or imprecise. As we pointed out in chapter 4, it allows us a certain amount of explication or 'rational reconstruction'. People may speak vaguely about a desire to 'do their own special thing', 'getting in contact with their real self', 'developing their potentials', etc. A scientific observer of the likes of Maslow may hit upon such fuzzy phrases, taking them to manifest a common underlying endeavour which, in reconstructed and bowdlerized terms, comes out as the desire for self-actualization.[13] This term effects a certain degree of theoretical systematization by subsuming a whole range of imprecise and somewhat metaphorical everyday action descriptions. (I am not, of course, making any comment here upon the actual fruitfulness of Maslow's hypothesis.)

Still, the fact remains that the special nature of human self-interpretation places strict limits upon theoretical advances in the dimension of generality. An agent's sincere avowal of his operative desires, made upon due reflection, is such a reliable source of information that it severely restricts the scope for redescription of these desires in more abstract and more inclusive terms. This point is not undermined by the observation that motivation is often complex and that introspective assessment of the relative strengths of the different impules is very difficult. What we are asking for here is merely a specification of the desires involved, not an indication of their strength. The latter would be of interest only to a predictive theory of action, not to the taxonomico-reductive kind that occupies us here.

Let us now turn to the other dimension of ontological integration, that of parsimony. To provide full ontological integration, a theory must not only introduce concepts of wider scope. It must also dispense with the narrow-scope terms in which common-sense describes the facts, and abstain from replacing these with narrow-scope terms of its own. It is easy to show that the desired interpretive theory of purposive action gets into trouble on this count.

Suppose I perform an action because it, or its upshot, possesses, *inter alia*, a desirability characteristic expressed by the term T belonging to our everyday vocabulary. This term we assume to be simple and definable only by ostension. It follows that T must have a synonymous counterpart in any putative scientific theory of purposive action. For given our inclusive use of the word 'desire' and the way desires are characterized in terms of their intentional objects, it follows that this particular action must spring from a desire to generate an upshot characterized by *T*. And there is no theoretical redescription of that desire which allows us to dispense with *T*. The only way to avoid the occurrence of this term in the characterization of the desire is to suppose that it is a compound of simpler, more general desires, the characterization of which nowhere involves the term *T*. But how could any set of desires not requiring *T* for their description add up to a desire for which *T* does figure in its description? For this to be possible, the descriptions of the simpler desires must include terms which combine semantically to yield the sense of *T*. But this is only possible if *T* is not a primitive term. And we assumed the opposite to be the case. No class of desires not featuring *T* in their descriptions can add up to a net desire to bring about something characterized by *T*.

To illustrate this general point with a concrete example, consider a simple everyday action such as my selection of a dish of pineapple from the restaurant menu. This description of the object of my action would presumably not be maximally specified: so let us stipulate that I choose pineapple not because of its reasonable price, say, or its low caloric content, but because of its delicious taste. In other words, I choose pineapple *qua* being an edible thing with pineapple taste. (Talking about the *object* of an action is a somewhat imprecise terminology. The end of my action is not the object itself, but doing something with it, *in casu* eating it. However, the condensed terminology is convenient for the purpose of the present argument.)

This desirability characterization suggests a decomposition of my motivation into a general desire for edibles and a subsidiary desire or preference, among things edible, for items that taste like pineapple. This makes it possible to view my action as one which fits into a general and infinitely varied pattern of human conduct, revolving around the acquisition and consumption of food. But this subsumption does not, of course, represent an advance beyond common sense, which is hardly oblivious of the fact that hunger is a strong and ubiquitous motive in man.

Let us now turn to the subsidiary conative factor, my preference for pineapple-tasting edibles. Is there any way to avoid reference to the taste of pineapple in the vocabulary of any theory strong enough to explain my action? If the answer is negative, we shall have failed to improve upon everyday understanding. In order to account for my selection of a pineapple-tasting thing, under that description, we must attribute to me a net desire for pineapple-tasting things. And the only way to avoid the occurrence of the term 'pineapple-tasting things' in the specification of that desire, is by construing that preference as the intersection of other, more general preferences (if they are not more general, the interests of parsimony will not have been served). But for this to be possible, the descriptions of those preferences must, when conjoined, add up to the net description, 'preference for pineapple taste'. This they cannot do unless that very description occurs in one of the component preferences, since 'pineapple taste' is (we may grant) a primitive predicate. It cannot emerge from the semantic compounding of simpler predicates. We cannot construe my desire for pineapple as the vectorial product of more general desires, but must admit it as an irreducible item in our ontology.

The upshot of this simple example generalizes to the conclusion that the ontology needed to explain purposive action in interpretive terms must be as rich as that embodied in common sense. It must admit as many undefined terms as the latter. Reduction will only be possible following the demonstration that the common-sense description is invalid and the terms used in it lacking actual application. Such demonstration may be presumed to be a rare occurrence since, in the first place, self-interpretations are especially reliable concerning the concrete *differentiae* of the desirability characterizations; and since, secondly, to eliminate a term from the action vocabulary, we must show that all action descriptions embodying it are mistaken, not just some of them. Barring this kind of simplification, our would-be theory of purposive action will be saddled with a vocabulary which is as compact and as finely discriminated as that of common sense. No progress will have been made in the dimension of ontological parsimony.

For the purpose of clarity, I have conducted the above analysis on the basis of a very simple and trivial example. This might generate the idea that my argument does not seriously damage the interpretive project. This idea may come from two sources.

The first one is the observation that many of the motivation theorists, following the lead of James and McDougall, were merely concerned with identifying the major thrusts of human action. They were well aware that we must abstain from explaining the fine detail of human conduct if we want a manageable theory. These 'major thrusts' are distinguished not merely by being responsible for large segments of human conduct; they are also *primary* in the sense that activation of other, secondary desires is dependent upon their prior activation. The desire for pineapple, for instance, only becomes operative if I desire food in the first place: if I am fully sated, that desire will not come into play at all. Thirdly, the primary desires are found in all human beings, individual divergencies in action merely reflecting differences in the secondary desires.

The critic might add, as a fourth point, that these three coinciding distinctions are also coextensive with the distinction between *innate* and *acquired* desires. However, the issue of innateness versus acquisition is one which deserves special attention, and I shall therefore return to it later. Confining our attention for the moment to the first three points, we must insist, in opposition to the critic, that even if we grant that the division introduced by him is a tenable one (and this might be questioned), it is hard to see how it serves to salvage interpretive theorizing. It is true that we are more interested in the urges shared by all mankind than in the finely discriminated preferences of a tiny group of connoisseurs, just as we are more interested in the motivations which determine the general direction of large sectors of human conduct—such as the desire for food—than those tastes which govern only its fine detail. Still these are not theoretically relevant considerations, at least not within an interpretive approach to action (they may be so within a biological–causal theory). From the point of view of interpretive theorizing, they amount to throwing in the towel, to admitting that such theorizing has little systematizing power and achieves a synoptic view of action only by arbitrarily restricting its subject matter.

The other source of dissatisfaction with my argument might be the idea that it is highly dependent upon the concrete example which, although genuine, is quite marginal. The example illustrates the problem of irreducible desirability characteristics by making play with simple sensory properties. But once we leave action directed at simple physical objects, it becomes much less obvious that the operative motivation behind concrete actions cannot be construed as the intersection of other, more general desires. Take an interest in philosophy, in sports, in music, or what have you. These could hardly be simple, unanalysable promptings like a longing for pineapple?

Yet it is questionable how far this suggestion will lead us. Let us look at your weakness for jazz. Notice, first, that it will not help us at all to analyse this affection into a general liking for music and a specific preference for jazz: this account will still leave the latter preference unreduced. We need to get at this very preference itself. Perhaps it would be possible to analyse your favourable attitude towards jazz, after a fashion. We might adopt the technique of factor analysis, trying to single out the characteristics of jazz music responsible for your enthusiasm by having you listen to a large number of tunes, jazz and non-jazz alike, and listing your reactions in detail. It might turn out that your attitude is determined by three qualities, *A*, *B* and *C*, found together only in jazz. (These qualities would have to occur singly in other kinds of music, too, in order for the corresponding terms to have wider scope than that of 'jazz'. Failing that, no ontological integration would have been achieved by the analysis.) We cannot conclude, however, that your attitude is the result of three more basic preferences–for *A*, *B* and *C*, respectively. It is quite likely that your weakness for jazz is a holistic phenomenon: you may be quite indifferent to qualities *A*, *B* and *C* when you meet them in isolation in pop music. Only in combination with the other two has any one of these characteristics any appeal to you. Your enthusiasm for jazz will be a unitary phenomenon after all, despite the complexity of its object. We have managed to produce a reductive characterization of the object of that enthusiasm, not a decompositional reduction of that conative state itself.

6

At this stage, the reader may have wanted to register a complaint for quite some time. Contrary to what was promised, the doubts raised concerning interpretive theorizing trade upon a particular feature of the concrete example chosen to illustrate such theorizing, namely, the instinct doctrine of James and McDougall, and their followers. These writers wanted to trace all human action back to a limited number of innate conative factors. The reasoning adduced may well be lethal for this programme. However, later theorists rejected the innateness assumption; in fact, a dissatisfaction with this assumption was the major sentiment which united the following generation of behavioural scientists. Central to their doctrines was a distinction between primary and secondary desires (although the term 'desire' was rarely used), that is between *innate* and *acquired* desires. Theories of this kind have no difficulty in handling the infinite variety of human objectives: they offer us a short list of innate impulses and trace the remainder back to some mechanism of desire generation, whether it be Hullian or Skinnerian conditioning; sublimation, transfer, or reaction formation as conceived by Freud; the drift towards congruity, 'balance' and consonance that has been demonstrated by such authors as Heider and Festinger; or any other proposal that has occurred in the literature.

To this charge, we can only reply that our reasoning does not presuppose an instinct theory as its object. It holds against any interpretive theory of purposive action. Innate or acquired, the list of conative states required by an adequate theory of purposive action can only be slightly less extensive than that embodied in the common sense understanding of action. It is correct that if the theories of desire acquisition cited are correct, then this gives us a theoretical handle on purposive action, permitting us to trace the endless variety of human desires back to a limited number of generative principles. But this kind of theoretical integration is a causal–genetic one, not the kind we seek in interpretive theorizing. It does not allow us to produce purposive accounts in which theoretically enriched concepts replace everyday ones within the scope of intentionalistic expressions. It does not give us any deeper understanding of the nature of human goals, but merely tells us how human beings come to pursue those goals. It effects theoretical systematization by focusing on the 'pushes' behind action, not the 'pulls'. But this is foreign to interpetive theorizing and does not further it in any way.

The fact that some theoretical systematization of purposive action is possible if we adopt a causal stance, serves to underscore the difficulties which beset interpretive theorizing in this field. It suggests that if we want to gain theoretical insight into human action, we should not look at the states *in* which it issues but rather at the states *from* which it issues. We should abandon the prospective way of looking at action in terms of its upshot in favour of a retrospective approach in terms of its cause. In brief, we should give up interpretive theorizing about purposive action.

7

I have tried to demonstrate how the fact that we cannot progress very much beyond the agent's own action descriptions constitutes a crucial obstacle to the theoretical understanding of purposive action. However, this is not to say that if this problem were to be solved it would be plain sailing for interpretive theorizing, but merely that this fact alone suffices to run it aground. As we noted in out initial examination of physics, the success of that discipline depends on the satisfaction of two conditions: first, the replaceability of the everyday vocabulary; secondly, the decompositional nature of physical redescriptions, a property which, of course, reflects the compositional nature of physical reality. We have now established that the first of these conditions is satisfied only to a limited degree in interpretive theorizing on purposive action. And although this demonstration is enough to show that the interpretive project is doomed to failure, I think that enough interest is attached to the second condition to make an examination of it also worthwhile. This is the case especially since the intensional property we invoked in the previous chapter to argue that everyday descriptions are not replaceable when they are true and maximally specified is a very strong one, requiring the (approximate) synonymy of substitutable expressions; so strong indeed that we might be tempted to dispense with it should it prove opportune to do so for certain purposes. Precisely one such purpose might be that of furthering a science of human action. We might fall back upon an intensionality of the same strength as that governing physical explanations, in which expressions are substitutable if their identity statement is necessarily true, although not analytically so. However, I shall now try to show that there are facts working against successful theorizing, even if we grant ourselves such licence with the strong intensionality of the action vocabulary.

The first thing to notice is that non-trivial redescription consistent with the weaker substitution constraint is only available for a minor segment of the objects of human desire. By non-trivial redescription, I mean description which goes beyond mere logical streamlining of the everyday description, one which introduces concepts that are genuinely non-synonymous with the everyday ones. Such redescription seems possible only when the objects are simple physical items or properties. Only such things possess 'real essences', fixed by their intrinsic properties as described in the vocabulary of theoretical physics, thus providing a characterization which may replace the everyday one. This kind of redescription will allow us to describe a man's desire for water as his desire for H_2O, his desire for salt as his desire for NaCl, and so on. But although the class of objects which permit of such redescription may be a central one, from the (non-theoretical) point of view of bodily survival, it is also a very narrow one. Even such a simple physical property as sweetness fails to gain admission to that class. Sweetness is not a natural kind: we do not consider it to be identical to that physical property—molecule shape, presumably—which causes experiences of sweetness in people. The observation that the sweet taste of some novel chemical compound was caused by a molecule having a different shape would not lead us to withhold the appellation of sweetness to it. And perhaps the same thing holds for all *determinate* sensory qualities, although the *determinable* ranges are identical to certain kinds of physical property. Redness is not identical to any particular bracket of electromagnetic radiation wavelengths, although it is probably true that we would refuse to call anything a colour unless it was experienced by virtue of the presence of electromagnetic radiation. Thus, even for human desires directed at simple physical objects or properties, the scope for non-trivial redescription is strictly limited.

The situation is even more hopeless when we turn to the more rarefied objectives of human endeavour. Man, after all, is not just a complicated homeostatic device, propelled by the urge to maintain his crucial physiological parameters at some stable level, and engaged only in purely physical interaction with the environment to secure this maintenance level. Man also craves such things as love, peace of mind, artistic creativity, self-determination, freedom, entertainment, and so on. And these abstracta have no 'real essences': there are no alternative, non-synonymous descriptions that might be combined with the everyday descriptions of these things in a necessarily true identity statement. Hence there are no non-trivial redescriptions that might be plugged into everyday action accounts without infringing even the weak intensionality on which we have fallen back. The only permissible kind of redescription is a trivial 'rational reconstruction' of the common-sense characterization in more precise, explicit terms. Such purely semantic touching-up can only result in marginal improvements in theoretical systematization, since it must respect most of the distinctions and discriminations made in the everyday description for fear of forfeiting its legitimacy. If the divergence between the everyday conception and its alleged scientific counterpart becomes too great, the latter cannot be admitted as a rational reconstruction of the former. A philosopher might persuade us, for instance, that to have True Freedom is to be resigned to the inevitable. But if Joe, who ranks freedom high on his list of desirables, denies that acquiescence appeals to him, we cannot override his protests and declare that this is the attitude he *really* wants to attain. Rather, we must conclude that he is not interested in True Freedom.

Moreover, even for those objects of human desire which possess a 'real essence' and for which a non-trivial, substitutable description is thus available, it is doubtful whether such substitution will issue in higher theoretical systematization. Take the desire for water and the desire for oxygen. The redescription of these objects in physical terms–as H_2O and O_2, respectively–reveals composition and structure in them and shows that the element O is present in both. This structural analysis makes for superior theoretical understanding of the chemical processes of which water and oxygen form a part. But the analysis does not transfer in any useful way when the physical description is plugged into an intentionalistic expression. The desire for H_2O is not the conjunction of a desire for hydrogen and a desire for oxygen; it does not have as a genuine component the desire for oxygen. Within the framework of an intentionalistic description, the desire for water is a unitary thing, perfectly unrelated to the desire for oxygen. No systematization by decomposition is possible. The theoretical superiority of the physical description of these objects only exists within the framework of a physiological, causal approach to action. It is lost when the description is placed inside the scope of those intentionalistic expressions that figure in interpretive accounts.

The objects of human desire thus retain most of their resistance to systematization, even if we disregard the strong intensionality of the action idiom, allowing ourselves the same degree of substitutivity as is available in physical accounts. So do the desires themselves, by the same token. We conclude that theoretical advance beyond the common-sense conception faces two obstacles in the field of purposive action. The first is the immunity of intentionalistic descriptions to replacement by other than (near-) synonymous counterparts, which, when combined with the general trustworthiness of everyday action descriptions, restricts replacement to false or incompletely specified descriptions. The second lies in the fact that, even if we dispense with the strong intensionality of the action idiom and introduce redescriptions of the objects of desire which were forbidden by the latter, the structure and interrelations between objects of desire which come to light do not carry over to the desires themselves. That structure does not exist in those things *qua* objects of conation.

8

Let us conclude by looking at a proposal for an integrative theory of purposive action that would achieve a high degree of integration despite the obstacles mentioned. The crucial idea of this proposal is that we drive the object of desire inside the agent's body. What we really desire, according to this construal, is to generate a certain condition in our own bodies. This idea can be fleshed out more fully as follows: if we look at the central nervous system (CNS) monitoring a purposive action on the model of a computer going through a routine—a conception worked out in some detail by

Miller, Galanter and Pribram in their *Plans and the Structure of Behaviour*–we realize that the CNS will occupy some 'mission accomplished'-state after having performed the last operation of that routine, which is that of checking whether the previous operations have brought about the intended upshot. Now it is possible that these terminal neural states are uniform across different routines; this is perhaps not too implausible if we look at operational sequences that are not sub-routines of larger routines, but are self-contained, being directed at upshots desired in themselves (according to the traditional interpretation). At any rate, it clearly is empirically possible that such uniformity prevails: we could construct a computer with this property. In this case, we should take the terminal neural state to be the common, ultimate goal of human action. It would seem to qualify for that status according to the characterization of goal-directedness in chapter 1, since the generation of that neural state is the common point towards which all human action gravitates. All successful action issues in this state, which hence may or indeed must be construed as the uniform, ultimate goal of human endeavour.

Notice that this theory avoids a number of pitfalls that mar other proposals which make play with neurophysiological facts. In the first place, the suggested interpretation need not embrace hedonism: it need not endorse the view that the terminal state of an action-guiding neural routine is a state of 'pleasure', and hence the view that all action aims at pleasure. This view is a common one in theorizing that attempts to marry the interpretive framework with neurophysiological fact or speculation. The classical example is Freud's early sketch of a neural interpretation of motivation, *Entwurf einer Psychologie*. Its fundamental axiom is that the CNS operates as an energy discharger. Any excitation of the CNS– endogeneous or exogeneous–will elicit a response, typically a bodily action, through which the system rids itself of this energy. This process is subjectively experienced as pleasure; indeed, it is the very physical aspect of pleasure. This kind of theorizing is vulnerable on two counts: in the first place, it falls prey to the standard objections to naive hedonism as charmingly set out by Ryle in *Concept of Mind*. Secondly, it is hurt by the dubious standing of the psycho-physical identity theory which is needed as a premise if a striving towards some neural state is to be interpreted as a striving towards pleasure. The theory sketched above stays clear of these difficulties by maintaining that the goal of action is the generation of some neural state, while refusing to apply any mentalistic description to that state.

But although it avoids these snares, we still suspect that something must have gone wrong on this proposal; and the flaw is not too far to seek. It is simply not true that our behavioural criteria for identifying goals force us to pick some such state as the uniform goal of human action, even if we grant for the sake of the argument that all successful action results in some such state. If this state were truly the goal of action, we should invariably choose the best, most certain way we knew of to bring it about. The fact is, however, that we do not. Consider the following example: some people dear to you are about to embark upon some activity which you know to involve perils of which they are ignorant; so you harbour a desperate urge to get a warning through to them, a project which faces serious practical obstacles and will most likely fail. Now suppose you are also aware that you could get your doctor to prescribe some pills that would put you in the very same neural condition that would ensue if you managed to get a warning through, the condition which, on the hypothesis examined here, is the uniform goal of all action. It is obvious that you would not consider this option for a moment, although it offers a much safer and much cheaper route to the alleged goal, but would put all your efforts into saving your loved ones from disaster. If you were successful, the same neural state would be generated; but the circumstances of its generation show that it cannot be construed as the goal of your action.

To highlight this fact, we may contrast the above case with one in which you harbour a similar fear of your beloved ones' safety, but where you recognize that fear to be perfectly irrational. In this situation, you will have no scruples about popping tranquillizers or consulting a hypnotist to get rid of this emotion. The proposal we examine here implies that all human action is really of this kind: the state normally considered as the goal is merely a means for the generation of some internal state.

The proposed interpretation of motivation reveals an interesting parallel to a kind of theorizing into which one is easily led in the theory of perception, one which was once advocated in a radical version by Russell. Seeing that perceptual awareness always coexists with some specific state of the afferent neural system (and seeing that this state is present even when no suitable external object is present), it is concluded that this neural state is the real and universal object of perception: all we ever see is part of our own brains, as Russell put it. The truth is, of course, that these neural processes are parts of the process through or by which we perceive objects external to us, not the objects of perception. In the same vein, certain states of the central nervous system are no doubt engaged when we establish that an action has been completed successfully. But these states cannot coherently be construed as the goal of action.

6

Rule accounts

1

In this chapter, we will assess the potentials of rule accounts for sustaining a theoretical treatment of human action. The kind of theorizing that will occupy us here is a narrowly specified one. In keeping with the formulation of our overall project, as decided on in chapter 5, we are looking for theories that will support rule accounts in which concepts of superior systematizing power replace everyday counterparts within the scope of intentionalistic expressions, in this case particularly the expression, 'N. N. subscribes to the rule that. . .' We can make the same point more simply by saying that we want to investigate whether or not it is possible to specify the *contents* of rules in ways surpassing the everyday mode with respect to systematizing power. Such specifications would be more general than those they supersede, allowing us to account for rule-governed action by means of fewer principles than are invoked in everyday accounts. What we hope to do is to unearth 'deep rules' of social action, a limited set of underlying principles reflected only fragmentarily in explicit common-sense codifications. These rules could then be mapped into an explanatory theory of superior integrative strength.

This reminder concerning the nature of our enquiry is apposite here, because most of the research and theorizing on rule-governed action undertaken by traditional social science—mostly under the name of 'role theory', to which we will return—has approached its subject in ways quite divergent from the one proposed here. This is increasingly the case the more such studies have aspired to going beyond mere description. Role literature abounds in detailed descriptive studies of particular rule systems as they are embodied in specific roles: the role of a policeman, a school superintendent, a physician, a psychiatrist, a college professor, and a chaplain, to mention just a few. However, whenever a more abstract, explanatory stance is adopted, it is accompanied by a change of categories. Instead of seeking more general principles in terms of which the contents of different social rules could be theoretically integrated, role theory has focused upon such issues as role conflict and its management; on socialization, that is the process through which the infant comes to master, among other things, the codes of conduct current in its social group; on the techniques of sanction brought to bear on offenders against rules; and on further such topics that are irrelevant to the kind of rule understanding we are aiming at here. These studies do not lead to a deepened insight into the contents of rules, but deal with processes at the interface between rule-governed action and other kinds of social events. The understanding they offer cannot be used to enrich rule accounts, but only to improve causal accounts; to replace, for instance, vague everyday ideas about rule learning with precise explanations in terms of operant conditioning or of the formation of a super-ego.

As we shall see in the course of the subsequent deliberations, this shift in emphasis is quite pat: there are good reasons why only little progress can be envisaged for a content-orientated rule approach. However, I do not think that these reasons had any part in shaping the actual course of rule theorizing. It merely followed a path of least resistance which led to the research interests outlined above. Hence it might be valuable to bring the obstacles to rule theorizing out into the open. This will be the objective of the present chapter.

2

As usual, we must deal with a number of preliminary issues before we can get on with our main business.

First, I would like to draw attention to the fact that an issue which loomed large in the previous chapter is much less pressing here. This issue concerned the constraints put upon theoretical redescription by our loyalty to the agents' self-descriptions. It is evident from what was said about rule-conforming conduct in chapter 1 that there would be no plausibility in pushing a counterpart to the Schützian Adequacy Postulate in the present field. The reason is that human beings may act under the guidance of rules which they are incapable of stating. And presumably the statements which they do offer could be false, since they are based upon much the same kind of evidence that is available to an observer. This is not to say that there are no constraints upon the vocabulary in which rule explicitations are expressed when we override the agent's own interpretation. Arguably, the terms of such vocabulary must satisfy the condition that the agent be capable of establishing their application or non-application to particular cases (cf. chapter 4, section 6). And perhaps further constraints may be derived from the fact that the evidence for such overriding interpretations must be wholly behavioural. But the fact remains that these constraints will be much less stringent than the one invoked in chapter 5.

The second issue has to do with the nature of the rule specifications which are to flow from rule theorizing and which are to replace the specifications occurring in everyday rule accounts. The theoretical specification is likely to diverge not merely by way of its superior generality, but also in its object. The everyday specification will often provide what we might call an *intrinsic* description of the prescribed conduct, that is, a fairly low-level description focusing on the very movements and gestures called for on a given occasion. The theoretical specification, on the other hand, will frequently refer to some outcome engendered by rule-following conduct, one which is detachable from the conduct itself (under a narrow description). An example: a trivial rule of etiquette requires you to shake hands when you meet an acquaintance. This rule specifies conduct in intrinsic, 'behavioural' terms. It would seem quite evident that under a description of this kind, such action is not open to theoretical illumination. In different parts of the world, the most diverse kinds of bodily movement count as greetings: nodding heads, shaking hands, embracing, rubbing noses, shaking clenched fists, etc. These differences are, by and large, due to historical accident and do not allow of explanation in terms of some general unified theory. Greetings and similar conduct governed by etiquette or ritual would seem to be resistant to theoretical treatment under its behavioural, intrinsic descriptions. (This chapter does not dogmatically ignore the possibility of such an approach: in section 10, I examine the prospects of a 'grammar' for the formal aspect of rule-governed action.) However, we sometimes recognize, even at the level of everyday understanding, that the accidental, conventional conduct prescribed by greeting rules hides a deeper aspect. Underneath their divergent conventional realizations, all greeting rules are recognized as having the same point: we perceive that they all order us to bring about some upshot, although this upshot is allowed to remain quite vague. In the case of greeting rules, the upshot is, very roughly, to show the other person one's respect and friendly intentions, and, more concretely, to signal that he may get on with his interactional business.

Notice, incidentally, that the abstract, non-behavioural characterization of greeting rules cannot be to the effect that they are precisely greeting rules. By calling something a greeting rule we say no more than that it is a rule prescribing what should be done in particular, well-defined situations–situations of initial contact between participants in an interaction. This says nothing about the point of the prescribed behaviour. This observation shows that the detection of 'social universals', types of rules prevalent in all societies, does not in itself constitute a theoretical advance of the kind we are seeking here. We gain no insight into the nature of the hand-shaking ritual by being told that it belongs to a class of rules found in all societies; no more so than we gain a deeper understanding of the biology of the spider *Araneus diadematus* by being told that it belongs to the class *Arachnida* which is represented on all seven continents.

Thus a theory of rule-governed action will often replace an everyday rule detailing the form of action with a counterpart specifying its outcome. I shall henceforth refer to an end state prescribed by rule as the *upshot* of the rule (thus notice that the upshot of a rule does not mean the broader consequences of adhering to it, or its function in the mechanics of social interaction; although the two things may, of course, coincide).

We now move on to another preliminary issue. If we look at rules as an overall category, we see that it falls into two classes, or perhaps better, into one precisely demarcated subclass and a residual class that is quite difficult to capture in a precise formula. The former class is that of technical rules: rules specifying the most efficient manner of bringing about some outcome. To the second group belong, first, rules for the regulation of human interaction in general, unconnected with any particular task: moral rules, rules of etiquette, certain rules of law, etc. Secondly, this latter group also encompasses rituals and ceremonies, which we may characterize as symbolic ways of doing things. I shall presently provide a more adequate characterization of non-technical rules. But first we must reflect upon technical rules and their standing in social science.

We noted in chapter 1 that technical rules have a purely factual core. Their formulations may often be seen as mere transpositions of purely factual principles into the prescriptive mode. The principles specifying the proper way, say, to prune roses, to insulate a house, or to cure a case of pneumonia, have twins of purely descriptive form expressing certain factual truths of botany, engineering, and medicine, respectively. The import of this observation, I believe, is that a social scientific discipline that wants to theorize about the contents of rules must leave technical rules out of consideration. For it would seem, to the extent that rule theory is to be a part of social science, that the rules dealt with must somehow reflect the nature of society and of man as a social animal. But technical rules reflect the nature of their subject matter. Thus the rules listed above reflect the nature of plants of the genus *Rosa*, the parameters of heat transmission from solid bodies, and physiological properties of the human body, respectively. They are parts of the sciences of botany, of engineering, and of physiology, not of social science. If a theory of rule-governed action were to occupy itself with such rules, it would acquire the status of a super-discipline encompassing all other branches of knowledge as proper sub-parts. This is hardly an attractive way to demarcate a social science sub-discipline.

Notice that technical rules are not automatically excluded on the grounds that they are not really *normative*, according to the definition presented in chapter 1. For we observed in that chapter that an agent may well adopt an attitude of commitment towards a principle which is really a general descriptive sentence in disguise. In that case, the principle counts as a rule in my sense. But it is a rule which has no birthright in a social science which tries to get a theoretical grasp upon the contents of rules.

The purging away of practical rules may not be as important in an approach to rule-governed action that is not concerned with the contents of rules. And we noted initially that traditional 'role theory' does not exhibit this concern. Many of the standard interests of role theory may well be pursued without regard of the above distinction, for instance issues concerning the learning of rules or concerning their enforcement. Still, I would maintain that, irrespective of theoretical orientation, neglect of the distinction between technical rules and their complement will issue in a subject field so heterogeneous as to leave little hope of progress in understanding. Hence it is surprising to find that this distinction is hardly ever heeded in standard expositions of role theory. To demonstrate the insouciance with which technical rules are allowed as a topic in role theory, we may quote from a standard textbook in the field.

> Many roles are imbedded within *social systems*, and the role concepts may easily be used for the analysis of complex organizations and other social forms. Most factories, for example, have a table of organization that lists the social positions of those who are its employees. Each of these positions is assigned a job to do, and each exhibits characteristic role behaviours. The roles of the various positions are specialized and interdependent. Moreover, production will often depend on the sequential performance of many complex roles. In a production line, for example, performance of several thousand roles may be necessary to generate an automobile, a vaccine, or a computer. In such a context, individuals must learn to accommodate a specialized role if they are to remain members of the organization. At the same time, even within the formal organization, roles are not wholly determined by job descriptions. . . .[1]

Even if we agree with the author's final contention, and moreover grant that the gap in determination is closed by truly societal determinants, the fact remains that reflection upon job descriptions will reveal very little about the nature of social interaction but all the more about the technology of mass production in the fields mentioned. Their inclusion within the scope of a social science investigation calls for justification beyond the fact that they may be described as 'rules' (or even 'roles'). At least such a move calls for very careful specification of those aspects of the rules (or roles) that are pertinent to social science.

It is a little more surprising to see the scant attention given to the distinction between technical and non-technical rules in a philosophically sophisticated contribution to social science methodology like Harré and Secord's *Explanation of Social Behaviour*, especially since this book outlines an approach focusing upon the contents of rules. The authors advocate the creation of a new social science discipline modelled upon ethology; they dub it *ethogeny*.[2] Ethologists try to identify the underlying patterns of instinctive behaviour in animals, especially social behaviour. Correspondingly, the proposed science of ethogeny is to extract the rules, most of them tacit, which underlie everyday social action in *homo sapiens*. That is, the proposed discipline is to deal with the content of social rules. Now, it is true that Harré and Secord single out a group of rules which corresponds roughly to my 'technical rules'; they refer to them as 'routines'. As an example of routines they mention 'the system of rules which must be followed in servicing a car'.[3] Yet they do not circumscribe this class of rules in order to dismiss it, but seem to regard it as a suitable object for the proposed science of ethogeny. But this is tantamount to glorifying any old car repair manual with the honorific title of a treatise in social science.

In the following deliberations on methodology, we shall be concerned only with those types of rule-governed action which possess proper credentials permitting inclusion in social science. We shall deal only with rules that do not just provide recipes for the technically efficient bringing-about of some end, with the exception of ends which are themselves social relationships. The rider is forced by the observation that theoretical analysis of social rules often depicts them as directed towards the creation or maintenance of certain social relationships or states (typically states of equilibrium or order). Rules suitable for safeguarding these interests could hardly fail to reflect crucial features of the conditions of societal living, and hence form a lawful part of the subject matter of social science. The qualification, 'technically efficient', is meant to prevent the formula from excluding action exploying ritualistic, symbolic ways of bringing about an end. For reasons which we will make clear presently, we want to keep rituals and ceremonies within the scope of our investigation.

Could not the undesirable rules be sequestered in another way, one, moreover, reflecting a traditional way of characterizing social action, namely, by introducing a distinction between rules of social interaction (the relevant class) and rules that do not essentially govern interaction? This formula would screen off technical rules as not essentially involving a plurality of actors. True, certain technical rules–such as those for the proper operation of a blast furnace, or for the launch of a manned space vehicle–may involve the co-ordination of the actions of several agents. But this is merely a reflection of the demanding nature of these tasks and of the physical and intellectual limitations of human beings. A person of superior bodily strength might be able to operate a blast furnace alone; a person with super-human intellectual powers might be able to launch a space vehicle single-handedly. The rules themselves, described in terms of their upshots, do not presuppose a plurality of agents.

However, a definition of this kind would be both too wide and too narrow. It would be too wide by including such rules as, for example, the rules for conducting official boxing matches. These rules are essentially rules for a two-person social episode. Still the rules (at least some of them) are clearly technically determined by the point of boxing matches: to decide which of the contestants is the better fighter. It would be too narrow, on the other hand, by excluding many ethical rules, not all of which can, in any straightforward sense, be said to govern human interaction. The maxim which says that I must not steal does not place constraints on my immediate social dealings with other people. Rather, it governs my behaviour to the extent that it may have repercussions on the interests of other people, some of whom may not yet be born at the time I contemplate the forbidden deed. As a matter of fact, moral rules may guide human conduct relating to people who are long dead. People will sometimes feel morally obliged to keep a promise given to a relative on his death bed. No interaction is involved here.

We must say a little more about the residual class which remains when technical rules have been screened away. Above, I divided that class into two roughly defined subgroups. No doubt a more fine-meshed classification would be needed for purposes other than our present ones; and perhaps that division is not exhaustive on a straightforward reading of the characterizations which I shall offer below. But I believe that even if there are types of rules that cannot be fitted into this dichotomy without some strain, the arguments to be provided will still suffice to assess their theory-generating powers. Hence the classification delivers what we ask of it in the present context. The first subgroup consists of rules with rather wide scope, regulating immediate human interaction in general, independently of the particular project engaged in by the interactants, as well as of rules regulating conduct not necessarily interactional, to the extent that it interferes with the interests of other people. Falling in (roughly) with a traditional sociological terminology, I shall refer to this subgroup as that of *mores*. We must introduce a distinction among *mores* that will become useful at a later stage. *Non-formal mores* enjoin the agent to bring about a certain end state (a certain upshot, in my terminology), or to abstain from bringing about certain other states. Moral rules belong to this group: they may oblige you to save the life of your next man if he is in danger, or to stop coveting his wife, but they do not ask you to go about the rescue in any particular way, nor do they specify any particular procedure you must follow in taking your mind off the girl. (Notice that this point holds even for deontological ethics: the rule that calls upon you to keep your promises does not prescribe any particular way in which the promised outcome is to be brought about. You may hire somebody else to do it, unless it is part of the promise that you do it yourself.) *Formal mores* involve the specification of a certain upshot, plus an indication of the way it is to be attained. The rules of the road require us to drive safely and attentively to avoid accidents. However, they do not leave it to our individual discretion to decide what conduct is most efficient to safeguard that interest, but order us to go about it in a particular way: to drive on the right side of the road; to stop at a red light; to use the turn signal when changing direction, etc. Rules of *etiquette* are also clearly formal *mores*. They qualify as *mores* because they have as their upshot the regulation of human interaction. However, in everyday affairs, their purely formal aspect is likely to be in the forefront of attention, to the near suppression of any thought of the underlying rationale. Interactants are not only supposed to act in a way that will facilitate the transaction; they are obliged to go about it by sticking to a number of fairly specific codes. Rules of etiquette diverge from the traffic code and similar rules by the nature of the connection between upshot and action: for traffic rules the connection is a causal one, whereas rules of etiquette involve symbolic ties as well. Action according to etiquette symbolizes and expresses certain attitudes in the interactants: attitudes of mutual respect and recognition.

The symbolic nature of etiquette is shared by the other main class of non-technical rules, namely, the class of ritual rules. I would characterize rituals as modal rules: rituals are ritual ways of doing things. And the ritual way is a symbolic way. As with etiquette, ritual action symbolically expresses certain attitudes in the agent, typically attitudes of deference and allegiance. Religious ritual, and the rituals surrounding birth, marriage and death, involve the symbolic manifestation of such attitudes. Still, as was also the case for etiquette, the manifestative side is by no means all there is to ritual: it often has an upshot as well (in the technical sense). And the expressive side and the upshot may be intimately linked. Take fertility rites as an example. These may be construed as religious services in which the natives pay tribute to the Powers and the order instituted by them. However, by affirming this order, the natives also assert their own position in it and the privileges it brings with it, including the right to a bountiful harvest or a successful hunt. A fertility rite is not an act of crop augmentation *cum* attitudinal display, but rather one of crop augmentation *by* attitudinal display.

Notice that to count as rules at all, in our technical sense, rituals must be obligatory, if only relative to the particular situation in which the agent finds himself, which may well be one of his own choosing. In the absence of this feature, they take on the status of mere constitutive rules, and as such are on a par with technical rules. Most activities that we commonly call rituals possess this normative aspect. Fertility rites, for instance, are not things that the native may perform or omit as he sees fit, as the modern farmer decides whether to use fertilizer; it would be utter profanity for the native to want to reap the harvest without paying tribute to the Powers of fecundity. Similarly, the ritual involved in a burial ceremony does not merely offer the participants a symbolic, conventional way of expressing their grief, but obliges them to behave in a way expressive of that emotion.

How does ritual fit into our present project which, as repeatedly stressed, is directed towards rules which may be assumed to reveal the nature of social reality and of man as a social agent? Does ritual not tie up with religious or metaphysical ideas that have to do with man's quest to understand reality, rather than having anything significant to do with his social nature? In response, I may point at a tradition in sociological thinking which asserts that (religious) ritual may possess a deeper meaning than that of which the participants are explicitly aware. I need only mention the name of Durkheim to indicate the theory I have in mind. The tie to rule theory would be provided by the suggestion that such deeper accounts of rituals, traditionally formulated within a functionalist framework, could profitably be interpreted as involving deeper-level *rules* tacitly heeded by social individuals. The latent function of ritual is to be construed as an upshot prescribed by deep rules operating far below the level of everyday consciousness. The general framework for such reinterpretation will be indicated in the following.

We have spent some time specifying the kind of behaviour with which a rule-orientated social science must deal. But it would seem that the topic of such a discipline also calls for another kind of demarcation. Several times I have stressed the point that the agent's attitude determines whether a certain principle occurring among the premises of the practical reasoning leading to an action guides him in the manner of a rule or of a merely factual principle. However, I also stated, in chapter 1, that I do not want to commit myself on the actual nature of the motivation behind rule-consonant action (i.e. action consistent with some rule but not necessarily motivated by 'respect for the rule'). This is a purely empirical issue which we cannot hope to resolve within the compass of the present study. But this stance appears to create a problem as to how the extension of the notion of rule-conforming conduct is to be fixed. And this is a problem that must be dealt with if we are to assess the prospects for a theoretical treatment of such conduct. How could we adjudicate this question without knowing, for example, whether action in accordance with ethical maxims counts as rule-conforming and hence belongs within the scope of rule-orientated social science? But in order to decide that question, we must determine whether moral rules are obeyed out of a genuine feeling of obligation or merely due to fear of repercussions. And this is precisely the kind of empirical issue on which I have refused to take a stand.

Fortunately, this problem is nullified by the observation that, first of all, in our methodological reflections, we deal with *types* of action rather than individual actions; and secondly, we must consider any type of action to be rule-conforming once certain tokens of this type are performed because of 'respect for the rule' (it follows that this mode of classification is non-exclusive: a type of action may be both purposive and rule-conforming at the same time and should therefore be treated under both headings). The latter principle is dictated by the consideration that the problems involved in dealing with an individual action in terms of a general theory have to do with the generic (typical) features of that action rather than with its unique features as a token. Hence if some type of action is *sometimes* performed out of respect for the rule, we are faced with the overall problem of devising theories to deal with this type. The frequency of tokens performed out of appropriately rule-abiding motives as compared to the frequency of tokens motivated by ulterior motives is irrelevant to this project. This upshot saves us from dependency upon detailed empirical investigation of actual motivation. For there can be little doubt that all types of social conduct which are ostensibly and officially performed out of respect for rules are indeed sometimes performed for that reason. Only extreme cynics would want to defend the position that the rules of morality, law, etiquette, etc. are always adhered to (if at all) for various less laudable reasons.

3

We cannot completely bypass the notion of a role in the present context. Traditionally, sociological theory has dealt with rule-governed behaviour under the heading of *role theory* (although, as indicated earlier, the concerns of role-theoretical research have been markedly different from those adopted here). The affinity between role theory and a theory of social rules is very close. Traditionally, a role is defined as the sum of expectations to which a person is subject, on the part of his fellows, *qua* holder of a certain position. However, not all expectations are part of something which may plausibly be called a role. Knowing that Jones is the coach of the football team, we may expect him to display emotion on the sidelines during the big game; yet this is hardly part of his role as a coach. Those coaches who make a point of appearing impassive under stress can hardly be charged with failing to live up to their roles. Thus, only the expectations that are warranted by the agent's position belong to his role *qua* occupant of that position. And the minute we include this element, we have introduced the aspect of normativity which, as I have argued, constitutes the essence of rules. The analysis of roles leads to the notion of a rule.

Role terminology might be thought to have a certain advantage over that of rules in relation to an issue previously discussed, namely, the delimitation of the scope of rule theory. For it might be suggested that the kind of rules which we want to exclude from consideration, that is, technical rules, are typically not tied to what we would call 'roles'. Although there may be rules for the proper care of garden plants, there is hardly such a thing as the role of a gardener; while there are rules for aircraft construction, there is no such thing as the role of an aircraft engineer. These are occupations or professions, not roles. However, the role terminology does not faithfully collect the kind of rules we want to examine; this is the case even if we stick to the everyday meaning of the term 'role', resisting the terminological anarchy of current role theory which, as we have seen, allows the worker's operations on the assembly line to count as a role. For instance, it is natural to talk of the role of a teacher, as well as that of a waiter, a captain, etc. All these roles involve some reference to functions and to associated technical rules of the sort we would like to exclude from a theory of rules. On other points, the role terminology is too narrow. Focusing on the notion of a role would lead to the neglect of one kind of rules in which we are keenly interested–moral rules. These apply across the board and are thus not relevant merely to persons occupying a certain position; that is, to particular roles.

Furthermore, there is a danger inherent in the role terminology. By what seems at times to be little more than the force of homonymy, talk about roles leads to the conception that role conduct is a species of acting in the theatrical sense of the term. Too often, writers on role theory can be found to move briskly on, with nothing by way of argument, from their initial endorsement of the notion of a role as a fruitful tool of sociological analysis to wholesale endorsement of the so-called 'dramaturgical' conception of social action. Social interaction is depicted as the creation of a dramatic illusion, a social mask or 'persona' behind which the social agent hides. Social commerce is an elaborately staged play in which the participants are actors and audience at the same time. Of course, there is no denying that such role-playing exists, and arguably it is much more frequent than is appreciated by the naive understanding of social life (cf chapter 4); Garfinkel and Goffman deserve eternal credit for having opened our eyes to this fact. Moreover, there is a link between rule-conforming behaviour, in my understanding of the term, and the dramaturgical conception of role playing. Many of the rules of social interaction call not only for a certain outward behaviour *vis-à-vis* one's fellows but also for an effort to mask the fact that the conduct is not spontaneous: the agent is supposed to feign a genuine concern for the other person. It remains true that this 'dramaturgical' element is not an essential part of rules and rule-following as defined in the present study. A large proportion of rule-following is not tied to any pretence of the above kind. Motorists faithfully abiding by the rules of the road are not pretending to be conscientious motorists (whatever that might involve); they *are* conscientious motorists.

The dramaturgical interpretation of rule-following conduct easily leads to a misapprehension of what is distinctive of that mode of action. Thus, in their study of social action, *Explanation of Social*

Behaviour, Harré and Secord take as the paradigm for rule-governed conduct that of an actor following a script.[4] But following a script does not display in a very clear manner that feature of normativity which I have claimed lies at the core of rule-following action. It is highly doubtful that a script is to be construed as an *ad hoc* rule governing the conduct of actors. When you read *Hamlet,* you do not think of yourself as perusing instructions to actors (remember that even the stage directions are not phrased as prescriptions but as descriptions). The way an actor playing a role is guided by the script is much closer to the way the behaviour of a hiker is guided by the trail map–which, after all, is just an iconic description of certain geographical formations–than, for example, to the way that interpersonal behaviour is constrained by moral rules.

Conceptual distinctions are relative to intellectual concerns; no distinction imposes itself upon us willy-nilly. And although I believe that crucial questions depend upon the distinction between rule-governed action and purposive action, both at the level of substantive social science and at the meta-level of methodological speculation, it would be dogmatic to assert that there is no investigation in which that distinction may be ignored. On the other hand, it would seem that the notion of rule-governed action adopted by Harré and Secord is open to the ultimate objection to a concept; namely, that it fails to achieve any partition at all; that it makes all things end up on the same side of the conceptual divide. Harré and Secord lay themselves open to this charge when they go on to construe intentions as short-term, *ad hoc* rules, as well they may once the normative aspect of rules has been done away with.[5] In this way it turns out that all intentional conduct is rule-following; the word pair, 'rule-following'/'non-rule-following' does not mark any applicable contrast at all.

I conclude that we will do well to stick to the terminology of rules rather than of roles. At any rate, analysis of the notion of a role brings to light that of a rule, as shown above. A theory of roles will perforce involve a theory of rule-following. It is just as well to go to that basic notion right away.

4

A final remark before we begin. We are about to examine theories supporting theoretically enriched rule accounts. Now as we pointed out in the previous chapter, this does not call for the accounts to be formally derivable from the theories. Such derivability is a function of the inferential strength of the theories, something quite independent of their degree of theoreticity as we understand that notion here.

The separation of the issues of systematizing power and inferential strength may be less controversial for rule-governed action than for purposive action. For there is a precedent that rule-governed conduct is handled by a particular type of weak theory, namely a theory of *competence*. A theory of competence delineates the agent's rule-following repertoire in the abstract, paying no attention to the way in which he actually uses this repertoire in actual conduct, nor to the degree to which he is successful in translating this repertoire into conduct when he decides to do so. His actual execution is likely not to be a mirror image of his abstract competence but to be marred by mistakes, sloppiness, interference from outside factors, etc. Accounting for these deviations from ideal competence, or at least some of them, is the task of a theory of *performance*. Hence a theory of competence will not allow any inference concerning what the agent will do on any concrete occasion. Nor will it license the converse inference, namely, from the performance to the competence, since I may perform a competence-governed action–utter a sentence, say– without that action springing from any competence on my part: I may simply have picked up that sentence from a phrase book. Thus, the relationship between competence theories and the conduct which they are used to explain is not one of derivability of the one from the other.

Let me make a few general remarks on the competence/ performance distinction, since we shall have to make use of it later. We may start by asking why this distinction seems to be native to rule-governed action, and *eo ipso* to human action. Why cannot a similar distinction be drawn in other fields? For is not the distinction between competence and performance, as defined above, just a special case of the distinction between an idealized theory and a lower-level empirical law for the same phenomenon? Is it not comparable with the distinction between, say, Galileo's law and some generalization about how bodies actually fall to the ground, not disregarding effects of air resistance, updrift, winds, etc.? (Granting for the moment that such a generalization could be produced at all.)

There is considerable truth in this observation. The distinction between theories of competence and theories of performance is indeed an instance of the distinction between idealized ¦theories and lower-level laws (given a realist interpretation of competence theories, for which I shall argue later). Still, theories of competence have properties which set them apart from the typical idealized theory and which explain why the competence/performance distinction has its home in the field of rule-governed action.

The crucial determinant is the normative character of the phenomena with which competence theories deal. Because rule-governed action is action subject to norms, we are invited, or indeed required, to draw up a more restricted, less inclusive ideal type in this field, that is, an ideal type encompassing fewer parameters and consequently relegating more parameters to the status of 'disturbing influences'. When drawing up idealized theories in physics, we are more or less at liberty to place the distinction between the two classes of parameters where we please: the only guidelines here are the rather soft ones of simplicity and computational manageability. However, when we are dealing with rule-governed action, there are additional constraints on model building. The chief one is to the effect that action not in accord with the model be regarded as somehow incorrect by the persons to whom the competence is ascribed, and conversely, that action must only be judged incorrect by the same persons if it is in conflict with the model. The presence of a given action in the agent's behavioural output does not automatically make room for that action in a theory explicitating his competence; nor, on the other hand, does its absence exclude it. Inclusion is decided by the agent's intuitions of the normative permissibility of his actions. The fact that the competence/performance distinction is tied up with normativity in this fashion makes it applicable only in the field of rule-conforming action.

An example from linguistics will be helpful in explaining this point. There can be no doubt that limitations on memory storage and on general information-processing capacity restrict the length of (spoken) sentences that a speaker will produce and a hearer 'take in'. These limits vary from speaker to speaker, and also depend upon the nature of the content communicated. However, let us imagine, contrary to fact, that such limitations were quite uniform among language users and quite independent of the semantic content of sentences, merely being a function of syntactic complexity. Let us assume, for instance, that the difficulties in sentence comprehension were simply measured by the number of nodes in the 'trees' used to display syntactic structure, and let us imagine that human beings could only take in spoken sentences of less than, say, twelve nodes.[6] The point is that this formally specifiable and hence quite precise limitation on sentence production and comprehension should not be accommodated in a theory of linguistic competence. For sentences transgressing the twelve-node limit would not be felt to be ill-formed, no more so than sentences which exceed our actual, less formally statable processing limitations. Thus, the uttering of such sentences would not break any linguistic rule. On the other hand, such cognitive and memory limitations would have to figure prominently in a theory of human speech performance. They would have to do so to account for the fact that human beings would never utter sentences of more than twelve nodes and that they were incapable of understanding such sentences when they were received auditively.

5

At last, we can now begin to examine the prospects for a theory of rule-conforming action, taking into account the restrictions of scope necessitated by the above deliberations. I shall go about this task by looking at a couple of concrete examples of such theorizing, criticizing them, and demonstrating that the criticism may be generalized into an argumentative strategy effective against all theories of the same overall form. The examples I adduce have not been put forth in exactly the same form in sociological literature, but rather represent extrapolations and recombinations of actual proposals.

We start by looking at a rather extreme version of rule theorizing which may be extrapolated from a recently vigorous trend in social theorizing, namely, that of *sociobiology*. This version takes its point of departure in a functionalist–evolutionist interpretation of social rules of the kind found in Hayek and others.[7] According to this position, extant human societies are the survivors of a contest of fitness which has been going on for hundreds of thousands of years. The engines of this evolutionary process are, on the one hand, a more or less random generation of different social customs and *mores* in different societies; on the other hand selectional pressures in the form of competition between neighbouring societies for scarce resources and of the individual society's struggle for survival in the face of adverse external conditions or of internal centrifugal forces. Societies with *mores* and customs of inferior efficiency as compared to those of their neighbours would be defeated and absorbed by the more vigorous societies.

This reflection upon simple mechanisms of cultural variation and selection allows us to infer that the societal norms and customs to emerge victorious from this process will be such as are attuned to the perpetuation of societal existence. The basic *mores* of extant societies will bestow a high probability of survival upon society if generally adhered to. In a Durkheimian vein, we may venture the hypothesis that the function of social rules is to organize human interaction such that the survival of society is thereby enhanced. However, this speculation takes us only a short step towards the conclusion we need. Accepting, for the sake of the argument, the above evolutionary story, what has been established is merely that the codes of current societies are such as serve *de facto* to enhance their survivability. It does not follow that social agents abide by these rules because they lead towards this upshot; that is, it does not follow that human beings obey existing social rules because such rules are recognized, however tacitly, to be the corollaries of some superior norm to which they swear allegiance (again tacitly), dictating them to adjust their behaviour to the ultimate goal of social survival. What we have so far is the formulation of a descriptive generalization concerning human action. It is not the formulation of a rule heeded in action. We need to drive this description inward, placing it within the scope of some such expression as, 'In society *S*, individuals abide by the rule that. . . .'

However, it is possible to strengthen the above tale, along lines familiar from evolutionist theory in biology, in such a way that the desired conclusion follows. In our first evolutionary narrative, we assumed that the unit of selection was society rather than its members. Societies, not social individuals, were said to compete for survival. But of course the competition between societies is also a competition between their members, since the fate of a society is also largely the fate of its members. When a society is conquered by another, the population of the vanquished society is likely to suffer decimation in the process. It is also likely to be demoted to a lowly social status where the conditions for successful reproduction are greatly impoverished: traditionally, the defeated people are enslaved by the victor. Hence, competition between societies will have a dramatic impact upon that crucial biological parameter, *differential reproduction rate*. The struggle for survival between societies is a struggle for survival between gene pools. This means that selectional pressures impinge not only on societies, but also on their members. Hence we must assume that the characteristics of the latter, too, are shaped by the evolutionary process in a direction enhancing the perpetuation of society.

One aspect of this adaptational process would be the generation of psychological tendencies in human beings which equip them for social living. At the theoretical limit–given sufficient time, and a perfectly stable social environment–this selectional process might well culminate in a human species in which functionally optimal codes were fully innate, the way they are in certain social animals, needing only a process of maturation to unfold. But given the rapidly changing socio-cultural environment in which man has his existence, the innate coding is more likely to take the form of 'learning rules'–innate tendencies which operate upon information gained through experience to produce patterns of social behaviour that are adaptive given the particular conditions (geographic, climatic, etc.) under which each individual society must reproduce itself.

If human beings were endowed with such tendencies, of whatever strength, we might express the situation by saying that man adjusts his conduct to a basic innate imperative ordering him to behave in such a manner that general adoption of that line of conduct would enhance the survivability of society. The generalizability requirement in this formulation, which suggests that human phylogeny may have anticipated Kantian ethics, reflects the biological observation that certain behavioural tendencies which are functional for the individual may be deleterious for the species. Aggressiveness towards co-specific individuals may be to the advantage of any particular member of the species, but will still tend to lower the survival chances of the species as such.

Thus the strengthened evolutionary story allows us to say not only that human beings act in accordance with social codes which are functional, but that they behave as they do because these codes are functional; that they obey these codes *as* functional. They do so in a deeply tacit manner, of course. The basic norm indicated is one which guides human action from behind the scenes and which cannot be raised to the level of explicit consciousness by mere self-reflection. It belongs to a deeply buried stratum of our psychological heritage. Hence the theory suggested introduces a third category into Merton's classical dualism of latent and manifest functions. The patterns of social interaction springing from the observance of deep rules are hardly manifestly functional: they do not possess a function which is clearly and expressly recognized by social agents. However, their function is not simply a latent one: the pattern of conduct is adopted on the basis of cognitive processes which select for functionality; processes, however, which are irretrievable by explicit consciousness. The concept for which the sociobiologist proposal carves out a place is much akin to the Freudian notion of an unconscious desire in its systematic position.

Theories of the kind outlined above will be familiar from the writings of sociobiologists. And details of the mechanisms involved in the development of adaptive patterns of social interaction have been worked out by the father of sociobiology, E. O. Wilson, in *Genes, Mind, and Culture*, a book written together with C. J. Lumsden. Central to the story is the notion of *epigenetic rules*.

Epigenetic rules are genetically fixed processes and procedures in man's cognitive make-up. They exist at several levels, according to Wilson and Lumsden, some at the superficial level of mere filters of sensory data, imposing certain structural features upon perception, others at the deeper level of secondary data processors, that is, at the level of directed thought, evaluation, and decision. Epigenetic rules shape human thought and action by affecting the likelihood that certain beliefs will be formed, or that certain tools, institutions, or norm systems will be adopted. The authors stress the fact that this influence is not one of rigid determination. Rather, epigenetic rules instill a certain drift or bias in human cognition and conation, resulting in a statistical tendency for thought and action to take a particular direction. The resulting probability distributions of action which reflect this drift are termed *bias curves* by Wilson and Lumsden.[8]

The bias curves for individual human beings are aggregated into *ethnographic curves* expressing the probability that society as a whole will exhibit a certain culture trait. Since such overall cultural patterns may possess different degrees of adaptiveness, that is, they may bestow differential genetic fitness rates upon their practitioners, they will be subject to the forces of selectional dynamics; and so will the practitioners themselves. As a consequence, those lineages whose genes fix epigenetic rules with a disposition for non-adaptive social conduct are eventually destined to extinction. Their harmful ways lead to lower reproduction rates and to their eventual disappearance from the scene. On the other hand, those whose genes guide them, through the mediation of epigenetic rules, towards selecting adaptive *mores* and customs, will be rewarded with enhanced genetic fitness. In this way, a creature is bred which is genetically adapted to the conditions of social living, his cognitive and conative apparatus informed by a number of innate structures that operate far below the level of everyday consciousness, but which are still at work shaping his most trivial everyday actions. More specifically, certain such structures govern man's normative assessments, the verdicts concerning what he must and must not do, which eventually issue in rule-conforming action. These epigenetic rules constitute a 'deep grammar' of social action, tacitly steering man towards lines of conduct that are adaptive and therefore able to safeguard the perpetuation of society.

It is interesting to note, incidentally, that the sociobiologist hypothesis extends to both kinds of rules that I have singled out for attention: those of *mores* and rituals. In an earlier book, *On Human Nature*, Wilson not only adopts the position (which may have some following even outside sociobiology) that certain moral rules, prominently the one dictating altruism, enhance inclusive genetic fitness and have therefore become encoded in human genes; he goes on to argue that the tendency to adopt certain religious rituals and practices are genetically fixed in the same way. For religious custom, too, even down to the fine detail of rituals, has repercussions upon the survival and reproduction chances of its votaries, and hence falls within the range of selectional forces.[9] Clearly, Wilson is not trying to tell us that religious liturgy is hard-wired into man and needs only a process of maturation to become actualized. He is merely proposing that the evolutionary process has instilled in man a tendency, only statistically detectable, to hang on to certain broad. kinds of ritual–those that are socially functional–once the random process of cultural innovation has brought them forth. With this theory, Wilson provides a biologico-evolutionary underpinning for views that are familiar from Durkheim, Malinowski, and others.

Let me hasten to point out that I use Wilson and Lumsden's doctrine only to throw light on the general mechanics of a functionalist–evolutionist theory of social action, not in order to indicate that they would underwrite the rule-theoretical speculation which I started out to sketch. I rather doubt that Wilson and Lumsden would endorse the radical view that not only various lower-level functional codes have become wired into the human intellectual apparatus, but that this has happened to the very maxim of functionality itself. True, there are certain hints that they embrace some such position. They remark, for example, (*Genes, Mind, and Culture,* p. 346) that 'the limbic system. . . serves as an "on-board" computer for assessing the ultimate genetic adaptiveness of contemplated actions', a statement that would seem to imply that the limbic system assesses action against the maxim that man must act in a way which will maximize the survival chances of the species, and hence aid the perpetuation of society. However, this may just be a sloppy formulation; at any rate, in the list of epigenetic rules in chapters 2 and 3 of *Genes, Mind, and Culture*, no such principle is included. The authors cite such low-level functional tendencies as the aversion to incest, tribalism, xenophobia, and a few others, to which may be added those of altruism, of dichotomization of objects into the sacred and the profane, hierarchical dominance systems, and a handful more mentioned by Wilson in *On Human Nature*. But the functionalist principle itself is not accorded the status of an epigenetic rule. I suspect that Wilson and Lumsden's reasons for refusing to construe it in this way are related to those which I shall introduce in a moment.

To repeat briefly, the theory, the merits of which we shall now assess, goes as follows: due to a process of gene-culture interaction which has been going on throughout the history of the human species, a general tendency has become genetically encoded in man to think and behave in ways that are conducive to the perpetuation of society. This tendency manifests itself in all departments of cognition and action; more specifically, it holds for the thought processes which control rule-conforming action. In this realm the epigenetic 'rules' may be construed as rules proper, that is, principles which motivate action via feelings of obligation or about 'what you are supposed to do'. We may interpret these facts to mean that rule-conforming action derives from a single basic norm to the effect that human beings must act in a way which will maximize the likelihood of survival of human society. This maxim promotes systematic integration of rule-conforming action by serving as a basic principle from which concrete social rules can be seen to follow as corollaries. For certain codes the derivation is obvious: the principle of altruism, the ban upon incest, the special obligations towards children, etc.; for others it may require more ingenuity.[10] But the suggestion is that eventually they can all be traced back to this fundamental maxim.

6

In the following, I shall try to show that the theory flowing from the above speculation cannot be sustained, involving as it does, a presupposition about man's innate cognitive endowment that is wildly implausible. Our speculation can only be upheld if we ascribe to man an immensely powerful innate theory regarding the possible forms of human society, a theory which allows him to generate a model of the particular society in which he lives on the basis of a very scant data.

The cognitive apparatus to be posited would be modelled upon that hypothesized by Noam Chomsky to account for the human infant's ability to acquire language. Chomsky argues–quite convincingly, to my mind–that the standard empiricist theories of learning cannot allow for the fact that human beings acquire the ability to utter and understand a potentially infinite class of sentences on the basis of a very small and somewhat degenerate body of data. There is no way that standard inductive procedures will permit the leap from that body of data to the model of language which the infant eventually constructs, in the form of a tacit, internalized grammar of the language. Nor will the process of random theory generation and testing do the trick, since the likelihood that the learner will hit upon the right theory, or one close enough to get an approximative process going, is effectively zero. We must conceive of the human infant as being 'wired' to learn language, that is, as being in possession of a general theory of the basic structure of language which drastically cuts down the possible models (grammars) that may be construed to fit any given body of linguistic data. The innate theory forms the basis of a strong abductive heuristic in language learning.

Now if we take human action to be governed by the fundamental epigenetic rule of functionality, obeyed in a deeply tacit manner, we must take man to be capable of a similar cognitive feat in the realm of social reality. To know which conduct is functional and which is dysfunctional, the agent must possess, however tacitly, a model of the society in which he carries on his business. That model will be generated on the basis of quite minimal and random data compatible with an indefinite number of models, unless strong constraints are placed upon model construction. These constraints are supplied by the general theory of social reality which specifies the possible forms of human society, and which hence allows agents to employ a strong abductive procedure in constructing a social model.

I believe that the assumption of such a cognitive mechanism is grossly implausible, and I shall make clear in a moment why this is the case. But first I shall use the affinity between the above speculation and the mechanism of language learning to deflect a couple of too simple-minded objections. In the first place, this hypothesis does not imply that we would all be capable of generating profound theorems about social reality on the basis of mere introspection: the sociological knowledge posited will be as resistant to explicitation through simple phenomenological methods as the rules of generative grammar. Secondly, there is the objection that dysfunctional conduct is rampant in today's societies as well as in those on historical record, a fact that would seem to disprove the hypothesis that man has the cognitive power, whether tacit or explicit, to discern dysfunctional conduct when he sees it. However, the tie to language learning suggests that dysfunctionality may be handled the way that ungrammatical material is handled by linguistic theory, which explains it as the result of interfering factors of various kinds and treats it in a theory of performance. The assumption that social agents possess a model of the society in which they live is clearly a theory of competence, and is thus not immediately falsified by performance data. One major factor serving to make performance fall short of competence lies on the conative side, in the form of countervailing motivations which tempt the agent to deviate from the narrow path of functional conduct. (There is no reason, of course, why we should take the hypothesized basic norm of human conduct to be incapable of being overpowered by egotistical desires and other strong impulses.)

Also, reflection on the linguistic analogy should stifle the objection that a cognitive mechanism of the required power just cannot be held as an innate possession. Equally, it defuses the objection that the alleged mechanism is not properly sensitive to information about the functionality of conduct collected through normal channels: people's spontaneous moral intuitions are often quite resistant to the demonstration that the preferred line of conduct leads to detrimental results if generally adhered to; although they may be able to override this intuition in the light of explicit reasoning. However, the information contained in an internalized grammar is equally insulated against information recorded in other, higher strata of the cognitive system. If it were at some time to be agreed by speakers that negation is henceforth to be placed in initial position in declarative sentences, this ruling would not immediately produce a linguistic intuition that sentences with the old word order were ill-formed; and the tendency to produce sentences according to the old pattern would be ever-present and could only be suppressed by a conscious effort.

A scruple of an altogether different kind might be the query as to why the rule theorist is saddled with a learning theory at all? After all, what he claims is merely that human beings abide by some tacit general rule to the effect that collectively dysfunctional conduct is to be avoided. Why must he take a stand on the question of the source of the information needed to apply this maxim? And if he must, what prevents him from simply pointing to such miscellaneous sources as offer themselves to the alert citizen, not excluding the reading of sociological tracts, newspaper editorials, political pamphlets, etc.? Why can the agent not be allowed to pick up the information needed through such standard channels as he goes along?

The trouble with this suggestion is that the basic social norms are quite firmly established in human beings at a fairly early stage of their childhood, a stage in which the information about the workings of society at large, which has been imparted to the child through traditional channels, is quite minimal. Hence it will be perfectly innocent of the information needed as premises for the practical reasoning leading to its adoption of lower-level rules of conduct as corollaries of the basic norm. Moreover, it is fairly obvious that the average adult is not in a much better position: his knowledge of social reality, as obtained in recognized ways, is typically quite exiguous and cannot account for the fixity of his moral opinions and the strength of his intuitions about normative matters in general. To insist that social codes are built on the basis of this kind of information would be like suggesting that first languages are learned from explicit instruction. The only way to salvage the hypothesis that human action is governed by some tacit basic norm prescribing functional conduct, is by stipulating a strong, tacit, genetically based theory to supply the needed factual premises. I shall now argue that there is a powerful reason for refusing to attribute to man a cognitive capacity of the suggested type.

It is hard to see how a process of random mutation and selection could ever have succeeded in generating a cognitive mechanism of the required power. Biological adaptation is a very slow process, requiring hundreds if not thousands of generations to bring about a major adaptive innovation.[11] Moreover, adaptation, even at this slow rate, will take place only in a fairly stable environment. Only selectional pressures operating in a consistent and unchanging manner will succeed in bringing about a functional adaptation. Constantly changing environmental conditions, and hence shifting selectional pressures, will fail to produce any unambiguous adaptive trend at all. However, the human environment clearly does not exhibit this stability. One crucial component of that environment, namely, the socio-cultural one, undergoes changes that are very rapid compared to the pace of biological selection. And the rapidity of societal change shows an accelerating tendency. Today profound changes in technology, political organization, etc. may take place within the lifetime of a single individual. In other words: the instruments of biological selection lag helplessly behind, leaving the human species no chance of evolving biological adaptations suiting it to its rapidly changing life circumstances. This holds for the suggested cognitive apparatus as a special case. How could *homo sapiens* ever have developed a genetically transmitted innate theory of social reality when some of the parameters which would have to be featured in such a theory have only emerged during the last couple of generations? How could an innate, tacit theory of 'social mechanics' be general enough to enable human beings to frame an integral model of modern 'information society', when many of the characteristic features of that society represent something completely novel in the history of the species? You might with more propriety have expected man to grow aerials for the direct reception of television broadcasts during the same span of time.

But maybe the rule theorist's grand hypothesis does not presuppose that human beings possess a cognitive apparatus attuned to *modern* society? Maybe he could get by on the assumption that human beings possess a cognitive apparatus attuned to the structure of human societies of early prehistoric times? There is little doubt that *homo sapiens* spent enough time within the very simple and very stable organizational structures prevalent in hunter-gatherer bands to adapt his cognitive anatomy to their functional needs.[12] If such a cognitive apparatus were granted, a relic in man's cognitive make-up, could the rule theorist not stick to his position that human conduct is indeed governed by the basic norm of functionality, assisted by a cognitive system determining what kinds of actions are conducive to social survival; adding only that the latter system is woefully inadequate? We cannot infer from the shortcomings of this system that man does not heed the basic norm after all; no more so than we may infer from a man's failure to implement his stated goal that he did not strive for that goal after all, if his failure were due to lack of knowledge concerning how to go about it.

This reasoning may appear attractive at first glance. However, I doubt whether it will meet success when we are dealing with a *tacit* theory and a *tacit* norm system of the kind involved here. To decide whether a person's failure to execute his declared intentions is due to a lack of resolve or to a lack of the required factual information, we may interrogate him for that information and, if we find it insufficient, supply him with the needed data. Continued failure must then be blamed on a lack of genuine intention. However, as pointed out in a previous paragraph, we must construe the alleged tacit cognitive structure as being insulated against information received through conscious channels. That means that we cannot expect information explicitly imparted to the agent about the dysfunctionality of his conduct to have any direct impact upon his spontaneous normative intuitions, as generated by that structure, and hence upon his conduct to the extent that it is controlled by these intuitions. This circumstance makes the assumption that man is tacitly governed by the maxim of social functionality, but fails to implement it due to a systematic shortage of relevant data, a perfectly vacuous one. It has become indistinguishable in its testable consequences from the hypothesis that man is not governed by some such general maxim. This is as much as to say that we cannot make proper sense of the former assumption.

7

We have arrived at a negative verdict on the question of the feasibility of a particular kind of rule theory, a theory extrapolating a line of thought encountered in sociobiology. However, this theory is admittedly an extreme one by virtue of the esoteric facts that have to be known for the basic epigenetic norm to be applied. Could it not be that action is governed by another kind of tacit norm that has equally broad scope as the functionality maxim, but which utilizes information that is readily available?

A cue for such a theory might be obtained from the re-interpretation of functionalist explanation in social science proposed by Philippe van Parijs in his article, 'Functional Explanation and the Linguistic Analogy'.[13] Van Parijs insists that if the power of functional explanations–of the form 'item i exists because it has the function F'–is to be salvaged, they must be strengthened *inter alia* by a premise to the effect, roughly, that i is embedded in a context C such that when i would produce F in that context, i will come to exist. Van Parijs observes that a premise to this effect may legitimately be assumed for functional explanations in biology: evolutionist theory puts at our disposal a general premise to the effect that a given species exposed to selectional pressures will tend to maximize its adaptedness to its current environment, within the constraints of its genetical flexibility (this is evidently a rough tendency statement which calls for numerous *ceteris paribus* clauses). Van Parijs goes on to observe that a similar mechanism of selection and adaptation has often been postulated for social systems, since societies with dysfunctional institutions and *mores* are thought to suffer a higher risk of dying out or breaking up than societies with functional institutions, this leading in the long run to a situation in which only highly functional societies prevail. Van Parijs rejects this proposal, on the grounds that there is no evidence of differential mortality rates of societies as a function of the nature of their institutions. He adds that the adaptive shaping of social institutions seems to be a process operating only within societies, determining the fortunes of social classes, organizations, etc.[14]

Instead, van Parijs invites us to conceive of the selectional mechanism as involving processes of reinforcement, primarily negative. Human beings tend to abandon modes of interaction and organization which lead to stresses and strains in social commerce, as a simple result of the aversive stimulation received. This is not a conscious process: it is, we may assume, as 'automatic' as the process through which the ratio of multi-syllabic words is raised in speakers' verbal outputs through a clever reinforcement regimen.

Van Parijs uses an example from linguistics to illustrate his point. The so-called functional approach in diacronic linguistics maintains that many features of language are to be understood in the light of the 'function' of language, which is communication. This holds for instance for the tendency towards maximum differentiation in the vowel system. If the vowels of a language are mapped into the phonological space defined by the two dimensions of open/closed and forward/back, it will transpire that the vowels employed are maximally spaced, in this way minimizing the risk of incorrect identification. The principle is most clearly seen to operate in cases of pronunciation change. If, in some initial state of maximum vowel differentiation, a phoneme moves away from its original position on the phonetic map, overcrowding will ensue in the region towards which it moves: the vowels in this area are now too close in phonetic value to be reliably distinguished. This creates a pressure on the original occupants of this area, serving to make them move further away in order to maintain differentiation. The mechanism of this adaptive process, according to van Parijs, is a largely unconscious one of negative reinforcement. A speaker who fails to adjust his phonological structure to re-establish differentiation is likely to be penalised by frequent misunderstandings of his linguistic output due to the phonetic proximity of the vowels. Such misunderstandings serve as aversive stimuli which prompt him to modify his pronunciation habits.

If we give a twist to van Parijs' position, it can be adapted to the rule framework. We break the association between reinforcement and the notions of reward and punishment which make reinforced action more naturally construable as purposive action (in the technical sense), and simply record the purely observational fact that certain experiences lead to a modification of rule-conforming behaviour, the modification being invariably pointed in the direction of minimizing stress and discomfort in social interaction.

We then interpret this tendency as the reflection of an implicit basic norm of social interaction to the effect that human beings must behave in a way facilitating social interaction. That is to say, we interpret the tendency as responding to *normative* pressures upon action. The ensuing rule does not make any extravagant demands upon man's cognitive powers: the stresses and strains are immediately felt and do not require a sophisticated innate theory for their detection.

So the proposal before us now is that rule-conforming action is ultimately derived from a basic norm requiring human beings to secure the smooth running of social interaction. This is the yardstick against which human customs and *mores* are constantly measured, and revised or rejected if they do not pass muster. If we now map the structure of this norm system into a theory of rule-conforming action, we get a theory very high in systematizing power. All its theorems will flow from the basic axiom that people subscribe to a norm directing them to facilitate interaction (which is of course not to imply that this norm will always prevail in the face of opposing urges). The rule is again a tacit one, shaping conduct from way below the level of everyday consciousness.

How should we adjudicate the credentials of this theory? Before we answer this question, we must first become clear about the strength of that property of hierarchical ordering which a rule system must display in order to be mapped into a strongly integrative explanatory theory. It is not enough that the lower-level norms which may be extracted from isolated segments of action are logically derivable from some common basic maxim, given additional premises detailing local conditions. The lower-level norms must actually be derived from the superordinate norm by the agent; that is, he must subscribe to the lower-level norms because he sees their connection with the more universal principle, if only implicitly. The logical ties between higher- and lower-level principles must map the channels through which the motivational forces travel downward from the superior norms, as it were. If these ties have no psychological reality, reference to the superordinate principle will fail to explain the agent's adherence to the lower-level rules, and hence to explain the actions flowing from them.

If this requirement be thought to be overly stringent, we can only reply that without it, the theoretical enterprise becomes too easy: its success will be secured in advance, but a success as empty as it is effortless. It only takes a little logical handiwork to achieve integration of the weaker kind. Suppose Mr N. N. subscribes to a rule bidding him to secure upshot (type) A under conditions a, and to a rule bidding him to bring about upshot (type) B under conditions b. We may now frame a more inclusive concept of a type of upshot C which is defined by the disjunction of the characteristics of A and B, and proceed to ascribe to Mr N. N. a more general maxim enjoining him to bring about upshots of type C. Indeed, utilizing this recipe, we could define a predicate which captures in a disjunctive specification the defining terms of all the upshots dictated by commonly recognized rules of action; this predicate would permit the explanation of all human rule-conforming action by means of one principle. But there is no guarantee that such a principle will have any psychological reality; no guarantee, that is, that agents actually derive their commitment to more specialized rules from this universal principle.[15]

The minute we spell out the assumptions to which rule theorizing commits us in this way, we realize that the hypothesis under examination is contradicted by ample commonplace experience as well as by recent empirical research. Let us start by noting that *mores* (on which we shall focus here) are not learned in an axiomatic way. During socialization, the child will pick up the relevant codes of conduct in a piecemeal and unsystematic fashion, entirely dependent upon the contingencies of disciplining and instruction to which it is subjected, and upon the influence of peer group pressures to which it is exposed. This much seems to be generally agreed upon by pedagogues and developmental psychologists, despite lingering disagreement concerning the mechanisms responsible for the acquisition of rule-conforming conduct.

However, this observation does not refute the hypothesis of a basic norm, since this hypothesis may be taken to assert that the hierarchical ordering of normative principles is something that is introduced at a later stage in the individual's psychological development, the result of a critical sifting of the norms to which he has been exposed during socialization. According to the hypothesis we examine here, the maxim of interaction facilitation operates upon a body of already existing rule-conforming action, as we will recall. That maxim does not in itself generate suggestions for ways to realize the prescribed upshot, but simply measures existing codes against that upshot. It is a normative filter, not a generator. (In this, there is a strong parallel to Wilson and Lumsden's proposal for a mechanism of gene-culture translation: the epigenetic rules are not taken to provide an effective procedure for generating functional *mores*, but only for assessing already existing customs in this respect. See, and compare, *Genes, Mind, and Culture*, chapter 4.)

The two-stage conception of norm generation which flows from this picture would mesh quite well with the most carefully worked-out theory of rule acquisition–more specifically, moral norm acquisition–that is available today, namely that put forth by Lawrence Kohlberg.[16] Kohlberg divides the evolution of normative thinking and action in the individual into three main stages. Of these, the first is really a pre-moral (and even a pre-normative) stage, in which the child obeys the precepts imposed by authority figures and by peers for purely prudential reasons: to avoid punishment, or to earn rewards and favours. This leaves us with two main stages of moral development proper, each, however, divided into sub-stages which need not detain us here. Suffice it to say that at the *first* of the two stages (that which Kohlberg dubs the conventional level), the child is guided by unquestioning commitment to the code in force in its family, peer group, or other circle of 'significant others'. Behaviour is guided by submission to authority and to fixed rules. Thus at this stage, we find the initial pre-rational adoption of moral codes that is presupposed by a theory which takes the superior norms to be filters applied to an already existing body of rule-conforming conduct. At the *second* of the two moral stages–in a strict sense only at the second and final sub-stage of this stage–a post-conventional, autonomous morality of universal principles arises. At this stage, the individual subjects the structure of received norms to the solvent of critical thought. Lower-level rules of action are examined and assessed in the light of higher principles. The cutting edge of the process is provided by the three notions of universality, comprehensiveness, and consistency.

If we take this process to be a tacit one, at least in part–which I believe that Kohlberg would be loath to accept, but which may still be closer to the truth than his own view–we get a story which is quite close to what is required by the proposed rule theory, based upon van Parijs' reinterpretation of functionalism.

I brought Kohlberg's doctrine into the picture because it is highly favourable to rule theory, suggesting that, contrary to appearances, the norm system governing human action has an underlying hierarchical, deductive structure which may be mapped directly into a highly integrative theory of rule-conforming action. Now, as was to be expected, Kohlberg's views have not remained unassailed; as it happens, many of the empirical studies which that proposal has generated seem to indicate that the pattern of moral development in man is neither as neatly segmented nor as universal as claimed by Kohlberg.[17] However, to give rule theory the benefit of the doubt–doubt, that is, concerning detailed empirical questions that are still quite undecided–I shall bypass all such objections. Instead, I shall argue that even if we accept Kohlberg's picture, closer scrutiny of its fine detail will show that it does not really support the proposed rule theory; rather the opposite, as a matter of fact.

In the first place, Kohlberg's theory does not state that at the final stage of moral development, systematization of moral judgements is achieved by tracing them all back to some basic rule of a substantive nature. Rather, what subjects strive for is merely *consistency* within the received norms which they have internalized, subject to certain purely formal constraints of which the most important one is that of universality (Kohlberg is clearly influenced by Hare's meta-ethics on this point). In other words, moral subjects try to establish a cognitive equilibrium in the structure of their moral intuitions, which is not the same as criticizing that structure in the light of some basic maxim imported from the outside. Securing internal consistency is much less than establishing hierarchical ordering and deductiveness: the former is compatible with the existence of a plethora of distinct moral principles, unrelated by deductive ties.

Secondly, one of Kohlberg's most clearcut empirical findings is the fact that a large proportion of human beings will never attain the third and final main stage of moral development, namely, that of an autonomous, post-conventional ethic. They will never embark upon the painful and arduous task of reflecting critically upon their own moral system, but will cleave to a path of least resistance, accepting without question the norms that were inculcated in them during childhood, with all their inconsistencies and irrationalities. Kohlberg's research indicates that only 25 per cent of humankind will ever reach the stage of a truly principled, autonomous morality.[18] The remaining 75 per cent are stuck with a conventional morality, a hodgepodge of unrelated or even inconsistent maxims.

Remember that the charge that this structure is a hodgepodge would not be refuted by the mere possiblity of subsuming the various specific norms adhered to under a common basic maxim. For such ordering can always be trivially accomplished, as we have seen. To deflect the charge, the ordering must be shown to be psychologically real, that is, the agent must subscribe to the subordinate norms because he subscribes to the superordinate ones and realizes, perhaps only tacitly, that the former are corollaries of the latter. If this condition is not satisfied, the more universal principles are explanatorily irrelevant to the lower-level principles and to the action to which they give rise. Thus, it will not help the rule theorist to object that conventional morality is, after all, not quite the unsystematic mosaic it was made out to be, but may be set out in a handful of simple maxims. Our concern here is explanatory theorizing, not normative reflection. And the obstacle we point to is the loose manner in which social agents' ethical competences are coupled. This is a comment upon the nature of agents' cognitive and conative make-up, not upon the rule system in the abstract.

We may add as a third point the observation that the above objections merely dealt with moral rules, and that other types of norms may be expected to be even less susceptible to theoretical systematization. As we have seen, the scope of such systematization is determined by the extent to which individuals subject the low-level rule intuitions, which have been instilled in them in a piecemeal fashion, to criticism in the light of higher-order principles. In the case of morals, there is considerable cognitive pressure towards such integration; although, if Kohlberg is to be trusted, this activity is only engaged in by a minority of human agents. But clearly the pressure is much weaker in the case of etiquette and other minor systems of *mores*. In the first place, matters of etiquette are much less urgent, which makes the question of consistency and system less urgent as well. As a matter of fact, in the case of etiquette, there is a tendency for people not to progress beyond unthinking obedience to the purely conventional forms dictated, failing entirely to glimpse the underlying rationale of rules of etiquette. Rules of etiquette are adhered to in a highly piecemeal fashion; if any evidence is needed for that contention, it is readily available in the fact that allegiance to such rules is quite resistant to critical reasoning appealing to higher principles. You may agree intellectually that some paragraph in the book of good manners is outdated or reflects a reactionary social philosophy, sexism, racism, or what have you, but still not be able to rid yourself of a gut intuition that this is somehow the right way to conduct yourself. Old ways die hard in the realm of etiquette. (Thus, the fact that etiquette was claimed on p. 238 to have a common ultimate upshot, namely, that of facilitating interaction, in terms of which it would seem to permit systematization, does not constitute an objection to what was just said. For that upshot may safely be taken to have little to do with the grounds for our actual adherence to this or that rule of etiquette, even when we are dimly aware of it.)

The above reflections can be applied to any kind of rule theory which focuses upon the upshot dictated by rules; they do not exploit any special feature of our most recent proposal for a rule theory based upon van Parijs' reinterpretation of functionalism. For that matter, they do not even presuppose a naturalistic conception of man or society, but are effective also against theories based upon the assumption that deep-level rules have been inscribed in the human mind by an omnipotent creator. Any theory asserting that rule-conforming conduct derives from a single deep rule, or a limited number of rules, must contend with the fact that in the psychological anatomy of most of us, rules exist as fairly insulated items. Man's rule-following competence for *mores* is a loose structure of insulated codes learned in a piecemeal fashion and never subsequently integrated into a unity.

Let me repeat that this observation is not contradicted by the fact that it would perhaps be possible to organize the maxims governing a person's conduct into a fairly parsimonious structure of hierarchical form; not even by the fact that when a person is called upon to justify his lower-level principles, he will readily appeal to higher norms from which the former are said to follow. The logical interrelationships thereby demonstrated need not correspond to any cognitive interrelations in the agent's competence structure; put more plainly, they need not reflect his actual reasons for sticking with the low-level rules. But these are the connections we require if we want to obtain a deeper *explanation* of the agent's rule-conforming conduct. The purely logical connections between the rules he swears allegiance to, or even between the ones he may adduce to rationalize his conduct, cannot provide explanation unless they form part of the actual cognitive–conative pedigree of the conduct. To point this out is simply to reiterate our general remarks on explanation and causality in chapter 3.

This reflection suggests that a scientific analysis of rule-conforming conduct, concerned with the content of rules, might actually produce a picture that is less integrative than the everyday version. In day-to-day affairs, we often mistake our own and other people's rationalizations of their rule-governed actions in terms of higher principles for the actual motivational dynamics of those actions. Scientific investigation of the actual motivations at play would reveal the mistake, in the process shattering the neatly organized hierarchy of rationalizing accounts, replacing it by a loosely-knit structure of mutually insulated low-level norms obeyed in a piecemeal fashion.

8

It is time to try a completely different tack. In the preceding discussion, we made frequent reference to grammar as a paradigm rule system. We used grammar and the process of language acquisition as a model for epigenetic rules and for the way they work to shape behaviour. This should have prepared the ground for the proposal that we use grammar as a paradigm in a much more substantive sense. Might there not be a 'grammar of social action', a set of rules related to social action in a way formally analogous to the way that grammatical rules are related to language acts?

How would such a project avoid the difficulties that beset the programme we have just criticized? In the previous discussion, we investigated the prospects for a theory of rule-conforming action concerned with what I termed the *upshot* of rules, in a somewhat technical sense, namely, the end state which rules dictate that we bring about. Grammatical rules, however, do not have an upshot; they do not oblige us to bring about some outcome detachable from the act of speaking or writing. They are *formal* rules, specifying conditions of well-formedness for a certain class of actions, but involving no prescriptions for the result of those actions. So I would propose that we abandon the search for a theory generalizing on the point of social rules and start looking instead for similarities at the formal level. The hopes which we may place on a theory of this form derive further fuel from a glance at the development which linguistics itself has undergone during the last couple of decades, a development that has been hailed as the introduction of genuine theorizing into that discipline. I refer, of course, to the 'Chomskyan Revolution' in linguistics. The following investigation of the potentials of a formal theory of rule-conforming action will use Chomskyan Transformational Grammar (hereafter TG) as its paradigm. This choice is natural not only in the light of the play made with Chomskyan linguistics in preceding sections, but also because many social scientists who have drawn on the analogy of linguistics have used TG as their model.

Let me provide a very brief sketch of TG to serve as a foil for the following deliberations. We may start by looking at the feature which most strongly sets TG apart from traditional structural grammar, namely, its *generative* aspect. It would appear that the notion of generation is used in two different, but related senses in Chomskyan linguistics.

In the primary sense of the word, generation (or 'generativeness') refers to a property of grammars considered as software, that is, as purely abstract sets of formulae. A grammar thus conceived generates the sentences of a language in much the same way that a mathematical formula generates numbers; the grammar is simply a mathematical model of the class of well-formed sentences of that language. According to Chomsky, generativeness in this sense constitutes the first and most obvious adequacy condition on grammars. To have any interest, a grammar for a natural language must at least be capable of generating all the sentences of that language, plus their associated structural descriptions.

The second way in which a grammar may generate a sentence, or a language, is by being realized in a physical medium, typically of course human nerve tissue, and contributing to the causal production of actual sentences. There is a certain ambiguity in the transformational grammarians' attitude to the question of whether the grammars proposed have a model in the speaker's mind (or brain). Since that question is crucial for the use of TG as a model for theory building in social science, we must treat of it at some length here.

It is natural to focus on the problem as it is manifested in the work of the major transformational grammarian, Noam Chomsky. I believe we can discern a certain development in Chomsky's position on the present issue. In *Syntactic Structures*, his seminal early work, Chomsky was only concerned with generation in the formal, mathematical sense. The chief point he wanted to make was that a fairly rich formal structure was needed to generate every sentence of English (the point was thought to hold for other natural languages as well); a structure considerably richer than was commonly supposed by mathematical linguists. Generation of sentences as a psychological process was not touched upon at all, apart from a brief paragraph disclaiming any connection between generative grammar and actual procedures of sentence production and comprehension.[19] However, in *Aspects of the Theory of Syntax*, causal generation enters the picture. Two lines of thought converge to necessitate its introduction. In the first place, Chomsky now views generative grammars as models of the speaker's *knowledge* of his language.[20] To construe them in this fashion is already to go beyond the minimal idea of a grammar as a mere mathematical model of the well-formed sentences of the language. For unless by 'knowledge' Chomsky simply means *what* is known, this word must be taken to refer to a concrete state or structure in the speaker possessing such knowledge. This conception is accompanied by that of a causal generation of linguistic output. For if this cognitive structure does not figure somewhere on the causal chain issuing in speech acts, the knowledge of language does not enter into the speaking (and understanding) of language at all: clearly a *reductio* of the assumption. And Chomsky indeed declares in *Aspects* that 'No doubt, a reasonable model of language use will incorporate, as a basic component, the generative grammar that expresses the speaker–hearer's knowledge of the language. . . .'[21] In the second place, we find a further line of thought in *Aspects* that will eventually mature into a full recognition of causal generation, although Chomsky does not seem to have appreciated its implications entirely at this stage. Chomsky introduces a distinction between grammars which are descriptively adequate *vis-à-vis* some particular language, and grammars which are explanatorily adequate (*Aspects*, Chpt. 1 §§4 and 6). Actually, the distinction is drawn not for grammars but for linguistic theories, that is, theories specifying the general form of grammars of natural languages. But the distinction transfers smoothly to the level of grammars.) Now if we aspire to developing theories that *explain* the form of linguistic output, we are forced to adopt a discriminatory attitude towards grammars that are descriptively equivalent–those which generate the same corpus of sentences: in keeping with any plausible construal of explanation, there cannot be a plurality of explanations of one and the same phenomenon based upon mutually incompatible premises. Thus the striving for explanatory adequacy forces us to ask which grammar is the 'true' or 'real' one. In *Aspects*, Chomsky seems to believe that we can answer this question by broadening the scope of our investigation: we construct a general theory of grammar detailing the common basic features of all languages. This theory will constrain the construction of grammars for particular languages by requiring that they be consonant with its overall principles; ideally, it will enable us to select the better grammar, relative to a given body of data, out of any two grammars proposed for some language. It follows from this characterization that such a theory of grammar may be taken as a model of the speech-acquisition device of human beings; and this is indeed how Chomsky sees it.[22] Still, it is not clear at this stage whether Chomsky has fully realized that the import of giving preferential treatment to one particular grammar out of a class with equal generative powers, attributing explanatory power to it, is a commitment to the assumption that that grammar is somehow realized in the speaker's mind (or brain). Suspicion on this count springs from the observation that Chomsky seems to consider only input–output data relevant to the choice, that is, data concerning sentences produced by speakers (including their interpretations of those sentences) supplemented only by further equally 'peripheral' data, such as data concerning the learnability of languages. But if by an 'explanatorily adequate grammar' we simply mean a grammar which is selected by our general theory of grammar in the light of such data, we cannot ascribe any more psychological reality to the preferred grammar than to any other grammar with the same generative power. I would agree with such critics as Quine[23] and Schwartz[24] that if we evaluate grammars only on the basis of their relationship to the corpus generated, then all grammars stand on an equal footing once they satisfy the basic requirement that they will generate all and only the sentences of the language. We may prefer one grammar over another because of its formal simplicity and elegance; because it is easy to work with; or because it is easy to handle with some current computer programme, thus facilitating work in machine translation. But this does not make that grammar more 'real' than its competitors. The status of different grammars here is equivalent to that of alternative ways of axiomatizing mathematics, or logic: we may consider one formalization superior to another on grounds of simplicity and compactness. But such considerations provide no warrant for declaring one axiomatization more 'real' than another. And the idea of explanation does not enter at this level at all.

Only in *Reflections on Language* does Chomsky fully take the step towards a realist interpretation of TG, and hence towards recognition of the idea of causal generation. In a rejoinder to Quine's and Schwartz's criticisms, Chomsky makes it clear that we may have to resort to an examination of the 'black box', that is, the neural structure which realizes the agent's competence, in order to select the grammar which actually governs his language.[25] And in later works–compare, for instance, *Rules and Representations*– Chomsky stresses time and again that the processes postulated by

TG are explanatory theoretical posits kin to the posits of natural science: linguistics is a branch of cognitive psychology, aimed at exploring the basic features of a certain human power, namely that of language use. The items which this theory postulates are as real as the postulates of theoretical physics.[26] This interpretation brings us to the notion which we wanted to establish, namely that of the causal generation of sentences by a grammar realized in the speaker's neural circuitry; because the postulated grammar can only serve to explain the form of the speaker's output if it is somehow causally coupled to that output.

How is the above sketch of Chomsky's position to be squared with his frequent insistence that TG does not provide a model of actual speech production but only of the

> knowledge of the language that provides the basis for actual use of language of a speaker–hearer. . . . When we say that a sentence has a certain derivation with respect to a particular grammar, we say nothing about how the speaker or hearer might proceed, in some practical or efficient way, to construct such a derivation. These questions belong to the theory of language use–the theory of performance.[27]

True, the sentence immediately following this passage is the one quoted on p. 269, where Chomsky seems to accept that a model of performance must include as a component a model of competence. However, he goes on to modify this with the remark that the generative grammar thus embedded 'does not, in itself, prescribe the character or functioning of a perceptual model or a model of speech production'.

The two may be reconciled if we appreciate that there are two distinct oppositions to be heeded in a proper statement of TG. One, which we have just laboured, is that between a grammar, realistically interpreted (i.e. as a structure in the speaker–hearer's cognitive anatomy), and a grammar as a purely formal, mathematical model. We might well express this as the contrast between the speaker's competence, realistically interpreted, and a mathematical model of what he knows. But that contrast must not be conflated with that between a speaker's competence (realistically construed) and his performance in using that competence. Even if we adopt a realist conception of competence, it is still true to say, with Chomsky, that a theory of competence is not a theory of performance. We discussed the difference between the two kinds of theory in a previous passage and need not repeat it here.

On the other hand, we must admit that the minute we interpret competence theories realistically, the relationship between theories of competence and theories of performance becomes very intimate. The overarching question in this area—whether competence structures are involved in performance at all—is no longer to be considered an open one to be decided empirically: it is settled ahead of time in the light of general methodological reflections. For if we picture competence as being in no way involved in performance, not even as something from which performance derives through a series of simplifying shortcuts, the use of fixed constructions, etc., we have no reason to believe that there is such a thing as competence at all, construed realistically. Competence is, after all, a theoretical posit, as Chomsky insists in his later works; it is postulated only because it appears to be needed to account for the facts of language use. But if we can explain these facts in terms of a performance theory which at no stage makes play with the competence structure, the latter must fall prey to Occam's razor: it is theoretically superfluous and should be done away with. The linguist who maintains that there is such a thing as a realistically conceived competence structure that plays no part in actual speech production or comprehension would be in the position of a nuclear chemist who declared that there are such things as electron shells, needed to explain (*inter alia*) the chemical 'competence' of substances (i.e. the valencies), adding, however, that these structures had nothing to do with the actual chemical bonding of atoms; this was said to be the product of an entirely different mechanism.

The observations on the relationship between competence and performance theories make this an appropriate place to issue a *caveat* concerning the following reflections on TG as a model for social science. Such reflections are perforce based upon current formulations of TG. This choice does not indicate that I consider TGs, in their current form, to represent the final word in linguistic theory. On the contrary, I suspect that TG may be in for comprehensive revision; and in particular I suspect that such revision will be prompted by the necessity of accommodating performance data: current research on speech production is not entirely favourable to existing versions of TG.[28] However, when discussing the suitability of TG as a methodological paradigm for social science, we have no other choice than to deal with TG as it exists today. We cannot base our discussion upon speculations about future versions which will probably be more consonant with performance data. Besides, it is quite obvious that this policy will not commit an injustice towards TG, since the property of transformational linguistics I shall focus upon in the following is so deep-seated that it will certainly be found in any future version deserving the name.

Let us now turn to a more substantive feature of TG, the one which has exerted such a strong fascination upon scientists from other fields. As mentioned, in *Syntactic Structures*, Chomsky tried to assess the logical power of the mathematical structure required to generate the sentences of English. He examined a couple of well-defined algorithms for their adequacy as models of that language. His conclusion was to the effect that the simplest structure tested, a so-called finite state grammar, was grossly inadequate in generative capacity. As for the second, somewhat more sophisticated structure (a phrase structure grammar), Chomsky concluded that it does not fall short of generative adequacy in the gross way a finite state grammar does, but that it can still only be used for the description and generation of English (and other natural languages) at the cost of great inelegancy.

To do justice to linguistic fact, Chomsky proposes a two-tiered device. It consists, first, of a set of base rules which are of a fairly simple form: in fact, they constitute a simple phrase structure grammar. These rules generate a class of *base strings*, each associated with a structural description termed a *base phrase marker*. The base strings and their phrase markers are the input to the second level of rules, the transformational rules. These rules map base strings, or sets of such strings, into other strings plus associated phrase markers; several such transformations may be applied in sequence. The resulting derived strings plus their phrase markers are then fed into the morphophonemic component which assigns to them a phonetic shape, thus turning them into full-dress sentences.

This sketch, of course, offers only the barest outline of the structure of transformational grammar. It is limited to the purely syntactic aspect of TG, bypassing the vexing question of the place of semantics within TG which currently occupies linguists. It suffices, however, to indicate that aspect of TG which has had particular appeal to social scientists, and which has made TG seem such a promising paradigm. It suggests that underneath the familiar phenomenal aspect of rule-conforming action, as captured in everyday codifications, there is a level of 'deep rules' of which the former are only the surface manifestations. These 'deep rules' are inevitably assimilated to unconscious, 'deep' motives of the kind uncovered by psychoanalysis; the esoteric true forces behind the familiar face of social action. The hope is that a 'depth grammar' of social reality might unearth similar secrets and thus give us an insight into the true ground-level dynamics of social action. By concerning itself with the *form* of action, this approach would side-step the strictures passed on a theory generalizing on the upshot of rule-conforming conduct.

9

I shall now try to demonstrate that whereas TG may be a useful model for social theorizing in other respects, it fails to qualify formally as a model for a rule-orientated social science, as far as its distinctive properties are concerned. The fact is that TG does not actually specify deeper rules of language, in addition to those captured in traditional structural grammars. The 'deep-structural rules' of TG–the base rules and transformational rules–are not norms against which linguistic output is measured; nor is anything else. Hence they are not rules in our present sense of that term. I shall now try to show that this is indeed the case.

Base rules and transformational rules are the principles of a recursive device the output of which is all and only the sentences of a given language. We found generation to be of two kinds, formal and causal. In the following we shall look at the two kinds of generation in turn, in an attempt to decide whether or not the principles governing the generative device qualify as rules of linguistic behaviour.

The first sense in which a grammar may be said to generate a corpus of sentences was analogous to that in which a mathematical formula can be said to generate a class of numbers. It is obvious, I think, that a grammar with sufficient logical power to generate in this sense the sentences of some language L will still not impose any additional rules upon speakers of L; if only for the reason that an infinite number of alternative grammars would possess the same generative capacity. None of these grammars can be assigned a preferential status; hence none of them can be taken to impose upon speakers the obligation that they generate their linguistic output in accordance with this particular grammar. Grammars, in the present sense, are purely formal devices for the economical, systematic description of linguistic data. They have no normative implications whatever; no prescription may be inferred from them.

The other sense of 'generation' applies to a hardware system which realizes some abstract grammar, and which is causally involved in the production of sentences. For this kind of grammar, the above argument, which appeals to an *embarras de richesse*, does not apply: there is one and only one grammar that is realized in an individual agent's neural circuitry. Does, then, the grammar which is thus realized impose any rules upon the use of linguistic forms? Do the principles of sentence generation which are actually embodied in human speech production—if only via the simplifications of a performance procedure—amount to a set of prescriptions for well-formed speech behind the surface rules recorded in traditional categorial grammars?

The answer again must be no. The grammar which has a hardware model in the human cognitive apparatus must be construed as simply an (idealized and partial) description of the workings of that apparatus. It does not impose any additional rules upon the linguistic ouput.

As an initial suggestion that this is the case, we may reflect upon the fact that no sin is perpetrated against the rules of grammar by a tourist mouthing a sentence in a language foreign to him, a sentence he has not construed himself according to the generative principles of grammar, but simply looked up in a phrase book and learned by heart. As long as the surface form of that sentence is all right, the tourist has given grammar all that is due to it. The pedigree of the sentence does not matter at all. Indeed, this example simply represents an extreme and unusual case of the simplification which is involved in much language performance, an extreme that is approximated in native speakers of the language only by such standard phrases as, 'thank you', 'how are you?', etc.; these are presumably generated as unstructured chunks.

However, this argument will inevitably elicit the rejoinder that it neglects the creative aspect of language, the fact that a native speaker of the language knows a potential infinitude of sentences. This unbounded capacity cannot be simulated by an (finite) device which learns sentences by heart as unstructured units. It was indeed reflection upon this fact which led linguists to postulate a recursive device to model linguistic competence. Thus, the normative force of the rules specified by TG resides in the fact that only if a person's linguistic output is generated in accordance with these rules will he be able to produce well-formed sentences over the entire infinite range which makes up his language. Any finite part of this general competence may be simulated by a simple storage device. Yet such a device must necessarily be inferior in generative power to a mature speaker of natural language. Thus, we appreciate the normative force of TG the minute we shift attention from the particular sentence, or any finite class of sentences, to the infinite class of possible sentences known by the native speaker; as the rule-theorist might argue.

This reasoning would perhaps be acceptable if there were only one way to generate the infinite corpus which makes up a natural language. But it is necessarily true that this is not the case. Once we have some algorithm that will generate the corpus, an infinite number of other algorithms with the same generative power may immediately be constructed, for example by adding paired introduction–deletion rules or other devices which effect a change at one point only to undo it later. Such empty epicycles may be added to the system *ad libitum*.

To illustrate this point in a concrete manner, we may consider an individual, let us call him Norman, who is the member of an English-speaking community. Norman is completely proficient in the local tongue, that is, his verbal output is such that everybody in the community will recognize it as quite acceptable. Still, Norman is different from the others: he does not generate his linguistic output the way other people do. The base component of his language-producing faculty produces strings which are all in the *passive* voice, whereas those of the normal speaker are all in the active voice (if TG is to be trusted on this matter). Norman brings himself in line with the majority by applying a device unique to him, an *Active Transformation*, to the greater part of his base strings (the exceptions are those strings which are allowed to be manifested in passive sentences). This transformation is the converse of that which, in normal speakers, takes base strings in the active into corresponding strings in the passive. It guarantees Norman a sentence-generating competence of exactly the same power as that of standard speakers.

Now it is obvious that, were his secret revealed to the community, Norman could not be censured for breaking any linguistic rules. As long as his linguistic output was indistinguishable from that of a normal speaker—as will clearly be the case—no charge of linguistic impropriety could be levelled against him. His situation would be much like that of a left-handed person who generates his written output in a non-standard way (his spoken output too, as a matter of fact: his speech is controlled by his *right* cerebral hemisphere). Now it is true that southpaws have traditionally been regarded as fit objects of censure, and that generations of schoolmasters have spent their best efforts in bringing such deviants into line with the rest of us. Still nobody in his right mind would ever suggest that the trouble with southpaws is that they infringe *linguistic* rules; that they sin against language in a manner parallel to someone who gets his inflections wrong. As far as linguistics is concerned, the left-handed person's peculiarities are purely factual matters of speech production, subject to no rules. In the same way, TG, in its distinctive properties, is a purely descriptive discipline with no normative implications at all. TG does not explicitate any rules over and above those specified in traditional categorial grammar.

We conclude that TG does not qualify as a paradigm for a rule-orientated social science, as far as its most distinctive feature is concerned: that is, its postulation of 'deep rules'. To the extent that transformational grammar is an explanatory theory at all, it is a branch of cognitive psychology, specifying the structure and capacity of a cognitive mechanism somehow involved in the production and comprehension of language. And this is indeed the way its creator, Noam Chomsky, views it today.[29] The explanations which can be derived from TG are causal ones, when written out in full. A social scientific discipline based upon TG would not be a rule theory of the kind we are concerned with here.

10

We have spent some time discussing TG as a model for rule-orientated theorizing in social science, because this doctrine enjoys considerable prestige in the sciences of human action and has had some impact here, if thus far primarily on terminology. Talk of 'deep structures' and of 'transformations' is a frequent stylistic embellishment, especially in the writings of social anthropologists. Our concern with TG arose out of the assumption that it imposes additional constraints upon the form of sentences, beyond those recorded in traditional categorial grammars. We were forced to conclude that this assumption was erroneous. There are several routes one could take from here. We could stick with TG as a model for social theorizing, while fully acknowledging that it is a cognitive theory. That is, we might use it to suggest possible lines of research into the cognitive processes which generate social action. This, we may mention in passing, is the approach adopted by Lévi-Strauss (in one of his doctrinal phases and according to one possible interpretation of his endeavours). Lévi-Strauss apparently considers himself to be engaged in the examination of deep cognitive structures which are manifested in certain patterns of human conduct and social organization: the narration of myths, the structure of kinship systems, etc.

However, this avenue is closed to us. As previously indicated, this approach, if blessed with success, would not produce interpretive theorizing. We need to move in another direction. The decision to examine TG was a move within the overall project of using grammar as a paradigm for a theory of rule-conforming action, focusing upon the form of action rather than its outcome. The demonstration that TG is not really relevant to this concern does not mean that this project cannot succeed. It may be able to find other guiding stars within the realm of linguistics; indeed, traditional categorial grammar is well suited for this purpose. Categorial grammars impose rules upon speakers which govern the form of their linguistic output. And clearly these rules, as formulated by theoretical linguistics, extend far beyond anything consciously entertained by everyday speakers. We may be allowed to nourish hopes of finding something similar for non-linguistic rule-governed action.

Below, I shall offer a few brief remarks upon the outlook for a social science seeking a paradigm in grammar. Let me begin by specifying what we imply, minimally, when we declare a sector of action to be governed by a 'grammar'. In the first place, we imply that actions in that sector can be segmented, in a non-arbitrary manner, into minimal structurally recognized elements. These are the 'words' (or 'morphemes') of that type of action. Secondly, we imply that some anatomically and physically possible sequences of these minimal structural units are classified as ill-formed: a grammar for a certain type of action must effect a partitioning into well-formed and ill-formed actions. Thirdly, we must have a type of description, not 'grammatical' itself, of the actions in the well-formed class such that when this description is fixed, it will single out a limited number of actions which are tied to it by a relation which we might call 'expressing'. In the case of language, the independent description is, of course, one which provides the meaning of the language act. What we are trying to capture here is the idea that grammatical form is a reflection of a deeper property of linguistic material, namely its content, and that this feature must have a counterpart in any system of rules to be dubbed appropriately as a 'grammar'.

Thus, the task before us is to assess the possibility that the application of this conceptual framework to rule-conforming action in general will bring to light formal constraints upon action which are 'deeper' than those embodied in everyday understanding: that it will unearth formal rules of wider scope than those ordinarily recognized and from which the everyday codes may be derived as corollaries.

As a preliminary, we may briefly recapitulate the types of rules which impose formal constraints upon action, as outlined on pp. 237–8. First, there is what I termed *formal mores*. These dictate an upshot of a certain kind, within the general area of the protection of human interests and the facilitation of human interaction, but direct us to observe certain forms in trying to bring it about. Traffic rules are examples of formal *mores*, as are rules of etiquette. Secondly, there are rules of ritual, which I characterized as symbolic ways of doing things, in the zero case simply expressing an attitude or emotion. By laying down the details of the symbolic manifestation, rituals count as formal rules.

Everyday understanding of action clearly embodies insight into rules of these kinds: we are all capable of citing rough explications of such rule systems. The rule theorist's hope is that these explications are merely the tip of the iceberg, hiding a deeply submerged part governing action in a tacit manner. To place ourselves in a position to decide whether this hope can be warranted, let us reflect upon the fact that if formal *mores* and rituals, in their rough-and-ready everyday codifications, are the manifestations of rules with much wider scope, then action governed by such rules must be projectible beyond everyday codifications. That is to say, it must be possible on the basis of knowledge of etiquette in one area, or knowledge of one isolated ritual, to determine the well-formedness of actions governed by other codes of etiquette or ritual. It must be the case that a person who is conversant with formal *mores* or ritual in one corner of social life will develop clear intuitions as to the well-formedness of action in other corners, provided that he is given the 'vocabulary' of those rules–the minimal action segments recognized by the latter. This is not to say that there must be unrestricted projectibility of rule-conforming action; that the 'grammar' elicited from one '*mos*' or ritual will govern all *mores* or rituals. But if the 'grammar' envisaged is to have wider scope than everyday rule codifications, and is to explain the latter, it must at least be projectible to *some* other type of action than that in which it was first picked up.

The agent must also develop intuitions of a more specialized kind: given a knowledge of the 'vocabulary' of a rule system otherwise unfamiliar to him, and given information about the content of a particular action within the scope of that system, the agent must be capable of deciding which sequences of actions 'express' this content, or even of specifying such sequences in advance. This is parallel to the way in which the native speaker will be capable of expressing new 'meanings' (propositions) in his language, given that he is supplied with the required vocabulary.

I think it is patently clear that neither of these powers is engendered in human beings who have been exposed to action governed by non-linguistic formal rules. If it be thought somewhat dogmatic to pronounce in this manner upon an issue which is, after all, an empirical one, without a firm basis in extensive research, I may defend my position by pointing to the way in which the linguist typically goes about his business. He relies on his own intuition as to the well-formedness of sentences and does not normally test a proposed rule of grammar through massive sampling of statistical data. The theoretical justification of this procedure lies in the consideration that the linguistic ability of a mature speaker is the product of a strong abductive mechanism which imposes its form upon the grammar adopted and which may be presumed to be identical in all mankind. To find large-scale differences here would be as surprising as to find radical differences in the way human beings digest their food. Now if the envisaged formal rules which govern non-linguistic action are strongly projectible, they must issue from a similar learning mechanism, which in turn must be presumed to be found in identical form in all of mankind. This mechanism will produce isomorphic rule systems in all agents, rendering the intuitions of well-formedness delivered by any single system generally valid. Thus, I presume to deem my findings of general import when I detect in myself no ability to project those rules of etiquette or ritual with which I am familiar. Nor do I find myself capable of generating creatively the outward form of a hypothetical ritual of which I am given the symbolic meaning, even if I am familiar with the 'vocabulary' of that ritual. There is no counterpart here to my ability to generate sentences in a language of which I know the grammar.

It is true, of course, that we are often capable of drawing *some* line between 'well-formed' and 'ill-formed' elements of ritual, relative to a specification of the symbolic content of the ritual. There are certain activities that may be *de rigueur* in a fraternity initiation ceremony, for instance, but which we know in advance would be quite improper as part of a church service. But this capacity does not reflect any 'deep' rules but merely simple everyday norms of decorum which everyone can produce on a moment's reflection. Moreover, this capacity does not enable us to generate in advance a liturgy expressing a given symbolic meaning, but only imposes certain very general conditions upon such a liturgy. The maxim that one must not engage in drunkenness or obscenity during a church service does not prescribe the precise form of this ritual.

A somewhat similar point holds for formal *mores*. Some of these—such as traffic rules—possess a certain projectibility. Anyone who reflects upon the conditions of safe road traffic will know in advance that there must be particularly stringent rules governing traffic in intersections and will be able to predict the general form of such rules: quite abstractly, the rules must establish a principle of precedence for traffic entering from different directions. However, this projectibility lacks the precision of that which follows from a 'grammar'. The form which it imposes upon traffic is utterly abstract and may be realized in an indefinite number of actual arrangements. It is worlds apart from the way that a precisely and fully specified semantic content will fix one or a few grammatical realizations.

The rule theorist might try to resist this entire reasoning by suggesting that it trades upon a conflation of the notion of projectibility and of what we might call *strong learnability*. To say that a rule is strongly learnable is to say that a human being will develop a 'knowledge' of that rule—if only in the form of a tacit competence—upon very slight exposure to action performed in accordance with it; more precisely, upon exposure that does not justify the assumption that the rule holds according to standard inductive procedures. Projectibility, the rule theorist would admit, is a property of any wide-scope rule system: after all, to say that a rule has wide scope is to say no more than that one and the same formula applies to a wide range of cases, and hence that the formula that is found to hold for one case will hold for the other cases as well; and this is precisely what we mean when we say that a rule is projectible. The feature of strong learnability, on the other hand, the feature that subjects are capable of *learning* general rules on the basis of minimal rule experience in a narrow segment of cases, is an exotic property that does not hold generally; or so the rule theorist might argue.

However, the issue of learnability is a red herring and does not better the rule theorist's position one bit. The rule theorist wants to invoke deep rules to explain social conduct. For such reference to be explanatory, it must be the case that the agents know the rules, however tacitly. But if they know them, they must also be able to decide what the rules dictate when applied to situations not yet encountered. This, after all, is what a tacit grasp of a (wide-scope) rule consists in. To declare that the agent knows the rule and then add that he still cannot determine what the rule prescribes on any novel occasion is to affirm and deny the same thing in one breath. It does not matter how the subject came by the rule in the first place, whether by simple induction or by some innate abductive procedure. Once he has such knowledge, it must be manifested in the ability to project the rule. The rule theorist's rejoinder really amounts to the observation that a general rule may in some sense be *valid* for a wide range of cases, without the agents' being in a position to know this in advance of encountering each new case. This description makes sense and happens to be true for cases, such as law codes, where rules are valid if they are enacted by some authoritative body which need not make its stipulations public. But, in addition to the obvious point that the tacit rules governing action are not created in this fashion, we must insist that rules which exist only in the form of codifications in statute books cannot serve to *explain* action: only rules that are known may do that. And rules that are known are *eo ipso* projectible. But we have found projectibility to be non-existent outside language.

Semantic accounts

1

In this chapter I examine the possibility of providing theoretical accounts of human action in terms of the notion of semantic meaning, the kind of meaning proper to languages. But at the outset the reader should be reminded of the restriction we put upon the scope of our investigation in chapter 1. We want to investigate the theory-sustaining power of semantic meaning outside the realm of language as it is commonly understood, that is, as referring to a spoken or written means of communication. We will also exclude action involving such recognized minor semiotic systems as semaphore, traffic signals, the football umpire's gesture language, and so on. These belong to the domain of linguistics and semiology, not to that of social science. As a basis for our enquiry we accept for the sake of the argument, that semantic theorizing is indeed possible for language in its traditional sense. Our task is to decide whether similar theorizing is possible for action outside this realm.

We shall look at two different ways in which a theory of human action would be, or would involve, a theory of semantic meaning. (1) The first way would follow from a demonstration that ostensibly non-semantic action does actually possess meaning of the very same kind as that possessed by spoken or written language. This would allow the construction of semantic theories for such action. (If such theories could be devised, they would show that certain types of apparently non-semantic action are semantic after all. Hence the need arises here for a technical term to mark the distinction between what is currently understood to be semantic action, and action which is now taken to be non-semantic but for which a semantic theory can actually be devised. I shall employ the subscript$_1$ to terms referring to action of the first kind, and the subscript$_2$ to terms signifying action of the second kind. That is, I shall talk about 'semantic$_1$ action' when I want to refer to acts of speaking and writing, and about 'semantic$_2$ action' when I refer to action outside this field to which semantic concepts may turn out to be applicable. I extend this neologism in an obvious manner to related terms, such as 'language', 'linguistic', 'meaning', 'utterance', etc. Whenever these terms are used without subscript, the distinction between the subscripted versions is neutralized, or the intended reference to either of them is evident from the context.) (2) The second way in which a theory of meaning could be shown to be, or be a component of, a theory of action would be through the demonstration that (to put it very crudely at first) the meaning of an action is a function of the linguistic$_1$ description assigned to it. If it could be shown that the meaning of action (here in the sense of, 'correct intentionalistic description of action') is somehow a product of the stock of linguistic$_1$ descriptions available to the agent, this would indicate that a full understanding of social action is only possible via the grasp of a semantic theory for the language spoken by the agent.

Let me remove any remaining danger of misconstruing the project outlined by emphasizing that we shall deal with affinities between semantic$_1$ and (ostensibly) non-semantic action only at the level of meaning. We shall bypass all other aspects of language$_1$ which have at one time or another supplied models for social theorizing: phonology (which is the main inspiration behind structuralist approaches to sociology and anthropology) and syntax (which, especially in its recent, transformational versions, has been looked to as a possible model by certain social scientists, and which we dealt with briefly in the previous chapter for that very reason). Our topic is precisely and narrowly that of examining suggestions to the effect that semantic meaning is embedded in non-semantic$_1$ action, and of examining to what extent this creates a foothold for semantic theorizing in the latter field.

Let me anticipate the conclusion towards which our investigation will lead us; this, I believe, will strengthen the reader's grip on the argument in a manner outweighing the resulting loss of suspense. I want to argue, concerning (1) above, that it is not tenable after all to ascribe a semantic content to non-linguistic$_1$ action; in other words, the notion of semantic$_2$ action has no extension. As for (2), I shall claim that the ties between non-semantic action and semantic$_1$ meaning are not tight enough to allow us to say that a semantic$_1$ theory is a part or component of any theory of non-semantic action.

2

Let us start out by briefly recapitulating the definitions of the semantic notions that will occupy us in this chapter. As set out in chapter 1, they were the following:

Speaker's meaning (meaning$_s$): S means that p in doing h iff
(1) S performs h, and
(2) intends (intention$_1$) that S's performance of h produce in A the belief that S is committed to it being the case that p, and
(3) intends (intention$_2$) that intention$_1$ be recognized by A and serve at least as part of A's reason for taking S to be committed to it being the case that p, and
(4) intention$_2$ is an iteratively public intention.

The notion of speaker's meaning, which is roughly equivalent to Grice's concept of non-natural meaning, is intended to capture a basic and primitive type of meaning which is independent of the existence of a conventional vehicle of communication, and which can be used to analyse the notion of convention-based meaning. (The definition provided pertains to constative meaning only, but can be easily modified to accommodate other illocutionary modes. We shall omit that exercise here.)

Sentence meaning (meaning$_x$) : x means that p in a group of people G iff it is a convention in G that members of G produce x only if they intend thereby to generate, in the manner specified in the definition of speaker's meaning, a belief in some audience that the utterer is committed to it being the case that p.

(This definition, too, may easily be extended to cover non-constative sentences.)

> *Saying*: S says that p in uttering the sentence x iff
> (1) S utters x
> (2) x is a sentence in S's language such that x means$_x$ that p in that language
> (3) S means$_s$ that p
> (4) S intends that the intention involved in (3) be grasped by the audience at least in part by virtue of their knowledge of the conventions of S's language.

Let me repeat the warning in chapter 1 that these are skeleton definitions only; much flesh must be put on these bones before they can be deemed satisfactory. Here I only provide such detail as is required by our present concerns, plus the additional filling needed for an intelligible presentation.

So far, we have only looked at the speech act aspect of meaning. But in chapter 1 we decided to understand by the term 'semantic meaning' a species of meaning having a vehicle of expression which satisfies certain formal conditions, namely, those of unboundedness, of compositeness, and of scrutability. By imposing these conditions, we screen away communicative systems for which only a trivial kind of semantics can be provided, one that at any rate does not go beyond the speaker's explicit grasp. To acquire a better understanding of these notions, we shall now examine how they are accommodated in recent theories of semantics for natural languages. This examination will serve a further purpose as well: it shows us what a theory of meaning looks like, thus giving us an idea of what we are asking when we enquire as to whether theories of meaning can be developed for non-linguistic$_1$ action.

The relevance for our current project of an examination of semantic theories for natural languages reflects our realization (see chapter 1, pp. 54–55) that it is only *qua* embodying a semantic *system* that semantic action calls for separate treatment. Or, to put it in Saussurean terms, it is only semantic action as manifesting a *langue* that lays claim to our attention; as mere *parole*, it is of no interest. The reason was given in chapter 1: *parole*, the sum total of communicative acts that are performed in some language, is not likely to present opportunities for theorizing significantly different from those presented by the parent classes of purposive and rule-conforming action. Put very crudely, a theory of *parole* is concerned with answering the following primary question, What do people say?, and with such subsidiary questions as, When do they say it? To whom do they say it? For what ultimate purpose?, etc. Given the analysis of semantic meaning just provided, this main question is a question concerning the communicative effect speakers seek to produce in their audiences. But, with the qualification noted on p. 36, these effects are likely to reflect the speaker's projects in life in general: if we disregard the restriction of communicative intentions to effects in the human sphere and look at their detailed contents, we see that they represent a cross-section of human goals and rule-dictated upshots in general. To assess whether *parole* is amenable to theorizing, we would only have to repeat the reasoning employed in chapters 5 and 6.

What is the form of a semantic theory, a theory of meaning in the dimension of *langue*? Quite generally, a semantic theory assigns to every well-formed symbol string of the object language a specification of its meaning, or meanings. This is what is minimally required to satisfy the criterion of success which should be imposed upon the exercise, namely that the theory is to model the native speaker's semantic competence. What is the structure of such a theory in more detailed terms? Here we are in the unfortunate situation that there is no generally accepted theory that might be pointed to as a paradigm. Indeed, there is even lack of agreement as to the proper form of such a theory among linguists (and philosophers). Moreover, to my knowledge, there has only been one attempt on the part of linguists to devise an overall theory of semantics aimed at living up to the criterion of adequacy mentioned, that is, a theory which tries to map out everything a native speaker knows about the interpretation of his language. This is the theory first sketched by Katz and Fodor, further developed by Katz and Postal in a classical work, and later expounded by Katz in a number of writings.[1]

In a nutshell, Katz–Postal (hereafter KP) semantics consists basically of two elements, a dictionary and a set of projection rules.

The dictionary lists the meaning, or meanings, of each of the lexical elements of the language. It is indeed quite similar to an ordinary college dictionary; however, instead of indicating the meaning of an entry in colloquial terms, it employs theoretical terms, so-called 'semantic markers' which are more precisely specified than everyday terms. These semantic markers allow of a uniform characterization of every lexical item of the object language and are furthermore thought to have universal application among natural languages. The projection rules specify how the meanings of larger semantic structures–sentences and sub-sentential expressions– derive from the meanings of lexical items when inserted into grammatical structures generated by the syntactic component of the grammar, and how the meanings of compound sentences are a function of the meanings of component sentences.

This capsule account is not enough, of course, to do justice to KP semantics. However, I shall not explore this theme any further, since KP semantics suffers from a crucial flaw which philosophers have been quick to point out:[2] it explicates the meaning of one language by translating it into another. In the dictionary, it aligns atomic expressions of the object language with expressions in a theoretical meta-language. Its projection rules tell us how to construct complex meta-language counterparts to every complex object–language expression. In this way, the theory fails to anchor the object language in any extra-linguistic reality: it only indicates which sentences in the meta-language translate which object language sentences. Moreover, the theory does not tell us in what linguistic meaning or linguistic understanding consists. If you know which English sentences translate which French sentences, you have a useful bit of knowledge (especially if you know English); but you do not know the first thing about what it means for one sentence to translate another. Indeed, you have no idea what it means for a sentence to have a meaning. KP semantics is particularly inadequate when conceived as a model of a speaker's semantic competence, since it seems to imply that semantic competence consists in the ability to translate one's native language into another language. This doctrine is either capricious, if the same treatment is not given to the semantics of the other language, or leads to an infinite regress if it is.

One way to progress beyond Katz–Postal—style semantics is by means of a transformation which may appear very slight. Instead of listing, that is, mentioning, the expressions of the meta-language which translate object language expressions, the former expressions should be *used*. More precisely, they should be used to indicate the truth conditions of the object language expressions, thus taking us outside the realm of signs and grounding semantics in the world.

To get an idea of what such a theory might look like, we must leave current linguistic theorizing and turn instead to the philosophy of language. The above proposal for a theory of meaning is not embodied in any linguistic theory that I know of but can only be found in a philosophical theory of meaning, namely that developed by Donald Davidson. Put very briefly, the basic technical trick of Davidson's theory is that of turning a Tarski-style truth theory for formal languages upside-down and extending its range to natural languages. Where Tarski's theory takes a notion of translation as an undefined primitive and constructs a recursive definition of truth in terms of it, Davidson's project takes a notion of truth and the related concept of satisfaction for granted and proceeds to characterize meaning in terms thereof. A Tarskian truth-theory, thus transformed, for a language L, is a recursive structure licensing inference, for every well-formed sentential string S_i of L, of a bi-conditional of the form, 'S_i is true iff p', where p is replaceable by a sentence of the meta-language.[3] To take the celebrated example of such bi-conditionals (so-called T-sentences), a meaning-theory for English would imply *inter alia* the theorem, ' "Snow is white" is true iff snow is white.'

The above specimen of a T-sentence may appear a bit trivial. This is in part to be blamed on the fact that the meta-language here is identical to the object language. The air of vacuousness would vanish if the object language were, say, Danish, or Swahili. However, even a homophonic (or homographic) meaning theory of the general form proposed by Davidson is really non-trivial, for a reason that is not apparent from reflection on single theorems derivable from it. By tracing the manner in which each T-sentence is derived from the axioms, the theory demonstrates how the meaning of composite linguistic structures is built up from the meanings of simpler units as inserted into semantically relevant syntactic form. By so doing, the theory accommodates and explains the three crucial features of language which we singled out as especially important, namely, those of unboundedness, compositeness, and scrutability. The way the theory does this (put very crudely) is by reading the familiar structure of quantificational logic into the object language. Thus the unboundedness, compositeness, and scrutability of the object language are shown fundamentally to be the unboundedness, compositeness and scrutability of quantificational logic. Quantificational logic is shown to be the true 'deep structure' of natural language, the underlying form which determines semantic interpretation and which embodies the basic recursive devices of natural language.

What I have just sketched is not the actual accomplishments of the Davidson programme, as it exists today, but rather the fond hopes that were nourished for it. This programme has yet to deliver what its proponents promised us. Scrutability, in particular, is a sore spot, the difficulty being largely that of accommodating the scrutability of propositional attitude sentences and other intensional contexts by means of a purely extensional logical apparatus.[4] The austere meta-language that Davidson wants to get by on also creates further well-known difficulties of a more global kind.[5] Hence I do not present this theory here as established dogma in the philosophy of language. Rather, I bring it in because as yet, there is no serious alternative on the market, and because, despite all its troubles, it illustrates a number of important features that should be accepted as *sine qua non*'s of semantic theorizing for natural languages and any other communication system exhibiting the properties of unboundedness, compositeness, and scrutability. Davidson's programme is interesting from the point of view of our current concerns, because we decided to make those features definitory of what we want to call a 'language' in the present context of enquiry. Whatever its ultimate fate, Davidson's proposal demonstrates to us the formal features of any theory powerful enough to handle a semantic system characterized by the triad of unboundedness, compositeness, and scrutability.

3

Drawing on speech act theorizing and current work in formal

semantics, I have adumbrated the concept of meaning that concerns us in the present chapter and have sketched the general form of theories in this field. The task ahead of us is to decide whether or not such theories are relevant for non-linguistic$_1$ action. Our investigation will fall into two parts. First we examine the possibility of developing an autonomous semantic theory for non-linguistic$_1$ action, a meaning-theory for segments of action that are not ordinarily construed as languages. Afterwards, we investigate whether or not semantic theory as it is commonly understood–more precisely, semantic theory of natural languages–can be said to constitute an indispenable part of any theory of non-linguistic action. We now turn to the first of these two projects.

The most serious and careful attempt to account for non-linguistic$_1$ action in terms of semantic categories that I know of is due to Roland Barthes. Barthes's position is developed in the two texts,[1] *Système de la Mode* and *Éléments de sémiologie*. In these works, Barthes cites as examples of linguistic$_2$ systems those of fashion, of food, of cars, of furniture, and of architecture.[6] In the following, we shall focus on the system to which Barthes himself has devoted the most attention, to the extent of making it the topic of an entire monograph, namely, that of fashion.

The statement that Barthes regards fashion as a semantic system calls for certain comment and qualification. At an early point in his investigation, he elects to shift his attention from apparel actually worn, to clothes as they are described and decreed in fashion magazines. I shall not go into Barthes's reasons for making this shift, beyond noting that in an uncharitable interpretation, they boil down to a suspicion on his part that the actual sociological phenomenon of wearing fashionable attire is not amenable to semantic analyses; hence the advisability of leaving the real world in favour of the cloudland conjured up by fashion journalism.[7] However, since Barthes indicates that his findings will, to a certain extent, transfer to fashion as an actual social institution, I presume to undo his methodological shift and return to the real world. This move does not perpetrate an injustice to Barthes in any case, since the objections that I shall raise later will be equally potent against a semantic analysis of fashion-as-described-in-women's-weeklies. What we gain by the shift is primarily access to a somewhat broader range of data than that made use of by Barthes, *inter alia* data which demonstrate correspondences between clothes and the world that are not established by particular fashions. These correspondences are on the whole more amenable to semantic construal than those adduced by Barthes. Thus, to some extent, the semiological position is strengthened by the methodological shift.

According to Barthes, semantic meaning accrues to articles of clothing by virtue of the relation of 'appropriateness' which exists between certain ways of dressing and certain occasions, activities, settings, etc.[8] Examples of the phenomenon are ubiquitous: light or casual clothes may, or even must, be worn for sporting activities, but are not permissible for the theatre or grandes soirées; skimpy garments are *de rigueur* on the beach, but are not to be sported at work; the clothes that are just right for the salons are entirely out of place around the campfire, etc.; the list can be continued *ad infinitum*.

If we venture beyond Barthes's own range of examples, we may also observe a clear connection between style of dress and certain key social parameters such as income level, social status, sex, age, education level, etc. This connection might once more be construed as a case of semantic coupling, the characteristics of the garments *signifying* the social parameters. Cases of this kind are actually the first to come to mind when we think about clothing as a language, and it is a topic dear to journalists and authors of popular sociological tracts.

In our introductory deliberations on semantic meaning, we dwelt upon the tie between this notion and that of communication. The examples of meaning suggested here accommodate this tie. For it does not seem strained to say that a person communicates certain facts about his social status, income, age, sex, etc. by the way he dresses. Nor, to turn to the examples examined by Barthes, is it wholly unnatural to say that the participants in some social event communicate to each other its status as, say, a formal gathering, by the clothes they wear.

Still, 'meaning' is a notoriously loose word, and 'communication' has several senses as well. So it remains to be demonstrated that the senses of these words as involved in the above descriptions are the same as those used in the analysis of semantic meaning. I do not believe such a demonstration can be given: there are crucial disparities between semantic meaning and the 'meaning' of a certain choice of clothes. Let us begin by examining whether or not the alleged garment language can be shown to satisfy the speech act component of semantic meaning, the conditions embodied in the notion of speaker's meaning. In preparation, let us recapitulate the definition of that notion in order to have its finer points readily available.

S means that p in doing h iff

(1) S performs h, and

(2) intends (intention$_1$) that S's performance of h produce in A (the audience) the belief that S is committed to it being the case that p, and

(3) intends (intention$_2$) that intention$_1$ be recognized by A and serve at least as part of A's reason for taking S to be committed to it being the case that p, and

(4) intention$_2$ is an iteratively public intention.

I shall argue that these conditions are not satisfied by the alleged cases of communication, and hence that the vehicle of communication involved–clothing–fails to qualify as a language. The way in which the communicative intentions influencing the choice of dress fall short of the conditions varies between the different cases listed above. I shall discuss them in turn.

Let us first examine the case in which a person uses style of clothing to indicate social position, financial status, educational level, etc. Here is a concrete example: Mrs Nouveau-Riche intends her 'audience' to recognize her fortunate economic situation by wearing a mink stole to the come-as-you-are-party. That is, she intends to generate in her audience the belief (realization) that she is very well off. Does this intention qualify as a semantic intention, in the technical sense? The answer must be in the negative: this intention falls short in several respects, of which I shall concentrate on one. Notice first, however, that I do not want to base my rejection upon the observation that the belief Mrs Nouveau-Riche intends to produce does not correspond exactly with that specified in the definition: the definition calls for the intention to be of the form, '*A* is to realize that *S* is committed to it being the case that *p*.' It would be inadvisable to base my argument on this point since Mrs Nouveau-Riche's intention is in accord with the original Grice analysis here, an analysis which still enjoys considerable following (we have seen that Schiffer accepts it). It would be unwise to ground our argument upon a component of the meaning analysis that is still the object of dispute.

Instead, I will direct attention to the fact that Mrs Nouveau-Riche fails to satisfy the reflexivity condition upon communicative intentions, the condition expressed in clause (3); this condition is shared by the Grice–Schiffer analysis and by every other proposal with which I am familiar. Mrs Nouveau-Riche fails to satisfy the reflexivity condition since, although she intends to generate in her audience a certain belief, she does not intend her audience to know she has this intention. She will want her intention of generating the indicated belief (plus an appropriate attitude of admiration) to remain covert, since effective concealment of that intention is crucial for the achievement of her purpose. If her intention were recognized by her audience, the attitude engendered would be one of disdain rather than admiration. Mrs Nouveau-Riche would be despised for flaunting her riches. Unlike communicative intentions, which are essentially (intended to be) public, the intentions involved in self-presentation of the kind engaged in in this example are necessarily covert. (This is why skilled practitioners of the art of self-display affect total obliviousness of the presence of onlookers: you cannot ascribe audience-directed intentions to a person who is utterly unaware that there are other people around.)[9]

We may strengthen this argument by noting that if Mrs Nouveau-Riche really satisfied the full conditions for meaning, she would literally be *saying* (albeit non-verbally) that she is very rich; and this our social code would stigmatize as unbearably gross. We should be charitable and not attribute to Mrs Nouveau-Riche such lowly intentions. But then we must also forgo attributing to her any communicative intentions, in the sense relevant to semantic meaning.

This analysis may be found not quite subtle enought to do justice to the phenomenon of self-presentation among true sophisticates. These do not intend their mien of obliviousness of the presence of an audience to be taken at face value: they know full well that their intention of 'impression management' will be recognized. But there is still a difference between such persons and a true communicator: the person who dresses ostentatiously will still not intend her primary 'communicative' intention to be recognized (and still less intend that recognition to be part of the audience's reason for adopting the intended belief); she just doesn't care whether it is recognized or not. Harking back to an example we used in chapter 1, we may compare the conspicuous dresser with a person who confronts his audience with a dead rat to let them know that their house is rat infested, not caring whether they recognize this intention or not, as long as the truth about the house sinks in.

Let me now turn to the use of clothes to communicate facts about age or sex. In this case there is no injunction against possessing the primary communicative intentions in question: there is nothing odious in intending other people to form (true) beliefs about one's age or sex, and hence no need to hide such intentions. There is even less of an odium against harbouring intentions of the slightly more complicated form stipulated by the analysis on p. 294, *in casu* that of intending the audience to believe that the speaker is committed to the fact of belonging to this or the other sex, or to some particular age group.

Still, such cases fail to qualify as communication in the technical sense. In the first place, there will normally be a simple absence of the appropriate primary communicative intentions: only rarely will we be able to unearth an intention, however implicit, of securing correct sexual or age identification as an actual motivation behind people's dress habits. And I dare say that intentions of being taken to stand committed to facts of these kinds are even less frequent. Moreover, even where such intentions are present, there will be a failure of the reflexivity condition expressed in the third clause of the meaning definition: there will be no higher-level intention that the basic communicative intention be recognized. Both sexes appear to resent being mistaken as members of the opposite sex and will, if necessary, see to it that they are dressed in a manner reducing the likelihood of such a mistake. However, as long as this goal is achieved, there is no endeavour to have this intention recognized in itself.

An even more radical failure of communicative intention obtains in situations where the alleged message consists in a definition of the social activity which the 'speaker' and his 'audience' are engaged in. We may, for instance, agree that certain types of garments, of conservative style and sombre colours, serve to 'indicate' that the occasion is a formal one (this example is of special interest because most of Barthes's concrete examples are of this kind). But 'indication' is not semantic meaning: there is no prospect in arguing that the participants in a funeral, for example, use their manner of dressing to generate in each other the belief that the gathering is a formal one. For they may all be presumed to know that already. Nor may they be taken to intend each other to understand that they are severally committed to the fact that the occasion is a formal one. The simple truth is that the participants obey a social custom which dictates a certain kind of dress for that kind of occasion. We need ascribe to the participants no intentions beyond that of obeying this rule.

The above remarks pertain directly only to Barthes's example of the garment 'language'. But they would seem to carry over immediately to all the other phenomena presented by Barthes as suitable topics for semantic analysis. Thus it is true that people use the food they serve, the cars they drive, the manner in which they furnish their homes, etc., to get across to their fellow men a certain image of themselves. But in all such cases, what matters to the 'speaker' is only that the appropriate beliefs (and the associated favourable attitudes) be generated. He will not, in addition, intend this communicative intention to be recognized but will intend that it remains secret. For in these cases, too, recognition of the primary intention will militate against realization of the ulterior goal. In brief, the phenomena cited by Barthes all serve at times as stage props in the game of self-presentation. But self-presentation does not amount to Gricean communication. The intentions behind self-presentation lack the complexity and reflexivity required for Gricean communication; and on one critical point they go directly counter to that notion, as we have seen.

4

However, it is perhaps unfair to Barthes to let the semantic interpretation of clothing rest solely upon the nature of wearer's intentions. It would seem that such a construal is also suggested to him by certain formal similarities between the semantics for natural languages and the dress code decreed by fashion. Barthes seems impressed by the fact that garments are describable in two dimensions, which, since Saussure, have been considered crucial for the analysis of language, namely, the *paradigmatic* axis (termed the associative axis by Saussure) and the *syntagmatic* axis. This is a distinction which applies to all levels of linguistic description, and thus to phonology and syntax as well as to semantics. Put very roughly, and restricted to semantics, the paradigmatic axis is a taxonomy classifying lexical items into kindred types. The criterion of classification is the commutation (or substitution) test. According to one possible version, this test would be concerned with substitutiveness *salva* meaningfulness. Such a criterion would collect all colour terms into one class; all terms applicable only to conscious beings into another class, and so forth. The paradigmatic dimension thus provides a typology, an ordered inventory, of the semantic building blocks of language. The syntagmatic dimension deals with the principles for the construction of the larger units (phrases and sentences) which may be built up with the simple elements pigeonholed in the paradigmatic system.

Barthes points out that a similar distribution of facts along two related axes can be accomplished for data on clothes.[10] Clothing possesses a paradigmatic (or, as he sometimes calls it, a 'systema-ic') and a syntagmatic dimension. The paradigmatic dimension is an abstract ordering of pieces, details and properties of clothes that cannot (physically) be displayed simultaneously on the same part of the body, of such a nature that replacing one item with another leads to a change of 'meaning'. The paradigmatic elements are combined in the syntagmatic dimension which deals with the concatenation of items from different paradigmatic classes in one single suit of clothes. An example: a deerstalker and a silk hat belong to the same paradigmatic category but have different 'meanings', the first indicating leisurely rural pursuits, the other formal urban activities. In an actual suit of clothes, the deerstalker may be combined with items from other paradigmatic categories, such as a trench coat and knickers, to form a syntagmatic unit.

Does the possibility of such a bi-axial distribution of data justify the construal of clothes as a semantic system? I take it to be obvious that it does not. It only takes a minimum of structure in a corpus of data to provide a foothold for the paradigm/syntagm distinction; the applicability of that contrast is almost universal and does not reveal any profound affinity with language. The facts of chemistry, for instance, are highly amenable to description in the paradigm/ syntagm matrix. The paradigmatic dimension would represent the classification of the chemical elements into genera with roughly similar properties (thus the periodic system belongs to the paradigmatic dimension). The syntagmatic dimension would specify the principles of chemical bonding, i.e. the theory of valencies. Yet these formal properties hardly go to show that chemistry is a semantic theory.

Nor does the garment 'language' display any of the formal properties which we singled out as characteristic of vehicles of semantic meaningfulness of a non-trivial kind. These were the properties of unboundedness, of compositeness, and of scrutability. Admittedly, the garment 'language' possesses an unboundedness of sorts: it permits the production of an infinite (or indefinite) set of different 'sentences'. For one may always expand the 'vocabulary' of that language by dressing innovatively and yet in a manner that will evoke a semantic reading, for instance, by wearing clothes made out of an exceedingly expensive space technology fibre in order to indicate one's wealth. Extension of this kind has no clear limits, thus rendering the language unbounded. But the generative mechanism responsible for this feature is altogether different from that of natural languages. It does not involve a compositional, recursive device building complex sentences out of simpler elements (including simpler sentences), but a general non-recursive principle tying together sign and significatum, roughly to the effect that any item of clothing the production of which requires great expenditure signifies wealth. This makes the unboundedness of the garment 'language' independent of structure: the generative principles do not work upon the form of sentences, but upon their simple constituents; not upon syntax, but upon the lexicon. This has dire consequences for the scrutability of the language, since it means that the workings of the generative semantic principles do not leave a structural imprint upon sentences, which can guide us in the process of interpretation. For the semantic principle of the garment 'language' mentioned above to be of any aid in interpretation, we need an extra bit of information in order to tie together this principle and the garment under scrutiny, namely, information to the effect that the garment is expensive. But this means that every time we extend the garment 'language' in the manner exemplified by the space-age suit, another clause must be added to the semantic theory for that 'language'. The extension destroys the scrutability of the language by introducing a 'sentence' that cannot be interpreted on the basis of the principles that sufficed for interpretation prior to its introduction.

Not only does the garment language lack any semantically relevant recursive structure; it is questionable whether it possesses any syntactic structure at all beyond lexical segmentation (and actually lexical segmentation is pretty arbitrary here: the commutation test yields highly ambiguous results). A syntagm of the garment language would seem to be a mere concacenation of elements. There is no counterpart in this language, say, to the noun phrase–verb phrase structure in English. It will not do to say that the Trouser–Jacket/Shirt/Sweater structure fills the bill, since no such structure really exists. What you have is a moral-*cum*-aesthetic maxim to the effect that both the upper and lower part of the torso must (normally) be covered; but there is no obligation that this be achieved by a two-piece garment. A one-piece suit will also do the trick.[11]

5

I have argued against Barthes's semantic interpretation of clothes by means of certain rather technical considerations designed to show that the garment 'language' falls short in both of the dimensions in which languages were characterized: clothes are not worn with the proper communicative intentions; nor does the garment system display the formal features of languages proper. However, I should like to clinch the case by adducing a less technical reflection which will serve to diminish the appeal of treating clothes and the other phenomena cited by Barthes as languages.

If we look at language as the possession of the human species rather than of the individual human being, it is patently clear that language is not just a medium for the convenient implementation of pre-existing communicative purposes. A large segment of human communicative intentions are such that they could hardly have existed if not for language. How, for instance, could one intend to communicate to one's fellows that one rejects the possibility of a phenomenalistic reduction of material objects if one did not possess a language? Indeed, how could one as much as ponder phenomenalism if one did not have a language? And how could one have any intentions involving phenomenalism, such as, say, that of finding a conclusive argument against it, if one were not endowed with a language?

This example shows that language is deeply intertwined with human thinking, willing, desiring and acting, once we get beyond the most primitive, biologically determined aspects of human existence. Language makes possible modes of life, objects of desire and avenues of thinking that are beyond the mute animal. The power of language in this respect is enhanced by what Putnam calls the linguistic division of labour.[12] To be able to use a word intelligently, it is not necessary to have a thorough grasp of the theoretical considerations that are its background assumptions or indeed its explicit content; the man in the street is capable of using the notions of theoretical physics quite productively in his everyday discourse without being able to give an account of the overall system in which they are embedded. Just by learning a language, human beings gain possession of a system of labels which point towards large stores of systematized experience extending far beyond what the individual could accumulate in a lifetime and towards possibilities of action that he could never himself have discovered or explored. Language provides man with a map of a cultural and intellectual landscape built up from the sediments of individual human action and thought through millennia, allowing him to direct his own thought and action along routes that would never have been suggested to him by his own limited experience.

I would contend that a similar point does not hold for Barthes's semiological systems. The facts communicated by these 'languages' are not made possible merely by the existence of these very languages. They are either facts which are independent of any language at all–such as facts about sex and age–or facts which are presumably dependent upon the existence of a language, but which could hardly be sustained merely by the particular semiotic code in which they are expressed: they presuppose the existence of a full-blown natural language. This probably holds for facts about social status, income, political attitude, and many more.

To express in a tangible way the relevance of this observation for our current discussion, let me relate a little fable. A Martian sociologist visits Earth and starts recording data on earthlings. Unfortunately, the Martian does not realize that the oral noises emitted by human beings has systematic significance (or maybe he simply lacks organs for detecting it: Martians live in a world without atmosphere and hence have no use for acoustic sensors). In other words, the Martian fails to recognize that human beings have a *language*. It is difficult to comprehend fully the impoverishment of the data which flows from his fateful oversight. But it is obvious that a glimpse in the Martian's field notes would reveal recordings only of the grossest biological aspects of human social intercourse.

Let us compare the relative enrichments of the Martian's data in either of two cases. (1) It suddenly dawns upon him that human speech (and writing) constitutes a language, which he then proceeds to decode. (2) The Martian hits upon the idea of construing clothes, food, and all the other Barthesian semiological systems as languages, which he then goes on to decode. He does this while still being oblivious of the fact that speech and writing constitute a language. It is evident that the resulting gains in data are dramatically different. In the first case, the Martian sociologist gets access not only to a vast body of novel data but to data of a completely different order of complexity than that with which he was acquainted before. The novelty resides not merely in the fact that the Martian now realizes, as he failed to do previously, that earthlings have communicative intentions. The chief novelty resides in the kinds of facts which earthlings communicate and in the subtle intentions, beliefs and emotions which the Martian may now ascribe to them on the basis of their verbal behaviour. Not so in the case where the Martian comes to understand only, for example, the garment 'language'. Apart from the very observation that the way people dress constitutes a language, the sociologist learns no new *kinds* of facts. For the facts communicated in the garment 'language' are of a sort with which the Martian is familiar already, such as facts about sex and age. If we are charitable enough to allow that facts about social status, position, political views, etc. are available to the Martian prior to his grasp of the 'real', spoken language, we may grant him the ability to realize that such facts, too, are communicated in the garment 'language'. But these facts are again of a kind which were available to him before he managed to decipher the language.

What I have attempted to illustrate with the above story is this. A special interest attaches to the interpretation of human language, in the commonly accepted sense, because it is a repository of that which is most distinctively human, and because the language of any particular community is a repository of that which most clearly distinguishes that community from its neighbours. If the sociologist does not understand the language of the people studied, he does not understand the most important things about them, no matter how impressive a body of data he has amassed. The semiological systems investigated by Barthes have a different status. By decoding them, we do not come to know kinds of facts that we did not know before. We only learn that social facts of a type with which we are familiar are being communicated through a channel not recognized so far. Barthes's theories, as well as those of other semiologists, may be said to amount to this piece of methodological advice: treat clothes, food, cars, etc., as languages for the purpose of sociological theorizing. In these remarks, I have tried to show that the gain in novel kinds of data that will accrue to us if we heed this advice is actually zero.

6

We have concluded that there is no future in the project of

developing a semantics for non-linguistic₁ action. However, the deliberations of the preceding section suggest another and perhaps more promising way of connecting semantic theorizing and social explanation. These remarks suggested that, although non-linguistic₁ action may not have its own, autonomous meaning content, such action may somehow embody meanings derived from language in the normal understanding of that word. Perhaps the meaning of an action is a function of the meaning of some linguistic₁ material somehow associated with it. If this were the case, understanding action would presuppose an understanding of language₁; a theory of action would incorporate as an essential part a theory of semantics₁, more precisely a semantics for natural language. We will dedicate the present section to a discussion of this proposal.

Note that the tie between linguistic₁ meaning and action that we are looking for here is a very strong and in a certain sense 'intrinsic' one. Thus, we could not support the hypothesis of such a tie merely by pointing to the fact that a convenient (or perhaps even unavoidable) way of expressing the logical form of intentionalistic states is to parse them as attitudes towards propositions (or, for those more parsimoniously inclined concerning ontology, attitudes towards sentences). My desire for a piece of cake may be construed as a desiring-true of the proposition that I have a piece of cake (or a desiring-true of the English sentence, 'I have a piece of cake', as spoken by me). My belief that I can get a cake by going to the baker's is my believing-true the proposition that I can get a cake by going to the baker's. However, these facts cannot be used to indicate an 'intrinsic' connection between action (and its attending motivational states) and language. Here, the reference to language and linguistic entities belongs solely to the meta-language (even granting that propositions are essentially linguistic entities, which is a questionable assumption). We do not imply that the linguistic items referred to are somehow part of the states described. This is apparent from the fact that we often feel justified (and at times even compelled) to use this terminology in the description of the behaviour of speechless creatures. When we agree, on the basis of convincing evidence, that Fido expects to be fed soon, we apply a description to Fido the logical parsing of which brings to light a proposition, or sentence: we attribute to him the propositional attitude, Fido expects-true that Fido will be fed soon. Clearly in this case we do not grant Fido a mastery of language in any sense. The reference to language belongs solely to our description of Fido's expectations (and this, of course, raises some thorny questions as to the precise relationship between the description and the behaviour displayed by Fido, and in general as to the empirical anchoring of intentionalistic descriptions).[13]

The connection between language and action which we are looking for must be even tighter. And here it may occur to us that our purposes might be served by a particular construal of the rather vague idea ventured in the preceding section to the effect that certain intentions could only be had by people in possession of a language. This idea might be spelled out and supported as follows. The reason why some intentions can be attributed only to beings endowed with a language lies in the fact that we can only grant such intentions to beings with the power of avowing them verbally. Some human intentions and their associated beliefs are so rarefied as to be effectively divorced from brute behavioural manifestation. Our only line onto them is the agent's readiness to confess to them when suitably prompted. That is, our only line onto the contents of such intentions is through semantic interpretation of the agent's avowals as couched in some natural language. This means that a semantic theory is *eo ipso* a theory of action; or, more precisely, those parts of it are tantamount to a theory of action which are necessary and sufficient for interpreting agents' avowals of intention (and this, of course, may involve very substantial parts of the semantic theory). The semantic theory is a theory of action in the sense that a grasp of that theory is a necessary and sufficient condition for grasping the contents of (at least some of) agents' intentions. For action embodying such intentions, the theory of action collapses into semantic theory.

A view which may be covered by the above formulation when carefully clarified and disambiguated has been presented by Jürgen Habermas. The main source is his study, *Zur Logik der Sozialwissenschaften*. In this work, Habermas attempts to show the inadequacy of a positivist approach to human action. The crucial stumbling block for this approach is said to lie in the language-impregnated character of human action. Since, according to Habermas, the phenomenon of language resists capture in terms of the conceptual machinery to which the positivist is restricted—one dealing with causal relationships between observationally ascertainable facts described in extensional terms—the language-impregnated nature of human action means that also non-linguistic action is intractable to him.[14]

In his discussion, Habermas refers to the kind of human action with which he is concerned as 'communicative action'. This suggests a trivializing interpretation of his position which takes 'communicative action' to mean the same as 'semantic action' in my sense. Clearly, semantic action is language-impregnated in a perfectly uncontroversial way. However, we find that by 'communicative action' Habermas means a much wider class than that of language acts: communicative action is action guided by social norms. The only thing excluded from communicative action (apart from purely reactive behaviour) is what Habermas calls 'strategic action', that is, rational calculating action directed towards the maximation of utility.[15] However, Habermas makes it clear that even this kind of action, although 'non-communicative', is still impregnated with linguistic meaning.[16] Thus, as it turns out, all human action, excepting purely reactive behaviour, is considered by Habermas to be language-impregnated.

Habermas presents his thesis to this effect in the following manner:[17]

Instead of controlled observation, what is required [in the sciences of action] is symbolic understanding, for subjectively intended meaning is given only in symbolic relations. . . . Here experience is not tied to private perception, the intersubjectivity of which is guaranteed in the context of experimental controls upon instrumental action, but rather to linguistic communication. . . . If we do not want to relinquish all access to intentional actions as data in the social sciences, then the context of experience within which those data are grounded must be that of linguistic communication and not communication-free observation.

If action and intention are bound together in such a way that action can be deduced from the statements which express intention, then the inverse thesis is also true: in principle, a subject can only engage in actions the intentions of which he is capable of describing. The limits of action are determined by a field of possible descriptions, and this is further determined by the structure of the language in which the understanding and world view of a social group is articulated. Thus, the limits of action are drawn from the limits of language.

The above statements are ambiguous in several ways. This ambiguity gives us an opportunity to dwell in somewhat more detail on the idea of the language-dependency of human action suggested in section 5. In the first place, we must distinguish between the claim that human action is informed by concepts and that it is informed by language (or, in a more careful formulation, informed by concepts which are essentially derived from a language). The position we examine here is the latter, stronger one; the former, weaker position, at least according to one reading, follows trivially from the observation that the criteria for the possession of at least certain concepts (to commit ourselves to nothing stronger here) are behavioural. Hence, if the criteria for the possession of a concept, C, are satisfied by the behaviour B, we may trivially say that B is impregnated with the concept C.

For our second clarification, we must emphasize the fact that the language-dependence of intentions which concerns us here is a logical, not a causal one. We take no interest in the, quite plausible, view that certain intentions owe their (individual) existence to the causal influence of the fact that language provides a separate designation for this kind of intention, or the desire embodied therein, and thus makes it available, prepackaged as it were, to speakers of that language. Man is a suggestible creature, and it is highly probable that the plans and intentions which he forms are to a large extent causally determined by the stock of descriptions which language puts at his disposal; this is indeed part of the point we made on p. 301 when we referred to the linguistic division of labour. Here we are only interested in a stronger dependency to the effect that certain intentions are such that a human being could not, logically, harbour such intentions if he did not master a language.

We have already indicated a way in which some such view could be supported. (I am not implying that this argument is used by Habermas, nor even that he would accept it.) It makes play with the criteria which we employ to determine the nature of certain intentions, or desires. It would seem that some desires are so ethereal that we could never hope to find conclusive grounds for their ascription in gross physical behaviour. The only solid handle upon such intentions is the subject's avowal that he harbours them. We may divide the class of such desires into two rough groups. To the first group belong desires with which no 'natural', non-linguistic behaviour, of a kind which could be taken to define these intentions, seems to be associated at all. What non-linguistic behaviour, for instance, would be associated in this way with the desire to demonstrate that a phenomenalistic reduction of material objects to classes of sense data cannot succeed? How could we ever attribute this desire to someone save on the basis of a verbal intimation that this is what he is up to? The second group consists of desires that do manifest themselves in characteristic non-linguistic behaviour in their general features, but which we will often want to describe with a fineness of nuance that seems beyond capture in purely behavioural terms. For instance, the desire to welcome one's master on the doorstep is one which may be displayed behaviourally. This is clear from the fact that it is a desire which we may ascribe both to a human being (like the butler) and to an animal (like a dog). But it would seem that only the butler could believe that his master will return the day after tomorrow; hence only the butler could desire to welcome his master on the doorstep the day after tomorrow. And we may agree with Wittgenstein that this has something to do with the fact that the butler has a language while a dog does not.[18] Thus language does not merely give man the ability to form completely novel kinds of desires, but also makes it (logically) possible for him to form desires with a fineness of nuance which are not conceivable in a speechless animal. And it could be argued that most everyday descriptions of desires are specified to a degree such that the states described, and the actions to which they give rise, would be inaccessible to organisms lacking a language.

Thus, the argument is this. There are classes of human desires, and aspects thereof, which have no adequate manifestation in pure non-verbal conduct. Our only handle upon such desires is agents' avowals. They can only be specified in terms of the semantic content of the utterances in which they are avowed. Semantic theory thus takes on the role of a theory of action, to the extent that such a theory licenses inference of the theorems which spell out the meaning of the avowals.

I have tried to present the strongest possible case for the language-dependency claim (or, as I shall dub it, the hermeneutical claim). And I hope that the above reasoning has made that position appear not altogether unattractive. However, I shall now go on to show that the adduced argument is incoherent.

We have maintained that our only line onto certain desires is agents' avowals. Let us be specific and concentrate on the desire D, expressed in the sentence P (of the form, 'I desire that so-and-so be the case'). Now notice first that our grounds for attributing D to some person cannot, even according to the hermeneutician, simply be his readiness to mouth P in the proper constative mood. P interests us only as expressing a certain proposition p in the avower's language. In another language where this proposition is expressed by some other sentence, Q, our grounds for ascribing D would be the subject's readiness to pronounce Q, not P. That is, our grounds for ascribing D, when characterized independently of reference to a particular language, is the agent's willingness to utter a sentence which means, in his native tongue, that p.

But here the analysis threatens to run around in a circle. Our only line onto the desire is the agent's readiness to sincerely assert that p. However, we are entitled to ask for the meaning of the proposition p. The meaning of p is a function, we may agree, of the truth conditions of that proposition (or its assertibility conditions; it does not matter for the present issue which we opt for). What are these conditions in the case at hand? They are the state of affairs of the agent harbouring the desire D. But our only line onto that desire is the agent's willingness to confess that p. So, until we know the meaning of the proposition which the agent avows, we do not know the nature of his desire. And until we know the nature of his desire, we do not know the meaning of the proposition which he avows.

The hermeneutician will object that our route with his argument is much too short. Maybe the above reasoning would hold water, he might admit, if language and meaning were atomistic; if no linguistic expressions and the meanings embodied therein were structurally related to each other. But we have spent considerable time in the preceding discussion celebrating precisely the compositional nature of language. We pointed out that language permits the construction of complex meanings out of the meanings of component elements. Thus, in order to give meaning to the sentence uttered by the agent in avowing his intention, *P*, all we need to know is the meaning of its semantically relevant structure and the meaning of the components inserted in that structure; *in casu* the meaning of the expression, 'I desire that. . .', and of the sentence which must be inserted in the blank to get *P*. A theory of meaning, properly construed, will show us precisely how the meaning of *P* can be constructed out of the meanings of its components.

Unfortunately, this rejoinder is of no avail. The compositeness of language will not deliver what the hermeneutician needs. The compositeness of language offers a simple and economical way of representing complex truth conditions, namely, as a function of the truth (and satisfaction) conditions of syntactic and lexical elements. Put succinctly, the compositeness of language saves us from having to invent an entirely novel sentence, perfectly unrelated to ones previously known, to express every novel fact (every novel set of truth conditions) we come across. In other words, the compositeness of language gives us a device for generating novel vehicles for expressing truth conditions. It does not enable us to create novel kinds of truth conditions, truth conditions which were somehow impossible until the formation of those vehicles. Still, this is the interpretation the hermeneutician needs. He requires that the sentence *P* ('I desire that so-and-so be the case') create its own truth conditions; not only the particular truth grounds which make it true on one particular occasion of utterance, but also the general kind of truth grounds which make it true whenever it is true. But, whatever the last statement really means, the compositeness of language will not deliver it.

However, the concern with compositeness was a side issue: our main topic is still whether or not language can somehow generate novel truth conditions, novel kinds of facts. To support his position on this issue, the hermeneutician might now try another tack. He might point to mathematics as a paradigm. Certainly the position is not absurd that mathematical language somehow generates mathematical reality, and mathematical truth. At least this is a view which has been defended seriously by an influential school in the philosophy of mathematics, namely intuitionism. There may perhaps be some intrinsic incoherency in the intuitionist position; or the general metaphysical reasoning behind it may apply only to mathematical reality, which is a rather peculiar domain to begin with, and not be transferable to empirical reality. But, the hermeneutician would go on, he is at least entitled to an argument in support of either of these claims. The *prima facie* plausibility of the intuitionist position in mathematics would seem to create an obligation on the part of the opponent of the hermeneutical hypothesis to defend either of the above alternatives.

However, it is possible to sidestep this challenge by demonstrating that the relationship between mathematical formalism and mathematical reality is different, even by the intuitionist's standards, from that between desires and the language in which they are expressed. The intuitionist's position is not that the mere introduction of mathematical terminology creates mathematical reality; if it were, intuitionism would be ontologically inflationary rather than contractive. The intuitionist's position is to the effect that mathematical truth, or mathematical reality, is created by mathematical *proof*. Mathematical reality is not generated by the mere putting together of mathematical expressions in a well-formed string of some formal system. Only the proof of mathematical formulae acccomplishes that.

The hermeneutician's case for desires is quite different from this. Here, the mere mouthing of lexical items inserted in a syntactic framework to form a novel sentence is thought to generate a new fact. But it is hard to see how the mere formulation of a sentence could accomplish this, even on the basis of a radical anti-realist conception of meaning of the kind motivating the mathematical intuitionist. What must be demonstrated, of course, is that this string of words is legitimate, that it has a coherent sense and is not a mere sequence of sounds or marks on paper. In mathematics, this is accomplished by giving a proof of the formula. The proof shows not only *that* the formula has a meaning, but also *what* meaning it has. But the notion of proof plays no part in the hermeneutician's argument.

But could not the hermeneutician retort that something more than the mere mouthing of a sentence is involved: what we have is the agent's sincere *endorsement* of the sentence which expresses his desire. This, while not being a proof in a formal sense, is still the closest thing to a proof that we can hope for in the realm of empirical fact. For we do not dispute the fact that an agent's sincere avowal of a desire carries great evidential weight.

This may be the case. The problem is that this 'proof' is extremely non-constructive, if I may be excused for a slight extension of this term as used by the intuitionist mathematician. The suggested proof of the ascription of a desire D to an agent A is merely A's sincere assertion that he harbours D. But the mere assertion of some sentence P, no matter how authoritative, tells us nothing about the sense of P. This is radically different from constructive proof in mathematics which is a complex logical structure that will inevitably reveal the essential properties of the sentence proved. The counterpart in mathematics of the hermeneutician's 'proof' would be the case of a mathematician to whom God spoke in a dream, declaring that some mathematical statement M is true. Now if the mathematician were a strong believer, he might accept this as incontrovertible evidence that M is indeed true. But even he could hardly maintain that this 'proof' made us very much wiser as to the meaning of M. For this 'proof' is as non-constructive as a proof can ever be. It is an extreme example of the kind of proof which is inadmissible according to intuitionist thinking. The hermeneutician can derive no support for his position by invoking a parallel to intuitionism in mathematics.

We have reached the conclusion that there could be no human desires such that their contents could only be specified in terms of agent's avowals. But now we have to square this upshot with the fact that the position to the contrary was based upon quite firm intuitions. It seemed to us entirely plausible, and will probably still do so, that only a person with mastery of a language may harbour plans of refuting phenomenalism or of meeting his master the day after tomorrow. While the argument just adduced may appear unassailable, it does little to weaken the hold of such examples.

However, a closer look at the examples shows that they do not actually contradict the abstract argument. Indeed, the examples indicate strongly that desires exist which could only be held by a creature endowed with a language. But it is false, as implied by the argument which we put into the mouth of the hermeneutician, that this is the case because our only criteria for the presence of such desires is the agent's verbal avowals. The agent's mastery of language enters the picture in another and much less direct way.

How would we actually determine that somebody wants to refute phenomenalism (apart from avowals)? In the first place, we would try to establish that he actually understands this philosophical doctrine; for although one may certainly intend to refute some position that one does not really understand–indeed, cynics would say that this is the rule in philosophy–it would clearly count against the ascription of some such intention if it could be demonstrated that the individual in question did not have the slightest grasp of the doctrine which he allegedly planned to refute. The criteria for establishing such understanding are actually quite trivial, although highly multifarious and very difficult to state with any precision. We would, for instance, check a person's ability to spot incompatibilities between phenomenalism and other philosophical views; to discern logical implications of phenomenalism; to detect and produce arguments in favour and disfavour of the doctrine, etc. His *desire* to produce an argument against phenomenalism might be discovered by way of the time he spends mulling over alleged refutations and counter-refutations; his joy when he (believes that he) has found a conclusive objection, etc.

Thus, the behaviour on the basis of which we would ascribe to someone the desire to refute phenomenalism is indeed largely verbal behaviour, namely the agent's occupation with arguments (i.e. sentential structures) directed against that view. The understanding of these arguments presupposes language; and it is difficult to conceive how anyone could be taken to seek a refutation of phenomenalism who did not possess the linguistic competence needed to handle such arguments. (It is true that Dr Johnson tried to refute phenomenalism in a non-verbal manner. But I dare say that we should not have been warranted in construing his conduct in this fashion if there had not been ample additional evidence, of a language-related kind, that this was indeed the Doctor's intention. Not any old kicking of a pebble counts as an attempted refutation of phenomenalism.) However, the tie between desire (and belief) and language is much less direct than alleged by the hermeneutician. The connection between someone's desire to refute phenomenalism and his habit of brooding over lines of thought which are antithetical to that position is not a linguistic connection. We do not decipher the desire in the brooding in the way we decipher it in the utterance, 'I want to construct a definitive case against phenomenalism.' Rather we discern it in the way that we discern someone's desire to climb Mount Everest in his constant brooding over maps of that area, his occupation with mountain-climbing equipment, and so on. Thus, the relationship between the behaviour and the desire is one of means–end rationality, as in all other purposive action. It is true that linguistic material plays a large part in the evidence on the basis of which we ascribe the desire mentioned to the agent. Still this desire is not avowed or otherwise stated in verbal form. It shows itself in what the agent does with the verbal material, and the attitude he adopts towards it.

Thus, it is not true, for desires of the kind discussed, that our only line onto them is agent's confessions. Nor, as a consequence, is there any warrant for the claim that a theory of semantics, which has, *inter alia*, the sentences expressing such confessions as its theorems, is the only kind of theory which will give us access to action arising out of such desires. The connection between language and action which we have examined gives us no grounds for saying that linguistic theory is, *inter alia*, a theory of non-linguistic$_1$ action. True, linguistic understanding is presupposed by any theory of action dealing with conduct above a certain level of sophistication. But in this auxiliary role such understanding is not different from, say, a theory of perception which may also be required for the interpretation of certain kinds of action.

7

In the preceding discussion, we placed a very strict interpretation upon the proposal that social science understands human action in terms of the concept of linguistic meaning. We took this to call for theories of social action to be of the same form as semantic theorizing in linguistics, or to be partly overlapping with such theories. This reading was dictated by our overall project which remains that of assessing the outlook for replacing everyday interpretive accounts with counterparts derived from genuine theories, *in casu* semantic theories.

However, many of the philosophers who have insisted on a tie between the understanding of action in general and the understanding of language have not intended to commit themselves to anything of this kind. They have not wanted to say that there is an affinity between semantic$_1$ theory and theories of (ostensibly) non-linguistic action, as finished products, but rather that there are crucial features in common between the methods employed to produce such theories. These methods have their original home in the understanding of a language, and are best understood within this realm, but are somehow projected into the domain of action understanding in general. In this way, the understanding of language comes to be viewed as a paradigm for the understanding of human action in the abstract. Since doctrines of this kind are quite widespread, we might be charged with neglecting a central theme in the language–action debate if we passed it by in silence. Thus, I shall end this chapter by subjecting this proposal to a brief examination.

A good example of an author who has advocated a position of the kind indicated is Charles Taylor. In his article, 'Interpretation and the Science of Man',[19] Taylor cites three respects in which the meaning of non-linguistic$_1$ human action is akin to that of linguistically articulated phenomena (texts). (1) In both cases we may, according to Taylor, talk about a 'field of objects' among which we can detect 'coherence or its absence, sense or nonsense'. (Taylor seems to regard meaning as a species of coherence.) (2) In both fields, we may distinguish between meaning and that in which it is embodied. (3) In both fields, meaning is meaning for some subject: there is no meaningfulness apart from someone or something for whom it is meaningful.[20]

All this is pretty vague. Fortunately, we need not bother with making it more precise. As it turns out, Taylor is not as much concerned with these features as with an additional one, allegedly shared by the interpretation of linguistic₁ and non-linguistic₁ action, but absent in the cognition of physical reality. This is the fact that the elicitation of textual meaning and action meaning involves an element of 'interpretation' or cognitive processing that is essentially non-algorithmic, that is, it cannot be pinned down to a purely mechanical, rule-governed procedure. As Taylor argues, the meaningful features of human action, linguistic and non-linguistic, are not *machine-decidable*: we could not design a programme for a (digital) computer such that the computer would put out true action descriptions on the basis of an input of brute behavioural (i.e. non-intentionalistic) data.[21] This is the case, according to Taylor, because whenever we attempt to validate attributions of meaning, our efforts take us through a circular movement: we start out to support the interpretation A, which cannot be shown true by mere inspection of reality but must be based discursively on further data and principles of inference, B. The data comprised by B are themselves non-brute and thus presuppose for their support still further data and inferential principles, C. Sooner or later this unravelling of assumptions and interdependencies will take us to some premise X which presupposes the truth of A, the interpretation from which we started. We have moved through a circle because the interpretation of action is a holistic process: there are no presuppositionless data, warranted by brute correspondence with reality, from which to proceed in a linear fashion, but only interpretations warranted by their fit with other interpretations and ultimately with our understanding of human action as a whole.

This is the background for the celebrated Hermeneutical Circle as a model for the interpretation of linguistic meaning. Interpretation proceeds in a circular motion in which all bits of information mutually support and modify each other, but where there is no way of getting outside of the circle to anchor the entire construction in a reality unvarnished by interpretation. According to Taylor, the affinity between action interpretation and textual interpretation shows itself precisely in the fact that theorizing in both fields is governed by the Hermeneutical Circle.[22] Moreover, Taylor invites us to see this affinity as in part the result of the language-permeation of action, of the kind we discussed in the previous section: human action is shaped and constituted by the concepts which agents use to describe it.[23]

So much for exposition of Taylor's doctrine, which echoes views canvassed by several generations of philosophers working within the phenomenological tradition (and recently also by authors within the analytical tradition).[24] To get a better grip upon this issue, we must drop the suggestive but unhelpful manner in which Taylor introduces it, that is, his talking about the machine-decidability of action descriptions. For at the moment, our understanding of what it takes for some task to be machine-computable is far too exiguous to offer a fruitful avenue of attack. As a matter of fact, there is no proof that the data processing that goes into the perception of physical objects is machine-computable; hence there may actually be no contrast between understanding of human action and perceptual recognition of physical objects in this respect.[25] At any rate, in the following we shall not be concerned with the alleged contrast between the understanding of action and language and the cognition of physical reality, but only with the claim that understanding in the first two domains is a unitary phenomenon in some deep sense. In particular, we shall examine the allegation that the common features of the two domains somehow originate in language and have a secondary and derived occurrence in non-linguistic₁ action.

To this end, we shall now embark upon an investigation of the central structural properties of linguistic understanding. We shall study the methodology of what is commonly called *radical interpretation*, that is, the interpretation of a language of which no prior linguistic knowledge exists. In so doing, we make a small but significant break with the hermeneutical approach, which typically deals with problems of interpreting utterances or texts couched in a language which we already understand. That case, which for historical reasons is central to the concerns of hermeneutics,[26] is a hybrid one and somewhat aberrant from an epistemological point of view. The pure case of radical interpretation is much more likely to reveal in a perspicuous fashion the crucial features of linguistic interpretation. It will come as no surprise that the following sketch will borrow heavily from the philosopher who initiated interest in radical interpretation, namely Quine.

We may start by agreeing that linguistic meaning is a matter of truth conditions, without committing ourselves on any of the controversial issues concerning the precise specification of meaning in terms of truth conditions (the question, for instance, whether or not such specification must involve the introduction of possible worlds, or the question whether or not truth conditions must be epistemically accessible). Hence the road to an interpretation of the object language of radical interpretation (or, as I shall call it, the native language) goes via the detection of the truth conditions of native sentences. That is, for every sentence of the native language, we must pin down the conditions under which an utterance of that sentence will be *true*.

The only way to get at these conditions is by observing the occasions on which native utterances are actually made, in the light of the assumption that the natives largely intend to assert what they think is true and that they are generally right in what they take to be the truth (this is very rough; more about the latter assumption in a moment).

It is obvious that not all sentences are equally well-suited for having their truth value determined in this fashion. For many sentences, we cannot fix their truth values merely by looking at the world: only observational sentences have this property. Hence, the entering wedge into the native language will be sentences describing the native's immediate surroundings as they are observed by the native and the linguist. However, the linguist is not restricted to passive recording of utterances volunteered by the natives for very long. Once he has grasped (tentatively, of course) a certain minimal segment of the native language (crucially involving the native expressions for assent and dissent), he will be in a position to offer observation sentences for the natives' verdict.

An additional benefit will also accrue from the linguist's (partial) grasp of the native language: it will allow him to identify the truth-functional apparatus (truth-functional connectives) found in the native discourse. Once the linguist has laid down, by questioning and passive observation, the truth conditions of a sample of native sentences, he may check any idiom which he suspects to be a truth-functional device by joining together sentences from the sample by that idiom. If native assent to the compound sentence depends in systematic ways on the truth values of its elements, a truth-functional connective has been identified. As the next step, the linguist will lay down the truth table for that idiom to find its counterpart among the connectives of his own language.

Once the logical connectives are in place, the linguist has acquired a powerful tool for progressing beyond the interpretation of observation sentences. For non-observational sentences, the linguist cannot, in the nature of the case, discover their meaning by observing the environment in which the natives are willing to assent to them. The only way for him to get at their meaning is to link them to the observational sentences which are relevant to their truth value. In the process of establishing such links, the linguist is greatly aided by his ability to offer sentences for the natives' assent or dissent and by his grasp of one crucial logical connective in the native language, namely, that which expresses material implication. He will offer, for the natives' verdict, sentences in which an observational sentence of known truth conditions is tied together, by material implication, with some non-observational sentences to which the linguist suspects that it is connected. By shrewd and lucky questioning of this kind, the linguist, slowly but surely, will manage to pin down the observational facts in which the natives' theoretical sentences are anchored.

Thus far, we have only allowed the linguist to treat native utterances as units, as whole sentences: he has only been concerned with the assignment of truth conditions. And truth conditions are the properties of sentences. However, to get a full grasp of the language, the linguist must, of course, penetrate to the inner structure of sentences. He needs to carve up sentences into smaller units and ascribe separate semantic import to them. He also needs to identify semantically relevant syntactic structure within sentences. He accomplishes this by means of what Quine terms analytical hypotheses.[27] These he gets at by noticing recurring elements in sentences, and by endeavouring to link them up with recurring elements in the total situations which make such sentences true.

The above account of radical interpretation should not be taken as indicating a temporal process (apart, perhaps, from the interpretation of simple observation sentences which must largely precede the other stages): the processes described are most likely to go hand in hand. For instance, the linguist would hardly be able to question the natives successfully without a certain grasp of the internal structure of native sentences. The above account describes analytically separable elements of the total, simultaneous process of interpretation.

What I have offered here is a purely skeletal account of the procedure of radical interpretation. The finer details of this process, and the way in which the various structures and elements of language emerge through it, do not really concern us here. Rather, we are interested in the general methodological–structural features of the theory of interpretation. It is at this level that crucial affinities exist between linguistic interpretation and the interpretation of action, according to the hermeneutician. These features may be seen as residing in a number of constraints to which radical interpretation is subject. We shall now examine these constraints, again drawing heavily upon such authors as Quine, Davidson, Lewis and others.

Let us begin by bringing out into the open an assumption which was built into the above procedure but which will not withstand closer scrutiny. This procedure presupposed that the natives form the same kind of observational beliefs as the linguist, and hence are likely to produce observational reports similar to his. *A fortiori*, it presupposes that the reports made in situations where the linguist will typically issue an observational report are also, correspondingly, observational reports in the native language. However, both assumptions may be questioned. Suppose the natives believe that rabbits are ancestors incarnate (cf. *Word and Object*, p. 69). In this case, the correct translation of their exclamation when a rabbit is in sight, 'Gavagai', would not mean, 'Lo, a rabbit', but rather, 'Lo, an ancestor incarnate.' We discover a need to identify the contents of native beliefs prior to fixing the meaning of native utterances.

How can we identify the contents of someone's beliefs? A time-tested method is, of course, to ask him. But this avenue is blocked in the present case, since we are not yet in a position to make sense of the answer. Instead, we must resort to the natives' extralinguistic behaviour. If we observe, for instance, that the natives capture, cook and consume the animals which they refer to as gavagais, we may safely assume that they regard gavagais as perfectly mundane creatures, and hence should lean towards 'rabbit' rather than 'ancestor incarnate' as the proper translation.

However, this conclusion really goes further than can be licensed by the evidence: the behavioural evidence only discredited one particular alternative to the 'natural' interpretation. It did not show in a positive fashion that 'rabbit' is indeed the proper translation. Moreover, it may be questioned whether it really suffices to rule out the alternative interpretation: maybe the natives take rabbits to be ancestors after all, but also believe that by eating rabbit meat, they may come to partake of the strength and wisdom of their forefathers who then assume some other animal form. (If this hypothesis seems too fanciful, consider the assumptions needed for a native interpreter to put the right construal upon the Catholic ritual of bread and wine in the Eucharist.)

To cut down on the underdetermination of interpretive theory, a number of methodological constraints have been suggested. Among these, most attention has been given to the so-called *Principle of Charity*. In a preliminary formulation, this principle tells us to grade interpretations in proportion to their tendency to make native beliefs come out *true* (or, which amounts to the same thing in practice, in proportion to their ability to maximize agreement between native beliefs and the beliefs of the linguist).

However, this principle will not do as it stands. It is simply not acceptable, when we are trying to translate, say, the language of a tribe at a near-neolithic stage of development, to assume any large-scale agreement between their beliefs and ours. Man at this stage cannot be taken to have arrived at the same conception of the world as that entertained by a member of a highly developed industrial society.

However, it is doubtful whether this crude version of the Principle of Charity was ever seriously and reflectively entertained by anyone. Davidson, who in earlier formulations appeared to be quite close to it, has later offered more circumspect phrasings: he now urges us to maximize agreement in belief, subject to, among other things, our 'knowledge of explicable error', that is, I take it, our knowledge of conditions under which people are likely to go wrong.[28] Thus, the Principle of Charity, in a more careful formulation, requires us to *minimize inexplicable error* on the part of the natives. Some such principle has been advocated by Lewis,[29] in a formulation which has received Davidson's endorsement.[30]

Is the Principle of Charity acceptable, thus amended? The answer depends, I think, on how much we require of an explanation of falsehood. If we require an explanation to make it deductively certain, or highly probable, that the natives commit themselves to a falshood, I think that the principle as amended will lead us to be overly charitable. Any standard anthropological text will offer numerous plausible interpretations of native action which saddle the natives with error of a kind for which we have no explanation of the required strength. The Principle of Charity would force us, quite counter-intuitively, to modify such interpretations, or to go looking for better ones.

Such a strong interpretation of the Principle of Charity is actually adopted by Lewis. He suggests that false native beliefs must be explicable in the sense that we must be able to point to some inductive method which would lead (with at least high probability, he seems to imply) to our current system of beliefs if given our life histories as data input, and which would yield (at least with high probability) the native system of beliefs when given native life histories as input.[31]

To show how this principle fails to accord with the practice of anthropologists—a practice which I think is legitimate—we might look at the traditional ascription of an *anthropomorphic* world view to natives. According to that view, nature is seen as embodying spirits, creatures with intelligence and appetite who are responsible for the behaviour of physical objects by using them as instruments for their actions. Now I doubt whether there is any determinate answer to the question as to whether our current 'inductive methods' (which, to be charitable to Lewis, we might read as meaning 'principles of theory selection') would lead to the adoption of an anthropomorphic world view if applied to the data available to the natives. But if there is one, I suspect that it is negative. After all, there is considerable difference between the behaviour of human beings and animals on the one hand–creatures to which we ascribe agency–and that of sticks and stones on the other. It would seem that our grounds for imputing agency, intelligence and appetites to the former do not carry over to the latter. Lewis's principle would force us to deem the anthropomorphic view inexplicable and would thus force us to seek another interpretation that would not saddle the natives with this view.

Lewis's prescription for accounting for mistakes is somewhat narrow, anyway: it merely allows explanations that show mistaken beliefs to be the outcome of rational reasoning which has been applied to false or insufficient data. But anthropological theory, or at least anthropological theory of a kind very popular in the past, would typically account for such beliefs in a different way. It would account for them by pointing to factors interfering with rational thinking about reality. Thus, for instance, it would account for the anthropomorphic views of pre-literate societies by representing them as accommodating the fears of these people, who were faced with a hostile and niggardly environment. By populating nature with spirits, the most powerful of which are thought to be favourably disposed towards man, a guarantee is postulated that the well-being of the individual and of society will prevail in the end.

Does this kind of explanation satisfy the modified Principle of Charity, according to a strong reading of the demand that error be explicable? I think not. Once again, we are not in a position to predict with any confidence what kind of beliefs, or overall world view, some community will adopt in the predicament mentioned. The lack of predictability is brought out by the observation that we would have little reason, *before* becoming acquainted with the native world view, to ascribe to them a fear of a hostile nature: that imputation is based solely upon the realization that it will explain the native world view. (And I would suggest that this remains the only evidence for that imputation, even *post hoc*, making it thus gravitate towards vacuity.)

To be acceptable, the Principle of Charity should call for explanation of false beliefs only in a weak sense, a 'why possibly'-sense, rather than a 'why necessarily'- (or 'why almost certainly'-) sense. In this sense, I think, we are indeed in a position to explain the anthropomorphic world view: it comes as no great surprise that man should derive his first models for the understanding of nature from the experience of himself as being endowed with intelligence and desires and with the power of agency. It is quite natural–although, again, not the inevitable consequence of some canon of theory selection common to the natives and us–that man should first populate the world with spirits and personalized forces, before the possibility dawned upon him of explaining natural phenomena by some more abstract notion of agency. When formulated in terms of this weaker concept of explanation, the Principle of Charity has considerable plausibility.

However things may stand regarding the Principle of Charity, it is evident that we need further ways to cut down on the underdetermination of interpretation. Let us return to the natives and the rabbits to see why this is the case. Suppose that the natives do indeed regard rabbits as ancestors incarnate and that they have no beliefs which might render it rational or permissible for them to consume their ancestors. But assume, furthermore, that the natives are the victims of an irresistible fondness of rabbit meat. The urge is so strong that, more often than not, it will get the better of them when they are in the immediate vicinity of a rabbit: they cannot help themselves, but kill and eat it, despite the rather flagrant violation of kinship sentiment involved in that action.

Now maybe we could stick to our interpretation that rabbits are considered to be ancestors incarnate, even in the face of such observations. The natives' reaction of horror and remorse after their deed might persuade us that this interpretation is valid after all. But if such acratic action became widespread, and the natives' pursuit of their long-term goals were constantly disrupted by short spells of pursuing contrary goals, our warrant for imputing desires to them, at least long-term ones, would become very tenuous. There would be too little constancy in the native behaviour to justify the ascription of long-term conative dispositions.

This observation suggests a constraint to the effect that our interpretations must not make people out to be overly susceptible to acratic action: we must avoid interpretations which represent people as exceedingly shifty. We might dub this the *Principle of Practical Rationality*, adding the remark that the rationality involved here is stronger than that primarily dealt with thus far in this study. The latter notion could be termed 'instant rationality', and might be captured in the principle that people act rationally in the light of their beliefs and desires in the instant of action. This notion does not exclude action which is acratic according to the stronger notion of rationality (i.e. action in pursuit of short-term goals of a kind incompatible with the accomplishment of long-term goals), but rather lays down a principle of desire attribution which permits us to say that, at the moment of action, the agent was prompted by a short-term desire to do so-and-so. (Note that the above stronger notion of rationality does not rule out *occasional* acratic action; it only tells us to avoid global action interpretations that imply very widespread acrasia. Thus it does not contradict, or supersede, the weaker notion of rationality.)

We have examined a couple of basic constraints on interpretation. Other, less fundamental constraints have been suggested in the literature and will be discussed briefly in a moment. However, I think enough has been said already for the outlines of a conclusion to emerge: the most important constraints on a theory of interpretation apply to it because a theory of interpretation is a part of, or an aspect of, a general theory of action and belief. What we learned from the examination of radical interpretation is that in order to fix the meaning of the sentences of a radically foreign language, we have to fix the beliefs of the foreign speakers. And to accomplish this, we have to acquire a grasp of the nature of the speakers' non-linguistic actions. Linguistic interpretation is attained only as an aspect of an overall interpretation of human action and belief. And the two constraints on interpretation which we have examined, the Principle of Charity and the Principle of Practical Rationality, enter the methodology of radical interpretation only because the core of a theory of interpretation simply *is* a theory of action and belief. Thus, there is no need to go on to examine the constraints on action interpretation, to determine whether there are affinities between these and the constraints on

linguistic interpretation as elucidated above; because the constraints on linguistic interpretation which we have examined *are*
constraints on action interpretation in general. They are
constraints on linguistic interpretation only because linguistic
interpretation incorporates a general interpretation of action and
belief. It is a foregone conclusion that the very same constraints will
emerge from an analysis of the interpretation of pure, non-linguistic
action. Any interpretation of (non-linguistic) action must
presuppose a grasp of agents' beliefs: we cannot hope to identify the
nature of an action unless we know what beliefs inspired the agent.
To get at the beliefs, we must invoke, *inter alia*, the Principle of
Charity in order to reduce the number of alternative interpretations
(we assume a situation of 'radical interpretation' of action, where
the agent's language is not yet understood and hence cannot be
used as a source of information). Furthermore, any interpretation
of non-linguistic action will be subject to the Principal of Practical
Rationality as a global constraint on the overall theory of action of
which it is a part, in a way which is perfectly parallel to what we
found in linguistic interpretation.

Thus, up to a point, our investigation may be said to bear out
the hermeneutician's claim. The analysis of radical interpretation
has disclosed important structural–methodological affinities
between linguistic interpretation and interpretation of action. Two
crucial methodological principles, the Principle of Charity and the
Principle of Practical Rationality, are involved in both. Moreover
the view has been vindicated that in both fields, the process of
interpretation traces a circular path (the Hermeneutical Circle). In
both fields, interpretation depends upon logically interlocked
assumptions concerning the agent's desires and beliefs. By virtue of
these interrelations, these assumptions all depend upon each other
in the final analysis, and even upon that particular interpretation
which concerns the interpreter at the moment and for which those
assumptions serve as the premises.

The embarrassment for the hermeneutician is the fact that the
direction of these affinities, if you allow the expression, is quite
opposite to what he claimed. It is not as if we have detected
structural features of action interpretation that somehow have their
source in the interpretation of language but which are imposed

upon the wider field due to the role of language in human action. It is not even the case that the features shared by the two fields are most clearly displayed, and hence most easily grasped, in the domain of language. Rather, what we have found is that there are familiar features of the interpretation of action–centrally, the epistemological and logical interrelatedness of attributions of desire and belief, and the constitutive role of rationality–that are also found in the sub-domain of linguistic interpretation, creating problems of a kind long familiar, for example, to economists trying to develop a theoretical vocabulary for the description of human choice.

But maybe this conclusion is premature. We have only examined two constraints on linguistic interpretation, albeit two very important ones. There might be further constraints on interpretation to which it is not subject *qua* theory of action but which could still be transferred to the latter in an illuminating manner.

Perhaps one further constraint may be elicited from the conjunction of two central features of language discussed earlier. Language is unbounded, permitting the construal of an infinite number of sentences. It is also scrutable, in that the meanings of an infinite class of sentences can be gathered from an inspection of those sentences, on the basis of a finite number of interpretive principles. It follows from such simultaneous possession of these two properties that language must be composite (and indeed recursive): the meaning of larger units must be a function of the meanings of smaller, component units, and of the structure in which they are combined.

The constraint which is suggested by this observation tells us to look for recurring structure in language and to grade interpretive theories in proportion to the extent that they ascribe the same meaning to identical lexical items and syntactic structures in different contexts. The bite of this constraint can be seen from the fact that it would require us to avoid, within limits set by the other constraints, the interpretation of large stretches of native discourse as *metaphorical*. Thus, it would count against the policy of certain anthropologists to interpret ostensibly metaphysical or religious statements as metaphorical discourse on social structures and processes. For metaphorical interpretation is precisely non-systematic, *ad hoc* interpretation which assigns different meanings to identical forms.

Does a similar principle hold for the interpretation of non-linguistic action? The answer must be no. The equivalent of linguistic atoms (words) would be basic acts, according to a strong, absolute reading of basicness which will not allow an action that is basic in one context to be non-basic in another. I shall bypass here the doubts that have been raised concerning the coherency of such a notion and merely point out that it is hardly the case that the 'meaning' of an action, at least under any description which is likely to interest us, is derivable from the 'meanings' of its component basic acts. Suppose, for instance, that I remove a number of paper slips from my wallet and hand them over to some other person. Assuming the validity of the theory of basic acts, this action would be re-describable as a sequence of basic acts, $A_1A_2A_3$. . . A_n. In a trivial sense, the meaning (*one* meaning) of the overall action would be derivable from a listing of these basic acts. For we may simply describe that action as the conjunction of those acts, $A_1+A_2+\ldots A_n$ (the '+' signifying temporal succession). But such a description of the overall action is perfectly uninteresting. The only kind of description which is likely to be of any use to us is one characterizing my action, for example, as that of buying a television set and paying for it in cash. This description cannot be inferred from a description of component basic acts in a way at all similar to that in which the meaning of a sentence can be derived from its components. The reason is, of course, that the connection between the locutionary act (the act of uttering certain words) and its semantic meaning is conventional, whereas the meaning of most non-linguistic$_1$ action depends heavily upon 'natural' (causal) connections. The semantic content of a sentence is built up out of the meaning-contributions of the component words, according to such principles of composition as those discussed in previous sections. A given component term makes the same contribution to every sentence, or a limited number of types of contributions in case of ambiguity. In the case of indexical expressions, the contribution may depend upon the context, but in systematically circumscribed ways specifiable in advance. The case of non-linguistic action is different. There is no presumption here that the same bodily movement makes the same contribution to total action meaning. Depending on the context, my act of raising my arm may count as an act of shooing away a fly, attracting someone's attention, bidding on a Picasso, pointing to the Morning Star, and so on, without end. The context is everything here, not, as in the linguistic case, merely something that cuts down upon the ambiguity left by interpretation according to purely intrinsic properties of the item interpreted.

Are there any other constraints on linguistic interpretation that might be transferable to the interpretation of action? When the topic of constraints on linguistic theorizing is brought up, the name of Noam Chomsky must inevitably come to mind. Chomsky argues that in order to explain the fact that infants succeed in learning language with surprising rapidity at an age when their general intellectual capacities are not yet very highly developed, we have to ascribe to them a strong innate capacity for ordering observational data involving language and for framing probable hypotheses for their explanation. The principles of this innate mechanism, when written out, will amount to constraints on the acceptability of grammars for particular languages. Chomsky refers to the total set of such principles as *Universal Grammar*. As examples of principles cited by Chomsky as belonging to Universal Grammar, we might mention the very principle that linguistic structures are generatable by a two-tiered algorithm, encompassing a phrase-structure component and a transformational component; the principle of *cyclic application*, which states that transformations apply to base strings in a certain order, namely, first to the innermost phrases, then to phrases containing these, and so on, up to complete, non-embedded strings; and the A-over-A principle to the effect that if a transformation applies to some embedded structure of a particular type T, that transformation must apply to the maximal structure of type T.[32] (In fairness to Chomsky, it must be stressed that these principles are offered in a very tentative spirit; this holds even more for a number of additional principles of a similar kind which are occasionally cited in Chomsky's works.)

However, the constraints listed by Chomsky are not relevant for our present enquiry. This has nothing to do with the fact that they are constraints upon theories of syntax rather than semantics: even syntactic constraints might at times be relevant for the choice between competing semantic theories. Rather, it is because we are only interested in constraints possessing a certain *a priori* standing *vis-à-vis* experience. Constraints upon theories of interpretation are meant to reduce somewhat the slack between data and theory. To be able to do this, they must possess an autonomy *vis-à-vis* the data such that we feel justified in applying them in an *a priori* fashion: they are principles we impose upon the data to order them, not principles we detect in the data. But despite the fact that Chomsky labels his methodologico-epistemological position one of 'rationalism'—a misnomer which has lead to much futile debate—he does not claim that we can demonstrate the validity of constraints of the kind listed above *a priori*. On the contrary, he insists that they hold true only as a matter of empirical fact, if they hold true at all. Hence, the Chomskyan principles of universal grammar do not possess the character of methodological constraints on theory construction in linguistics; and the question as to whether they may be fruitfully transferred to the understanding of non-linguistic action does not arise at all.

To sum up our reflections on the hermeneutic view, the view that all action is somehow permeated with language and must hence be grasped through methods and procedures that are borrowed from linguistic understanding: the hermeneutician is right, after a fashion, that the interpretation of non-linguistic action exhibits certain crucial structural similarities to that of semantic interpretation, as manifested in the constraints upon the latter. He is also right that there are important methodologico-epistemological features common to the two fields in the holistic nature of interpretation and the resulting 'hermeneutical circularity' of the process. But he is wrong in suggesting that this affinity means that human action in general is 'language-like', if this means that the common features have their source in language, and that there are methodological lessons for a science of action that can only be learned from reflection on linguistic interpretation. As we have seen, rather than action being language-like, it is really language that is action-like: a theory of linguistic meaning is a specialized theory of action and comes into being only as a part of an overall interpretation of behaviour. Reflection on the phenomenon of radical interpretation helps dispel the aura of mystery in which linguistic interpretation is often shrouded in hermeneutical writings. Linguistic interpretation is not an occult, transempirical process, but a branch of empirical enquiry at large. More relevant to our concerns, such reflection reveals the falsity of the view that the problems of action interpretation infest it because of its association with linguistic interpretation, which is thought to be the original source of these maladies. Indeed, the problems besetting linguistic understanding are at their root the very problems of action understanding as such.

Epilogue

1

The time has come to take stock and to recapitulate briefly the answer we have reached to the query raised in the Introduction: are there considerations of principle working against our producing systematizations of our knowledge of social action which are superior in theoreticity to current common-sense understanding of action, and which will support theoretically-enriched interpretive accounts? The notion of theoreticity appealed to was defined as a function of the generality of the principles we invoke and the economy of the ontology we posit in order to express our knowledge.

We have come up with an affirmative answer to this question, or better, a number of affirmative answers, as we found it necessary to divide the investigation into a number of independent, parallel sub-investigations corresponding to the different arguments needed to establish an answer to our question for each of the different modes of interpretive accounts. We singled out three such modes, namely purposive accounts, rule accounts, and semantic accounts.

In purposive accounts, the crucial block to gains in theoreticity was found to be the semantic shallowness of the intentionalistic vocabulary in which they, and other interpretive accounts, are couched. This feature marks an important dissimilarity between intentionalistic terms and those employed to explain natural processes. The latter typically apply to things united by the possession of some unspecified 'real essence', a description of which may replace the term used in everyday accounts, *salva veritate*. The replacing descriptions are normally more analytical than the expressions they supersede, revealing structure and complexity in the things described and thereby paving the way for a reduction of heterogeneous macro-phenomena to an organized set of homogeneous micro-phenomena explicable by means of a limited number of principles. By contrast, intentionalistic terms are mere surface, from the semantic point of view, pointing to no 'deeper' descriptions. They possess no theoretical counterparts with which they may be exchanged in explanatory contexts, *salva veritate*.

But this result does not by itself preclude theoretical gains in purposive explanation: everyday accounts might still be replaced by theoretical ones if the former could be shown to be largely false. But I argued that human beings enjoy a privileged epistemic access to their motivational impulses which renders this route to theoretical progress rather unpromising. True, this privilege is a qualified one, as is demonstrated in Freud's work: people may on occasion be genuinely mistaken about their own motivation. On the other hand, erroneous self-understanding has to be exceptionally widespread and consistent to make room for theoretical advance along these lines: *every* self-interpretation involving a particular motivational term must be deemed incorrect for that term to be eliminable from the theoretical vocabulary and a gain in ontological parsimony thus secured. This is an exceedingly strong demand which will only be satisfied in very few, if any, cases.

The reasoning applied to purposive accounts did not carry over to rule accounts, since the agent's epistemic position is less favourable in this case: it is a fact of everyday experience that people may act in accordance with rules which they are incapable of specifyng (grammatical rules are a case in point). This circumstance nullifies the effect of the semantic shallowness of intentionalistic terms. Instead, we found blocks to theoretical advance in rule explanation of another, more empirical kind. We restricted our investigation to a class of rules dubbed '*mores*', comprising rules regulating human interaction and human interests, and to the class of ritual rules; for only these rules are specifically social in their content.

Within an interpretive approach, theoretical gains in the investigation of rule-following conduct are achieved by subsuming the rule explications volunteered by agents under more general, more inclusive formulations not known to common sense. (If the everyday explication is rejected as *false*, there may of course be theoretical gains without subsumption.) However, we made much of the point that the interests of an explanatory theory of rule-following action are not served by a mere codification of everyday rules as corollaries of more general principles, as a purely logical exercise: the inferential ties explicated in such a codification must map the actual pathways of motivational forces in agents, as it were. Rules higher in the hierarchy must not only subsume rules further down, as a matter of pure logic, but must express the agent's reason for abiding by the latter rules. If not, the theoretically posited rule just represents a rationalistic misrepresentation of the actual motivational dynamics of rule-governed action.

Once this point is savoured, we realize that the hopes for theoretical gains in the understanding of rules, of a kind suited to enrich interpretive accounts, are very slight. As a matter of fact, a faithful scientific picture of the motivation of rule-governed action may show *less* cognitive integration (of the desired type) than the everyday picture which is likely to embody considerable idealization and rationalization. We get an indication of this by reflecting on the way in which the rules regulating human interaction are *learnt*. Such rules are learnt piecemeal during infancy and adolescence, and are not imparted through the inculcation of a basic norm from which the rest are then derived as corollaries. And although there may be some subsequent effort to rearrange and interconnect that which has been learnt, it is doubtful whether this activity succeeds in generating a motivational structure which is as simple and as integrated as everyday conception has it. That conception is in part modelled upon the rule codification to which social agents appeal in the normative–critical use of norms; that is, in the enterprise of justifying and criticizing each other's conduct. The everyday understanding of rule-following conduct is tainted by the dual use of norms in a critical as well as an explanatory function, and illicitly borrows some of the axiomatic regimentation which has its home in the former use. A scientific model of the competence structure behind rule-governed social interaction will be less integrated than the rationalization offered by common sense.

As for ritual rules, we investigated the proposal that grammatical rules be taken as a paradigm for theorizing in this area, and the hope that we may make the same kind of progress beyond everyday understanding here as has been achieved in the study of syntax. However, the lack of projectibility of ritual rules shows this hope to be vain: if ritual rules were the manifestation of a more abstract, underlying 'grammar', the learning of ritual conduct in one corner of social life would result in a command of ritual conduct in other areas as well, with no additional instruction being necessary. But no non-trivial 'generalization of learning' is actually found in ritual rules.

The problem in a theoretical strengthening of semantic accounts was entirely different from those encountered in the two other modes. Here, the theoretical effort will not even get under way, for the simple reason that semantic notions do not apply to action outside of language. We may if we like describe action as 'meaningful' to set it over against purely natural processes; but the notion of 'meaning' employed here is far less specific and far less complex than the one used to characterize semantically significant elements of language. Central to the notion of semantic meaning is the concept of 'speaker's meaning', that is, the concept of someone meaning something in doing something. That concept unfolds into a specification of a highly complicated, iterative sequence of communicative intentions which is just not found outside of language. Moreover, the vehicle of semantic meaning–the semantic system–displays the formal properties of compositeness, un-boundedness, and scrutability which are similarly unique to linguistic action. The question of whether we can devise theories of action on the model of semantic theories in linguistics–or rather, on the model of those semantic theories which linguists hope someday to construct, and the general form of which has been explored by philosophers–does not arise at all. The use of semantic terms to describe non-linguistic action is a metaphor which may on occasion be illuminating, although I suspect that it is more often misleading and dangerous. But that use is not founded upon deep-seated affinities which could warrant the hopes for successful theorizing in social science modelled upon linguistic semantics.

We conclude that there are narrow limits to theoretical progress in the interpretive approach to action. As long as we remain loyal to our common-sense ways of accounting for action, emphasizing purposiveness and rule-following, we must renounce a more theoretical, more unified picture of human motivation. The boundless richness and diversity which human action displays to the everyday observer will not reduce to orderliness and system as long as we explain it in terms of purposes and rules. Purposiveness and rule-following are just not the intellectual categories that make action reveal the unity we seek in theoretical enquiry. There is no short list of 'ultimate ends' to which all human endeavour can be reduced; indeed, the class of such ends has indefinite extension. Nor can we detect 'deep rules' of social action of which the everyday rule codifications are merely the surface manifestations. The use of interpretive methods flatters our sense of being unique, of being something set apart from the rest of reality, and produces a reassuringly familiar picture of social action, displaying that 'faithfulness to social reality as it is experienced by the agents themselves' which is cherished by interpretive theorists. But these virtues are bought at the price of being stuck with a shallow understanding of the phenomena. To get beyond the everyday understanding, we must shift to a causal approach: we must examine the conditions which shape action from behind, as it were, rather than the ends towards which it steers and the rules to which it seeks to conform. Here, as elsewhere in science, we can only create order in the welter of experience by abandoning our everyday ways of explanation. This is not to say that the needed shift is a radical one: there is no call for us to give up *describing* action in intentionalistic terms, identifying it via its goal or governing rule. It is only when we aspire to *theoretical explanation* of action that we have to abandon our accustomed ways. Nor of course is causal explanation of action unknown to common sense. But our findings call for a shift of emphasis in action explanation from the rule-following purposive aspect stressed by common sense to the causal aspect which is less prevalent in that conception.

2

This conclusion may strike the reader as unsupported on its

positive side, that is, in its recommendation of a causalist turn. After all, what has been shown in the preceding chapters is merely that little is to be expected from the interpretive way. But this is hardly a certification of the causal approach: I myself deplored, in the Introduction, the tendency of the interpretivists to take any demonstrated weakness in the rival view to signal a virtue in their own position. Still I seem to commit the same fallacy here, taking the breakdown of the interpretivist programme to prove the viability of a causalist approach. To ward off this charge, I shall round out this essay with a few remarks to indicate where I see room for theoretical progress within a causalist approach to individual action in social science. In the process, I shall draw a distinction between two varieties of causal explanation of action, one of which turns out to be afflicted with the same weakness as interpretive accounts, whereas the other one offers some genuine promise of theoretical progress.

The first type of causal explanation seeks to account for action as a function of extrinsic eliciting and controlling conditions which are typically simultaneous with, or immediately antecedent to, the action. This approach might grow out of the observation that intentionalistically described motivational states are broadly dis-positional, as we saw in chapter 1. Put very crudely, the positing of a motivational state links the specification of certain events and conditions in the agent's environment with the specification of the actions which he performs *vis-à-vis* that environment. Using an oldfashioned terminology, we might say that motivational states are *intervening variables* in a functional relationship between the environment (the independent variable) and human action (the dependent variable). The motorist's hunger is an intervening variable which links his spotting a billboard at the roadside announcing a restaurant up ahead with his subsequent action of getting off at the next ramp. His obedience to the traffic rules is an intervening variable which ties his glance at the speedometer with his subsequent act of easing on the accelerator, etc.

Given this analysis, we may characterize interpretive accounts as explanations in which, out of the total set of variables controlling action, only the intervening variables are mentioned, whereas the independent variables which control action through the inter-mediation of these variables are left out. In interpretive explanation, we account for the driver's getting off the road by citing his hunger and his knowledge that there is a roadside restaurant up ahead, leaving unmentioned the eliciting event of the billboard catching his eye. And we cite his obedience to the speed limit to explain why he slows down, leaving out the triggering event of his checking the speedometer. (This is the typical case. However, at times such information is actually included in interpretive ac-counts. But then its function is to supply, in an indirect fashion, a specification of the beliefs on which the agent acted. An account of the motorist's act of reducing speed may mention that he checked the speedometer, but only as a way of conveying his recognition (belief) that he was going too fast. At any rate, interpretive explanation does not *require* that such information be included.)

Now the causalist's proposal is that we shift the focus of action explanation by tracing the determination of action back past the intervening variables to the independent variables, thereby turning interpretive accounts into causal accounts. This move would introduce a whole new range of parameters into action accounts, namely the parameters detailing the eliciting and controlling variables. And the causalist's hope is that this range might be more amenable to theoretical systematization than the intervening variables.

There are notorious problems involved in producing causal explanations of human action of the type sketched here, problems reflecting the difficulty of formulating adequate general laws in the face of the complexity and idiosyncrasy of human beings, the difficulty of generating precise measurements of the strength of motivational forces, the difficulty of defining action terms with sufficient precision, the difficulty of conducting experiments, and many more. I shall bypass these traditional worries for causal explanation here, and instead focus upon a consideration which is more in line with the general argument of this book. I shall demonstrate that the proposed explanations cannot secure a gain in *theoreticity*.

The fact is that causal accounts of the kind outlined partake of the weaknesses suffered by interpretive accounts. The vocabulary needed to describe the conditions which trigger and control action–and hence the vocabulary to be used in the laws subsuming these events–must be as rich as the vocabulary needed to describe the intentionalistic states referred to in interpretive accounts. In part, the two vocabularies are identical. For the conditions which causally elicit and control action do so by being thought by the agent to be instrumental or detrimental, as the case may be, to the realization of his goals or of the upshots dictated by rules to which he subscribes. At least, their causal efficacy is due to some associative nexus with those goals and upshots. That is, the causally relevant aspect of those conditions (or better, one such aspect) requires for its description a reference to the agent's relevant goals and rule commitments. A full specification of the causally relevant features of the eliciting and controlling events must thus incorporate a description of the goals and upshots to which they are tied, and hence must make use of the vocabulary employed to characterize those goals and upshots. Thus the vocabulary used to describe the immediate causal conditions of action must be at least as rich as the language employed in interpretive explanation, a language which we have shown to be resistant to significant theoretical enrichment.

This point is related to an observation which is often adduced in the debate over causal explanation of human action: human beings do not respond to the purely physical aspect of the stimuli which impinge upon their senses, but instead to these stimuli as they *interpret* them. That is, it is not (or at least not only) the physical parameters of the stimuli which are relevant for the causal explanation of action (as long as we conceive action as action, that is, intentionalistically), but rather the higher-order descriptions which agents assign to them. For instance, it is not the purely acoustic properties of your vocalization that elicits my hostile response, but the insulting semantical content which I read into it. (The acoustic properties are not irrelevant, however: they are the properties I interpret to get at the semantical reading. But the point is that the acoustic properties alone do not explain my reaction.) This fact is troublesome for the causal analysis of human action since the investigator can never know in advance which parameters will be relevant in a given situation; there is not even a fixed stock from which those parameters will be selected. The natural scientist examining a physical system can quickly establish which kinds of forces are at work in it and thereby determine which variables are relevant to explain it. In the case of a 'behavioural system', for instance a group of human beings in interaction, it can never be determined which parameters are relevant on the basis of a brief inspection. Certain aspects of the situation may be vested with a significance—social, religious, emotional, etc.—which is crucial for the dynamics of that system but which is not revealed by a simple observation of the interactants or the setting. This makes the social scientist's task of producing reliable predictions an exasperating one, with the exception of highly formalized situations, typically of a rule-bound nature, where some kind of implicit 'script' determines which features of the situation the participants are obliged to notice and react to. We have now found that the same property of human action—the interposition of an 'interpretive' process between stimulus and response—makes for a boundless richness of the vocabulary needed to explain action even in causal terms.

The language required to formulate causal explanation of action in terms of proximal eliciting and controlling stimuli must be as rich as the intentionalistic language. It is in part identical with that language, projected onto physical reality, as it were. This is no surprise, since the proximal stimuli work upon the intentionalistic states of the agent and hence partake, in their characterization, of the diversity and irreducibility of the latter. Thus, to make any progress in causal theorizing, we must look beyond the immediate causes and the motivational states with which they interact, to the conditions which generated those states. We must try to create some order in the facts of human action by seeing the rich variation of motivation as springing from a limited number of generative mechanisms to which they owe their existence.

As it happens, this is an approach frequently adopted in social psychology. Much work in this discipline is focused upon the forces moulding man's behavioural tendencies. For instance, there is extensive speculation about primary socialization, the debate centring on the nature of the processes by which social norms are instilled into the young. Various mechanisms have been proposed, such as the formation of a super-ego proposed by Freud, modelling, the pressure towards conformity, fear of punishment, but also purely cognitive processes, as in the theories of Piaget and Kohlberg. A grand attempt to account for the genesis of human motivation in terms of a single mechanism is made in Skinner's theory of operant conditioning, which places the process of reinforcement at the basis of all significant action in man. A more specific mechanism of generation and modification of human impulses is examined in the theory of cognitive dissonance (which I believe is mislabelled as a *cognitive* theory). This theory deals with the tensions that may exist between certain beliefs or evaluations and certain behaviours, tensions which release themselves through the modification of these beliefs and evaluations. A related theory, known under the name of 'balance theory', deals with the way in which pro- and con-attitudes tend to form a stable equilibrium; for instance, people tend to develop a dislike of that which is despised by persons whom they admire. This is different from the mere tendency towards conformity, the latter being the individual's inclination to align himself with the consensus in his social group, whether represented by people liked or disliked. Another hypothesis is the doctrine of 'Mere Exposure', the suggestion that the mere exposure to some thing or situation leads to the liking of that thing or situation, at least in certain specified cases.[1]

Evidently, each of these theories only supplies a tiny piece of the overall puzzle, and even when taken together, they cannot stand alone. Since they deal only with the social determinants of action—inherently, or in the use to which we put them in social science—they must be combined with theories from psychology, biology and physiology to provide a more complete picture. But here we are merely concerned with the social aspect of the processes through which human conative tendencies are shaped.

There is also interesting work on the *cognitive* dimension of motivation. Studies have been conducted to determine how human beings process the information on the basis of which they settle for a particular line of action. The results are far from trivial, revealing countless surprising and unflattering facts about Man the Decision-Maker. His assessment of probabilities is heavily subject to distortion; he uses numerous heuristic shortcuts of questionable validity; and he normally fails to utilize the full information before him because of cognitive overload.

These findings on the conative and cognitive aspect of motivation represent genuine advances in our knowlege of human action,
and specifically a gain in theoreticity. Admittedly, this gain was
easy to come by since common sense has fairly little to say on these
issues, but is none the worse for that. True, it is hardly a secret to
common sense that rules are somehow transmitted to children as
they grow up, and that people are prone to take over the attitudes
of those they consort with; but the precise mechanisms at work are
not known to common sense. And many of the curious facts
brought to light by dissonance theory and balance theory are
entirely beyond common sense, as is the case with certain aspects of
operant conditioning theory. The advance over common sense is
even greater in the area of cognitive processes, on which topic
everyday knowledge is all but silent.

3

However, this favourable assessment of the accomplishments of a
causal-genetic approach is subject to a serious qualification which
takes us back to the topic of interpretive accounts and adds to the
significance of our results concerning them. The point is that
although the shift to a causal-genetic approach opens up new
opportunities for theorizing, it does not allow us to get by without
reliance on interpretive accounts with their inherent shallowness.
These will remain with us as a low-theoretical lacuna in action
explanation. The reason is the failure of genetic accounts to get a
hold on particular action: they explain only the existence of general
behavioural tendencies, but are too weak to account for the
particular actions manifesting those tendencies. To close the gap,
social science must resort to interpretive accounts. These connect
the genetic story and the particular action by rationalizing the
latter in the light of the motivational factors explained in the
former.

But why should it not be possible to develop genetic theories
strong enough to be explanatorily relevant to particular action? (In
the following, I shall refer to such theories as (genetic) theories of
performance, while I term theories dealing with the acquisition of

general inclinations and rule commitments (genetic) theories of *repertoire*.) As I myself pointed out in chapter 2, explanatory power in causal accounts is not contingent upon a strong inferential connection between the explanans and the explanandum: at times, explanation may be provided by citing a cause which is only (known to be) a counterfactually *necessary* condition of the explanandum, with no (known) determinate statistical correlation with that event. Certainly the processes through which inclinations and rule commitments are acquired are necessary conditions for the subsequent actions manifesting them, and hence should be granted explanatory relevance.

To meet this objection, we have to get a better understanding of the task which the genetic theorist faces. His goal is to devise accounts of individual action which can replace interpretive accounts. This means we must impose an additional requirement upon the explanations he offers, namely, that they provide a grip on particular action which is at least as tight as that offered by interpretive accounts: if not, the shift to causal-genetic explanation involves a loss of explanatory power. That is, we require that the causal possibility space in which a genetic account places an action be no more extensive than the rational-option space in which a purposive account of the same action places it, or than the permitted-option space in which a rule account places it.

An example will illustrate the differences in explanatory tightness which typically obtain between a genetic account and an interpretive account of the same action, and the adverse effect of this upon the usefulness of the former account: Jimmy is taking extra mathematics lessons to raise the grade point average of his BA degree. In terms of purposes, the explanation is that Jimmy hopes for a career as an engineer and wants to improve his chances of getting accepted by one of the top universities or colleges in the field. This account provides a fairly tight hold on Jimmy's action: given that the schools on which he has set his sights maintain stringent entrance requirements in mathematics, there is little for him to do but to take extra classes in the subject. He might try to get help from his fellow students, or even consider cheating on the exam; but apart from these possibilities, which are more remote, there are few options open to him but the one actually chosen.

If we turn to a genetic explanation of the same action, we get a far less satisfactory account. Suppose Jimmy's ambitions about a future as an engineer were shaped by the high esteem in which his father–Jimmy's model figure–held that profession. A genetic account of Jimmy's academic activities would thus point to this process of modelling. However, this account provides only a very tenuous hold, in purely inferential terms, upon Jimmy's current actions. After all, Jimmy might have rebelled against his father's middle-class values long ago and have dropped out of the career game, or have found an even more powerful model figure later in adolescence and have decided to become a football star. He might also have shown a great gift for music and have chosen a career in this field instead. Even if his father's influence had remained decisive, Jimmy might have found other ways to live up to his expectations than in the choice of career, or have decided that a more average school would satisfy his ambitions; and so on without end. The causal impact of the socializing influences is transmitted to present action through an infinity of mediating links, some of which counteract it rather than conduct it. Hence, the statistical, inferential connection between the socializing events in the agent's past and his current actions will be very weak, exerting only a feeble explanatory grip on particular actions. Such explanations are inferior to interpretive accounts which set forth action in its rational interconnections with the agent's goals or the rules to which he subscribes. (It is important for the proper comparison of the two types of explanations that the genetic account does not take on any illicit explanatory power of the interpretive kind. This is hard to avoid in a fully stated genetic account, since it will comprise a specification of the agent's relevant goal, or his relevant rule commitments, as a psychological factor contributing to the generation of his action. It must be kept in mind that the specific nature of the events or states which make up the causal ancestry of the action are not allowed to make any difference to its explanatory power: only the tightness of the causal connection is allowed to make any difference in a genetic account.)

There is another fact we must keep in mind to appreciate fully the magnitude of the genetic theorist's task: the information which allows a genetic account to reach all the way to particular actions must derive from the theory itself. It is not enough that the gap is closed by mere collateral information. Such information does not strengthen the grip of the theory upon the explanandum, but merely provides independent evidence for the occurrence of that event. For instance, we know from the commonest everyday experience that people will almost invariably perform some greeting ritual when they meet. Such action is no doubt a consequence, *inter alia*, of parental drill in early childhood, and we may want to explain it by referring to that event. But the tight inferential connection between occasions of people meeting and the performance of greeting ceremonies is not the corollary of any general theory of rule learning, and is not presented as a function of any particular feature of the learning process (such as the length of the period of instruction, the learner's emotional attachment to the instructor, the severity of sanctions in case of infraction, and so on). The information which licenses prediction is no part of the theory, and does not strengthen theoretical explanation.

The reason why social science faces difficulties in closing the gap between theory and particular action is that social science is an *incomplete* discipline, in May Brodbeck's sense.[2] An incomplete discipline is one the parameters of which interact with variables not covered by the discipline, and in which, as a consequence, the former variables are subject to influences not explicable within the theory. But we must distinguish two kinds of incompleteness to characterize the predicament of social science more accurately: for the simple incompleteness of a discipline does not necessarily rob it of a strong inferential power in certain applications. Mechanics is an incomplete discipline, since some of its variables–for instance, acceleration–figure in other disciplines such as electrodynamics as well. The inferential virtues of mechanics are due to the fact that many physical systems are, or approach, pure mechanical systems, that is, systems in which non-mechanical forces are absent or negligible. We may call a discipline for which a similar condition holds *weakly incomplete*. A *strongly incomplete* discipline then is one in which no pure systems exist, that is, no systems in which only variables unique to that discipline are at play.

It hardly needs an argument that social science is a strongly incomplete discipline. Social science as we conceive it in this study deals with human action as socially determined, and with the social determinants of action.[3] Countless variables relevant to the determination of action will fall outside the scope of social science thus defined, as they will on the basis of any sensible demarcation of this discipline one might care to adopt. First, there are the psychological parameters, specifying stable as well as more transitory characteristics of agents. To the former belong such properties as intelligence, character, and personality, to the latter such conditions as mood, emotion, and set. Secondly, there are the physiological parameters of health, metabolic rate, hormone balance, blood chemistry, and others.[4] These psychological and physiological parameters constitute variable boundary conditions and interfering factors which disrupt and modify the link between the process through which a certain behavioural repertoire is acquired and the actual performance, and render the idea of an inferentially strong social science perfectly utopian. Inferentially strong theories can only be hoped for if these further parameters are taken into consideration along with the social ones. But to include them in this manner would make our theories plunge below the level at which social science operates. Social science must rest content with providing only a partial picture of action, sustaining only very weak causal explanations of particular action.

Admittedly, social science could still achieve some quasi-completeness, and the explanatory tightness that goes with it, if the psychological and physiological parameters showed no individual variation. Social science could then bracket off these parameters, as it were, relegating them to the status of standing conditions to be handled by an omnibus reference to a uniform human nature or human physiology. However, individual variation in psychological and somatic characteristics is a fact of life, as is variation in these parameters over time in each individual. Hence, the particular values of these parameters in the individual under scrutiny will have to be spelled out in detail, and the nature of their interaction with the purely social variables explained, if accounts of particular actions are to be forthcoming. Those accounts must hence cite, in equitable fashion, parameters belonging to the societal realm as well as to individual psychology and physiology. And the theories which sustain them cannot be drawn from social science alone, but from these fields as well.

It might be revealing to test my argument against a genetic theory which, if valid, would refute it, namely Skinner's theory of operant conditioning. Skinner claims to be able to explain not only how a repertoire is instilled into an agent, but even the occurrence of particular displays of that repertoire. However, a closer look at the devices employed by Skinner to accomplish this actually serves to confirm our conclusion. In the first place, Skinner obtains the pertinent results using rats and pigeons rather than human beings. This wise choice makes it possible for him to establish a fairly tight inferential nexus between conditioning and actual performance, since these creatures show much less indi-vidual variation than human beings: whereas there is no perfectly uniform human nature to serve as a stable background condition for social theory, there is something approaching a uniform rat nature or pigeon nature to serve in this role. (As it happens, rats and pigeons are sufficiently different for Skinner's findings not to be generalizable in their precise numerical values, such as those pertaining to extinction rate, etc. And even the qualitative aspects of his results are only valid if animals with gross physiological or psychological abnormalities are sifted out beforehand.) Secondly, and crucially, Skinner relies on the device of keeping his test subjects in strict solitary confinement in a box-like chamber with little to do to pass the time except depressing a bar, and of keeping them suitably hungry and hence concerned with the food they earn through that effort. Skinner's theory has little to say about what a (well-fed) pigeon or rat at large will do in the next instant–let alone about what to expect from a human being.

Thus, causal theorists do well to stick to genetic theories of repertoire, leaving explanation of particular action alone. True, the incompleteness of social science makes itself felt in this kind of theory, too: psychological and physiological differences prevent the formulation of exceptionless laws linking certain determinate events in people's biographies with their subsequent acquisition of a specific behavioural repertoire. Certain people will never develop a liking for music, regardless of the amount of 'mere exposure' to which you subject them; others will never internalize the social norms, despite immense efforts on the part of parents, teachers, psychiatrists, and prison authorities. Still, in the case of genetic theories of repertoire, we can establish acceptably strong statistical relationships without citing the exogenous variables in detail: all we need to do is to exclude grossly pathological cases, whereafter the rest can be taken care of by a general reference to human nature as a standing background condition. This strategy, which we rejected in the case of genetic accounts of performance, works for repertoire theories because they set their sights so much lower. They explain the mere genesis of an item in the agent's repertoire, but have nothing to say about the conditions which subsequently maintain it, nor about its strength or any other characteristic relevant to the way in which it interacts with other items in this repertoire, and hence relevant to the prediction of the agent's actual performance on any particular occasion. Genetic accounts of repertoire trade off empirical content for a strengthening of the inferential tie between the explanans and the explanandum.

Moreover, in the case of genetic explanations of repertoire, we are willing to settle for accounts which offer only a modest statistical correlation between the explanans and the explanandum since there is no alternative type of explanation available to render the service which they offer. Unlike genetic theories of performance, theories of repertoire do not compete with interpretive accounts for our attention.

The fact remains, however, that these virtues of repertoire accounts are bought at the cost of their failure to make contact with individual action. They cannot explain, in a manner satisfying our needs, why a person performed a particular action within his repertoire on a particular occasion. And in its effort to close this gap, the causal-genetic approach is to some degree caught in the very difficulties which we hoped to put behind us by taking the causalist turn. The genetic approach fills the lacuna in action explanation by invoking interpretive explanations which take the preference structure and normative commitments, the origin of which is explained in the causal account, as premises of an account which rationalizes performance in the light of these motivational states. Such accounts do not help establish a tight inferential connection between repertoire and action, since interpretive accounts are themselves inferentially weak, and do not even specify any determinate inferential connection between the motivational states and the ensuing action. They do, nevertheless, establish an explanatory tie between the repertoire-generating events and the particular action, a tie in which a causal and an interpretive component are combined in tandem. The explanation of individual action within a social science framework is thus a two-stage process, involving elements belonging to two different modes of explanation. But this device makes interpretive accounts permanent parts of the explanation of particular action in social science, and thus brings the arguments we have explored in the bulk of this work to bear upon the genetic approach as well, if only indirectly and partially. The genetic approach will show the same resistance to theoretical improvement, in one of its components, as we detected in interpretive accounts. It emerges that social science accounts of particular action, even on the basis of a causal approach, are inevitably burdened with an ingredient that is doomed to theoretical shallowness, this being the price we have to pay for the privilege of conceiving action as action and of describing it in the favoured, intentionalistic categories.

Notes

Chapter 1

1. Cf. Peter Alexander, 'Rational behaviour and psychoanalytic explanation', *Mind*, 71, 1962. It should be noted that Alexander doubts whether this condition can ever be satisfied by psychoanalytic interpretations.
2. It may be objected that this comparison is skew, and that the data garnered in psychoanalytic practice really do show that even unconscious aims are somehow present to consciousness. For these are essentially repressed motivations, it might be pointed out; and how could the mind keep such undesirable elements from entering the gate to full awareness, so to speak, unless it knew their indentities and knew that they were undesirable? This interpretation creates the well-known 'paradoxes of self-deception', eloquently set forth by Sartre in *L'être et le néant*. I cannot go into these issues here, but will simply refer to a paper by David Pears which demonstrates how these paradoxes may be avoided and the objection to my remarks on unconscious aims be defused: 'Freud, Sartre, and Self-Deception', in Richard Wollheim (ed.), *Freud. A Collection of Critical Essays*.
3. Cf. Norman Malcolm, 'The conceivability of mechanism', *Philosophical Review*, 77, 1968.
4. In *Content and Consciousness*, chapter 5, D. C. Dennett provides a sketch of how such a hook-up might work, using a computer and its print-out facility as a model. I find Dennett's account illuminating, although I take exception to the way in which he tries to explain the alleged epistemic authority of first-person avowals of intentions (and other first-person 'introspective reports') in terms of the model.
5. Cf. *The Stratification of Behaviour*, p. 160.
6. A. Rosenblueth, N. Wiener, and J. Bigelow, 'Behavior, purpose and teleology', *Philosophy of Science*, 10, 1943; R. B. Braithwaite, *Scientific Explanation*, chapter 10.
7. For an excellent exposition of these, see Andrew Woodfield, *Teleology*, chapters 3 and 4.
8. The view that intentionalistic descriptions are supervenient upon physical descriptions was proposed by Davidson in 'Mental events' (in L. Foster and J. W. Swanson (eds), *Experience and Theory*) and has since won many adherents.

9. My remarks on the intentionalistic proto-theory are much indebted to the 'functionalist' position expounded by such authors as Putnam, Fodor, Dennett, and others. My debt is especially great to the work of Dennett; cf. *Content and Consciousness* as well as the articles collected in *Brainstorms*. However, I go along with Dennett's analysis only as far as the psychological notions comprised in the 'matrix of motivation' are concerned. That analysis meets with difficulty when extended to such phenomenal states as pains, the purely sensory aspect of experience, etc. This is indeed not surprising, since these states are not on the face of it intentionalistic at all. (For Dennett's gallant attempt to make his analysis stick for phenomenal states as well, see 'Toward a cognitive theory of consciousness', in C. Wade Savage (ed.), *Minnesota Studies in the Philosophy of Science*, vol. IX.)

10. The interpretation of psychological notions as theoretical terms is suggested by Carnap in the article, 'The methodological character of theoretical concepts', in Feigl and Scriven (eds), *Minnesota Studies in the Philosophy of Science*, vol. I. It has since been worked out in more detail by Richard Brandt and Jaegvon Kim in 'Wants as explanations of action', *Journal of Philosophy*, 60, 1963, and by William P. Alston in 'Wants, actions, and causal explanations', in H. N. Castaneda (ed.), *Minds, Intentionality, and Perception*.

11. Cf. 'The meaning of "meaning" ', in K. Gunderson (ed.), *Minnesota Studies in the Philosophy of Science*, vol. VII.

12. Cf. 'Naming and necessity', in D. Davidson and G. Harman (eds), *Semantics of Natural Language*.

13. A. Goldman: *A Theory of Human Action*, chapter 2.

14. Cf. 'The logical form of action sentences', in N. Rescher (ed.), *The Logic of Decision and Action*.

15. H. L. A. Hart: *The Concept of Law*, p. 87 f.

16. Cf. Thomas Nagel, 'Linguistics and epistemology', in Sidney Hook (ed.), *Language and Philosophy*.

17. 'Reply: semantic theory and tacit knowledge', in S. Holtzman and C. Leich (eds), *Wittgenstein: to Follow a Rule*, p. 130 ff.

18. *The Language of Morals*, chapter 3, section 2.

19. This is closely related to what has been dubbed the *Convention of Truthfulness* : cf. David Lewis, *Convention*, p. 177 ff. Compare also with the definition of 'meaning$_x$' below.

20. Grice's explorations into this concept of meaning can be traced in the papers 'Meaning', *Philosophical Review*, 66, 1957; 'Utterer's meaning and intentions', *Philosophical Review*, 78, 1969; and 'Utterer's meaning, sentence-meaning, and word-meaning', *Foundations of Language*, 4, 1968.

21. Cf. John Searle, *Speech Acts*; Stephen Schiffer, *Meaning*.

22. 'Meaning', here cited after P. F. Strawson (ed.), *Philosophical Logic*, p. 43.

23. Cf. 'Intention and convention in speech acts' as reprinted in *Logico-Linguistic Papers*, p. 156. The present rendition is basically Schiffer's elaboration in *Meaning*, pp. 17–18.

24. Cf. *Meaning*, p. 18.

25. *Meaning*, chapter 2.

26. There might be a certain doubt as to the power of the iterative device to plug the hole in the definition for which it was designed. Can we not embarrass it with a counter-example of the familiar kind, this time involving a person who satisfies clauses 3 and 4 of the definition but intends this fact to be secret? But in the way that these clauses are specified, there is no room for such an intention. S's iteratively public intention that q is equivalent to the class of intentions of the form, 'S intends that A realize that S intends that A realize that S intends that A realize. . . that S intends that q'. However, for every intention I_m of that form there is, within the class of S's intentions, another intention I_n to the effect that I_m be known to A. That is, if S's iteratively public intention (intention$_2$) is realized, then for every component intention I_m of that intention, A knows that I_m is had by S. But this is incompatible with A lacking knowledge that S satisfies clauses 3 and 4. Hence S cannot coherently entertain intention$_2$ as an iteratively public intention while at the same time intending that fact to be unknown to A.

27. *Meaning*, p. 71.

Chapter 2

1. The epistemological notion of theoreticity, for all its centrality in other philosophical contexts, is not useful for our present concerns. There are two reasons for this. In the first place, the notion of unobservables is most fruitfully invoked in connection with the phenomenon of micro-reduction which does not seem to have any legitimate place in an intentionalistic approach to human action. Interpretive social science has no use for the method of dividing macroscopic, perceivable action into elements which fall below the sensory threshold. Secondly, lack of observationality is not a happy choice as a measure of theoreticity, at least as we understand it here, since that notion is thought of as a virtue in a scientific discipline. But involvement with unobservables is not a desirable thing *per se*. As a matter of fact, from the point of view of epistemology, it is a distinct liability: by resisting full capture in terms of observation, unobservables offend the empiricist sensitivities of science. The repeated attempts to dispose of unobservables in philosophical reconstructions of science bear witness to this (I have in mind

especially Ramsey's and Craig's elimination programmes). If the positing of unobservables is sometimes taken as an index of scientific sophistication, this is only because the introduction of such notions typically brings with it a gain in systematization of the kind I explicate in the following pages. But lack of observationality *per se* has nothing to recommend it as a criterion of theoretical excellence.

2. Does the notion of a suppressed wish exemplify the kind of theoretical advance we are looking for, thus allowing us to call off the search right away? The answer is no. The concept of a suppressed wish does indeed effect a systematic integration of previously unrelated data, but not one from which theoretically enriched interpretive accounts can be inferred. In the first place, not all the phenomena subsumed by the notion of a suppressed wish are actions at all (dreams and memory lapses hardly qualify). Secondly, for those manifestations of suppressed wishes that count as actions, the achievement of the Freudian theory is not that it offers a deeper interpretive account, but that it offers an interpretive account at all. For common sense denies these phenomena the status of action, and hence places them beyond the reach of interpretive explanation. In brief, the theory of suppressed wishes cannot deliver the order we placed in the Introduction (the basis for this rejection will become clearer with the further clarifications of our query in chapter 5).

3. In *Minnesota Studies in the Philosophy of Science*, vol. II.

4. The most forceful statement of that doctrine is made in Habermas's *Erkenntnis und Interesse. (Knowledge and Human Interests)*.

5. In *Science, Language, and Human Rights*.

6. In the article mentioned, Hempel actually makes a brief reference to ideal types in economics, but in a way that underestimates their fruitfulness.

7. Weber's most careful presentation of the notion of ideal types is given in the article 'Die "Objektivität" sozialwissenschaftlicher und sozialpolitischer Erkenntnis', in *Gesammelte Aufsätze zur Wissenschaftslehre*. An English translation, ' "Objectivity" in social science and social policy', is found in Edward A. Shils and Henry A. Finch (eds), *The Methodology of the Social Sciences*.

In the article, '*Homo oeconomicus* and his class mates' (in Maurice Natanson (ed.), *Phenomenology and Social Reality: Essays in Memory of Alfred Schutz*), Fritz Machlup recommends a number of non-economic ideal types to the social scientist's attention. Although the tone of this recommendation is somewhat playful—among Machlup's examples are *homo cholericus, homo alcoholicus* and *homo amorosus*—I do not think it unsporting to point out that the little vignettes with which Machlup illustrates his ideal types do not inspire much confidence in their fruitfullness. His little narratives simply illustrate some of the—very loosely specified—conditions which justify us in describing a person as lovestruck, as choleric, or as an alcoholic. This is semantics rather than social science.

8. See for instance C. G. Hempel, *Aspects of Scientific Explanation*, pp. 334–5.

9. Cf. *Aspects of Scientific Explanation*, pp. 366–7.

10. *Aspects of Scientific Explanation*, p. 426.

11. For a careful attempt, see Sylvain Bromberger, 'An approach to explanation', in R. J. Butler (ed.), *Studies in Analytical Philosophy*, First Series. Bromberger's work is expanded upon in Peter Achinstein, *Laws and Explanation*, chapter 4.

12. Most of the standard objections to the covering law analysis on the points that concern us here were first raised by Michael Scriven in the course of a sustained campaign against that analysis, with the main blows being struck in his articles 'Truisms as the grounds for historical explanations' (in P. Gardiner (ed.), *Theories of History*) and 'Explanations, predictions, and laws' (in Feigl and Maxwell (eds), *Minnesota Studies in the Philosophy of Science*, vol. III). Another important source is William Dray, *Laws and Explanation in History*.

13. *Philosophy of Science*, 15, 1948, p. 137.

14. Ibid., pp. 139–40 and p. 164.

15. In Feigl and Maxwell (eds), *Minnesota Studies in the Philosophy of Science*, vol. III.

16. This essay appears in the volume *Aspects of Scientific Explanation*.

17. An alternative construal of statistical explanation retains deductiveness between the explanans and the explanandum, at the cost of a probabilistic reformulation of the explanandum (i.e. instead of the explanandum sentence p, we get a sentence of the form: 'There is a probability r that p.' This is not the place to go into Hempel's reasons for preferring the former rendition; suffice it to say that nothing of present concern hangs upon the choice. In particular, the deductive reconstruction does not safeguard explanatory tightness (see below) any better than the i-s construal does, but merely relocates the explanatory slack.

18. *Aspects of Scientific Explanation*, pp. 367–8.

19. Ibid., p. 335.

20. N. Rescher: *Scientific Explanation*, pp. 65–6.

21. Rescher stresses the logical independence of these two measures, and refers to the properties measured as 'explanatory power' and 'comparative strength', respectively. But I think we may be allowed to treat them under one heading here.

22. In the article 'A pragmatic approach to explanations' (*Philosophy of Science*, 47, 1980), Peter Gärdenfors presents a theory of statistical explanation built around the notion of an increase in prior probability.

23. Cf. 'Statistical explanation', here as reprinted in *Statistical Explanation and Statistical Relevance*, p. 78 and pp. 53–5.

24. Cf. W. Salmon: *Statistical Explanation and Statistical Relevance*, p. 55

25. See his article 'Theoretical explanation', in S. Körner (ed.), *Explanation*.

26. *Statistical Explanation and Statistical Relevance*, p.78.
27. Ibid., p. 79.
28. Salmon tries to explicate this crude intuitive notion by means of the concept of degree of inhomogeneity of the reference class; cf. *Statistical Explanation and Statistical Relevance*, pp. 51–3.
29. Cf. 'Truisms as the grounds for historical explanations', in P. Gardiner (ed.), *Theories of History*.
30. *Aspects of Scientific Explanation*, pp. 360–1.
31. K. Marc-Wogau, 'On historical explanation', *Theoria*, xxviii, 1962, p. 228 f.
32. 'Causes and counterfactuals', *Journal of Philosophy*, 70, 1973.
33. In 'Can man be a subject for science?', *Philosophy and Phenomenological Research*, 31, 1970–1, p. 593.

Chapter 3

1. In 'Explaining action', *Inquiry*, 13, 1970, p. 61.
2. *Journal of Philosophy*, 60, 1963, p. 691.
3. The example is an emended version of one given by Roderick Chisholm in 'The descriptive element in the concept of action', *Journal of Philosophy*, 61, 1964. To my knowledge, Chisholm was the first to see the importance for action theory of what was later to be called 'deviant causal chains'.
4. As it happens, Davidson actually adopts the latter analysis in 'Freedom to act', in Ted Honderich (ed.), *Essays on freedom of action*.
5. Recognition of the importance of background information is frequent in the recent literature on explanation. See, for example, Charles Travis, 'Why', *American Philosophical Quarterly*, 15, 1978; Alan Garfinkel, *Forms of Explanation*, Chapters 1 and 2; Peter Gärdenfors, 'A pragmatic approach to explanations', *Philosophy of Science*, 47, 1980
6. Cf. *Aspects of Scientific Explanation*, pp. 477–8.
7. 'Man as a subject for science', quoted from *Metaphysics and Common Sense*, pp. 232–3.
8. The example involves an allusion to one adduced by Donald Davidson (cf. 'Actions, reasons, and causes', *Journal of Philosophy*, 60, 1963, p. 698). As it happens, Davidson implies that the intentionalistic description of motivational states is causally irrelevant in the sense specified below, but seems rather unperturbed by this. However, this attitude may be legitimate, since to Davidson the rationalizing effect of the intentionalistic terms is non-explanatory. For more detail of Davidson's view of the relationship between intentionalistic and physical descriptions, see his 'Mental events', in L. Foster and J. Swanson (eds), *Experience and Theory*.
9. In *Holistic Explanation*, chapter 3, Section 4, Christopher Peacocke

offers a penetrating discussion of what he calls the *conjunction restriction* on explanations. Although Peacocke does not mention the LCA, the conjunction restriction actually accommodates the force of the LCA as presented here.

10. See for instance Putnam's article, 'The mental life of some machines', in H. Castaneda (ed.), *Intentionality, Minds and Perception*.

11. 'The explanation of purposive behaviour', in R. Borger and F. Cioffi (eds), *Explanation in the Behavioural Sciences*.

12. Cf. 'What is a theory of meaning? (II)', in G. Evans and J. McDowell (eds), *Truth and Meaning*, p. 89.

Chapter 4

1. One example is Peter Winch; cf. *The Idea of a Social Science*, and 'Understanding a primitive society', *American Philosophical Quarterly*, 1, 1964.

2. *Philosophy and Phenomenological Research*, 14, 1953, p. 34. Further presentation of Schütz's methodological position is found in the articles 'Concept and theory formation in the Social Sciences', *Journal of Philosophy*, 51, 1954, and 'The social world and the theory of social action', *Social Research*, 27, 1960.

3. Cf. 'Concept and theory formation in the social sciences', *Journal of Philosophy*, 51, 1954, p. 267.

4. I take the Postulate to apply only to theory construction in social science, as we understand that term in this study (cf. the Introduction). Hence, with this somewhat artificial restriction, there is no direct clash between Freudian theorizing and the Postulate, since psychoanalysis falls outside the scope of that definition. But as we shall see later, this insulation is difficult to uphold.

5. See, for instance, 'Common-sense and scientific interpretation of human action', *Philosophy and Phenomenological Research*, 14, 1953, p. 4.

6. Ibid., p. 34.

7. The terms to which the Postulate applies all refer to intentions and motivations; cf. 'Common-sense and scientific interpretation of human action', p. 31 ff.

8. In stating that Schütz committed himself only to a weaker version of the Postulate, we take perhaps a certain licence regarding his position. At one point, he cites with approval W. I. Thomas's principle that anything is real which is so defined by social agents, adding that to the inhabitants of Salem in the seventeenth century, witchcraft was a reality and should be recognized as such by social theorizing ('Concept and theory formation in the social sciences', *Journal of Philosophy*, 51, 1954, p. 263). Still it is not clear that Schütz would want this to commit him to anything stronger than the position just outlined, namely that

the ontology of the everyday interpretation must be endorsed as the intentional, not as the real object of action and motivation. At any rate, our objective here is not Schützian scholarship, and we granted ourselves at the outset the freedom to diverge from Schütz's actual position in case this would produce a more defensible view. The reader may take the above interpretation as an exercise of this right.

9. This position has been most forcefully argued for the case in which the interpreter and the target culture are separated by a historical rather than a geographical barrier, notably by representatives of the school of hermeneutics. The classical work is H.-G. Gadamer, *Wahrheit und Methode* (*Truth and Method*). Gadamer's reasoning only partially overlaps with the one I suggest here.

10. A similar point is made in John Skorupski, 'The meaning of another culture's beliefs', in C. Hookway and P. Pettit (eds), *Action and Interpretation*, p. 94. The idea that semantic holism makes language impossible to learn is questioned by Mark Platts who suggests that the learner may generate a provisional semantic hypothesis on the basis of exposure to a limited segment of the language, anticipating the rest of the semantic system (cf. *Ways of Meaning*, p. 49 ff.). But if this observation salvages the learnability of the native language by natives, by the same token it shows it to be learnable by outsiders, too: for there is no reason why outsiders should not form the same kind of semantic hypotheses.

11. 'Common-sense and scientific interpretation of human action', p. 3.

12. Cf. 'Rule-following, objectivity and the theory of meaning', in S. Holzman and C. Leich (eds), *Wittgenstein: to Follow a Rule*, p. 99f.

13. This device is actually invoked by such authors as Apel and Habermas who endorse what they term 'a consensus theory of truth' (Cf. Jürgen Habermas, 'Wahrheitstheorien', in H. Fahrenbach (ed.), *Wirklichkeit und Reflexion: Walter Schulz zum 60. Gerburtstag).* It should be noted that these authors do not employ the consensus theory to support relativism; hence they are unaffected by the objections to such a use.

14. At first sight, the proposed constraint might even be thought to be entirely vacuous, since there would seem to be no independent access to the natives' beliefs, inference patterns and standards of rationality when they function to determine the natives' interpretations of each others' utterances. To put it another way, the inference patterns and rationality canons (etc.) which are to be read (by us) into the natives' practical and cognitive dealings with reality, and those which are to be read (by us) into native acts of interpreting other aliens, get fixed on the basis of the same body of data, namely data having to do with native dealings with physical reality, whereas native acts of interpreting other natives offer no additional and independent data. But this objection overlooks the fact that within the native community, there may be explicit discussion of the proper interpretation of concrete utterances thought to be puzzling, in the course of which explicit or implicit appeal will be made

to standards of rationality and canons of inference. One party to the debate may reject the other's interpretation on the grounds that it attributes bizarre beliefs or excessive muddleheadedness to the interpretee. We may even come across explicit pronouncements such as 'Contradictory beliefs in the interpretee are always the product of bad translation' in the record of these discussions. I do not think such evidence could be declared out of bounds even according to the most fastidious canons of radical interpretation. And if it is admitted as legitimate, it must also be accorded some evidential weight in interpretation.

15. After finishing the manuscript of this book, I have come across a sketch of an argument similar to my rebuttal of the phenomenologist in Martin Hollis's article 'The social destruction of reality', in Martin Hollis and Steven Lukes (eds) *Rationality and Relativism*. However, Hollis uses the argument for a slightly different purpose, namely to dispose of cultural relativism in the standard sense to the effect that rationality canons vary between cultures. In this role, the argument is less efficient, since a cultural relativist in the standard sense is not committed to the idealist premise which reduces the phenomenologist's argument to incoherency. That is, a relativist need not involve himself with the view that social reality is socially constituted.

16. My remarks here, and in the following, are based upon a Kripkean semantics for natural kind terms. Cf. 'Naming and necessity', in Donald Davidson and Gilbert Harman (eds), *Semantics of Natural Language*.

Neeedless to say, this semantics is not without its problems, which I cannot deal with here, however. Not all these problems constitute threats to the argument I present here (such as, for instance, the problem of the precise role of causality in semantics). The point I make on the basis of Kripkean semantics remains sound as long as we can uphold the idea of a term picking out a referent by means of an associated description which does not, however, give the meaning of that term. Certain philosophers of language would not be willing to concede this possibility; but the current state of semantic theorizing hardly allows any authoritative resolution to this issue. My confidence in Kripkean semantics on this point springs from the conviction that demonstrative devices indeed exhibit the debated property. Demonstrative expressions single out their referent by means of contextual clues and paralinguistic accompaniments (gestures, etc.). But a description of these features could in no way be termed the *meaning* of those expressions.

17. For a good illustration of the diversity of theories in this field, see the papers and selections found in *Witchcraft and Sorcery*, an anthology edited by Max Marwick.

18. The most persuasive and appealing study of such phenomena remains the one that started it all, Goffman's *The Presentation of Self in Everyday Life*.

19. I here adopt the standard reconstruction of functionalist explanation as offered, among others, by Hempel; cf. 'The logic of functional analysis', in L. Gross (ed.), *Symposium on Sociological Theory*.

20. For the view that agents' concepts rather than their beliefs (or 'theories') should be respected, see P. Winch, 'Comment to I. C. Jarvie, "Understanding and explanation in sociology and social anthropology" ', in R. Borger and F. Cioffi (eds), *Explanation in the Behavioural Sciences*.

Chapter 5

1. The most eloquent proponent of this position is Jürgen Habermas, and his work, *Erkenntnis und Interesse* (*Knowledge and Human Interests*) the most ambitious attempt to support it.

2. Published in *Les Fondements Philosophiques des Systèmes Économiques. Textes de Jacques Rueff et Essais rédigés en son Honneur*, edited by Emil M. Claassen. An English version is found in David Miller (ed.), *A Pocket Popper*.

3. K. R. Popper: 'La rationalité', p. 144

4. It may help to explain this feature of Popper's model if we appreciate the fact that he originally introduced it to support an anti-psychological stance in social science. His idea was that social action could be explained by the 'logic of the situation', that is, by features of the situation in which the agent found himself. The problem is, of course, that the action provoked by a given objective situation depends crucially upon the agent's subjective concerns. Compare *The Open Society and its Enemies*, vol. 2, chapter 14.

5. It is true that there are procedures which will extract, for any person P and any event E, a figure that may be construed as the subjective probability assigned to E by P. However, it is questionable whether such procedures will always satisfy a basic condition for counting as measurements, namely, that the figure elicited is independent of the process of measurement. There is reason to believe that the fact measured is sometimes generated by, or at least strongly influenced by, the very process of measurement. Compare Jon Elster, *Ulysses and the Sirens*, chapter 3, section 4.

6. Trouble arises when obedience to rules is taken to lead to so-called lexicographic preferences which cannot be handled by the mathematical methods applied to standard utility functions. However, they will still fit into the general rationality framework as described previously. Moreover, rule commitment does not necessarily translate into lexicographic preference functions. Cf. Elster, *Ulysses and the Sirens*, chapter 3, section 3.

7. This conception was first presented in the article, 'A behavioral theory of rational choice' in the *Quaterly Journal of Economics*, 69, 1954, and later elaborated in numerous publications.

8. The objection might be raised that such examples do not demonstrate any role for maximizing considerations in purposive accounts, but merely reflect the fact that when we fail to find a suitably optimal connection between a person's goals and the action engaged in, this raises a *further* question, namely, as to the nature of the beliefs which made that course of action seem optimal. However, I doubt that there is any natural way to divide up the total sum of information sufficient to still our doubts about Norbert's action into distinct, self-contained part-accounts, each addressing a different aspect of our puzzlement. Remember that our query concerning Norbert's action might have been prompted precisely by our surprise at seeing him, the millionaire, engaged in such a lowly activity as lawn-mowing. Any account adequate to dispel that puzzlement must somehow embody the information that Norbert's huge assets are not at his disposal at the moment.

9. For a review of such research, see Ward Edwards, 'Behavioral decision theory', reprinted in Ward Edwards and Amos Twersky (eds), *Decision Making*.

10. A lucid discussion of the logical status of the principles of mechanics is found in Ernest Nagel, *The Structure of Science*, chapter 7.

11. In the 1930s and 1940s, the tradition was perpetuated in the person of H. A. Murray. More recently, the most important names are Abraham Maslow (especially in *Motivation and Personality*) and Charlotte Bühler. Both hold the concern with goals of human action rather than its causal determinants to be a part of a 'humanistic reorientation' in the science of human action.

12. Cf. the following passages from the *Dynamics of Behavior* :

The main contention of this book–seemingly a perfectly obvious and innocent view–is that behavior consists in active give and take between the organism and the objective environment. This interrelationship may be called 'dealing with the environment'. . . . Here we are making the claim that this direction of receptive and motor activity toward the environment is the fundamental tendency of animal and human behavior and that it is the all-pervasive primary motivation of behavior (pp. 124–5).

The behavior-primacy theory regards the tendency to deal with the environment as a primary drive, and indeed as *the* primary drive in behavior. The various capacities for dealing with the environment afford outlets for the general behavior drive and give it different forms–given the necessary environmental opportunities. So the manifold human interests are predictable from the combination (p. 133).

13. For Maslow's theory, see his *Motivation and Personality*.

Chapter 6

1. Bruce J. Biddle, *Role Theory*, pp. 6–7.
2. R. Harré and P. F. Secord: *The Explanation of Social Behaviour*, p. 9.
3. Ibid., p. 201.
4. Ibid., chapter 10.
5. Ibid., pp. 202–3.
6. The idea of measuring the structural complication of sentences in terms of the number of nodes is suggested in Miller and Chomsky, 'Finitary models of language users', in Luce, Bush, and Galanter (eds), *Handbook in Mathematical Psychology*, vol. II. Miller and Chomsky's proposal is considerably more complicated than the one I provide here.
7. Cf. F. A. Hayek, 'Notes on the evolution of systems of rules of conduct', in *Studies in Philosophy, Politics and Economics*.
8. E. O. Wilson and C. J. Lumsden: *Genes, Mind, and Culture*, p. 7.
9. E. O. Wilson: *On Human Nature*, chapter 8.
10. For an attempt to derive some particular human customs and norms from evolutionist premises, see David P. Barash, *Sociobiology and Human Behavior*, chapter 10.
11. Cf. David P. Barash, *Sociobiology and Human Behavior*, p. 312. Also, *Genes, Mind, and Culture*, p. 295 ff.
12. Cf. *Genes, Mind, and Culture*, p. 296.
13. 'Functional explanation and the linguistic analogy', *Philosophy of the Social Sciences*, 9, 1979.
14. Van Parijs: 'Functional explanation', p. 432.
15. Notice that the construction of norms of such spurious universality embodies a mistake similar to the mobilk fallacy exposed in the previous chapter.
16. For a statement of Kohlberg's views, see for instance 'From is to ought: how to commit the naturalistic fallacy and get away with it in the study of moral development', in *Cognitive Development and Epistemology*, edited by T. Mischel, and 'The claim to moral adequacy of a highest stage of moral judgment', *Journal of Philosophy*, 70, 1973.
17. A review of the literature is given in Martin L. Hoffman, 'Moral internalization: current theory and research', in *Advances in Experimental Social Psychology*, vol. 10, edited by L. Berkowitz.
18. Cf. 'From is to ought', *Cognitive Development and Epistemology*, p. 200.
19. N. Chomsky: *Syntactic Structures*, p. 48.
20. N. Chomsky: *Aspects*, p. 9.
21. Ibid., p. 9.
22. *Aspects*, Chapter 1, sections 4 and 6.
23. 'Methodological reflections on current linguistic theory', in G. Harman (ed.), *On Noam Chomsky: Critical Essays*.
24. Robert Schwartz, 'On knowing a grammar', in S. Hook (ed.), *Language and Philosophy*.

25. N. Chomsky: *Reflections*, p. 175.
26. Cf. *Rules and Representations*, pp. 189–92.
27. *Aspects*, p. 9.
28. For a review of the literature, see J. A. Fodor, T. G. Bever and M. A. Garrett, *The Psychology of Language*, chapter 5.
29. Cf. *Rules and Representations*.

Chapter 7

1. J. J. Katz and J. A. Fodor, 'The structure of semantic theory', *Language*, 39, 1963; J. J. Katz and P. M. Postal, *An Integrated Theory of Linguistic Descriptions*; J. J. Katz, *Linguistic Philosophy*.
2. Cf. David Lewis, 'General semantics', in Donald Davidson and Gilbert Harman (eds), *Semantics of Natural Language*, p. 169 f; also Bruce Vermazen, review of *An Integrated Theory of Linguistic Descriptions, in Synthese*, 17, 1967.
3. Cf. Donald Davidson, 'Truth and meaning', *Synthese*, 17, 1967.
4. Davidson grapples with this problem in 'On saying that', *Synthese*, 19, 1969.
5. Cf. J. A. Foster, 'Meaning and truth theory', and Brian Loar, 'Two theories of meaning', both in G. Evans and J. McDowell (eds), *Truth and Meaning*.
6. Cf. *Éléments de sémiologie* (*Elements of Semiology*), chapter I 2.2–2.4.
7. Cf. *Système de la Mode*, chapter 1.5.
8. Ibid., chapter 2.13. Strictly speaking, Barthes maintains that semantic meaning may derive from another source as well: even without being tied to any particular occasion or activity, fashion styles will always signify something, namely, fashion itself (2.3). But this would seem to be a confusion of syntax and semantics in the alleged fashion language; it is equivalent to saying that every well-formed sentence refers to or signifies its own well-formedness; as if every well-formed sentence meant, 'This sentence is well-formed.'
9. A similar point is suggested in David Papineau, *For Science in the Social Sciences*, p. 100 f.
10. *Système de la Mode*, chapter 12.
11. As it happens, Barthes claims to find a constant formal structure in fashion-clothes-as-described, dubbed by him a *matrice* (*Système de la Mode*, chapter 5.4). A matrice is a tripartite structure, consisting of the *object*, which is the bearer of meaning, the *variant*, which is the producer of meaning, and the *support*, which is the material substratum of the variant. Thus, in an open-collared shirt, the openness is the semantically operative feature (the variant) which, 'supported' by the collar, bestows upon the shirt (as object) its semantic meaning (which is

roughly that of 'casual, leisurely activities'). But it would seem that such tripartition cannot always be found. If fashion insist that clothes have a particular colour, obedience to that maxim does not impose upon the clothes any such structure. A closer examination of Barthes's discussion shows that, in order to find his tripartite structure everywhere, he is forced to make heavy play with the fluid character of the garment language lexicon, as well as to introduce a dummy element: the presence/absence of a support is allowed to count as a variant (cf. chapter 5.4). With this much elasticity in the way elements are identified and counted, we could never fail to find a tripartite structure.

12. Cf. 'The meaning of "meaning" ', here as reprinted in *Philosophical Papers*, vol. 2, p. 227 f.

13. Some philosophers, such as Jerry Fodor, maintain that the use of an intentionalistic idiom does indeed imply that the subject of description manipulates propositions expressed in a 'brain language'; see for instance 'Propositional attitudes', *Monist*, 61, 1978. For a forceful criticism of this idea, see D. C. Dennett, 'Critical notice: *The Language of Thought* by Jerry Fodor', *Mind*, 86, 1977.

14. This paragraph is a rough condensation of chapter 4 of the work cited.

15. Cf. J. Habermas: *Zur Logik der Sozialwissenschaften*, pp. 140–1.

16. Ibid., p. 141, pp. 162–4.

17. Ibid., pp. 139–40 and p. 161. The translation is based upon the draft of an English edition of 'Zur Logik der Sozialwissenschaften', to be published by the MIT Press under the title *The Logic of the Social Sciences*.

18. Cf. *Philosophical Investigations*, p. 174.

19. *Review of Metaphysics*, 25, 1971–2.

20. C. Taylor: 'Interpretation', pp. 3–5.

21. Ibid., p. 9.

22. Ibid., pp. 12–14.

23. Ibid., pp. 15–17.

24. See, for instance, Hilary Putnam, *Meaning and the Moral Sciences*, Lecture 6.

25. The doctrine that digital computers cannot be programmed to produce (true) perceptual statements about material objects is argued by Hubert Dreyfus in *What Computers Can't Do* (cf. chapter 1). As it happens, Dreyfus's argument is very similar to the one used by Taylor to draw a contrast between interpretation of action and description of physical reality.

26. 'Hermeneutics' was originally the name of a discipline ancillary to theology, devoted to the authoritative interpretation of the sacred texts.

27. *Word and Object*, chapter 2, § 15.

28. 'On the very idea of a conceptual scheme', *APA Proceedings and Addresses*, 1973–4, p. 19.

29. 'Radical interpretation', *Synthese*, 23, 1974, p. 336–7.

30. Ibid., p. 346.
31. Ibid., pp. 336–7.
32. For an exposition of these principles, see, for example, 'Linguistic contributions to the study of mind: present' in *Language and Mind*.

Epilogue

1. For a survey of pertinent work in social psychology, see R. P. Abelson, 'Social psychology's rational man', in S. I. Benn and G. W. Mortimore (eds), *Rationality and the Social Sciences*. A review of the work on 'mere exposure' is provided in Albert A. Harrison, 'Mere exposure', in L. Berkowitz (ed.), *Advances in Experimental Social Psychology*, vol. 10.
2. Cf. 'Methodological individualisms: definition and reduction', *Philosophy of Science*, 25, 1958.
3. This conception is not meant to exclude such traditional topics as the study of social structure and macro-dynamics as proper parts of social science. The point is merely that these fall outside our present interests.
4. It might be argued that some of the psychological parameters, such as those expressing personality traits, are really social, since they deal with aspects of the way people interact socially (traits such as introversion, assertiveness, etc.). I disagree with this reading, holding these terms to refer to *dispositions* in human beings to respond in certain characteristic ways to specified social situations; and these dispositions may be ascribed even to a solitary human being. However, the logic of these terms may be somewhat fuzzy in everyday language, and many philosophers have claimed that the ascription of these traits carries an implication that they have actually sometimes been manifested. Since the manifestations are social, according to my definition, the overall trait is social, too. However, I suspect that the oddity of ascribing a dispositional trait to somebody, while admitting that he has never had the opportunity to manifest it, is not a matter of semantics, but of conversational implicature, having to do with our grounds for such an ascription: we could hardly know somebody to possess a certain character trait unless we had observed its manifestations at least once. At any rate, it must be allowed that there are no logical objections to the idea of a disposition that is never manifested (such a disposition must have a categorical basis; but that is a different matter). Such latent dispositions, which may or may not be the referents of our everyday psychological vocabulary, belong to a realm alongside and independent of the social. They cannot be spirited away or reduced to the social, since they are correlated with, and presupposed by, the social, being precisely dispositions to respond to social situations in specified ways.

Bibliography

This list only contains titles cited in the text.

Abelson, R. P. 'Social psychology's rational man'. In S. I. Benn and G. W. Mortimore (eds), *Rationality and the Social Sciences*. London: Routledge & Kegan Paul (1976).

Achinstein, Peter. *Laws and Explanation*. Oxford: Clarendon Press (1971).

Alexander, Peter. 'Rational behaviour and psychoanalytic explanation'. *Mind*, 71 (1962).

Alston, William P. 'Wants, actions, and causal explanations'. In H. N. Castaneda (ed.), *Intentionality, Minds, and Perception*. Detroit: Wayne Books (1967).

Ayer, Alfred J. 'Man as a subject for science'. *Metaphysics and Common Sense*. London: Macmillan and Co. (1969).

Barash, David P. *Sociobiology and Human Behavior*. New York: Elsevier (1977).

Barthes, Roland. 'Éléments de sémiologie'. *Communications*, 4 (1964). English edn: *Elements of Semiology*. London: Cape (1969).

—*Système de la Mode*. Paris: Éditions de Seuil (1967).

Bernard, L. L. *Instinct*. New York: Holt (1924).

Biddle, Bruce J. *Role Theory*. New York: Academic Press (1979).

Braithwaite, Richard B. *Scientific Explanation*. Cambridge: Cambridge University Press (1953).

Brandt, Richard and Kim, Jaegwon. 'Wants as explanations of action'. *Journal of Philosophy*, 60 (1963).

Brodbeck, May. 'Methodological individualisms: definition and reduction'. *Philosophy of Science*, 25 (1958).

Bromberger, Sylvain. 'An approach to explanation'. In R. J. Butler (ed.), *Analytical Philosophy*, first series. Oxford: Basil Blackwell (1965).

Carnap, Rudolf. 'The methodological character of theoretical concepts'. In H. Feigl and M. Scriven (eds), *Minnesota Studies in the Philosophy of Science*, vol. I. Minneapolis: University of Minnesota Press (1956).

Chisholm, Roderick. 'The descriptive element in the concept of action'. *Journal of Philosophy*, 61 (1964).

Chomsky, Noam. *Syntactic Structures*. The Hague: Mouton (1957).

—*Aspects of the Theory of Syntax*. Cambridge, Mass: MIT Press (1965).

—*Language and Mind*. New York: Harcourt Brace Jovanovich (enlarged edn, 1972).

—*Reflections on Language*. New York: Pantheon (1975).

—*Rules and Representations*. Oxford: Basil Blackwell (1980).

Davidson, Donald. 'Actions, reasons, and causes', *Journal of Philosophy*, 60 (1963).

—'The logical form of action sentences'. In N. Rescher (ed.), *The Logic of Decision and Action*. Pittsburgh: University of Pittsburgh Press (1966).

—'Truth and meaning'. *Synthese*, 17 (1967).

—'On saying that'. *Synthese*, 19 (1969).

—'Freedom to act'. In Ted Honderich (ed.), *Essays on freedom of action*. London: Routledge & Kegan Paul (1969).

—'On the very idea of a conceptual scheme'. *APA Proceedings and Addresses*, 1973–74.

Dennett, Daniel C. *Content and Consciousness*. London: Routledge & Kegan Paul (1969).

—'Critical notice: *The Language of Thought* by Jerry Fodor'. *Mind*, 86 (1977).

—'Toward a cognitive theory of consciousness'. In C. Wade Savage (ed.), *Minnesota Studies in the Philosophy of Science*, vol. ix. Minneapolis: University of Minnesota Press (1978).

—*Brainstorms*. Brighton: Harvester Press (1979).

Dray, William. *Laws and Explanation in History*. Oxford: Clarendon Press (1957).

Dreyfus, Hubert L. *What Computers Can't Do*. New York: Harper & Row (Revised edn, 1979).

Dummett, Michael. 'What is a theory of meaning? (ii)'. In G. Evans and J. McDowell (eds), *Truth and Meaning*. Oxford: Oxford University Press (1976).

Edwards, Ward. 'Behavioral decision theory'. In W. Edwards and A. Twersky (eds), *Decision Making*. Harmondsworth: Penguin Books (1967).

Elster, Jon. *Ulysses and the Sirens*. Cambridge: Cambridge University Press (1979).

Evans, Gareth. 'Reply: semantic theory and tacit knowledge'. In S. H. Holtzman and C. M. Leich (eds), *Wittgenstein: to Follow a Rule*. London: Routledge & Kegan Paul (1981).

Fodor, Jerry. 'Propositional attitudes', *Monist*, 61 (1978).

Fodor, Jerry, Bever, T. G. and Garrett, M. A. *The Psychology of Language*. New York: McGraw-Hill (1974)

Foster, J. A. 'Meaning and truth theory'. In G. Evans and J. McDowell (eds), *Truth and Meaning*. Oxford: Oxford University Press (1976).

Freud, Sigmund. 'Entwurf einer Psychologie'. In M. Bonaparte, A. Freud and E. Kris (eds), *Aus den Anfängen der Psychoanalyse*. London: Imago Publishing Co. (1950). English translation, 'Project for a scientific psychology', in vol. I of *The Standard Edition of the Complete Psychological Works of Sigmund Freud*. London: Hogarth Press (1966).

Gadamer, Hans-Georg. *Wahrheit und Methode*. Tübingen: J. C. B. Mohr (Paul Siebeck) (third edn, 1972). English edn: *Truth and Method*. London: Sheed & Ward (1975).

Gärdenfors, Peter. 'A pragmatic approach to explanations'. *Philosophy of Science*, 47 (1980).

Garfinkel, Alan. *Forms of Explanation*. New Haven: Yale University Press (1981).

Goffman, Erving. *The Presentation of Self in Everyday Life*. Garden City: Doubleday (1959).

Goldman, Alvin. *A Theory of Human Action*. New Jersey: Prentice-Hall (1970).

Greenstein, Harold. 'Can man be a subject for science?' *Philosophy and Phenomenological Research*, 31 (1970–1).

Grice, H. P. 'Meaning'. *Philosophical Review*, 66 (1957). Reprinted in P. F. Strawson (ed.), *Philosophical Logic*. Oxford: Oxford University Press (1967).

—'Utterer's meaning, sentence-meaning, and word-meaning'. *Foundations of Language*, 4 (1968).

—'Utterer's meaning and intentions'. *Philosophical Review*, 78 (1969).

Habermas, Jürgen. 'Zur Logik der Sozialwissenschaften'. Beiheft 5, *Philosophische Rundschau*. Tübingen: Siebeck und Mohr (1967). Reprinted in J. Habermas, *Zur Logik der Sozialwissenschaften*. Frankfurt-on-Main: Suhrkamp (1970). English edn; *The Logic of the Social Sciences*. Cambridge, Mass: MIT Press (forthcoming).

—*Erkenntnis und Interesse*. Frankfurt-on-Main: Suhrkamp (second edn, 1973). English edn: *Knowledge and Human Interests*. Boston: Beacon Press (1971).

—'Wahrheitstheorien'. In H. Fahrenbach (ed.), *Wirklichkeit und Reflexion: Walter Schulz zum 60. Geburtstag*. Pfullingen: Neske (1974).

Hare, R. M. *The Language of Morals*. Oxford: Clarendon Press (1952).

Harré, Rom and Secord, P. F. *The Explanation of Social Behaviour*. Oxford: Basil Blackwell (1972).

Harrison, A. H. 'Mere exposure'. In L. Berkowitz (ed.), *Advances in Experimental Social Psychology*, vol. 10. New York: Academic Press (1977).

Hart, H. L. A. *The Concept of Law*. Oxford: Clarendon Press (1961).

Hayek, F. A. 'Notes on the evolution of systems of rules of conduct'. In *Studies in Philosophy, Politics and Economics*. London: Routledge & Kegan Paul (1967).

Hempel, Carl G. 'Typological methods in the natural and the social sciences'. In *Science, Language, and Human Rights*. Philadelphia: University of Pennsylvania Press (1952).

—'The theoretician's dilemma'. In H. Feigl, M. Scriven and G. Maxwell (eds), *Minnesota Studies in the Philosophy of Science*, vol. II. Minneapolis: University of Minnesota Press (1958).

—'The logic of functional analyses'. In Llewellyn Gross (ed.), *Symposium on Sociological Theory*. New York: Harper & Row (1959).

—'Deductive-nomological vs statistical explanation'. In H. Feigl and G. Maxwell (eds), *Minnesota Studies in the Philosophy of Science*, vol. III. Minneapolis: University of Minnesota Press (1962).

—'Aspects of scientific explanation'. In *Aspects of Scientific Explanation*. New York: The Free Press (1965).

—*Aspects of Scientific Explanation*. New York: The Free Press (1965).

Hempel, Carl G. and Oppenheim, P. 'Studies in the logic of explanation'. *Philosophy of Science*, 15 (1948).

Hoffman, M. L. 'Moral internalization: current theory and research'. In L. Berkowitz (ed.), *Advances in Experimental Social Psychology*, vol. 10. New York: Academic Press (1977).

Hollis, Martin. 'The social destruction of reality'. In M. Hollis and S. Lukes (eds), *Rationality and Relativism*. Oxford: Basil Blackwell (1982).

James, William. *The Principles of Psychology*. London: Macmillan (1891).

Katz, Jerrold J. *Linguistic Philosophy*. London: Allen & Unwin (1972).

Katz, Jerrold J. and Fodor, J. 'The structure of semantic theory'. *Language*, 39 (1963).

Katz, Jerrold J. and Postal, P. M. *An Integrated Theory of Linguistic Descriptions*. Cambridge, Mass: MIT Press (1964).

Kim, Jaegvon. 'Causes and counterfactuals'. *Journal of Philosophy*, 70 (1973).

Kohlberg, Lawrence. 'From is to ought: how to commit the naturalistic fallacy and get away with it in the study of moral development'. In T. Mischel (ed.), *Cognitive Development and Epistemology*. New York: Academic Press (1971).

—'The claim to moral adequacy of a highest stage of moral judgment'. *Journal of Philosophy*, 70 (1973).

Kripke, Saul. 'Naming and necessity'. In D. Davidson and G. Harman (eds), *Semantics of Natural Language*. Dordrecht: D. Reidel (1972).

Lewis, David. *Convention*. Cambridge, Mass: Harvard University Press (1969).

—'General semantics'. In D. Davidson and G. Harman (eds), *Semantics of Natural Language*. Dordrecht: D. Reidel (1972).

—'Radical interpretation'. *Synthese*, 23 (1974).

Loar, Brian. 'Two theories of meaning'. In G. Evans and J. McDowell (eds), *Truth and Meaning*. Oxford: Oxford University Press (1976).

McDougall, William. *Social Psychology*. London: Methuen (1908).

Machlup, Fritz. 'Homo oeconomicus and his class mates'. In M. Natanson (ed.), *Phenomenology and Social Reality: Essays in Memory of Alfred Schutz*. The Hague: Martinus Nijhoff (1970).

Mackie, John L. *The Cement of the Universe*. Oxford: Clarendon Press (1974).

Malcolm, Norman. 'The conceivability of mechanism'. *Philosophical Review*, 77 (1968).

Marc-Wogau, Konrad. 'On historical explanation'. *Theoria*, 28 (1962).

Marwick, Max. (ed.) *Witchcraft and Sorcery*. Harmondsworth: Penguin Books (1970).

Maslow, Abraham. *Motivation and Personality*. New York: Harper & Bros (1954).

Miller, G. A. and Chomsky, N. 'Finitary models of language users'. In R. D. Luce, R. Bush and E. Galanter (eds), *Handbook of Mathematical Psychology*, vol. 2. New York: Wiley (1963).

Miller, G. A., Galanter, E. and Pribram, K. H. *Plans and the Structure of Behavior*. New York: Holt, Rinehart and Winston (1960).

Nagel, Ernest. *The Structure of Science*. London: Routledge & Kegan Paul (1961).

Nagel, Thomas. 'Linguistics and epistemology'. In Sidney Hook (ed.), *Language and Philosophy*. New York: New York University Press (1969).

Papineau, David. *For Science in the Social Sciences*. London: Macmillan (1978)

Parijs, Philippe van. 'Functional explanation and the linguistic analogy'. *Philosophy of the Social Sciences*, 9 (1979).

Parsons, Talcott. *The Social System*. Glencoe, Illinois: The Free Press (1951).

Peacocke, Christopher. *Holistic Explanation*. Oxford: Clarendon Press (1981).

Pears, David. 'Freud, Sartre, and self-deception'. In R. Wollheim (ed.), *Freud. A Collection of Critical Essays*. Garden City: Doubleday (1974).

Platts, Mark. *Ways of Meaning*. London: Routledge & Kegan Paul (1979).

Popper, Karl R. *The Open Society and its Enemies*. London: Routledge & Kegan Paul (fifth edn, 1966).

—'La rationalité et le statut de principe de rationalité'. In E. M. Claassen (ed.), *Les Fondements Philosophiques des Systèmes Économiques. Textes de Jacques Rueff et Essais rédigés en son Honneur*. Paris: Payot (1967). An English version, 'The rationality principle', is included in David Miller (ed.), *A Pocket Popper*. Oxford: Fontana Paperbacks (1983).

Putnam, Hilary. 'The mental life of some machines'. In H. Castaneda (ed.), *Intentionality, Minds, and Perception*. Detroit: Wayne Books (1967).

—'The meaning of "meaning" '. In K. Gunderson (ed.), *Minnesota Studies in the Philosophy of Science*, vol. VII. Minneapolis: University of Minnesota Press (1975). Reprinted in *Philosophical Papers*, vol. 2. Cambridge: Cambridge University Press (1975).

—*Meaning and the Moral Sciences*. London: Routledge & Kegan Paul (1978).

Quine, Willard V. O. *Word and Object*. Cambridge, Mass: MIT Press (1960).

—'Methodological reflections on current linguistic theory'. In G. Harman (ed.), *On Noam Chomsky: Critical Essays*. Garden City: Doubleday (1974).

Rescher, Nicholas. *Scientific Explanation*. New York: The Free Press (1970).

Rosenblueth, A., Wiener, N., and Bigelow, J. 'Behavior, purpose and teleology'. *Philosophy of Science*, 10 (1943).

Ryle, Gilbert. *The Concept of Mind*. Harmondsworth: Penguin Books (1963).

Salmon, Wesley. 'Statistical explanation'. In R. G. Colodny (ed.), *Nature and Function of Scientific Theories*. Pittsburgh: University of Pittsburgh Press (1970). Reprinted in *Statistical Explanation and Statistical Relevance*. Pittsburgh: University of Pittsburgh Press (1971).

—'Theoretical explanation'. In Stephan Körner (ed.), *Explanation*. Oxford: Basil Blackwell (1975).

Sartre, Jean-Paul. *L'être et le néant*. Paris: Gallimard (1943). English edn: *Being and Nothingness*. London: Methuen (1958).

Schiffer, Stephen. *Meaning*. Oxford: Clarendon Press (1972).

Schütz, Alfred. 'Common-sense and scientific interpretation of human action'. *Philosophy and Phenomenological Research*, 14 (1953).

—'Concept and theory formation in the social sciences'. *Journal of Philosophy*, 51 (1954).

—'The social world and the theory of social action'. *Social Research*, 27 (1960).

Schwartz, Robert. 'On knowing a grammar'. In S. Hook (ed.), *Language and Philosophy*. New York: New York University Press (1969).

Scriven, Michael. 'Truisms as the grounds for historical explanations'. In P. Gardiner (ed.), *Theories of History*. New York: The Free Press (1959).

—'Explanations, predictions, and laws'. In H. Feigl and G. Maxwell (eds), *Minnesota Studies in the Philosophy of Science*, vol. III. Minneapolis: University of Minnesota Press (1962).

Searle, John. *Speech Acts*. Cambridge: Cambridge University Press (1970).

Shwayder, David S. *The Stratification of Behaviour*. London: Routledge & Kegan Paul (1965).

Simon, Herbert A. 'A behavioral theory of rational choice'. *Quarterly Journal of Economics*, 69 (1954).

Skorupski, John. 'The meaning of another culture's beliefs'. In C. Hookway and P. Pettit (eds), *Action and Interpretation*. Cambridge: Cambridge University Press (1978).

Strawson, Peter F. 'Intention and convention in speech acts'. *Philosophical Review*, 73 (1964). Reprinted in *Logico-Linguistic Papers*. London: Methuen (1971).

Taylor, Charles. 'Explaining action'. *Inquiry*, 13 (1970).

—'The explanation of purposive behaviour'. In R. Borger and F. Cioffi (eds), *Explanation in the Behavioural Sciences*. Cambridge: Cambridge University Press (1970).

—'Interpretation and the science of man'. *Review of Metaphysics*, 25 (1971–2).

Travis, Charles. 'Why'. *American Philosophical Quarterly*, (1978).

Vermazen, Bruce. 'Review: *An Integrated Theory of Linguistic Descriptions*'. *Synthese*, 17 (1967).

Weber, Max. 'Die "Objektivität" sozialwissenschaftlicher und sozialpolitischer Erkenntnis'. *Archiv für Sozialwissenschaft und Sozialpolitik*, 19 (1904). Reprinted in *Gesammelte Aufsätze zur Wissenschaftslehre*. Tübingen: J. C. B. Mohr (Paul Siebeck) (second edn, 1951). An English translation, ' "Objectivity" in social science and social policy', is included in Edward A. Shils and Henry A. Finch (eds), *The Methodology of the Social Sciences*. New York: The Free Press (1949).

Wilson, Edward O. *On Human Nature*. Cambridge, Mass: Harvard University Press (1978).

Wilson, Edward O. and Lumsden, C. J. *Genes, Mind, and Culture*. Cambridge, Mass: Harvard University Press (1981).

Winch, Peter. *The Idea of a Social Science*. London: Routledge & Kegan Paul (1958).

—'Understanding a primitive society'. *American Philosophical Quarterly*, 1 (1964).

—'Comment to I. C. Jarvie: "Understanding and explanation in sociology and social anthropology" '. In R. Borger and F. Cioffi (eds), *Explanation in the Behavioural Sciences*. Cambridge: Cambridge University Press (1970).

Wittgenstein, Ludwig. *Philosophical Investigations*. Oxford: Basil Blackwell (1968).

Woodfield, Andrew. *Teleology*. Cambridge: Cambridge University Press (1976).

Woodworth, Robert S. *The Dynamics of Behaviour*. New York: Holt, Rinehart & Winston (1958).

Wright, Crispin. 'Rule-following, objectivity and the theory of meaning'. In S. H. Holtzman and C. M. Leich (eds), *Wittgenstein: to Follow a Rule*. London: Routledge & Kegan Paul (1981).

Wright, Georg Henrik von. *Explanation and Understanding*. London: Routledge & Kegan Paul (1971).

Index